The ADIRONDACK Book

A Complete Guide

James Swedberg

THE ADIRONDACK BOOK

A Complete Guide

Fourth Edition

Elizabeth Folwell
with Amy Godine and Galen Crane

Berkshire House Publishers
Lee, Massachusetts

On the Cover and Frontispiece:
Front Cover: *"Bog River,"* photo by James Swedberg
Frontispiece: *Adirondack Canoe (Saranac Lake)* Photo by Mark Kurtz
Back cover: Author's photo by Nancie Battaglia

Library of Congress Cataloging-in-Publication Data

Folwell, Elizabeth.
The Adirondack book : a complete guide / Elizabeth Folwell ; with Amy Godine and Galen Crane.— 4th ed.
p. cm. — (Great destinations series, ISSN 1056-7968)
Includes bibliographical references and index.
ISBN 1-58157-014-7
1. Adirondack Mountains Region (N.Y.)—Guidebooks. 2. Adirondack Park (N.Y.)—Guidebooks. I. Godine, Amy. II. Crane, Galen. III. Title. IV. Series.

F127.A2 F55 2000
917.47'50443—dc21

99-056678

ISBN: 1-58157-014-7
ISSN: 1056-7968 (series)

Editor: Susan Minnich, Managing Editor: Philip Rich. Design and composition: Dianne Pinkowitz. Cover design and composition: Jane McWhorter. Index: Diane Brenner.

Berkshire House books are available at substantial discounts for bulk purchases by corporations and other organizations for promotions and premiums. Special personalized editions can also be produced in large quantities. For more information, contact:

Berkshire House Publishers
480 Pleasant St., Suite 5; Lee, Massachusetts 01238
800-321-8526
E-mail: info@berkshirehouse.com
Website: www.berkshirehouse.com

Manufactured in the United States of America
First printing 2000
10 9 8 7 6 5 4 3 2 1

No complimentary meals or lodgings were accepted by the author and reviewers in gathering information for this work.

Berkshire House Publishers'
Great Destinations™ travel guidebook series

Right on the money.

— THE NEW YORK TIMES

. . . a crisp and critical approach, for travelers who want to live like locals.

— USA TODAY

Great Destinations™ guidebooks are known for their comprehensive, critical coverage of regions of extraordinary cultural interest and natural beauty. The authors in this series are professional travel writers who have lived for many years in the regions they describe. Each title in this series is continuously updated with each printing, in order to insure accurate and timely information. All of the books contain over 100 photographs and maps.

Neither the publisher, the authors, the reviewers, nor other contributors accept complimentary lodgings, meals, or any other consideration (such as advertising) while gathering information for any book in this series.

Current titles available:
The Adirondack Book
The Berkshire Book
The Charleston, Savannah & Coastal Islands Book
The Chesapeake Bay Book
The Coast of Maine Book
The Hamptons Book
The Monterey Bay, Big Sur & Gold Coast Wine Country Book
The Nantucket Book
The Newport & Narragansett Bay Book
The Napa & Sonoma Book
The Santa Fe & Taos Book
The Sarasota, Sanibel Island & Naples Book
The Texas Hill Country Book
Wineries of the Eastern States

If you are traveling to, moving to, residing in, or just interested in any (or all!) of these enchanting regions, a **Great Destinations™** guidebook is a superior companion. Honest and painstakingly critical, full of information only a local can provide, **Great Destinations™** guidebooks give you all the practical knowledge you need to enjoy the best of each region. Why not own them all?

Acknowledgments

Just as the Adirondack Park is a combination of many different places, the fourth edition of *The Adirondack Book* represents the combined efforts of many people who spent hours hunkered over their computer keyboards, days in the darkroom, or evenings at far-flung restaurant tables. Coauthors Amy Godine and Galen Crane deserve the first round of heartfelt thanks for making this book a fresh, new endeavor: Amy's approach to local history is always lively, always informative, and Galen's look at regional transportation and information services leaves no stone unturned, no road unremarked, no website unexamined.

James Swedberg, from Long Lake, earns kudos for bringing scores of new images to the book, from all corners of the Adirondacks, and for introducing readers to other noteworthy North Country photographers. I also thank Edward Comstock Jr., of Old Forge, who gracious loaned numerous historical postcards from his private collection, images that amuse and instruct.

To my intrepid team of restaurant reviewers, I send my appreciation and the admonishment to loosen those belts one more notch: the difficult work of discovering and detailing Adirondack eateries never ends. Thanks to Cali Brooks, Galen Crane, Jim Gies, Ken Sprague, Leslie Aylsworth, Mark McCullough, Leigh Ann Couch, Lohr McKinstry, and Brandy Saxton.

To my *Adirondack Life* co-workers — every last one of you — thanks for keeping me informed of new businesses of all stripes, and for being such a copacetic bunch no matter which deadline was looming.

Tom Warrington, my husband, once again proved to be the guy I could count on, to go on one more road trip, try one more obscure diner, seek out one more antique shop, and deserves special commendation for service beyond the call of duty for chaperoning lots of other people's children at Enchanted Forest.

The last word of thanks, naturally, goes to all the Adirondack innkeepers, restaurateurs, craftspeople, shop keepers, boatbuilders, guides, and others who add the human dimension to this wild and wonderful place.

Contents

STATE OF NEW YORK
EXECUTIVE CHAMBER
ALBANY 12224

GEORGE E. PATAKI
GOVERNOR

Dear Friends:

From its incredible glacial beginnings to its spectacular beauty today, New York's Adirondack region offers a remarkable diversity that few places in the world can rival.

As one of the largest and oldest state parks in America, the Adirondack Park is a unique resource. Created more than 100 years ago, its six million acres include public land protected as "forever wild" by the New York State Constitution and private land where careful forest management, tourism and other natural resource-based industries support some ten million visitors annually. The park is home to 130,000 permanent residents and 70,000 seasonal residents.

The Adirondack Park provides countless places to experience and things to see. Its 46 mountains over 4000 feet, 2600 lakes and ponds and 1800 miles of river, millions of acres of forest and abundant wildlife provide endless recreational opportunities. From scenic drives along mountain roads to week-long hikes in the back country, from bird-watching to fishing, the Adirondack Park is an exciting and sometimes challenging place to live, work and visit.

The Park's small towns, historic sites and museums are gateways to the Adirondacks' rich culture and history of military conflict, rustic architecture, logging, hunting, fishing, trapping and natural resource conservation.

From my own experience visiting the Park with my children, I have found that the Adirondacks are a place of discovery and renewal -- discovery of the working of nature, history and tradition; renewal of our own spirit and enthusiasm for life as we walk majestic mountain trails and canoe in clear lakes surrounded by a timeless forest.

I welcome you to share these experiences and to use this comprehensive guidebook when you visit the Adirondacks this year and for years to come.

Very truly yours,

George E. Pataki

Introduction

New York's Adirondack Park is a big park: bigger than Yellowstone and Yosemite put together and larger than any of the national parks in the lower forty-eight. This park is better than national parks in many ways, too. You don't pay an entry fee when you cross the so-called Blue Line, the park's boundary; you don't need a permit to hike, climb a mountain, canoe, or explore the backcountry. People make this park their home and have lived here for many generations, giving this region a distinctive culture and offering an array of services to visitors.

The park covers six million acres, about the size of the state of Vermont. Land owned by New York State is about 2.5 million acres, and large landowners, especially timber companies, own about a million acres more and contribute significantly to the local economy. The year-round population of the Adirondack Park is about 130,000 residents, although Hamilton County, where I live, has only three or four people per square mile.

I've lived in the Adirondacks all my adult life, and I've enjoyed visiting many different communities, exploring wild places, and learning about the region. Although the landscape appears timeless, human endeavors change frequently. That's the impetus behind the fourth edition of *The Adirondack Book* — to supply information about new places and updates on classic spots. I hope that these pages encourage you to explore this great place.

Betsy Folwell
Blue Mountain Lake

THE WAY THIS BOOK WORKS

There are eight chapters in this book — History, Transportation, Lodging, Culture, Restaurants and Food Purveyors, Recreation, Shopping, and Information — and many maps and indexes. Within in each chapters, you'll find a subheading — "Fishing," for example — and under that topic is general information that's true for the whole park. Then specific services and businesses are grouped geographically by region: **Lake George and Southeastern Adirondacks, Champlain Valley, High Peaks and Northern Adirondacks, Northwest Lakes,** and **Central Adirondack** (which includes the southwestern Adirondacks). Towns are listed alphabetically in the regions. So, Bolton Landing may be the first town listed in the Lake George area, and pertinent businesses in that town will then be listed alphabetically.

Many of the entries have "information blocks" on the left side of the page, listing phone numbers, addresses, and so forth. We've checked these facts as close to the book's publication date as possible, but businesses do change hands and change policies. It's always a good idea to call ahead — a long-distance call is a whole lot cheaper than a tank of gas.

For the same reason, you won't find specific prices listed for restaurants, lodgings, greens fees, and so forth; we indicated a range of prices, which you'll find at the beginnings of the chapters or directly under the specific heading. Lodging prices are based on a per-room rate, double occupancy, during the high season, so that we had consistent standard for comparison; off-season and mid-week rates are generally cheaper. Restaurant price ratings show the cost of one meal including appetizer, entrée, and dessert, but not cocktails, wine, tax, or tip.

	Lodging	**Dining**
Very Inexpensive	Under $40 per night, double occupancy	
Inexpensive	$40–$70	Up to $15
Moderate	$70–$100	$15–$20
Expensive	$100–$200	$20–$35
Very Expensive	Over $200	Over $35

Credit Cards are abbreviated as follows:

AE — American Express	DC — Diner's Club
CB — Carte Blanche	MC — Master Card
D — Discover Card	V — Visa

The ADIRONDACK Book

A Complete Guide

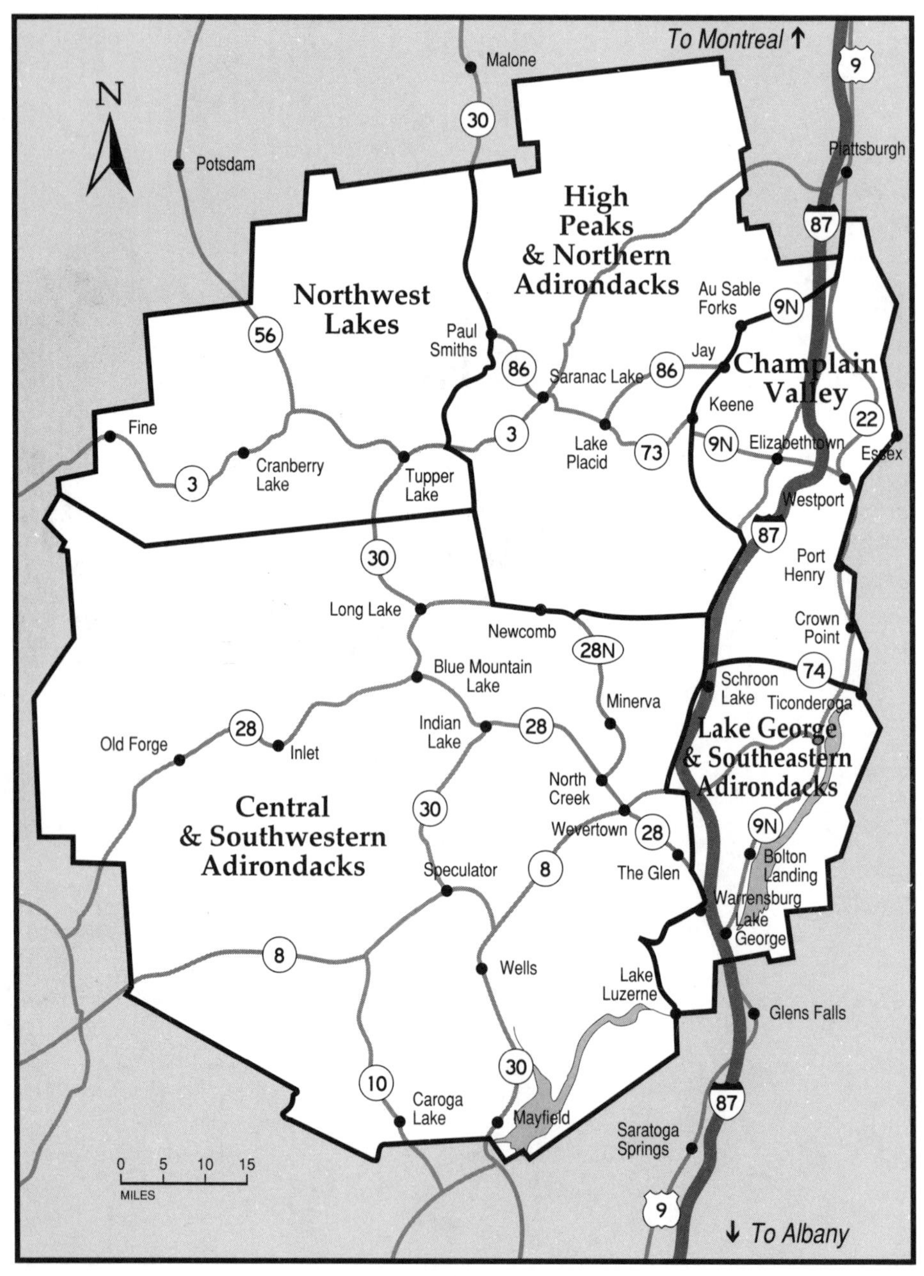

THE ADIRONDACKS IN FIVE REGIONS

CHAPTER ONE

The People's Park

HISTORY

Courtesy of Keene Valley Library

Even a century ago, the elements of an Adirondack vacation were the same as today: fresh air, clear lakes, and wild mountains. Boating party on the Ausable lakes.

Planning a trip to the Adirondacks in northern New York? Bring a road map, bring your bug spray, and by all means bring this book. But above all, bring your love of mystery and your capacity for wonder, for nothing is exactly as it seems here, and a taste for contradiction can only sweeten your encounter with a park bigger than the state of Vermont. How is it, for example, that over half of this so-called "Park" is in private hands? What kind of park is that? Lakes and rivers, cataracts and rugged peaks you were expecting, but weed-capped cones of hundred-year-old iron ore tailings? Wyoming-worthy dude ranches and a hundred little towns? You keep reading in your pocket history book that Indians never really *lived* here — a "trackless wilderness" it was known as — yet here's another two-room town museum with a display case full of local arrowheads and beads. You keep hearing about these fabulous Adirondack Great Camps, rustic summer compounds as imperial and capacious, some of them, as European duchies, and one or two even open for a tour. But nobody prepared you for the moody rows of former company housing in Lyon Mountain or the kitschy miniature golf courses of Lake George. You thought these mountains, woods, and moonlit bogs were about as far from multi-ethnic city life as you could get, yet here, lost on a back road, is an Irishtown, and there a Spanish Settlement Road, and farther west, in Tupper Lake, a synagogue built by eastern European immigrant peddlers before the First World War.

As for the seemingly unchanging forest, that also tells a more problematic story than what first meets the eye. It turns out that your favorite view of Edenic woods was once, and not so long ago, a veritable moonscape of slash and dust and ugly stumps; the gin-clear stream where you saw a moose standing up to its knobby knees was once turbid with the stinking liquor of tannery waste.

The Adirondack forest primeval? Not exactly. "Forever wild" is only one small version of what's in store. There is also — and no less dramatically — the forest recovered and the forest redeemed, the forest industrial, and, sadly, the forest failing under the sour burden of acid rain. There is the Adirondacks of the solitary footpath lifting toward a rock-slick summit, and the rolling, easy Adirondacks that flanks the western shore of Lake Champlain, a mirror image of Vermont with its bosky apple orchards and tidy Yankee farmsteads. There is the watery, idyllic Adirondacks of the summer camp, and the Adirondacks of the boarded-over, passed-by village Main Street. Downstate politicians with a second home in Westport cherish one kind of Adirondacks. Sixth-generation Franco-Americans juggling several backwoods jobs to keep afloat — maybe running a string of housekeeping cottages in the summer, doing a little wood chopping, and some road work for the county — know and love another. Sometimes these Adirondacks intersect, but often they seem to belong to quite different, mutually uncomprehending worlds.

Of course, the region's greatest enduring mystery belongs to history. How came it to pass that a vast swath of forest so relatively close to so many eastern cities was among the last in the lower 48 to gain the eye and expertise of the surveyor, cartographer, and lawmaker? Such marvelous proximity, and yet, for so long, so lightly valued and little known! So proudly venerable — yet so recent an addition to our pantheon of great parks! Like the proverbial girl next door who turns out to be a heart-stopping knockout, the Adirondack region has been, in terms of our appreciation of it, a very late bloomer. It took time for us to get wise to its rare beauty, time to learn to see and cherish the quiet treasure in our own backyard.

And maybe that's just as well, because the same forces that delayed a loving valuation of the region also stalled our rolling in and making an unholy hash of it (though the combined assault of extractive industries like mining, logging, and tanning, took a hard toll). Start with the Native Americans, for whom the Champlain Valley corridor was long a borderland between hereditary enemies, the Iroquois and the Algonquin, or more particularly, the easternmost Iroquois tribe, the Mohawks, and from the other side of the lake, the Abenaki, westernmost of the wide-ranging Algonquins. Borderlands that double as sporadic war zones are no place to settle down, and permanent Indian encampments were accordingly unknown. (Migratory visitations, on the other hand, have been going on for some eight thousand years, the summer-to-fall residency that accounts for those relics you'll keep seeing in the local village museum display case.)

The Adirondack region was not a draw for European settlers in the seventeenth and eighteenth centuries, when a distant, long-lived imperial conflict pitted the British Crown against the soldiers of New France in one bloody raid and

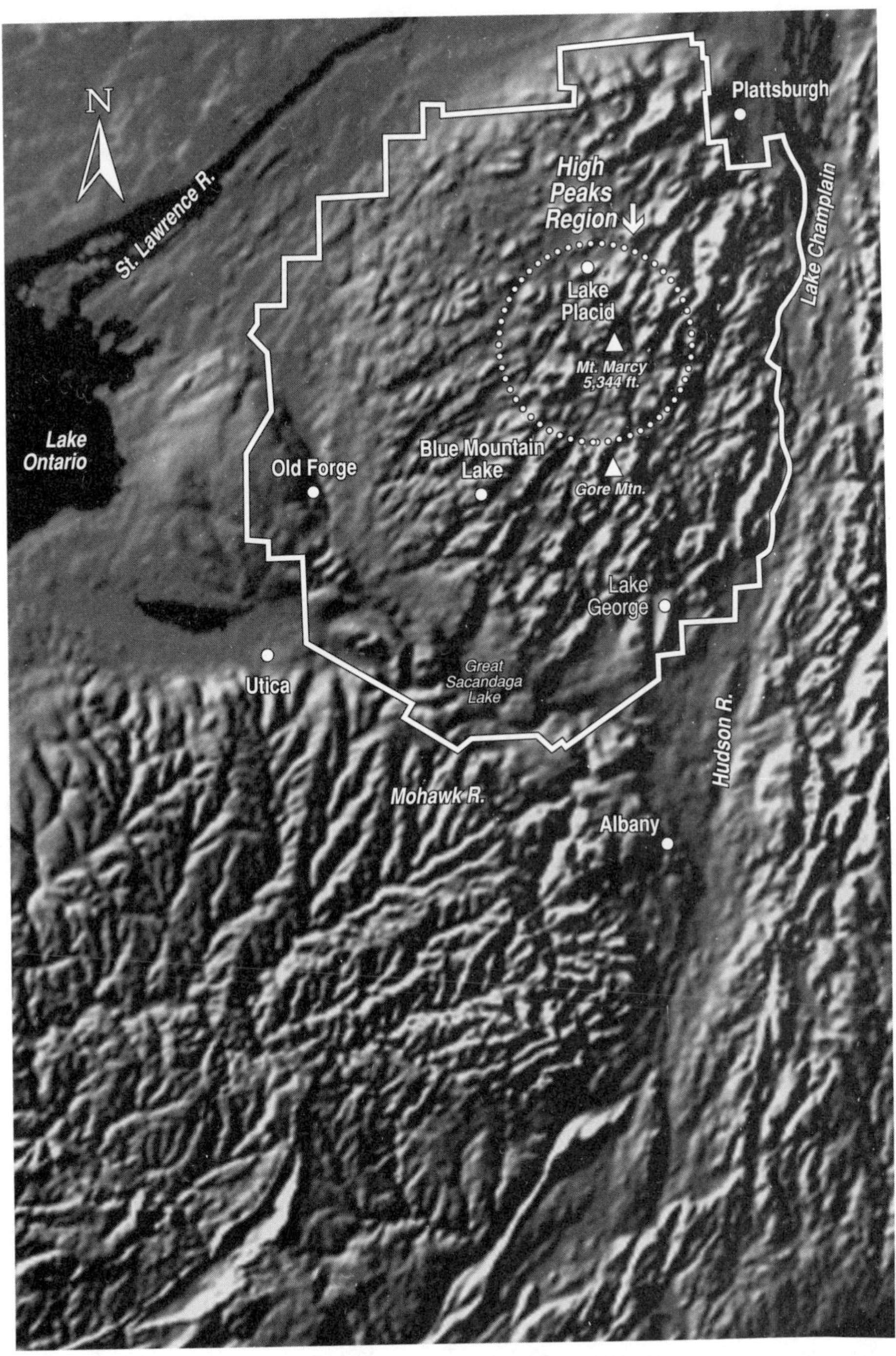

ADIRONDACK TOPOGRAPHY

In 1609, Samuel de Champlain sailed down the lake that now bears his name. Near present-day Ticonderoga, his troops and their Algonquin guides overpowered the resident Iroquois, continuing the age-old enmity between the native groups.

Courtesy of Cornell University Library

skirmish after another, culminating, of course, in the French and Indian War. In the Champlain Valley in particular, much more was at stake than a mere show of military muscle. Each nation was as hot to lay claim to this commercially strategic thoroughfare as it was keen to edge the other out. This key waterway (Lake Champlain and Lake George) was the conduit for the kind of abundant timber (including arrow-straight white pines that could mast a royal navy) that a wood-starved Europe hadn't seen for a century. It provided habitat and transport for enough furs to cloak all of gay Paree. Indeed, whosoever ruled these waters owned the markets that lined the royal purse. The upshot of this imperial conflict for the Adirondack region was inevitable. The eastern Adirondack region on the west flank of Lake Champlain gained a reputation of, if not a full-blown war zone, at least a pretty darned dicey place to settle. And so, for the first two-thirds or so of the eighteenth century, settlers stayed away.

Or mostly. In 1730, soldier-farmers from New France colonized a settlement on the west side of Lake Champlain where the banks are close as pincers. Fort Saint Frederic, at present-day Crown Point, thrived for another thirty years, time enough for the French pioneers to raise families, build a trading post, mill, and chapel, and befriend the traveling bands of Native Americans. But in 1758, hearing of the imminent approach of British troops under the tireless Lord Jeffrey Amherst, the French homemakers of the region's first European enclave destroyed their Adirondack Roanoke and fled to Canada, leaving the charred remains to be rebuilt and re-invented as His Majesty's massive fort, Crown Point.

The French and Indian War also gave American and British soldiers their first glimpse of this virgin wilderness, and some of them liked what they saw well enough to come back at the conflict's end. Bands of Quakers found the region too, and gave Quaker names to several early settlements in the southern and eastern Adirondacks, among them, Wing's Falls, later called Glens Falls, the bustling mill town at the Adirondack's southeastern edge.

Laboring under the delusion that the underpopulated Adirondack region might somehow escape the ever-growing tension between native-born Americans grown restive under British rule and those loyal to the Crown, the peaceable Quakers were in for a rude surprise. Once again, during the Revolution and for some years after, the eastern Adirondack corridor between Montreal and Saratoga emerged as a bloody frontier warpath, and settlers hunkered down at their peril.

Among the ranks of the veterans who were nonetheless attracted to this dangerous frontier were many Scots, survivors of the Highlander regiments that fought with fabled valor at Lake George and Fort Ticonderoga. In the southern Adirondacks, Sir William Johnson, the high-living Irish-born veteran and brilliant liaison between the Iroquois and the British Crown, bought himself a sweet chunk of real estate from the British-allied Mohawks and set about parlaying his riverside homestead into a wilderness fiefdom worthy of Joseph Conrad's Kurtz. (Proud local legends insist that the tireless Johnson sired seven hundred progeny, donned a kilt with his Scottish Highlander immigrant tenants, and reveled with the Mohawk braves who routinely camped and feasted on his baronial front lawns.) But the Johnson family was pro-British, and when William Johnson died and the patriotic fever of the Revolution took the Mohawk Valley by storm, his sons exiled themselves to Canada, their faithful Scottish tenants with them, and the old man's upstate kingdom was seized and broken up, never to be restored.

Johnson wasn't the only land baron to lose his hard-won Adirondack empire to the winds of revolution. The Scotsman Sir Philip Skene sowed his fertile corner of the Adirondacks near today's Whitehall (formerly Skenesborough) with sawmills, iron forges, settlers, and his own small crew of African-American slaves. Sir William Gilliland, a Scots-Irish immigrant and like Skene and Johnson, a veteran of His Majesty's Forces, set his dogged sights on the "howling wilderness" (his words) at the mouth of the Boquet River, near Willsboro (which he named for himself). Come the Revolution, the exiled Skene saw his shipyard seized, his slaves dispersed, and his pioneering iron forges used to fashion the cannonballs that stalled the British navy at the Battle of Valcour. Gilliland should have had better luck: he, at least, backed the winning party, even feeding three thousand shell-shocked American soldiers in weary retreat from a disastrous foray into Canada. But patriot or not, Gilliland's grand feudal ambitions were ill suited to the democratic temper of his times. Benedict Arnold (of all people!) charged Gilliland with treason: Gilliland went to jail, lost his holdings and his farms to marauding Loyalists, landed in debtor's prison, and wound up freezing to death in the Adirondack woods, leaving a handful of Adirondack villages to honor his good work with Gilliland family names.

The ill-starred, quixotic sagas of these dreamy speculators have dominated the pages of most Adirondack histories. To the names of Johnson, Gilliland, and Skene, add Alexander Macomb, brief owner in 1791 of almost four million Adirondack acres; add the Rhode Island merchant John Brown, whose "Tract" would encompass much of today's Park before it reverted to New York State for taxes; add John Thurman, the New York City businessman who recruited Scottish pioneers to the region near the village that bears his name today. Little wonder we should still be fascinated: their stories make such satisfying copy. The energetic Thurman: gored to death in his prime by a bull! The ever-hopeful Brown (who named his ghostly, never-settled townships things like Frugality, Sobriety, and Perseverance) lost his land agent, a son-in-law, to suicide, and his holdings to the state! The impecunious Macomb who wound up in debtors' prison, half-mad!

More enduring, if less flamboyantly dramatic, was the experience of the nameless pioneers who discovered the region in the half century or so after the Revolution when a close-to-bankrupt New York State took over the crown lands of the northern wilderness and sold upstate parcels by the thousands. Only then did the region see anything like a real influx of settlers, many of them veterans of the continental army. In they poured from the worked-over, exhausted hill farms of New England, and it wasn't long, maybe a decade, maybe two, before sod huts and log shanties donned neat suits of locally milled clapboard, and every crossroads settlement could boast an inn, tavern, and makeshift church. Historians call it the Yankee Migration, and Puritan-descended Yankees these land-starved settlers mostly were. But there were Hessians too, and bands of Scots-Irish from northern Ireland, and once again Quakers trickling northward from the Hudson Valley, and coming south after 1816, both French and Anglo-Canadian homesteaders looking to make a fresh start after the quashing of the failed Canadian Rebellion.

Some came of their own accord, others in response to the propagandistic broadsides and handbills of land agents working for downstate speculators; speculators who had every reason to assume their settler-tenants would improve the value of their investment with each swing of the ax, even when they failed to pay rent or give over a portion of their crops. This time-honored colonial strategy had worked well enough elsewhere along the Eastern seaboard. What went wrong up here? Why did one Adirondack empire after another fail to prosper?

It is true that many of these so-called "harpy land barons" would not live on or anywhere near their tracts, and not a few tenant farmers chafed under the high-handed, semi-feudal expectations of their absentee landlords. But far more demoralizing than a long-distance landlord was the daily, blunt, implacable resistance of the terrain. If it wasn't the bitter thinness of the Adirondack soil (a few lush river valleys aside), it was the length and harshness of the winters, the stinginess of the growing season, the roughness of the topography, or the dread ferocity of predators — wolves and panthers, bugs and bears. Nor was the situation eased by the absence of transportation routes that might have eased the settlers' transition from subsistence to a market economy. What did it profit them to grow the sweetest hops, the fattest turnips, the reddest apples in their township, if they lacked wagon route or railhead or boat landing to get their crops to market? To be sure, there were

The Adsit log cabin, on Willsboro Point, was built by Yankee settlers in the 1790s.

James Swedberg

snug farming settlements in places as far-flung as Lake Placid and Lake Luzerne, but once other options were open (tourism especially), agriculture as the prime force of the local economy quickly took a back seat.

The fact that the nineteenth century Adirondack region was unvisited by marauding bands of horse-borne, painted Indians, or masked banditos, has made it hard for us to see it as a frontier territory every bit as dangerous and seemingly remote as the highlands of New Mexico or Arizona, but this is surely how it felt to the first lonely, forest-bound pioneers. As Adirondack cultural historian Philip Terrie has observed, "The only thing that distinguished the Adirondacks from western frontier regions was that exploitation of local riches — real or imaginary — did not involve the removal or slaughter of indigenous peoples."

Everybody knew the Adirondacks was no place for a farmer with any kind of means. Settlers moved there mostly when they couldn't afford better pickings elsewhere. But how many of these hopeful pioneers could guess at a glance that such fair-seeming country could make a poor man poorer still? Little wonder that so many from this first generation of Adirondack pioneers pushed on to greener pastures farther west when the Erie canal opened for business in 1825, or hastened home to long-settled New England. At the same time, as the rough reality of Adirondack climate and topography eroded the Jeffersonian dream scape of a thousand well-tended, self-sufficient little farms, another kind of vision cast its own enduring spell — the view of the Adirondack woodlands not as a hindrance to a farmer's fortune but as a fortune in itself, rich as Croesus in the two crops that are the bane of any farmer's existence: namely, tall trees and big rocks thickly seamed with iron ore.

It wasn't that these native crops weren't right there for the harvesting all along or that the colonists and the Indians before them were unmindful of them. But in 1700, what New Hampshire homesteader was thinking about the

Courtesy Edward Comstock Jr.

Adirondack rivers were declared public highways so that logs could travel freely downstream to cities like Glens Falls and Lyons Falls.

red spruce of the Adirondack interior? All the timber a colonist could hope for was right there in the back forty. It would take the depletion of the New England and southern New York forests to force a deeper move into northern New York, an advance that only quickened as innovations in the woods industries made it easier to get trees out. In the early 1800s, legislation that declared New York rivers public highways launched the great age of the Adirondack river drive. By mid-century fast-running Adirondack rivers — the Saranac, the Grasse, the Schroon, the Hudson — were sometimes so densely shingled over with floating logs a skilled river driver could hop from log to log for half a mile with nary a glimpse of the water roiling underneath.

By 1850 New York State led the nation in timber production. Tiny sawmills that once catered to the basic needs of pioneers now shipped and sledded their product north to Canada or south to Albany. The feudal land baron was supplanted by the capitalist lumber baron, and the homesteader once as game to burn a tree as look at it now added skilled logger or river driver to his resume. Every tree, it seemed, had its use: white pine and red spruce for ships' masts and house construction; hardwood for charcoal; hemlock for the bark whose tannin-rich liquor was essential in the curing of leather, a particularly vital Adirondack industry from 1860 to 1880. In the last two decades of the nineteenth century, the shift from rags to wood pulp in the papermaking industry brought a whole new world of trees into the loggers' line of fire. Pulp-grinding machinery didn't care how straight or true or old or long the wood it used. Cellulose fiber did the trick, and trees as skinny as three inches round were fair game.

As for that other bumper Adirondack crop, iron ore, it too owned a hearty appetite for vast stands of wood. Ore was so abundant in the northeastern Adirondacks you could see it plainly in the outcrops along Lake Champlain, and so famously pure, some of it, you could work it fresh from the seam. Better than two hundred forges operated in the nineteenth century Adirondacks, almost half of them along the iron-russet banks of two Adirondack rivers, the Ausable and the Saranac. Of the scores of remote hamlets that owed their founding to these charcoal-hungry forges, many are now ghost towns or little more than a cluster of leafy sinkholes in the woods, but in 1850, New York State led the nation in iron ore production. The lumber barons who had overtaken the "harpy land barons" were now joined in their pursuit of wood by mining magnates, whose prolific crews of woodchoppers and colliers (charcoal makers) kept their forges bright with burning charcoal. Thanks to those mining magnates, the Adirondack forest suffered its first scarifying clearcuts. Indeed, it was the mining industry, much more than lumbering, that did so much to load the quills of illustrators whose before-and-after engravings of the Adirondacks (virgin, then denuded) in magazines like *Harper's* and *Frank Leslie's Illustrated Weekly*, spurred an outraged readership to support the notion of an Adirondack forest preserve. Consider: it took two and a quarter cords of wood to make one hundred bushels of charcoal, and up to 500 bushels of charcoal to generate a ton of Adirondack ore. The hills were alive with the sound of crashing hardwoods. Music to some ears, perhaps, but to others, an infernal racket.

As industrialization stepped up the demand for the extractive products of the northern New York wilderness — tanbark, logs, pulpwood, ore — settlers found plenty of pick-up work to buttress the meager output from their hardscrabble farms. And a good thing too: the flexible, seasonally responsive diversification of the Adirondack home economy — a potato farm in the summer, a logging gig in the winter, a little hauling, a little millwork, a job guiding city fishermen to favorite streams — was the key to survival, and this tradition, long honored by migratory bands of Native Americans, defines the Adirondack lifestyle even now.

But when local hands proved too few to meet the labor needs of fast-growing mining towns, tannery hamlets, and logging camps, another source of labor was introduced: immigrants and migratory workers. To an extent, different industries generated different ethnic enclaves. Irish immigrants, for example, were often drawn to tannery towns. French Canadians worked in the woods, Italians on the railroad tracks, Poles and Lithuanians in the mines. But no single ethnic group monopolized any single industry to the exclusion of any other. St. Regis Mohawk Indians worked on river drives and in Adirondack tanneries as well. In Lyon Mountain, Witherbee, or Mineville, eastern European miners worked cheek by jowl with Italians, Spaniards, Irish laborers, and African Americans; indeed, the first iron miners in the Adirondacks were the land baron Philip Skene's black slaves. The logging camp at Wanakena featured a

Old Rocks, New Mountains

Mount Marcy (below the moon) and other previously jagged High Peaks were rounded off by glacial ice thousands of years ago.

Katherine E. McClelland photograph courtesy of Smith College Archives

The rocks beneath Adirondack peaks and valleys were formed from sediments laid down in shallow seas some 1.3 billion years ago. Though that sounds like a tranquil enough beginning, the intervening millennia between the Grenville period and modern times was a chaotic riot of rumpling, folding, shearing, compressing, cracking, and colliding. Himalayan-like peaks rose, then were beaten down by weather and wave; the land was then stretched and cloven as continents crashed into one another. The metamorphic rocks we walk on today, atop Mount Marcy or even along a southern Adirondack stream, were once buried fifteen to twenty miles beneath the surface.

Today's mountain ranges, though, were ultimately shaped by the scraping action of a mile-thick glacier 10,000-plus years ago. This moving wall of ice took the jagged peaks down to their hardest bedrock, deposited sand as sinuous eskers, and left behind giant boulders — erratics — as calling cards. The Adirondacks are rising still, reaching up at a rate of two or three centimeters a year, thanks to a hot spot deep within the Earth.

From the high points of land, hundreds of rivers drain north into the St. Lawrence River, east to Lake Champlain, and south to the Hudson and Mohawk valleys. Lakes often fill the ancient fault valleys, in diagonal lines between the mountains.

Swedish sauna, and up near Chazy an encampment of Italian stonemasons built themselves a hive-shaped bread oven in the woods.

Because these rough-hewn, company-built settlements rose and dispersed with the success and decline of the industries that founded them, their story has excited little notice among Adirondack historians. If anything, the Adirondacks has enjoyed a certain nativist reputation as a demographic land apart, free and clear of "outsiders," the monolithic stronghold of the Yankee pioneer. But northern New York was never exempt from the demographic trends that salted so much of rural America with ethnic enclaves during the

Ads, Dacks, and Adirondacks

The word "Adirondack" reportedly comes from an Iroquois word that means "they eat bark," an insult referring to the Algonquin's allegedly lousy woodcraft skills. That can't be proven, though (neither their ineptitude nor the etymology); using romantic native-sounding words has long been a favorite pastime of map-makers, writers, and even politicians. What can be defined, though are some North Country specifics:

The Adirondack Park: Established in 1892, it covers 6.1 million acres of public and private land in a shield shape that includes much of the northern third of New York State. It's the largest state park in the nation. It's not all wilderness: everything within, from the summits of the highest peaks to the most remote bog to Main Street in Lake Placid, is in the park.

• **The Adirondack Forest Preserve:** Established in 1885, this is about 42 percent of the Adirondack Park that is public land, and preserved as wilderness, wild forest, or primitive areas. It's composed of many scattered parcels, not one contiguous unit, although some wilderness areas are vast enough to take days to cross on foot. In a nutshell, if you're on Forest Preserve land you're free to hike, hunt, fish, canoe, and do almost whatever else you want, although wilderness areas are off-limits to motorized vehicles (e.g., snowmobiles and motorboats). If you're not on public land, you're trespassing on somebody's property, unless you have permission to be there. Odd as it may seem to come across private land inside a state park, please respect it. If you want to go for a walk in the woods, look for trailheads with state Department of Environmental Conservation signs, they are on public land.

• **The Adirondack Mountains:** The tallest summits — the celebrated High Peaks — occupy the northeast quarter of the Adirondack Park, but there are chains of mountains and scattered monadnocks throughout the region. They generally lie in parallel fault valleys, making a southwest to northeast diagonal across the park.

great age of industrialization. If a migratory lifestyle deprived many of these immigrant communities of a place in the written historical record, you can still trace the evidence of an ethnic presence in the tongue-twisting nomenclature of early headstones, the sunken remains of one-time railroad tracks, the French or Irish street names in Adirondack towns.

Not every nineteenth century Adirondack railroad spur bore carloads full of hemlock bark or iron ore, pulpwood or massive logs. Some were built specially to ferry a special cargo *to* the woods: namely, the sightseers and "city sports" for whom, from 1870 to 1910 or so, a visit to the distant Adirondacks held all the exotic cachet of an African safari. The burgeoning resort scene was an inevitable extension of the "Grand Tour" of the North Country that already encompassed toney Saratoga Springs and elegant Lake George. And where railroad sleepers left off, stagecoaches and steamboats picked up — another source of seasonal employment for enterprising locals, some of who would parlay modest stagecoach routes into backwoods transportation empires.

This new, bourgeois resort clientele expected rather different lodgings than

In the 19th century, steamboats delivered thousands of guests to lakefront hotels, from Blue Mountain Lake (pictured here) to Lake George and the Saranac Lakes.

Courtesy of Edward Comstock Jr.

the circuit riders and traveling peddlers who preceded them, and Adirondack hostelries made haste to adjust. The proverbial backcountry tavern with its rough pallets in the attic begat the North Country inn, which in turn begat the double-balconied hotel, with uniformed black waiters, Irish cooks, and ready stable of picturesque, authentically gruff Adirondack guides. More socially positioned visitors were lucky enough to enjoy an invitation to one of the Adirondack Great Camps, private compounds sometimes as built-up as a small town. Here guests were plied with the bubbliest champagne, the mildest Cuban stogies, and the most delicious six-course feasts that the ruthlessly gotten gains of the Gilded Age could buy.

Wilderness no longer had to justify itself as a means to an agricultural or industrial end; it was increasingly an end in itself, good, it was held, for spirit, soul, and body, especially those bodies in the early grip of tuberculosis. Lots of rest and good clean air, that pretty much summed up the homely prescription of Dr. Edward Livingston Trudeau, the great champion of the "Adirondack cure," and that's what a six-week stint in the screened-in porch of a Saranac Lake village cure cottage delivered. In this hill-bound hamlet, there were, in addition to Trudeau's well-known sanatorium, cure cottages for Lower East Side tenement girls, for Cuban aristocrats, for show business mavens, and for Hungarian aesthetes. Robert Louis Stevenson did a turn at Saranac Lake. So did the gangster "Legs" Diamond. You sat, you ate, you rested, you got bored out of your mind. But as often as not, you did get better. And if you didn't, your problem was you found the Adirondacks just too late to do you good.

What happened when the tourists and the travelers collided with the worked-over, roughed-up landscape of the Adirondack industrialist and his heavy-booted teams of loggers, tanners, river drivers, and millworkers? No matter how pristine the eventual destination, the view from the stagecoach or sleeper window almost certainly exposed the Adirondack adventurer to the occasional glimpse of clear-cut hillsides and tangled slash. Sometimes it

Great Camp décor was often an eclectic mix of twigs, logs, bark, and stone – plus Japanese lanterns, Oriental rugs, and Indian baskets. Camp Cedars interior, Forked Lake.

Adirondack Museum

seemed the more prolific the newly converted admirers of the region, the faster it was changing, and not for the better. Was it an accident that in the same year (1864) an anonymous editorial in *The New York Times* suggested that the Adirondack region be preserved as a "Central Park for the world" and George Perkins Marsh published his seminal book, *Man and Nature*, on the delicate relationship between a healthy forest and a secure watershed?

Cut too much, Marsh argued, and you set the scene for a tidal wave of muddy run-off, and unleash the threat of flood and drought. Too much cutting can even make the climate change, and diminish rainfall, which in turn would damage agricultural production. No more rain: no more farms, no more food — worst case scenario, *no more people*! In New York State specifically, as surveyor Verplanck Colvin pointed out, a ravaged watershed in the north could mean lower water levels for the Hudson and the Erie Canal — a disaster for commercial and transportation interests, and for downstate politicians. A healthy watershed was also a safeguard against water-borne disease, a concern of no small moment to the epidemic-leery voters of metropolitan New York.

Though it would take a few more decades to gather steam enough to win the necessary political support, here was a perfectly utilitarian rationale for the founding of a preserve. No early advocate ever argued for the Adirondack Park in aesthetic terms alone. It helped that the region was gorgeous, but it was health and public safety, not good looks and recreation, that won the day in 1885 with the creation of the Adirondack Forest Preserve, then comprised of almost 700,000 acres scattered over eleven counties. Five years later the state began to consolidate its holdings with further purchases, and the expectation was expressed that someday all the land within the penciled "Blue Line" that outlined the edges of this new park would comprise "One Grand, Unbroken Domain."

In 1892, the Adirondack Park was officially defined. Three years after that, a new state constitution declared these Forest Preserve lands should be "forever kept as wild forest lands." Private land could still be logged, but state land was off-limits, allowed to grow up and fall down without interference from man. It was, notes the historian Philip Terrie, a provision that made the Adirondack

Presidents in Residence

Although we can't claim that George Washington slept here, the father of our country was certainly aware of the vital importance of fortifications at Ticonderoga and Crown Point along Lake Champlain's western shore. **Thomas Jefferson** and **James Madison** visited Lake George in 1791, on a summer reconnoiter to Vermont that doubled as a vacation; Jefferson, a seasoned world traveler, described the lake as one of the most beautiful he'd ever seen.

In 1817, **James Monroe** skirted the wild edge of what would become the Adirondack Park in a trip from Champlain to Sackets Harbor, on the St. Lawrence River. **Andrew Jackson**, who served in Congress from 1827–1829, was a close friend of Richard Keese II, after whom the village of Keeseville is named. Jackson ("Old Hickory") went north to see Keese, and in honor of the occasion, a hickory sapling was sought to plant in the front yard of the homestead. But no hickories could be found for miles around, so a bitter walnut was substituted. It thrived.

Chester A. Arthur stayed at Mart Moody's Mount Morris House, near Tupper Lake, in 1869, and slept on the floor like everyone else. When he was president, in 1881, Arthur named the guide and innkeeper postmaster of a new settlement named — surprisingly enough — Moody.

Grover Cleveland also knew Moody as a guide. While hunting near Big Wolf Pond, Cleveland reportedly said to him, "There's no wolves, here, darn it! But — there ain't a hundred pencils here, either, goin' every minute to take down everything I say." The president returned to the Adirondacks for his honeymoon, and also stayed at posh places like the Grand View, in Lake Placid, and the Saranac Inn.

President **Benjamin Harrison** visited his vice-presidential candidate Whitelaw Reid at Loon Lake during the 1892 campaign, and he whistle-stopped in Crown Point, Lyon Mtn., Bloomingdale, and Saranac Lake. Along the way, he was feted with band concerts and pageants, and given gifts of iron ore and wildflower arrangements. In 1895, Harrison built a rustic log camp named Berkeley Lodge on Second Lake, near Old Forge.

William McKinley made a special trip here to John Brown's grave in 1897, but it was his assassination that led to one of the most exciting footnotes in Adirondack history. **Theodore Roosevelt**, who first came to the mountains as a teenager in 1871, was climbing Mt. Marcy when news of McKinley's imminent demise was cabled north. A guide scrambled up the peak to tell T.R., who made it down in record time. Three relays of teams and wagons whisked him in the murk of night from the Tahawus Club to North Creek, and Roosevelt learned he had become the twenty-sixth president on September 14, 1901, in the North Creek railroad station.

Calvin Coolidge established a summer White House at White Pine Camp, on Osgood Pond, in 1926. This was at the height of Prohibition; silent Cal's place was a mere stone's throw away from Gabriels, a hotbed of bootleg activity.

Franklin D. Roosevelt was no stranger to the North Country. He officiated at the opening of the 1932 Winter Olympics, dedicated the Whiteface Memorial Highway in 1935, and celebrated the fiftieth anniversary of the Forest Preserve in Lake Placid that same year.

Forest Preserve "one of the best protected landscapes in the world." And enacted not a day too soon: late nineteenth-century innovations in pulpmaking meant that virtually *all* the woods were fair game for the lumber magnates, and between 1890 and 1910, the very years the Park was birthed, logging activity on privately held lands within the park actually peaked. Of course, the more frenetic the pace of logging, the faster the non-state-owned forest was depleted, and as shortages occurred, many lumber companies began to move their logging operations elsewhere, to tree-cloaked Quebec, for instance, or to the temperate South.

And what was moving in about this time, sputtering exhaust and spitting gravel and scaring horses half to death? Infernal combustion. Automobiles were rare enough in the Adirondack region in the early 1900s, but within a generation roads were snaking between passes. And in their dusty wake followed not only carloads of vacationers, but trailheads that met the roads and led hikers to remote summits; roadside auto courts, housekeeping cabins, and filling stations; and roadside attractions with music, dancing, and even dancing bears.

Was it the end of the Adirondack Park or the beginning? Certainly the age of the automobile spelled the death of the Adirondacks' vaunted isolation and mystique. You didn't need to come for a season anymore. From the necklace of mid-size cities that outline the Adirondack region (Glens Falls, Plattsburgh, Ogdensburg, Watertown, Amsterdam, Gloversville, Massena, Malone), you could do it in a day! Or chug up from Albany or even Brooklyn for a nice long weekend: pack the trunk with tent and camping gear, throw the kids in back under a blanket, check the oil, kick the tires — you're off. No two-week stay at one hotel; you could play connect-the-dots between lakeside campgrounds under the towering white pines, cook your own chow over an open fire instead of dealing with a stuck-up waiter in a uniform at some swank hotel. You didn't need to hire a guide; a good map and one of those new wood-canvas canoes could do you just as well.

Roads democratized the Adirondack experience as no paper legislation ever could, and with the ease of access, the reputation of the region as a recreational nirvana grew by leaps and bounds. Small towns reeling under the recent loss or exodus of the extractive industries rebounded with a plethora of services aimed squarely at the car-borne tourist: diners, supper clubs (maybe, during Prohibition, with speakeasy in back), motels, and souvenir shops (Step right up! Get your genuine Mohawk-made balsam pillows! Your German porcelain souvenir plaques! Your maple sugar candy and your Japanese paper flowers!). As the century wore on, those small town storefronts would increasingly include the recreational outfitter and the real estate office. Nothing like the completion of a super-highway, the "Northway," or Interstate 87, in 1967, to whet the appetite of city dwellers keen to build their Adirondack getaway.

Indeed, so rapid was the proliferation of Adirondack second homes in the

Virgin Trees and Charismatic Megafauna

The Adirondack forest primeval — which survives today in scattered tracts of old growth in remote wilderness areas like the Five Ponds and West Canadas — varies according to elevation and soil. At the very tops of some mountains, only alpine shrubs and flowers grow, and below them are stunted trees known as the *krummholz*, which can be hundreds of years old yet only a few feet high. Lower down, thick spruce-fir forests grow; on steep, inaccessible slopes some patches have remained undisturbed for centuries. White pine and spruce take over at an elevation of 2,500 feet or so, with mixed hardwood forests — yellow birch, beech, sugar maple, plus eastern hemlock — covering miles and miles of the central Adirondacks. The understory in this woodland is the classic Adirondack landscape, with beautiful ferns and wildflowers like trillium, lady's slipper, and jack in the pulpit.

James Swedberg

Moose disappeared from the Adirondacks between 1870–1970, but are now making a comeback, especially near Lewey Lake. Road sign on Rt. 30.

White pine towering 150 feet tall and enormous spruce were the first to fall before the woodsman's ax. These logs were floated downstream to towns and sawmills as early as 1812, and following the Civil War, when paper-making technology made the great leap from rags to wood pulp, softwood forests were stripped bare. Hemlocks too had great commercial value; bark was a necessary ingredient in leather tanning, but the wood itself was left to rot where it fell. Many towns in the central and southern Adirondacks owe their existence to tanneries that processed South American hides into American shoe parts.

Early records show a wide variety of wildlife ranging through the different habitats of woods and waters. Elk lived in the St. Lawrence and Mohawk river valleys as late as the 1820s, and moose were common throughout the lake country until about 1870. Mountain lions and wolves posed a serious threat to settlement, but generous bounties paid out by counties (in the mid-1800s, some locales paid more for bounties in a year than they spent on schools) decreased the numbers of predators considerably. Mountain lions are occasionally spotted today, although conservation officials deny any breeding population; questions linger about wolves. Did gray wolves ever really live in upstate New York, or are the smaller, reddish canines we call coyotes the historic Adirondack wolf?

Black bears have adapted remarkably well to life with humans; their numbers have been stable over this century. Other carnivores like fisher, pine marten, and bobcat are thriving in the forest. Lynx once were found in the High Peaks and other rugged countryside, preying on snowshoe hares, but disappeared due to hunting and habitat changes. Efforts to reintroduce the species in the 1980s have proven fruitless.

The big reintroduction success story is the beaver. For three centuries, well before maps and military expeditions, there was lively trade in beaver pelts, with furs shipped to Fort Orange (now Albany) and Montreal. Beaver hair pressed into felt was used in fashionable hats, and demand soon exceeded the supply. By 1894 beavers were virtually extinct; in the early 1900s, they were reintroduced to the Old Forge area. By 1910 the animals had spread throughout the central Adirondacks, busily building dams and flooding woodlands. Today you can see evidence of their engineering on almost any Adirondack waterway.

In addition to the lakes, forests and peaks, these beavers' engineering efforts create habitat for the Adirondack bird population. Loons, revered for their haunting songs, inhabit many larger Adirondack lakes and ponds. With luck you may see an osprey, peregrine falcon, or bald eagle soaring on warm currents over a lakeshore or cliff. Hawks are fairly easy to spot; songbirds – especially warblers – are plentiful during warm weather; and at least ten varieties of ducks nest near the waterways of the park. For more birding information, see "Wildlife" in Chapter Six, *Recreation*.

sixties, and so potentially damaging was their impact on the landscape, that Governor Nelson Rockefeller appointed a commission that recommended a new agency just to oversee land use and development. Thus was spawned the controversial Adirondack Park Agency (APA) in 1974. Many are the local objections to the APA's unwieldy bureaucratic mandate (to guide development on public and private lands), but on one thing its critics can almost all wholeheartedly agree: the establishment over a hundred years ago of the Adirondack Park was a miracle of timing, foresight, and good luck. It could not have happened any sooner, and it certainly could not have happened since. Love the park for its variety and beauty, and you won't be disappointed, but love it for its hidden history as well — the lost loggers, the vanished tannery towns, the boarded-over mine shafts, the stagecoaches, the peddlers, and the wedding cake hotels — and your love and understanding of it can only be enhanced.

CHAPTER TWO

Over the Rivers and Through the Woods

TRANSPORTATION

On any road map of New York State, the Adirondack Park shows up as a green, shield-shaped polygon. Looking closer, you'll notice that the park boundary encloses a lot of empty space, crossed by few highways and dotted by towns. This reflects the large portion of the park that's public land, and it doesn't mean that those spidery thin lines are bad roads. Major roads through the Adirondacks are well-maintained two-lane blacktop, the lifelines of the region. Come winter, an army of snowplows and sand trucks keeps the roads clear; two feet of snow here causes far less trouble here than two inches, in say, Washington, D.C.

Courtesy of Edward Comstock Jr.

Stagecoaches traveled between most Adirondack towns in the 19th century, offering a quick, but dusty and bone-jarring ride.

On that map, you'll notice lots of blue rivers and lakes, the region's original travel corridors. By canoe or by snowshoe over the ice, Native Americans and the first Europeans followed these paths of least resistance. Although no river provided passage through the entire rugged region, it was possible to travel from the southwest to northeast corners via the Moose, Raquette, and Saranac river systems with but a few short "carries," the Adirondack word for "portage." The importance of the rivers is underscored by the fact that in the early 1800s many streams were declared public highways for the purpose of floating logs to market on them.

The first roads were hacked out of the forest in the early 1800s, to transport iron ore, charcoal, and other commodities between settlements. Later, some of these dirt tracks were corduroyed (paved with logs), but they were never very good, not much more than wide trails. A stagecoach ride on one could be a bone-jarring, tooth-loosening experience, and a special passenger wagon, the "buckboard," with a long, springy board between the front and back wheels, evolved to make the best of terrible roads.

Even into the beginnings of the tourist era, waterways remained principal transportation routes, and most towns were built along a lake or river that allowed people to connect with the larger world. In response, specific vessels were developed: the guideboat — light, fast, and maneuverable, easy for one man to carry overland — with oars rather than paddles, marvelous for fishing and hunting on Adirondack ponds; and tiny steamboats, built to fit the small lakes of the interior.

The first widespread, modern means of movement was the railroad. Originally built to haul timber out, the railroads quickly became a profitable, convenient way to haul tourists in. Beginning about 1900, a web of lines throughout the region saw several passenger trains a day speeding north from East Coast cities to destinations in the park. One of the most popular targets, Blue Mountain Lake, could be reached by a remarkable trip that involved an overnight train ride from New York via Utica, transfer to a steamboat, change to the world's shortest standard-gauge railroad (less than a mile long), and a final transfer to another steamboat for delivery to your hotel of choice.

Courtesy of Saranac Lake Free Library, Adirondack Collection

A novelty in the 1900s, the automobile proved to be the best way to navigate around the Adirondack Park.

By the 1920s, with the growing popularity of the automobile, roads were gradually improved until they eventually surpassed the railroads, although such special offerings as ski trains enabled passenger service to struggle along until well after World War II. The late 1960s were a watershed time; the last passenger train serving the interior, the Adirondack Division of the New York Central (the Utica-to-Lake Placid line), rolled to a stop in 1965, and the Adirondack Northway, the only interstate highway in the region, was completed along the eastern edge of the park in 1967. This event seemed at once to assure that the family car would be the way the vast majority of people would travel to the Adirondacks for years to come, and to discourage the development of a public transportation system.

So, if you want to get around in the 21st century Adirondacks, you'll need your own wheels. If you don't own a car, rent one before you get to the North Country. Even if you come here by some other means, once you arrive it can be difficult to do much without one. Public transportation is scarce and not always convenient.

The following information gives you the best routes for access to the Adirondacks, and for getting around once you're here. We start with the most practical means of transportation — your car — and also provide details on bus, train, and air service. Routes that incorporate a ferry crossing are also described. A selection of taxi services in principal communities is listed as well. For car rentals within the Adirondacks (availability has expanded in recent years), we suggest you contact the chamber of commerce or visitor information center of the area you plan to visit; you'll find phone numbers and addresses under "Tourist Information" in Chapter Eight, *Information.*

BY CAR

HIGHWAYS TO GET YOU HERE

Major highways can get you to the perimeter of the Adirondack Park from all points:

• ***From New York City:*** Take I-87 north. This is the New York State (or Thomas E. Dewey) Thruway, a toll road, to Albany (Exit 24); then it becomes the toll-free Adirondack Northway. Principal exits off the Northway for the interior are 21 (Lake George), roughly four hours from metro New York; 23 (Warrensburg, North Creek, and Blue Mtn. Lake), about 15 minutes farther north; 28 (Schroon Lake, Paradox Lake, and Ticonderoga), about five hours from New York; and 30 (for Lake Placid, Saranac Lake, and the High Peaks), another 15 minutes up the line.

• ***From Philadelphia and South:*** Take the Northeast Extension of the Pennsylvania Turnpike and then I-81 north to Syracuse. From Syracuse take I-90 east to entry points such as Utica and Amsterdam, or I-81 farther north and then east on Rte. 3 at Watertown to reach the northern areas. Either way, it's

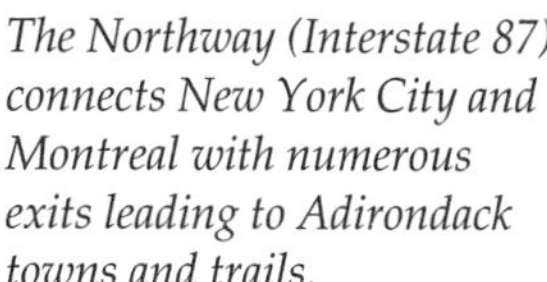

The Northway (Interstate 87) connects New York City and Montreal with numerous exits leading to Adirondack towns and trails.

Melody Thomas

not as far as you might think — you can reach the southwest edge of the park in about six hours from Philadelphia. Or you can take I-88 from Binghamton to Schenectady, go east two exits on I-90 and head north on I-87 from Albany; see above, "From New York." And there's always the Garden State Parkway to the New York Thruway, then proceed as above.

• ***From Buffalo, Cleveland, and West:*** Take I-90 east to Syracuse, then proceed as directed above ("From Philadelphia"). From Buffalo to the edge of the park north of Utica is a little over four hours.

• ***From Toronto and Detroit:*** Take Rte. 401 toward Montreal. Three toll bridges cross the St. Lawrence River. The one that provides the most direct access not only to the edge of the park but also to such interior locations as Lake Placid and Blue Mtn. Lake leaps from Prescott (Highway 16 exit) to Ogdensburg; the toll is $2.00 U.S. one way. On the U.S. side, take Rte. 37 west a couple of miles to Rte. 68 south to Colton, and Rte. 56 into the park. From Toronto it's about five hours to the edge of the park and seven to the center.

• ***From Ottawa:*** Take Highway 16 to the Prescott–Ogdensburg toll bridge and proceed as directed above ("From Toronto"). Allow two hours to the edge of the park, four to central points.

• ***From Montreal:*** Take Highway 15 south; this becomes I-87, the Adirondack Northway, at the border. Principal jumping-off exits for the interior are 38 (Plattsburgh), only an hour (plus customs wait, which can be lengthy) from the outskirts of Montreal; and 34 (Keeseville), 20 minutes south of Exit 38.

• ***From Boston:*** Take the Mass. Pike, I-90, to I-87, then head north and follow the directions given under "From New York," above, to get past Albany. Or, take I-93 north to I-89, to one of the Lake Champlain ferry crossings described below. Via Albany, the Adirondacks are about four hours from Boston; via the ferries they're closer to five, but the ferries are fun.

HIGHWAYS TO GET YOU AROUND ONCE YOU GET HERE

North and South

Not surprisingly, four of the five north-south highways that traverse the Adirondacks do so in the narrow corridor between Lake Champlain and the mountains. This is where much of the region's population and many of its attractions are located, and it's also on a direct line between two concentrations of population: New York City and Montreal. These routes are:

• ***NY Rte. 9N,*** which rambles through lovely rolling countryside from Saratoga Springs northwest to Corinth and Lake Luzerne, then east to Lake George village, then up to Hague, and to Lake Champlain at Ticonderoga, where it meets . . .

• ***NY Rte. 22,*** which hugs Lake Champlain all the way from Whitehall, up to Ticonderoga, where it joins 9N. The combined routes have expansive views of the lake on the east and farmland in the valley beneath the High Peaks on the west, passing through Crown Point and Port Henry. At Westport, Rte. 22 follows the lake valley north to Willsboro, while 9N heads west to Elizabethtown, over Spruce Hill and on to Keene. This historic route passes through Upper Jay, Jay, and Au Sable Forks, paralleling the Ausable River, and connects again with Rte. 22 at Keeseville.

• ***U.S. Rte. 9*** begins in the park just north of Glens Falls and skirts Schroon Lake and the Schroon and Boquet rivers, but its route has been mostly supplanted by . . .

• ***I-87,*** the Adirondack Northway, a honest-to-goodness interstate highway named "America's Most Scenic Highway," in 1966–1967.

• ***NY Rte. 30,*** the fifth north-south route, bisects the region from Gloversville via Speculator, Indian Lake, Blue Mtn. Lake, Long Lake, Tupper Lake, and Paul Smiths to Malone. The remote and lightly populated western half of the region has no north-south highways.

East and West

Reflecting the reality that most travel in the Adirondacks always has been north-south, only three highways traverse the entire region on the east-west axis, and two of them cover some of the same territory. These are:

• ***NY Rte. 28,*** which forms a semicircle from Warrensburg through North Creek, Indian Lake, Blue Mtn. Lake, Inlet, Old Forge, and down to Utica.

• ***NY Rte. 8,*** which zigzags west from Hague, on Lake George, through Brant Lake, Chestertown, Johnsburg, Speculator, Lake Pleasant, Piseco, Hoffmeister, and southwest to Utica.

• ***NY Rte. 3,*** which crosses the northern part of the park from Plattsburgh, to Redford, Vermontville, Bloomingdale, Saranac Lake, Tupper Lake, Piercefield, Childwold, Cranberry Lake, Star Lake, and exits the Blue Line west to Watertown.

ADIRONDACK ACCESS

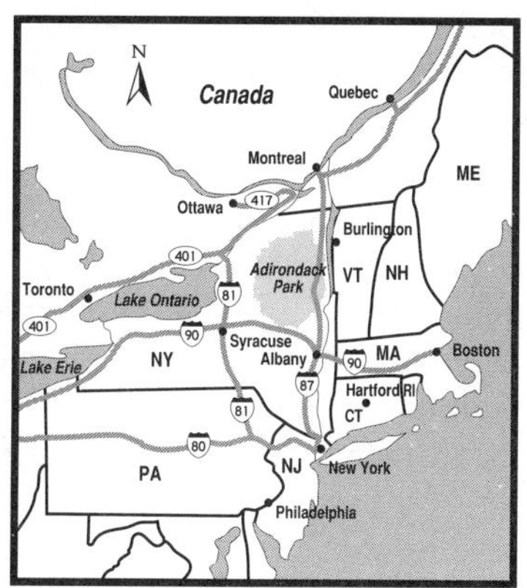

Blue Mtn. Lake is central — it's $1^1/2$ to 2 hours to the edge of the park in every direction — so this location will serve as a reference point in determining about how long a drive to the Adirondacks will take:

CITY	MILES TO BLUE MTN. LAKE	APPROXIMATE TIME TO BLUE MTN. LAKE
Albany	105	2 hrs
Binghamton	220	4 hrs
Boston (via Albany)	270	5 1/2 hrs
Buffalo	280	5 1/2 hrs
Burlington, VT	100	3 hrs (involves ferry)
Montreal	165	3 1/2 hrs*
New York	260	5 1/2 hrs
Ottawa	150	3 1/2 hrs*
Philadelphia	390	8 hrs
Rochester	210	4 1/2 hrs
Syracuse	140	3 hrs
Toronto	320	7 hrs*
Utica	90	2 hrs

*plus possible delays crossing border

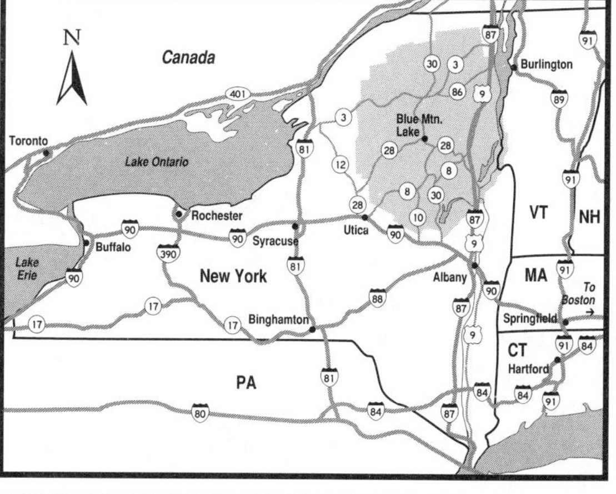

Additional Routes

Other shorter but scenic routes in the Adirondacks include:

• ***Northeast on NY Rte. 73*** from Underwood (Exit 30 of the Northway) to Lake Placid, which offers a 45-minute panorama of the High Peaks.

• ***West on NY Rte. 86*** from Jay, past the foot of Whiteface Mtn. and through dramatic Wilmington Notch to Lake Placid, then on to Saranac Lake and Paul Smiths.

• ***East on NY Rte. 374*** from Chateaugay, past the Chateaugay lakes and Lyon Mtn. to Plattsburgh, which, in addition to views of the Adirondacks, provides a long-distance scan across Lake Champlain to the Green Mountains of Vermont as it drops down Dannemora Mtn.

• ***Northwest on NY Rte. 28N*** from North Creek on Rte. 28 to Long Lake. Be sure to stop at the roadside rest area at Newcomb, where a display identifies the High Peaks panorama to the north.

• ***East on the "Number Four" Road*** from Lowville, past Stillwater Reservoir and on to Big Moose and Eagle Bay, which is on NY Rte. 28. This drive offers not so much great views as a sense of the forest depths. About half of the 45 miles is gravel or graded dirt, and there are no services over the full distance.

The Adirondack North Country Association (ANCA) has designed several driving tours both in and around the Adirondacks. These are arranged so as to hit scenic vistas, historic markers, craft shops, and so on. You can pick up a map of these routes at tourist centers and chambers of commerce, or call ANCA at 518-891-6200.

BY BUS

Considering the size of the Adirondack region — you could fit Connecticut inside it — it's astonishing how little bus service exists. There's only one round trip a day that's of any use, and once you get off the bus you're dependent on traveling by foot, or finding sparse taxi service and even sparser rental car possibilities. If you do plan to use bus service, here are your options:

• ***Greyhound Lines, Inc.***, plies the I-87 ("Northway") route on the eastern edge of the park a couple times a day, but declines to stop anywhere within the Blue Line. The best you can do is Glens Falls or Plattsburgh. For more information: 518-434-8095 (Albany terminal), 518-793-5052 (Glens Falls), or 518-563-1480 (Plattsburgh).

• ***CHAMP Express*** offers service within Essex County and between Lake Placid and Plattsburgh, connecting with Greyhound buses there. For more information: 518-523-4431.

• ***Adirondack Trailways*** is your best bet for bus access, and offers the following routes:

Daily trips into the interior: You can escape Manhattan as early as 7am from the Port Authority Bus Terminal, from gates 60–65 for Lake George, and by 10:30am to towns further north, like Schroon Lake, Keene Valley, Lake Placid, Saranac Lake, and Tupper Lake. Allow five hours to reach Warrensburg, one of the southernmost Adirondack stops. Other Trailways buses leave at semi-regular intervals in the afternoon; call ahead for a schedule. A one-way ticket from New York City to Warrensburg cost just under $40 in 1999. Southbound trips leave Canton at 9:15am daily and arrive in New York at 7:20pm.

Some of the stops on this run help you realize you're not in urban America anymore. The "bus station" in Keene Valley, for example, is the Noon Mark Diner; in Lake Placid, it's at Lake Placid Video.

Five other buses from New York/Albany north: Two penetrate the Adirondacks as far as Warrensburg and the other three give it up in Glens Falls, just outside the Adirondack Park. There's also summer-only service along the west shore of Lake George to Ticonderoga.

For more information: Adirondack Trailways, 800-225-6815.

In Chapter Three, *Lodging*, accommodations within walking distance of local bus stops are noted.

BY TRAIN

AMTRAK

Amtrak operates one train a day each way between New York City and Montreal, which was brought to national attention in the 1997 PBS special *America's Scenic Rail Journeys*. ***"The Adirondack"*** leaves each city in the morning and reaches its destination the same evening (schedules are different on Sundays), closely following the west shore of Lake Champlain for the better part of 90 miles through the park. The New York departure is from Penn Station (212-582-6875). It makes several stops in the Adirondacks, but how to get around once you are deposited at these places is problematic. You can arrange, in advance, for shuttle service from the handsome Victorian depot in Westport to Lake Placid (or Elizabethtown or Keene) by calling 518-523-4431 or 518-523-1475. It may not be what it once was, but compared to buses and puddle-jumper airplanes, this remains the most relaxing, scenic way to get to the Adirondacks.

The trip is spectacular, involving tunnels, high trestles, rocky ledges 150 feet above the waters of Lake Champlain, and vistas of farm and forest, river, lake, and mountain that simply cannot be had any other way. The Champlain Valley Heritage Network has published a descriptive map of the route (available from the Essex County Visitors Bureau, 800-44PLACID), which also lists local taxi service. The least expensive Fort Edward–Plattsburgh round-trip fare was $32 in 1999.

Amtrak service to Westport and other towns parallels Lake Champlain, offering beautiful views of water, mountains, farms, and villages.

James Swedberg

In addition, ***Amtrak's Empire Service*** leaves New York's Penn Station several times a day and stops in Albany-Rensselaer, Schenectady, and Utica, where you can arrange to rent a car by calling 800-654-3131 (Hertz) or 800-331-1212 (Avis). One train a day from Boston hooks up with this route at Albany-Rensselaer. Coming from the west, Empire Service originates in Buffalo; Chicago–Boston/New York and Toronto–New York Amtrak trains also ply this route.

For more information: 800-USA-RAIL (872-7245) or 800-523-5700.

In spring 1999, an Amtrak passenger train began trips from Utica to Thendara/Old Forge, marking the rebirth of at least semi-regular train service to the southwestern Adirondacks. Trains run primarily on weekends and holidays from spring through fall, at least one round trip per day. The ride takes approximately 2 1/2 hours; an adult round-trip fare is about $20. Once you're in Old Forge, there's a shuttle bus to take you to the Enchanted Forest and shops on Main Street. This run was not in Amtrak's database at press time, so call Adirondack Scenic Railroad's Utica office at 315-724-0700 for schedule and fare information, or visit www.adirondackrr.com.

TOURIST TRAINS

The ***Adirondack Scenic Railroad*** operates a popular short line from its Thendara station from spring through fall, with round-trip runs south along the Moose River to Otter Lake, and north to Carter Station. Look for special events (Train Robbery Tuesdays) and unique travel opportunities (the ASR allows mountain bikers and canoeists—and their respective conveyance—to use the train as part of their explorations). Fares in 1999 were between $7–$10 for adults, depending on the trip. For fare and schedule information, call 315-369-6290 or visit www.adirondackrr.com.

The ***Adirondack Railway Preservation Society,*** the nonprofit outfit that operates the Adirondack Scenic, hopes by fall 2000 to be running an excursion line on the eight miles of track between Saranac Lake and Lake Placid. Initial approvals to revitalize the entire rail corridor between Carter Station and Lake Placid — which hasn't seen a train in 20 years, and of which the Placid–Saranac line would be the first part — were granted by the state in August 1999.

And beginning in 1999, the Adirondack Scenic Railroad was no longer the only tourist train around, with the opening of the ***Upper Hudson River Railroad*** (UHRR), out of the North Creek Depot. The depot earned a place in history in September 1901 as the spot where Teddy Roosevelt, then vice president, learned that his boss William McKinley had died in Buffalo, and that he was the next president of the United States. A museum is planned for the North Creek station.

The UHRR runs 8.5 miles along the Hudson River to the beautifully restored Riverside Station in Riparius, where passengers can disembark (there's a small refreshment stand) for thirty minutes or so before the return trip. The entire journey takes about 2 hours, 15 minutes.

The 1999 fare was $9 per passenger, with discounts for seniors and children. Daily trips in July and August run at 10am and 1pm from North Creek, with a reduced schedule from April–June and in September and October. Bicyclists can arrange to ride one way and pedal the other; plans are in the works to add a car to haul canoes and kayaks so that paddlers can make an exciting whitewater run downstream and ride in style back to their cars. Call the UHRR at 518-251-5334 to learn about fares and schedules.

Like the Adirondack Scenic, the Upper Hudson has big plans too, to connect with Saratoga Springs to the south. Real passenger service is still years off, but this is one line rail fans should keep an eye on.

BY FERRY

The only way to get to the Adirondacks from the east is to cross Lake Champlain, largest freshwater lake in America after the Great Lakes. You can do that on the bridge at Port Henry, which has a nice view that lasts for about 30 seconds, but why not savor the journey and take one of the Lake Champlain ferries? The views last for up to an hour and you don't have to steer. Three of the four crossings are operated by the oldest continuously running inland navigation company in America. Rates vary depending upon type of vehicle, number and age of persons in it, etc.; those shown are for car and driver, one way, in 1999.

• ***From Charlotte, Vermont, to Essex:*** This may be the most scenic route, seeming to deliver you truly into the mountains. Crossing time is 20 minutes; trips run from approximately April 1 to New Year's (service is usually expanded if ice fails to form from January to March), departing Charlotte on

Car ferries cross Lake Champlain in four places. The trip from Essex, NY, to Charlotte, VT, takes w about 20 minutes.

James Swedberg

the hour and on the half hour, from 6:30am to 11:30pm during the summer season. $7. For more information call 802-864-9804.

• ***From Burlington, Vermont, to Port Kent:*** This is almost as scenic, and delightful for its relaxing hour-long crossing of the widest part of the lake. Trips run several times a day from mid-May through mid-October. A gift shop and a counter serving snacks and beverages (alcoholic and non-), can be found on board. $12.75. 802-864-9804.

• ***From Grand Isle, Vermont, north of Burlington, to Plattsburgh:*** A bit north of the Adirondacks, this route provides a decent if long-distance view of them. It operates 24 hours a day year-round, blasting through ice packs in even the coldest snaps, generally every 20 minutes (every 40 minutes in the dead of night). Crossing time is 12 minutes. $7.00. 802-864-9804.

• ***From Orwell, Vermont, to Fort Ticonderoga:*** This crossing is a living museum. Following a route that's been in use since the British army arrived in the 1700s, it brings you to the foot of the promontory on which the restored fort reposes. This is one of the few cable-guided ferries left in America: The cable is attached at each landing and a tugboat provides power. Crossing time is six minutes; the one-way fare is about $6 per car, and trips run from 8am to 6pm, from early May through late October, and from 7am to 8pm July 1 through Labor Day. There's no set schedule; "We just go back and forth," says the captain. In summer 1999, a friendly lamb was the ferry mascot, wandering from passenger to passenger expecting a pat on the head or a snack. For more information: 802-897-7999.

Visitors to the fort at Crown Point (see "Historic Buildings and Districts" in Chapter Four, *Culture*) may soon have an interesting way to get to Vermont: a pedestrian/bicycle ferry is planned between Crown Point and Chimney Point, Vermont. Though the search continues for funding sources, the boat will be a 45-foot wooden working replica of a 19th-century historic sailing vessel, outfit-

Deer Crossing

Keep your eyes peeled for deer as you drive through the Adirondacks — not only to see them, which will be a pleasant memory of your trip, but also to avoid hitting them.

Deer are most active in the late afternoon and evening, and particularly just after sunset, when they're also hardest to see. They often travel in pairs or small groups; if one crosses the road ahead of you, others are likely to follow. They're especially mobile during fall, for several reasons: that's their breeding season; they have to travel more to find food; and hunters disrupt their daily routines. In winter they seek out plowed roads since the going is easier. Around Old Forge, especially Rte. 28 and the South Shore Rd., deer are as common as squirrels, all year.

One more thing: the instinctive reaction of a deer caught by car headlights is to freeze, not to scramble out of the way. It's up to you to miss. Your best bet: drive alertly, obey speed limits — and take those "DEER CROSSING, X MILES" signs seriously.

On Rte. 30 between Speculator and Lewey Lake, "Moose Crossing" signs have been installed; they're not just a tourist gimmick but a real warning of a potential hazard. Pay special attention in the fall, when thousand-pound bulls can come crashing out of the forest directly into your lane, and at night, when your headlights may shine *under* their bodies, without reflecting in their eyes.

ted with a motor. For more information, call the Essex County Visitors Information Center, Crown Point, at 518-597-4646.

BY AIR

COMMERCIAL AIRPORTS

In all this vast territory there's only one commercial airport: Adirondack Airport at Lake Clear, about 15 minutes from Saranac Lake and 30 from Lake Placid. In 1999 it was served by USAirways (800-428-4322), flying 19-seat Beechcraft planes that look like cigars with wings. Service consists of three direct round trips — one morning, one afternoon, one evening, Monday through Friday — from Albany, scene of USAir connections. On Saturday there is only one morning flight; on Sunday there is one morning and one afternoon flight. Fares depend on the time of year, how far ahead you purchase your ticket, and so forth. In a random sampling, the nonrefundable price in fall 1999 for a flight from Albany to Saranac Lake was $301 round trip or $179 one way, with 21-day notice. There are occasional discounts, sometimes as low as $200 round trip.

As these commuter airlines come and go, it's best to call first to make sure this one's still using Lake Clear. The airport number is 518-891-2290. If you're

Winter Driving

The Adirondack climate that dumps ten or more *feet* of snow in an average winter may be great news for skiers and snowmobilers, but what about the road conditions, you might wonder. Throughout the Park, the state and county highway departments have fleets of snowplows that toil night and day to keep roads clear. For several years, a "bare roads" policy has been in effect here, meaning that sand and salt are applied liberally when roads may be slippery. Another plus for winter driving these days is the prevalence of four-wheel- and front-wheel-drive cars, which handle better on slick roads than the traditional rear-wheel-drive vehicles. (If you're coming to the wintry Adirondacks in a pickup truck, van, or passenger car with rear-wheel drive, try putting at least 150 pounds of weight — concrete blocks, sandbags, whatever — over your rear axle to help traction.)

The worst driving scenarios often occur at the beginning or end of winter, when temperatures hovering at the freezing point can cause a mixture of snow, rain, and sleet, with fog near lakes and low cold spots. Then it's best to consider your options: can you wait out the storm at your lodgings, or are you prepared to rest at a remote pullout if conditions deteriorate? Every winter traveler's car should carry a sleeping bag, a small shovel, a snow scraper, extra windshield-washing fluid, a powerful flashlight, and some candy bars, just in case you need to dig out of a snowbank, or sit quietly beside the road for a few hours as the weather takes its course. Cell-phone owners beware: coverage is spotty at best, so don't count on it.

calling another airport or a travel agent, ask about "Saranac Lake," not "Adirondack." Car rentals are available at the airport: USAirways can help you book with Hertz or call the agency at 800-654-3131.

Cities just outside the Adirondacks that offer air service are Albany, Syracuse, and Burlington, Vermont (amenities such as jets and a variety of rental cars), and Watertown and Plattsburgh (puddle-jumpers). The best source of up-to-date information about these options is your travel agent or Internet sites like Travelocity (www.travelocity.com).

PRIVATE AIRPORTS

Private airports, ranging from a tarmac strip down to a patch of grass in the woods, can be found scattered about the Adirondacks, in places like Schroon Lake, Ticonderoga, North Creek, and Westport. Consult a good navigational map. The most significant is on the outskirts of Lake Placid, with a 4300-foot runway, pilots' lounge and other facilities: 518-523-2473. Another is at Piseco, at which pick-up can be arranged by calling Don Bird's taxi service, fifty miles away in Inlet, 315-357-3631. Better be prepared to be met at most of the others; taxi service and cars to rent are nowhere to be found in most cases, and it can be a hike to get to town. For the truly adventuresome, you can charter a seaplane to pick you up on the East River, at 23rd St. and Waterside Plaza, New York City; check under "Scenic Flights" in Chapter Six, *Recreation*, for seaplane services.

CHAPTER THREE

Rustic, Classic, and Basic

LODGING

Travelers to the eastern Adirondacks in the early 1800s were welcomed at inns and taverns, although accommodations occasionally fell short of expectations: a visitor to the Pavilion, a hotel near Ticonderoga, described the place in 1855 as "noisy and ill-conducted. . . . The food is bad, the cooking worse, the rooms are small, the bedsteads large, and you have your choice between a feather-bed and one made of corn-husks, with now and then a corn-cob thrown in by way of variety."

Courtesy *Adirondack Life* magazine

Lake George's original Fort William Henry hotel set a standard for elegance in the 19th century.

After the Civil War, and the publication of *Adventures in the Wilderness* by William H.H. Murray, the entire Adirondack region — from the High Peaks to the lake country — became popular as a tourist destination. The demand for lodging — luxurious lodging that could compare with hotels in Newport or Saratoga Springs — grew, and huge hotels multiplied on lakeshores from Blue Mtn. Lake to Westport, Bolton Landing to Lake Placid. Lake George's Fort William Henry Hotel had scores of rooms and tiers of piazzas; the Mansion House, in Elizabethtown, boasted rooms for 200 guests; Paul Smith's St. Regis House was described as "first class in every respect, and patronized by the very best class of people in the country."

Those vast hotels succumbed to fire and/or the changing tastes of the traveling public. The Adirondacks in the late 19th century were an exclusive place, a destination that was difficult to reach, and with the advent of modern steamship travel, the spas of Europe became accessible to the wealthy. At the same time, the middle class was increasing in numbers, automobiles were becoming affordable, and ordinary people started taking vacations. They eschewed stodgy old hotels and headed for tent campgrounds, resorts, and roadside cabins.

By the 1930s, Adirondack guests had come to expect all the modern amenities plus a sophisticated atmosphere. Rondaxe Hotel lobby, near Old Forge.

Courtesy Edward Comstock Jr.

Resorts of the 1920s combined planned activities like dances, waterfront contests, and games for kids with amenities such as common dining rooms and private cabins. The housekeeping-cottage colonies — groups of buildings without a central dining facility — took that notion of privacy a step further, and became popular because families could prepare all their meals. Motels, designed for people who just wanted a clean place to rest overnight, were built on the edges of many towns.

The 1980 Winter Olympics in Lake Placid led economic planners to worry that not enough rooms would be available for the legions of spectators. Many homeowners took the plunge into accommodating guests, and the Olympic legacy is many freshly converted bed & breakfasts. B&Bs continue to thrive, with a flurry of businesses opening in 1999, as owners of historic properties in the Champlain Valley and the central Adirondacks began taking in guests.

A word here differentiating the various lodging terms: generally, in New York, a *bed & breakfast* is defined as a place that holds 10 or fewer guests. Breakfast is served and the owner usually lives on the premises. An *inn* is larger, often serves dinner or lunch as well as breakfast, and has to comply with state codes for public safety and food service. Then there is the *bed-&-breakfast inn*, which is a place that's bigger than a B&B, is regularly inspected by the state, and offers the morning meal in the price of a night's stay. As long as we're on the subject of definitions, a *housekeeping cabin* includes a kitchen or kitchenette, so guests can cook meals.

Nowadays the variety of Adirondack lodgings covers the full spectrum: there are country lodges that offer hearty meals and access to hiking or cross-country skiing; vast old hotels filled with antiques; lakeside resorts with a full roster of activities; housekeeping cottages nestled by the beach; and motels. For many visitors, the classic Adirondack vacation is a week on the lake in the same housekeeping cottage that they enjoyed as a child. Some families come back the same week every year, and for that reason, many of the nicest places are booked years in advance. If you want to try a housekeeping cabin and have flexibility in your vacation time, consider May–June or September– October.

Listed in this chapter you'll find a whole range of accommodations. Our criteria for selection was to seek out places with a special approach — an individual personality — that offer comfort, cleanliness, and hospitality. For some listings, the setting is a primary consideration; in others, it's wonderful architecture; some sites offer first-class amenities and services; in still others, it's the hosts and hostesses that set the place apart. With this kind of intuitive categorization, you'll find positive notes on a few modest, inexpensive places that succeed at what they're trying to do, just as you'll find perhaps briefer mention of the highly acclaimed spots. Above all, we try to offer a range of prices and options.

At the end of the chapter, you'll find a listing of motels, simple cabins, and private campgrounds. There are many, many more places to stay in the Adirondacks than you'll read about in this book (if we catalogued all the places in Lake George village alone that would fill this entire chapter); phone numbers and World Wide Web addresses for tourist information offices can be found in Chapter Eight, *Information*. To learn about various lodgings on-line, click on Bed and Breakfast.com, www.innsmart.com/newyork, or www.adirondack inns.com. Or search for the particular town or region you plan to visit.

ADIRONDACK LODGING NOTES

RATES

Some cottages and resorts are available only by the week during July and August, and this is indicated in the "Min. Stay" section of the information box. Extrapolate the per-night, double-occupancy rate by six, and you should get an idea of what a week's visit costs. It's possible for a single woman to stay at Wiawaka Holiday House, on Lake George, for $200 per week, just as a couple can spend upwards of $900 for a single night at The Point.

Rates quoted are for per-room, double occupancy during the prime tourist season, which in most cases is July and August. Some places that are open year-round charge more during January–March because of increased heating costs. You can usually expect lower rates for midweek stays, off-season rentals, or package deals; it's definitely worthwhile to ask. In places described as bed & breakfasts, you can expect that breakfast is included in the price of your room; many resorts and inns offer full or modified American meal plans.

Some places add ten or fifteen percent gratuity to the bill, and motel and hotel rooms are subject to New York's seven-percent sales tax. Also, Essex County, which includes Lake Placid and much of the Champlain Valley, enacted a three-percent bed tax in November 1999. The rates that are listed here don't reflect those additional charges.

Very Inexpensive	Under $40 per night, double occupancy
Inexpensive	$40–$70
Moderate	$70–$100
Expensive	$100–$200
Very Expensive	Over $200

MINIMUM STAY

Many of the resorts and housekeeping cabins rent units by the week only in the summer, with guests arriving and leaving on a Saturday or Sunday. In the winter, some accommodations ask for a two-night minimum stay in order to make it worthwhile to turn up the heat in the cabin. Midweek in the off-season many places will happily welcome overnight guests; if no minimum stay is specified, you can assume that one night is fine.

DEPOSIT/CANCELLATION

Reservation arrangements vary greatly from place to place. Some resorts and cottages that rent by the week ask for a 50-percent deposit; some winter-season places have a "no-snow" cancellation policy so that guests don't get stuck if the weather fails to cooperate. A handful of bed & breakfasts ask for full payment of one night's stay 14 days in advance.

PRIVATE RENTALS AND RESERVATION SERVICES

Most real-estate agents handle private summer-home rentals. These places might be anything from backwoods camps to new condominiums to lovely old houses with private lakefront, boats, and all the up-to-date creature comforts. *Adirondack Vacation Home Rentals* (Richard Knight; 315-369-6242; PO Box 190, Old Forge NY 13420) offers scores of spotless private camps (including the Albedor mansion, with room for dozens of your closest friends) and houses year-round in the Old Forge, Big Moose, and Inlet area. The Mt. Marcy Marketplace classifieds, found in the bimonthly *Adirondack Life* magazine (518-946-2191; PO Box 410, Jay NY 12941), can be a terrific source for vacation rentals throughout the region. Securing private accommodations takes considerable planning, but can be ideal if you're traveling with pets or have a large family in tow.

Some private campgrounds are listed in this chapter, but a list of all of the Department of Environmental Conservation campgrounds in the Adirondack Park can be found in Chapter Six, *Recreation*.

For some, the quintessential lodging remains the Adirondack lean-to and the best bed one made from balsam boughs.

Courtesy Edward Comstock Jr.

CREDIT CARDS

Credit cards are abbreviated as follows:

AE: American Express
CB: Carte Blanche
D: Discover
DC: Diners Club
MC: MasterCard
V: Visa

LODGING IN THE ADIRONDACKS

LAKE GEORGE AND SOUTHEASTERN ADIRONDACKS

Bolton Landing

HILLTOP COTTAGE BED & BREAKFAST
Owners: Anita and Charlie Richards.
518-644-2492.
6883 Lakeshore Dr.
Open: Year-round.
Price: Inexpensive.
Credit Cards: MC, V.
Special Features: No pets; no small children; no smoking.

The Bolton Landing to Lake George road was originally known as "Millionaires' Row," and Hilltop Cottage belonged to a caretaker for one of the grand estates. It's directly across the street from the Marcella Sembrich Memorial Studio, a museum honoring the Romanian-born diva, and once housed her music students. The clapboard cottage has three guest rooms upstairs; one has a queen-size bed and a private bath, while the other two share a bath. Anita, a former German teacher, and Charlie, a retired guidance counselor, bought the 11-room house in 1985 and opened as it a B&B three years later. Hilltop Cottage is a friendly, homey place, and after a breakfast of German apple pancakes on the screen porch, you can walk over to Bolton's tennis courts and lakefront parks.

THE INN AT BOLTON LANDING
Innkeeper: Jeffrey O'Connor.
518-644-5253 or 800-981-5656.
www.boltonlandingrentals.com.
4913 Lakeshore Dr.
Open: Winter weekends; daily late Apr.–late Oct.
Price: Moderate to Expensive.
Credit Cards: MC, V.
Special Features: No pets; no small children; no

Behind a prim white picket fence on the edge of "downtown" Bolton Landing is this lovely three-story Colonial-style home. Built in 1815, the six-bedroom inn is one of the oldest buildings in the village. All guest rooms have beautiful queen-size beds, private baths, and air conditioning; the Morgan Suite contains two adjoining bedrooms that share a bath. Three white clapboard cottages set on the four-acre property have complete kitchens and accommodate up to six people each. On a sunny spring day, the two-story atrium is a great place to plan the day's activities, like a trip to the beach — just across the street, in Rogers Park. Rates include a continental breakfast.

Melody Thomas

The Sagamore Hotel is on a island in Lake George, and boasts gourmet dining, championship golf, a full-service spa, and lovely accommodations.

THE SAGAMORE HOTEL
Managing Director: W. Robert McIntosh.
518-644-9400.
www.thesagamore.com.
Sagamore Rd.
Open: Year-round.
Price: Expensive to Very Expensive.
Credit Cards: AE, DC, MC, V.
Handicap Access: Several units; elevators in hotel.
Special Features: 2 gourmet restaurants; spa; fitness

For more than a century there's been a Sagamore Hotel overlooking Lake George. Completed in 1883, the grand lodge has survived two fires and weathered the Depression, but gradually declined during the seventies. In 1983 the island property was bought by a real-estate developer who launched extensive renovations. Today the Sagamore Hotel is the pride of the community and winner of numerous awards for excellence in serving the traveling public.

The elegantly appointed public areas include a conservatory with lake views, the Trillium Dining Room, the Sagamore Dining Room, a casual pub, an art gallery, and a gift shop. Guests have 350 center; tennis courts; conference facilities; children welcome; no pets.

deluxe units to choose from, including suites, hotel bedrooms, lakeside lodges, and executive retreats with lofts. The list of Sagamore amenities is impressive: a huge indoor pool, spa, and fitness center; miniature golf; an indoor tennis-and-racquetball facility; outdoor tennis courts; playground; a beautiful sandy beach; docks for guests' boats; and a Donald Ross–designed championship golf course two miles away.

The Sagamore Hotel is a popular spot for conferences, offering excellent facilities for large and small groups. There's no need to leave the kids at home if one or both parents are attending meetings: the social department has plenty of supervised activities for children.

Chestertown

THE CHESTER INN
Owners: Bruce and Suzanne Robbins.
518-494-4148.
www.thechesterinn.com.
Main St./Rte. 9, near the town hall.
Open: Year-round.
Price: Moderate.
Credit Cards: MC, V.
Special Features: No pets; children over 12 welcome; smoking in designated areas only.

One of Chestertown's beautiful homes that is listed on the National Register of Historic Places, this Greek Revival inn dates back to 1837. Beyond the grand hall, with its mahogany railings and grain-painted woodwork, there are four lovely second-floor guest rooms with private baths, including the Victorian Suite, which has its own sitting room and bath with a deep, old-fashioned tub. Downstairs is a common room with a TV/VCR and plenty of books. Guests are welcome to explore the 13-acre property, which has gardens, a horse barn, smokehouse, and an early cemetery; during Chestertown's bicentennial celebration in 1999, archeologists explored the property and found the inn's ancient privy to be a treasure trove of artifacts.

Nondrivers take note: Chestertown is a regular stop on the Adirondack Trailways bus line, and this inn is just a block from the station. It's also a short walk to the Main Street Ice Cream Parlor or to a movie at the Carol Theatre.

THE FRIENDS LAKE INN
Owners: Sharon and Greg Taylor.
518-494-4751.
www.friendslake.com.
Friends Lake Rd.
Open: Year-round.
Price: Expensive, MAP; Moderate, B&B.
Credit Cards: AE, MC, V.
Min. Stay: 2 nights on weekends; 3 nights on

For most of its 130-year history, the Friends Lake Inn has been a hostelry of one kind or another, although its first tenants, the tannery workers, would marvel to see people rather than cowhides soaking in the enormous wooden hot tub outdoors. Sharon and Greg have completed extensive renovations on the building and guests now enjoy 14 comfortable rooms and small suites, all with private baths. Bedrooms have brass or iron bedsteads, patchwork quilts, and antiques; many have fire-

holiday weekends; 1 night midweek.
Special Features: Outdoor hot tub; cross-country ski trails; mountain-bike rentals; guide service for outdoor treks; gourmet restaurant; extensive wine list.

places, whirlpool tubs, and views of Friends Lake.

Truly an inn for all seasons, guests can enjoy sleigh rides and cross-country skiing on 32 kilometers of groomed trails here in the winter; fishing in the spring; swimming and mountain biking in the summer; hiking in the fall. From time to time, there are wine-, Scotch-, or beer-tasting dinners and murder-mystery weekends. Small business conferences are easily accommodated. There's no need to travel far for dinner — the restaurant on the first floor is delightful. Inquire about seasonal packages that combine lodging with golf, rafting, or skiing; midweek bed & breakfast stays and two-night romantic getaways are reasonably priced.

LANDON HILL BED & BREAKFAST
Owners: Judy and Carl Johnson.
518-494-2599.
www.bedbreakfast.net.
Landon Hill Rd.
Open: Year-round.
Price: Moderate.
Credit Cards: MC, V.
Min. Stay: 2 nights on weekends
Special Features: Children welcome; no pets; no smoking.

In 1995 this lovely Victorian home set among rolling hills on a country lane was opened as a bed & breakfast. The place is peaceful and comfortable. A beautiful oak spiral staircase leads you to the four tastefully decorated guest rooms upstairs (two with private baths), and downstairs are a guest room and bath that are handicap accessible. Before breakfast, have coffee and fresh muffins by the wood stove, then, after stoking up on homemade quiche and fresh fruit, explore the Johnsons' 89 acres, or head for Chestertown's historic district or the nearby Schroon River for fishing and canoeing. Landon Hill is just a mile from I-87, the Northway, so it's a convenient jumping-off spot for further adventures. Inquire about art workshops occasionally offered here.

Diamond Point

CANOE ISLAND LODGE
Owners: Jane and William Busch.
518-668-5592.
www.canoeislandlodge.com.
Lake Shore Dr.
Closed: Mid-Oct.–mid-May.
Price: Expensive.
Min. Stay: 3 nights.
Credit Cards: None.
Special Features: Private island; sand beach; sailboats; rowboats;

Back in 1943 Bill Busch financed the down payment on Canoe Island with a couple hundred bushels of buckwheat, and in June 1946 he welcomed the first guests to his lodge. The 21-acre, 25-building complex now offers all kinds of family vacation options from quaint log cabins to modern suites and private chalets. There are clay tennis courts, a sandy beach on Lake George, hiking trails, and numerous boats to sail. Perhaps the best part of a stay here, though, is the chance to enjoy the lodge's very own 5-acre island, about 3/4 mile offshore. Regularly scheduled shuttle boats take guests

Canoe Island Lodge has its own one-design sailboats for exploring Lake George.

James Swedberg

windsurfers; tennis; children welcome.

to the island where they can swim, snorkel, fish, sunbathe, and explore a beautiful, undeveloped part of the lake.

The Busch family takes great pride in offering hearty European-style meals with homegrown vegetables, homemade bread and pastries, and treasured old-country recipes. On Thursdays, there are island picnics and on Sundays, gala buffets; dances, movies, and special children's programs are also on tap, although there's no pressure to join in.

The lodge accommodates 175 people at peak capacity. In spring and fall, rates include breakfast, lunch, and dinner; from July 1–Sept. 7, a modified American plan is in effect.

Hadley

SARATOGA ROSE INN
Owners: Nancy and Anthony Merlino.
518-696-2861 or 800-942-5025.
www.saratogarose.com.
Rockwell St.
Open: Year-round.
Price: Moderate to Expensive.
Min. Stay: 2 nights on weekends.
Credit Cards: MC, V.
Special Features: Fireplaces; no children under 12; smoking permitted downstairs only.

In its heyday Hadley was a bustling community with a variety of waterpowered businesses relying on the Hudson River. Well-to-do mill owners built elaborate mansions in town, and today, one of them has been restored to its former glory by Nancy and Anthony Merlino. Saratoga Rose — on sedate, tree-lined Rockwell Street, it's a surprising sight in exuberant shades of buff, shocking pink, and mauve — is now a bed-and-breakfast inn with four second-floor guest rooms, each with private bath and air conditioning. The Queen Anne Room has a king-size bed and working fireplace; the Garden Room has a private sun porch and spa tub. The Carriage House has a very private large chamber with a queen-size canopy bed, fireplace, and a secluded deck with Jacuzzi. All rooms are decorated with period antiques and prints.

Two-night packages are available to inn guests, with perks like clubhouse passes to the Saratoga harness-racing track, guided horseback-riding trips, scenic airplane flights, or a visit to Saratoga Springs for a mineral-water bath and relaxing massage.

Saratoga Rose has a very good restaurant (see Chapter Five, *Restaurants*) that's open to the public year-round and a small pub; in the summer, the wide, geranium-draped veranda is a pleasant spot to enjoy supper.

Hague

THE LOCUST INN
Innkeeper: James Coates.
518-543-6035 or 888-593-7712.
www.locustinn.com.
Rtes. 9N & 8.
Open: Year-round; house rents as a 5 bedroom home in summer.
Price: Moderate.
Min. Stay: 2 nights.
Credit Cards: D, MC, V.
Special Features: 1 handicap access room; beach; boat ramp; children welcome; no pets.

A graceful homestead built in 1865, the Locust Inn was renovated in 1992 and launched as a bed & breakfast. It's packed with antiques and art, and conveniently next to the town beach and boat ramp on Lake George.

The three attractively appointed guest suites — all with lake views — have queen beds, private baths, sitting areas, and TV/VCRs. The Penthouse, under the eaves, is quite charming. The carriage house is a separate cottage located on Hague Brook. Note that the bed & breakfast effectively closes in July and August, when the entire five-bedroom house is rented as one unit.

RUAH BED & BREAKFAST
Owners: Judy and Peter Foster.
518-543-8816.
www.ruahbb.com.
Lake Shore Dr.
Open: Year-round.
Price: Moderate to Expensive.
Credit Cards: D, MC, V.
Special Features: Hiking trails; fireplace; balconies; children under 12 by special arrangement.

Such an appealing place naturally has amusing legends: this stone mansion was designed by Stanford White; part of the estate was won in a poker game; the Lake George monster — the biggest hoax ever seen in northern New York — was created in the studio of the original owner, artist Harry Watrous. Visit Ruah and you'll have your own stories to tell — about visiting a lovely inn overlooking a beautiful lake.

The four guest chambers are all upstairs and have private baths. The Queen of the Lakes is outstanding, quite spacious, with access to the balcony and views from every window. The Watrous Suite is a separate wing with two adjoining bedrooms and balconies. Common rooms downstairs include a vast living room with a fieldstone fireplace and an antique grand piano, a cozy library, and an elegant dining room. To give you an idea of the scale of this inn, the veranda stretches across the front of the house and measures about 80 feet long.

Guests at Ruah can enjoy breakfast from the glassed-in porch overlooking Lake George.

James Swedberg

TROUT HOUSE VILLAGE RESORT
Owners: The Patchett Family.
518-543-6088 or 800-368-6088.
www.trouthouse.com.
Lake Shore Dr./Rte. 9N.
Open: Year-round.
Price: Moderate.
Min. Stay: 2 nights on weekends.
Credit Cards: AE, D, MC, V.
Special Features: 400-foot sandy beach; boats and bikes for guests; fireplaces; cable TV with HBO; children welcome; no pets.

One of the few four-season resorts on the quiet northern portion of Lake George, Trout House is a handsomely maintained complex of log cabins and chalets. Many of the cabins have fireplaces, decks, and complete kitchen facilities (including dishwashers); there are numerous suites and rooms in the main lodge, all with private baths. In the summer, there are canoes, rowboats, sailboats, kayaks, bikes, and even a 9-hole putting green for guests. Trout House is a short distance from historic sites such as Fort Ticonderoga and Crown Point, while the Ticonderoga Country Club — a challenging 18-hole course — is just up the road.

By January, the atmosphere changes from that of an active resort to a quiet country inn. Cross-country skiers, snowshoers, skaters, ice fishermen, and snowmobilers can go out right from the front or back doors to explore miles of countryside.

Lake George

ALPINE VILLAGE
Owners: Lil and Ernest Ippisch.
518-668-2193.
Rte. 9N.
Closed: Dec. 1–May 1.
Price: Moderate.
Min. Stay: 3 nights.

The sitting room of the main lodge is an Adirondack gem, and log cabins of all sizes, from the spacious main lodge to cute duplex cottages with fireplaces, characterize this lakeside resort. The grounds are nicely landscaped, leading down to a private beach; other amenities include rowboats and canoes for guests, a recreation room,

Credit Cards: D, MC, V.
Special Features: Private beach; tennis; children welcome; no pets.

tennis court, and some dock space for visitors' boats. In the summer, breakfast is included in the room rate. Folks here will even pick you up at the bus station if you make advance arrangements.

DUNHAM'S BAY LODGE
Managers: Kathy and John Salvador.
518-656-9242.
www.adirondack.net/tour/dunhamsbay.
Rte. 9L, on the east side of the lake at Dunham's Bay.
Closed: Mid-Oct.–late May.
Price: Expensive.
Credit Cards: AE, MC, V.
Min. Stay: 3 days on summer weekends.
Special Features: Sandy beach; tennis; pool; play area; restaurant; children welcome; no pets.

The centerpiece of this stylish resort on the less-developed side of Lake George is a massive stone lodge built by a well-to-do Glens Falls dentist in 1911. Inside the lobby and restaurant, Dunham's Bay is spacious and sunlit; there's a new indoor/outdoor pool complex with a Jacuzzi, and for a cool drink at the end of the day, there's a swank cocktail lounge with a pool table.

Accommodations range from one- or two-bedroom housekeeping cabins in a shady grove to large modern rooms in the main lodge or motel. Cottages rent by the week only in the summer, while during the off-season, from Memorial Day to mid-June, there's a two-night minimum stay; daily rates are considerably less. There's a restaurant and snack bar on the premises offering breakfast, lunch, and dinner.

FORT WILLIAM HENRY MOTOR INN
Manager: Sam Luciano.
518-668-3081 or 800-234-0267.
www.fortwilliamhenry.com.
Canada St./Rte. 9.
Open: Year-round.
Price: Inexpensive to Expensive, depending on season.
Credit Cards: AE, D, DC, MC, V.
Handicap Access: Yes.
Special Features: Restaurants; pool; in-room phones; cable TV; handicap-access rooms; children welcome; small pets accommodated.

For more than 125 years there's been a hotel named Fort William Henry on this bluff overlooking Lake George. The current version is a brand-new complex with 288 rooms, an indoor pool, a heated outdoor pool, and 18 acres of manicured grounds. The motor inn has four restaurants, including the Lookout Cafe, serving lunch in a pleasant outdoor setting, and the Trolley, which specializes in steak and seafood. Interesting package options are available, such as a two-night bicycle adventure that includes breakfast, dinner, bike rentals, and a trail map, or a golfer's getaway. Note also that rates for Labor Day–late June are less than half price compared to the summer season.

Right next door is the Fort William Henry museum, portraying French and Indian War history on the site of the original fort: cannons boom, muskets blaze, and uniformed soldiers go through their drills. If modern amusements are more to your taste, there's miniature golf and the Million Dollar Beach a short walk away.

LAKE GEORGE BED & BREAKFAST INN
Innkeepers: Filomena and Tom Egan.
518-668-5477 or 800-348-5113.
www.lakegeorgebb.com.
47 Montcalm St.
Open: Year-round.
Price: Moderate to Expensive.
Credit Cards: All major.
Special features: no smoking; no pets; no young children.

Finding an inn with character — rather than generic motel decor — is a challenge in the heart of Lake George. The village has scores of modern motor inns packed cheek by jowl, but not many other options. This big, lovely home, offering eight rooms with private baths, is set away from Canada Street, but not so far you can't stroll on down for an ice cream cone or a concert in the park. The Million Dollar Beach is five or ten minutes from the inn.

ROCKLEDGE
Owners: Jack and Pat Barry.
518-668-5348.
Lake Shore Dr.
Closed: Mid-Sept.–June 1.
Price: Moderate to Expensive.
Credit Cards: MC, V.
Special Features: 540 feet of lakefront; sandy beach; pool; children welcome; no pets.

The original "Rockledge," a three-story mansion built in 1886, stands guard under the pines on this 14-acre lakefront property. Although the historic house isn't open to guests, the building's gracious presence adds a special touch to this otherwise thoroughly modern resort.

Rockledge offers one- or two-bedroom housekeeping cottages, motel rooms, and suites. Cottages are generally available by the week only. There's an outdoor pool, a sandy beach, and room for badminton, volleyball, and shuffleboard.

WIAWAKA HOLIDAY HOUSE
518-668-9892.
Rte. 9L; RR 1 Box 1072.
Closed: Mid-Sept.–early June.
Price: Very Inexpensive.
Credit Cards: None.
Special Features: Private beach; dockage; primarily for women.

Founded in 1903 as a place where working women could take inexpensive vacations, Wiawaka offers clean, simple accommodations in three pretty Victorian cottages, a rustic dormitory reputedly designed by Stanford White, and a motel. Set on 60 unspoiled acres on the east side of Lake George, the place is remarkably peaceful.

Vacationing at Wiawaka is a bit like staying at a YWCA camp: no smoking or alcohol is allowed on the premises; guests are expected to make their own beds and sweep out their rooms; swimming, boating, and horseshoe pitching are part of the fun. Three meals a day are included in the room rate; taking a room without meals is not permitted. In 1990 the first male guests were welcomed here (before that, they had to stay elsewhere in Lake George). Children are not allowed.

Lake Luzerne

The Coral Room at the Lamplight Inn has a four-poster bed and nice views of the grounds.

Courtesy of Lamplight Inn

THE LAMPLIGHT INN BED & BREAKFAST
Owners: Linda and Gene Merlino.
518-696-5294 or 800-262-4668.
www.lamplightinn.com.
2129 Lake Ave.
Open: Year-round.
Price: Moderate to Expensive.
Min. Stay: 2 nights on weekends.
Credit Cards: AE, MC, V.
Special Features: Fireplaces; no pets; smoking permitted in parlor only; children over 12 welcome.

Built a century ago as the bachelor "cottage" for a wealthy lumberman, the Lamplight Inn has been painstakingly refurbished by Gene and Linda Merlino. The public room has rich chestnut wainscoting; high, beamed ceilings; two fireplaces; Oriental rugs; lace curtains; and lots of antiques. The spacious, sunny dining room, although a recent addition, is entirely in keeping with the Victorian style.

An ornate keyhole staircase leads upstairs to the 10 guest chambers (all with private baths), and five of the rooms have gas-burning fireplaces. The furniture and decor are quite different and delightful in each room: for example, the Skylight Room has a high coffered ceiling, skylight, and a high-back old-fashioned oak bedstead, while the Victoria Room has a queen-size canopied four-poster bed. The handsome carriage house has five suites, all with queen-size beds, gas-burning fireplaces, phones, cable TV, and air conditioning. The house next door contains two lovely suites with fireplaces, TVs, and phones. Breakfast, which is included in the room rate, includes fresh fruit and sweet breads or cake, homemade granola, omelettes, and daily specials like apple crêpes or Belgian waffles.

The Lamplight Inn is close to the Saratoga Racetrack and tends to be busy in August. November through April room rates are offered at special savings, with packages for leaf-peepers, holiday shoppers, cross-country and downhill skiers, and couples hoping for a romantic break during dreary mud season.

Paradox

LAKE PARADOX CLUB RENTAL HOUSES
Owner: Helen Wildman.
518-532-7734.
Sawmill Rd. & Rte. 74 (Paradox); Box 125 (Severance NY 12872).
Closed: Most cabins mid-Oct.–mid-May; 2 cabins & B&B open year-round.
Price: Inexpensive to Moderate.
Credit Cards: None.
Min. Stay: 1 week for houses July–Aug.
Special Features: Children welcome; pets accommodated with prior arrangements for cabins; private sand beach; boats; no smoking at Red House.

Helen Wildman's family has owned hundreds of acres on the western end of Paradox Lake for more than a century; eight of the 11 lakefront rental houses were built by her grandfather. These places are big — four to six bedrooms — and have full kitchens, old-fashioned stone fireplaces, and screen porches. There's nice swimming at the club's private beach, canoes and rowboats for exploring pretty Paradox Lake, plus tennis, horseshoes, hiking trails, and a baseball field. Guests can rent outboards for fishing, or Sunfish for sailing around the lake. Helen says, "Many of our tenants return regularly, year after year, but there's always room for newcomers, especially if your vacation plans are flexible."

In spring and fall, weekly rental rates are about half the July–August fees. Two of the houses are completely winterized, great for ice fishermen and cross-country skiers who'd like to discover nearby Pharaoh Lake Wilderness Area.

ROLLING HILL BED & BREAKFAST
Owners: Jewel and Lou Ady.
518-532-9286.
Rte. 74 (Paradox); Box 32 (Severance NY 12872).
Closed: Nov.–Mid-May.
Price: Inexpensive.
Credit Cards: None.

A restored 1840s-vintage farmhouse near Paradox, Pyramid, and Eagle lakes, Rolling Hill offers country hospitality and a hearty homemade breakfast. Guests share bathrooms for the four pleasant, antique-filled rooms upstairs, and just off the dining room there's a spacious screen porch, a real plus during bug season. For hikers and fishermen, the action is east (Paradox Lake) or west (Pharaoh Lake Wilderness), with miles of trails and dozens of trout ponds. This is good terrain for bicyclists, too, with lots of quiet back roads to explore.

Schroon Lake

CLADDAGH INN
Hosts: Bill and Donna Wilson.
518-532-0315.
www.claddagh-inn.com.
Rte. 9 south of town.
Open: Year-round.
Price: Moderate.
Credit Cards: No.

Schroon Lake has regular bus service from points south, a movie theater, tennis courts, plenty of small restaurants and interesting shops, and Claddagh Inn is within walking distance of everything. There are five guest rooms, all with private baths; three have queen beds, two have twins. A small beach at the end of the property's pleasant lawn means that guests can swim or launch a canoe

Most rooms at Claddagh Inn have queen-size beds and views of Schroon Lake.

James Swedberg

Min. Stay: 2 nights on summer weekends.

and be back in time for breakfast, served from 7:30–10am.

SCHROON LAKE BED & BREAKFAST
Innkeepers: Rita and Bob Skojec.
518-532-7042.
www.schroonbb.com.
Rte. 9.
Open: Year-round.
Price: Moderate.
Credit Cards: MC, V.
Min. Stay: 2 nights on weekends.
Special Features: Fireplace; no smoking; no pets; children over 12 welcome.

Only minutes off the Northway (I-87) is this lovely country inn with five attractive guest rooms, all with sparkling private baths. The living room has a stone fireplace, shelves of books and magazines, and comfortable sofas for curling up with the novel of your choice. Guest quarters have polished hardwood floors, Oriental rugs, fine antiques, patchwork quilts, and thick terrycloth robes in the closet. Just across the lawn is a gourmet restaurant serving lunch and dinner.

SILVER SPRUCE INN
Innkeepers: Phyllis and Cliff Rogers.
518-532-7031.
www.silverspruce.com.
Rte. 9.
Open: Year-round.
Price: Moderate.
Credit Cards: D, MC, V.
Min. Stay: 2 nights on weekends; inquire.
Special Features: Fireplaces; no smoking; no children.

This historic home is a true gem. Encompassing more than 8,000 square feet and containing 28 rooms, the place manages to be luxurious and unpretentious, rustic and elegant, at the same time. At present there are two guest rooms with queen beds and two large suites with king-size waterbeds; all accommodations have wonderful oversize bathrooms with deep porcelain tubs that date back to the days when the building belonged to the owners of a major plumbing-supply company. Silver Spruce would be an ideal setting for friends traveling together or a small corporate retreat.

The lovely great room spans the entire width of the building, with plenty of couches and chairs, a piano, and an electric organ clustered by a huge fireplace. Running the length of the building is a spacious sunporch with wicker furniture. In the basement is an intriguing surprise, a rustic tavern that dates back to Prohibition days, complete with bookshelves that hide secret stashes of liquor and a back bar that once graced the Waldorf Astoria Hotel.

Restoration of a huge barn is ongoing, with plans to offer a few more suites in the future.

Courtesy Catherine W. Querns

Wraparound porches at Schroon Lake's Wood's Lodge are ideal for watching waterfront activities.

WOOD'S LODGE
Innkeeper: Catherine Wood Querns.
518-532-7529.
East St.
Closed: Mid-Oct.–May 10.
Price: Moderate.
Min. Stay: 2 nights on summer weekends.
Credit Cards: None.
Special Features: Private beach; children welcome; no pets.

The Lake House, a Steamboat Gothic hotel perched over Schroon Lake, is just one part of the four-acre complex at Wood's Lodge, a waterfront hostelry that's been owned and operated by the same family since 1912. The Lake House has two tiers of delightful gingerbread-trimmed porches wrapping around the building, and antiques in every room. There's also a chalet with several suites and private rooms, a main lodge with two-room suites, and five lakeside cabins. Many of the accommodations have kitchen facilities, but for those without, there's a modern community kitchen and an elegant dining room with a beautiful lake view.

Wood's Lodge is a short walk from what downtown Schroon Lake has to offer (barbecue at Pitkin's, weekly square dances by the lake), and there's a private beach, tennis court, and shuffleboard court on the property. The bus stop is a block away.

WORD OF LIFE INN
Manager: Don Lough.
518-532-7771.
www.wol.org.
Rte. 9.
Open: Year-round.
Price: Inexpensive to Expensive.
Credit Cards: D, MC, V.
Handicap Access: 6 rooms available.
Special Features: Indoor pool; children welcome; Christian atmosphere; recreational facilities; summer camps for youth.

A full-service Christian resort, the Word of Life Inn offers all kinds of accommodations from chalets and rustic lakeside cabins to deluxe executive and honeymoon suites. There's a complete roster of activities, concerts, and inspirational speakers, plus tennis, miniature golf, swimming, boating, hiking, and special events. Besides the inn, which is just south of Schroon Lake village, there's a family campground farther down the lake with sites for tents, travel trailers, and motor homes (some sites have electrical, water, and sewer hookups), plus several housekeeping cabins. Videos showing the facilities are available for a small fee.

Silver Bay

NORTHERN LAKE GEORGE RESORT
Owners: The Martucci Family.
518-543-6528.
Rte. 9N.
Open: Year-round.
Price: Inexpensive to Expensive.
Credit Cards: MC, V.
Handicap Access: Some accommodations.
Special Features: 400 feet of lakefront; sandy beach; free rowboats and canoes; hiking trails nearby; children welcome; dive shop.

Opened as the Hotel Uncas in 1896, the Northern Lake George Resort bills itself as the last of the lake's original old hotels still open to the public. The main lodge has been changed significantly over the years, though: the third floor with dormer windows was removed in the 1950s, and balconies and porches were added. The Great Room still maintains the appeal of an old Adirondack lodge with its stone fireplace and polished wood floors.

Inn guests can select from rooms on the lodge's second floor with private balconies providing views of the lake; new, winterized lakeside villas with fireplaces, kitchens, cable TV, and decks; or motel rooms. There's a cocktail lounge and public restaurant on the premises, open from late June through early September.

The depths of Lake George hold numerous wrecks from French and Indian War bateaux to sidewheel steamboats. The Northern Lake George Resort has a full-service dive shop offering tank fills and supplies; special dive charters to underwater historic sites can be arranged for groups.

Silver Bay Association offers workshops and conferences as well as private lodging in a variety of historic structures.

James Swedberg

SILVER BAY ASSOCIATION YMCA CONFERENCE CENTER
518-543-8833.
Silver Bay Rd., off Rte. 9N.
Open: Year-round.
Price: Inexpensive to Moderate.
Credit Cards: MC, V.
Handicap Access: Yes.
Special Features: Full conference facilities; planned activities; waterfront.

With nearly a square mile of picturesque property on Lake George and 65 buildings, Silver Bay Association is an awesome complex. Many of the structures hark back to the turn of the century in graceful Victorian architecture, yet meals and amenities are thoroughly modern. The list of activities is almost endless, from swimming and fishing to crafts and aerobics classes. Hiking and cross-country ski trails weave among the hillsides, and there's ice skating on the lake. A day-care center, open weekdays, is part of the complex.

Accommodations run the full range from tidy double rooms in old-time lodges to cozy cabins; it's possible to stay here without being part of a workshop or conference by joining the association, which costs about a hundred dollars a year for a family or $50 for an individual.

Warrensburg

ALLYN'S BUTTERFLY INN
518-623-9390 or 800-221-2390.
www.butterflyinn.com.
Rte. 28, near Rte. 9.
Open: Year-round.

Formerly known as The House on the Hill, this grand old house is under new ownership since 1999. Public areas are elegantly appointed, and the huge wraparound porch invites lingering on a summer day to watch the real butterflies visiting the garden.

Min. Stay: 2 nights July–August.
Price: Moderate to Expensive.
Credit Cards: Inquire.
Special Features: One room handicap accessible; no smoking; air conditioning.

All guest chambers are named after native butterflies, with the Skipper Room set up for mobility-impaired guests. Three rooms have private bath; all have in-room coffee makers and small refrigerators. A full country breakfast is served from 7:30–10:30am. Ask about off-season midweek discounts.

COUNTRY ROAD LODGE
Owners: Sandi and Steve Parisi.
518-623-2207.
www.countryroadlodge.com.
Hickory Hill Rd.
Open: Year-round.
Price: Inexpensive.
Credit Cards: None.
Special Features: Cross-country ski trails; no pets.

In 1974, Steve Parisi began transforming an old farmhouse on the banks of the Hudson River into a year-round bed & breakfast that's a haven for cross-country skiers. Country Road Lodge is decidedly off the beaten path, well suited to bird watchers, hikers, and others who want to explore the secluded 35-acre property and adjacent state lands. Hickory Hill downhill ski center, a low-key facility with an impressive vertical drop, is right next door, and Warren County's cross-country ski and hiking trails start at the back door.

There are four comfortable guest rooms, two with private baths. Special winter weekend packages include meals plus après-ski treats. There's no TV at Country Road Lodge, but plenty of books, magazines, a piano, board games, and a panoramic view of the Hudson River and Sugarloaf Mtn.

DONEGAL MANOR BED & BREAKFAST
Owner: Dorothy Dill Wright.
518-623-3549.
117 Main St.
Open: Year-round.
Price: Moderate to Expensive.
Min. Stay: 2 nights on holidays and some weekends.
Credit Cards: MC, V.
Special Features: Fireplace; children over 6 welcome; no pets.

James Fenimore Cooper was a guest at Peletiah Richards's house when he was researching *The Last of the Mohicans*, and according to one of Richards's children, Peletiah reportedly grumbled, "That young man has made some mistakes in describing the journey of the Munro-Hayward party that was guided by Uncas." In those days, the house was among the grandest in town, and later in the 19th century this place became more elaborate still, with the addition of an Italianate tower, a long veranda, and a bay window. Details inside Donegal Manor are lovely: there's an ornate fireplace in the parlor, a beautiful coffered wood ceiling above the staircase, and antiques throughout.

Two guest rooms with private baths are upstairs. A section of the house that dates from 1820 has been renovated into a handsome suite with a corner fireplace in the living room, queen-size bed, and spacious bathroom. Downstairs is an antique shop and more collectibles can be found for sale in the barn.

The best part about Donegal Manor can't be described in architectural or decorative terms — it's Dorothy Dill Wright, the innkeeper, and her genuine Irish charm. We suspect she's the real reason that folks return time and again to this bed & breakfast.

THE MERRILL MAGEE HOUSE
Innkeepers: The Carrington Family.
518-623-2449.
wwwwebny.com/merrillmageehouse.
2 Hudson St.
Open: Year-round.
Price: Expensive.
Credit Cards: AE, D, MC, V.
Min. Stay: 2 nights on holidays and weekends.
Handicap Access: 1 room.
Special Features: Restaurant; tavern; pool; hot tub.

Before 1981, when Florence and Ken Carrington purchased this lovely Greek Revival house in the center of town, the property had remained in the same family all the way back to 1839. The oldest part of the original house is now the tavern and reception rooms; the back portion of the restaurant, circa 1812, actually came from another homestead some miles away. Merrill Magee House is listed on the National Register of Historic Places.

The new Peletiah Richards Guest House, behind the inn, combines 20th-century conveniences, like private baths and a glassed-in spa room, with 19th-century decor: each room has its own fireplace, brass or four-poster bed, and handmade quilt. These rooms are all named after herbs, and "Parsley" is wheelchair accessible.

Merrill Magee's grounds are beautifully landscaped, with flower gardens, shady nooks, and a swimming pool. In the summer, you can sit on the porch and listen to evening concerts held in the bandshell just on the other side of the white picket fence. Special events include an annual Beaujolais Nouveau celebration that features wild game on the menu; conferences and meetings are cheerfully accommodated.

RIDIN'-HY RANCH
Managers: Andy and Susan Beadnell.
518-494-2742.
Sherman Lake, several mi. N. of Warrensburg & W. of Bolton Landing.
Closed: Dec. 1–26.
Price: Moderate.
Credit Cards: AE, D, MC, V.
Min. Stay: 2 nights.
Special Features: Horseback riding; indoor pool; restaurant; children welcome; no pets.

Western-style dude ranches were once abundant in the southeastern Adirondacks, but many have closed in the last few years. Ridin'-Hy, an 800-acre complex on Sherman Lake, continues to prosper, offering everything from a private intermediate-level downhill ski area to rodeos. There are 50 miles of trails for snowmobiling, cross-country skiing, or horseback riding: you can ride Old Paint year-round, for as many hours or days as you please. In warmer weather, guests can swim, row, or water-ski on Sherman Lake, and fish in Burnt Pond or the Schroon River.

The centerpiece of the ranch is an enormous two-story log cabin that contains a cocktail lounge, living room, game room, and restaurant. Accommodations include new chalets, lodge rooms, and motel units, all finished with natural wood. Numerous midweek and off-season packages are available.

CHAMPLAIN VALLEY

Crown Point

CROWN POINT BED & BREAKFAST
Owners: Sandy and Hugh Johnson.
518-597-3651.
www.crownpointbandb.com.
3A Main St.
Open: Year-round.
Price: Inexpensive to Moderate.
Credit Cards: AE, MC, V.
Special Features: Children welcome; no smoking; no pets.

Built by a banker in 1887, this stately 18-room mansion is a testament to Victorian craftsmanship. The woodwork — made of cherry, mahogany, oak, chestnut, walnut, and pine — gleams in paneling, window trim, pocket doors, floors, and an ornate staircase. There are three parlors, three porches, four fireplaces, and five acres of gardens and grounds for guests to enjoy. It's a five-minute walk to Lake Champlain or a short bike ride to the ruins at Crown Point.

There are five guest rooms, all with private baths and decorated with antique bedsteads and dressers. Guests can gather in the new Adirondack room, which has a wood stove, TV/VCR, lots of books and games, and a casual, rustic atmosphere.

Elizabethtown

THE BALSAMS MOUNTAIN LODGE
Owners: Deborah and Dane Stanley.
518-873-9536 or 888-267-4833.
www.adirondackinns.com/balsams.
Cobble Hill Rd.
Open: Year-round.
Price: Moderate to Expensive.
Credit Cards: None.
Special Features: Therapeutic touch massage; hot tub room with fireplace; reduced rates for visiting clergy.

This grand old shingle-style home perched high on Cobble Hill, above Elizabethtown's golf course, was built in 1902 by a Manhattan banker whose friends included J. P. Morgan. In the 1920s, the house was the centerpiece of the Kilkenny Club, which operated several lodges and the golf course. More recently, the building was run as Paradise Lodge, a summer music colony, then a boys' camp; in the 1970s, the place was abandoned to the elements.

The Stanleys bought the house in 1992 and rebuilt it practically top to bottom, substituting highly adorned Edwardian-style decor for the dark, rustic elements of the original house's public spaces. The porches, though, remain expansive, twig-framed gems.

Four guest rooms with private baths are upstairs. The grandest is the J. P. Morgan suite, a thousand square feet, with its own second-story porch, gas fireplace, sitting area, whirlpool tub encircled by Spanish tile, cedar closet, TV, queen-size bed, and views galore. The Helen Keller room, named in honor of her visit many years ago, is tucked under the eaves, with antique oak furniture and bold wall coverings and window treatments. The Buckley room (William and James Buckley stayed with the original owners) is more subtly decorated, with a hardwood floor and its own porch with views of Raven Hill. The Elizabeth room also has its own porch, and lovely light streaming through windows above the queen-size bed.

Breakfast — made to order omelets, French toast, Belgian waffles, or low-cholesterol choices — is served whenever guests arise.

OLD MILL BED & BREAKFAST
Owners: Beki Maurello-Pushee and Bruce Pushee.
518-873-2294.
www.adirondackinns.com/oldmill.
Rte. 9N.
Closed: Mon.–Thurs. fall–winter; inquire.
Price: Moderate.
Credit Cards: AE, D, MC, V.

In the thirties and forties this lovely property — bounded on two sides by the Boquet River — was an art school run by landscape painter Wayman Adams. Now it's a lovely bed & breakfast packed with antiques, Oriental rugs, paintings, and sculpture. Four guest rooms (three with private baths) are in the main house; students from the Meadowmount School of Music often bunk in the studio building during the summer.

Breakfast, served 7:30–8:30am, is decidedly a highlight here. On sunny, warm mornings it's served on the enclosed patio that has a fountain as its centerpiece, and the rest of the time the feast is presented in the formal dining room. Muffins, juice, poached pears with cream or baked grapefruit with honey are the starters, followed by bourbon French toast, lemon soufflé pancakes, or perhaps quiche with garden-fresh tomatoes.

STONELEIGH BED & BREAKFAST
Owners: Rosemary Remington and William Ames.
518-873-2669 or 888-222-9789.
www.adirondackinns.com/stoneleigh.
Union St.
Open: Year-round.
Price: Inexpensive.
Credit Cards: AE, MC, V.
Special Features: Fireplace; older children welcome.

Richard Harrison, a Boston-based architect, designed this imposing Germanic-looking castle for New York State Supreme Court Justice Arthur Smith in 1882. The house has a fine library, as befits a country judge, and several porches and balconies under the tree-shaded, secluded grounds. There's also a TV room and a living room for guests.

Downstairs, there's a suite with private bath that is wheelchair accessible; upstairs, four spacious rooms share a bath and a half.

Essex

CUPOLA HOUSE
Manager: Donna Lou Sonnett.
518-963-7222.
S. Main St.
Open: Year-round.
Price: Moderate to Expensive.
Credit Cards: MC, V.
Special Features: Boat slips; no smoking; children welcome.

A prim and proper Greek Revival with wonderful two-story porches, Cupola House has two handsome apartments decorated with antiques and Adirondack furniture that are just a quick walk up from the Essex Marina. Both have complete kitchens and full baths and access to the upstairs porch; rates include a boat slip at the marina. The south apartment nicely accommodates two couples or a family; the north apartment has one bedroom with a wood stove.

If you need transportation to or from the Westport train station or nearby airports, it's available at no charge. Cupola House is just two blocks from the ferry to Vermont and conveniently close to all of Essex's shops and restaurants.

THE ESSEX INN
Owners: Trish and John Walker.
518-963-8821.
Lake Shore Rd.
Open: Year-round.
Price: Moderate.
Credit Cards: AE, MC, V.
Handicap Access: 2 downstairs suites.

Stretching along Main Street with two tiers of porches is this lovely, carefully restored inn. The building is surprisingly narrow — just one room and the hallway wide — with a cafe, courtyard, and dining room, plus two spacious guest suites downstairs. Upstairs there are three bedrooms, plus two more suites: one includes a bedroom, bath, and kitchenette, while the other has two bedrooms, a sitting room, and bath.

The hotel is full of antiques, plus handsome period engravings and photographs. In 1995 new owners took over the Essex Inn and set to work making the landmark as friendly as it is historic. The food's good, too.

THE STONEHOUSE
Innkeeper: Sylvia Hobbs.
518-963-7713.
Church & Elm Sts.
Closed: Nov.–Apr.
Price: Moderate to Expensive.
Credit Cards: None.
Special Features: Fireplaces; bikes for guests.

Step into this 1826 Georgian stone house and you feel as if you've entered a classic English country house. Tall windows suffuse dappled light into the living spaces; private gardens ring the property. Two lovely suites with private baths and two rooms with a shared bath occupy the second floor; renovations to the top floor transformed the space into an exceptional 20′ x 30′ room with exposed beams, exposed stone walls, and French doors that open onto a rooftop deck with a view of Lake Champlain.

Breakfast could be categorized as first-rate continental, with fresh baked goods from Montreal, seasonal fruits, and gourmet coffee and tea. Note that the Stonehouse is located across the street from one of Essex's historic churches and is available for receptions and private gatherings.

Port Henry

THE KING'S INN
Innkeepers: Linda Mullin and Nancy Masher.
518-546-7633 or 800-600-7633.
109 Broad St.
Open: Year-round.
Price: Moderate.
Credit Cards: AE, D, MC, V.
Special Features: Pub serving lunch and dinner; fireplaces.

Slowly but surely downtown Port Henry is refurbishing neglected buildings from the town's heyday as an iron-mining center. One bright spot is the restored King's Inn, an 1893 mansion on a hill overlooking the lake. There are nine nice rooms upstairs, all with private baths. Three have working fireplaces; two have views of the lake. The best room in the house has a canopy bed, a big sitting area with two east-facing windows (there's even a telescope for spotting sailboats on Lake Champlain), and a great big bathroom with a deep porcelain tub.

Folks traveling by train or boat take note: pick-up and delivery to the marina or depot can be easily arranged, and Port Henry's shops, historic sites, and waterfront are within walking distance. There's no need to walk very far for a good meal, though: the restaurant on the first floor is quite good, and you can enjoy a cocktail sitting in an antique wicker chair on the wraparound porch.

Ticonderoga

The cobblestone facade at Stone Wells is a landmark in downtown Ticonderoga.

James Swedberg

STONE WELLS FARM BED & BREAKFAST
Innkeepers: Jeff and Susan Wells.
518-585-6324 or 888-261-5800.

A wonderful cobblestone facade sets off this surprisingly large Craftsman-style bungalow at the foot of Ticonderoga's main street. Inside, chestnut woodwork, vest-pocket windows, and airy, comfortable rooms make an amiable haven for

www.stonewellsbb.com.
331 Montcalm St.
Open: Year-round.
Price: Moderate.
Credit Cards: AE, MC, V.
Special Features: No smoking or alcohol on premises.

guests. Two rooms share a bath on the first floor, and three rooms and two baths are located on the second floor. Ask for the "blue room" if you'd like a private bath.

Hearty breakfasts are served from 7–9:30am, and you're off to spend a day at Fort Ticonderoga.

Westport

The Inn on the Library Lawn has ten rooms for guests, plus a lovely dining room open on summer weekends.

James Swedberg

ALL TUCKED INN
Innkeepers: Tom Haley and Claudia Ryan.
518-962-4400; 888-ALL-TUCK.
www.alltuckedinn.com.
53 S. Main St.
Closed: 2 weeks in Mar.
Price: Moderate.
Credit Cards: None.
Special Features: Children over 6 welcome; dinners by prior arrangement.

A grand old Dutch Colonial home, All Tucked Inn occupies a prominent spot on Westport's Main Street. There are nine lovely rooms (all with private bath); five have views of Lake Champlain. A suite on the first floor has its own porch and fireplace. From the inn, you can walk to the Westport Yacht Club, the marina, Westport Trading Company, tennis courts, and even the eighteen-hole golf course.

THE INN ON THE LIBRARY LAWN
Innkeepers: Susann and Don Thompson.
518-962-8666.
www.innonthelibrarylawn.com.
1 Washington St.
Closed: Mar.–Apr.
Price: Moderate.

As you might imagine, this charming little hotel — which dates back to 1875 — is situated just across from Westport's wonderful old library. Extensive renovations have created peaceful, refined public areas and 10 elegant, comfortable rooms, all with private baths. On the second floor there's a library and lounge area; a sitting room with fireplace welcomes visitors downstairs.

Min. Stay: 2 nights on holiday weekends.
Credit Cards: AE, MC, V.
Special Features: No smoking; children welcome.

Breakfast (soufflés, waffles, pastries, and fresh fruit) is included with the room rate. On summer weekends, the pretty dining room is open for lunch.

THE VICTORIAN LADY
Innkeepers: Doris and Wayne Deswert.
57 S. Main St.
518-962-2345.
Open: Year-round.
Price: Moderate.
Credit Cards: None.
Special Features: Children welcome; no smoking.

Three architectural styles are exuberantly (and successfully) combined at the Victorian Lady, a newcomer to Westport's list of fine lodgings. Inside, you'll see evidence of the original Greek Revival home, but outside, Second Empire shows up in a square tower and mansard roof. The full-length porch is Eastlake and offers a fine place for reading a novel or looking out over lovely gardens.

Three guest rooms all have private baths; there's a room with bunk beds that shares a bath. While in Westport, be sure to take the self-guided walking tour of historic buildings.

THE WESTPORT HOTEL
Innkeepers: Rita and Ralph Warren.
518-962-4501.
114 Pleasant St., Rte. 9N across from the Amtrak station.
Open: Year-round.
Price: Moderate.
Credit Cards: D, MC, V.
Special Features: Restaurant; children and leashed pets welcome.

When the railroad came to Westport in 1876, Albert Gates opened his hotel on the other side of the tracks. Ever since, the spacious clapboard building has been operated as an inn. Guests can now choose from 10 refurbished rooms decorated with antiques and hand-stenciled walls; most have private baths. In warm weather, use the breezy wraparound porch for watching the world go by on Route 9N or enjoying a meal from the hotel's fine kitchen.

Folks who are traveling without a car should note that there's daily Amtrak service to Westport, and many of the town's charms, from the Essex County Fair and Depot Theater to the lakefront, are nearby. From Columbus Day through Memorial Day, package deals with lodging, dinner, and breakfast for two are quite affordable.

Willsboro

ADIRONDACK MEADOWS
Innkeepers: Debra Whitson and John Haverlick.
518-963-4075 or 877-963-4075.
277 Lake Shore Rd., Rte. 22 bet. Essex & Willsboro.

Two miles up the road from the historic settlement of Essex is a lovely Greek Revival home, operated for the last decade as a bed & breakfast. Adirondack Meadows has a sweeping view of Lake Champlain, with four simple, appealing guest rooms upstairs that share baths. An efficiency

Open: Year-round.
Price: Inexpensive.
Credit Cards: MC, V.
Special Features: Lake views; bikes; children and well-behaved pets welcome.

apartment in a nearby building is perfect for families or for an extended stay. Three beaches are within a few miles of the inn; several golf courses are a short distance away in Willsboro, Westport, and Peru. Bicycles, cross-country skis, and a canoe are on hand for guests who'd like to explore.

HIGH PEAKS AND NORTHERN ADIRONDACKS

Elk Lake

At Elk Lake Lodge, you can hike, canoe, fish for brook trout, or just sit in an Adirondack loveseat under tall pines.

James Swedberg

ELK LAKE LODGE
Managers: Janet and Percy Fleming.
518-532-7616.
Elk Lake Rd., off Blue Ridge Rd. (Elk Lake); Box 59 (North Hudson NY 12855).
Closed: Nov.–early May.
Price: Expensive; includes all meals.
Credit Cards: None.
Min. Stay: 2 nights.
Special Features: Private lake and pond; mountain hiking trails; canoes and rowboats for guests; fishing; children welcome; no pets.

In a nutshell, Elk Lake Lodge is the quintessential Adirondack lodge. Set on a breathtaking private lake ringed by the High Peaks, in the midst of a 12,000-acre preserve, the place offers everything an outdoorsperson could ask for: great fishing, unlimited wilderness hiking, and canoeing on an island-studded lake that's off-limits to motorboats. Of course, if just hanging out, listening to the loons, and admiring the view are your kinds of recreation, this place has that in spades.

There are six rooms in the turn-of-the-century lodge, all with twin beds and private baths. Around the lakeshore there are seven cottages, ranging from Little Tom, a cozy spot under the trees for two, to Emerson Lodge, which sleeps up to 12. Several of the cabins are equipped with kitchens and have fireplaces, or have decks overlooking the lake; all are nicely decorated. The price of a stay at Elk Lake includes all meals, which are served in the dining room where huge picture windows reveal the mountains and lake.

Jay

THE BOOK AND BLANKET
Innkeeper: Kathy Recchia and Fred Balzac.
518-946-8323.
Rte. 9N.
Open: Year-round.
Price: Inexpensive to Moderate.
Min. Stay: 2 nights on holiday weekends.
Credit Cards: None.
Special Features: Children welcome; inquire about pets.

Rooms in this restored Greek Revival home are named for authors: the Jack London number has a north-woods ambiance, queen-size bed, and private bath with a whirlpool tub; the Jane Austen room has a queen-size bed and a quiet nook for reading; the F. Scott Fitzgerald room has a double bed and shares a bath. All of the rooms — upstairs and down — have lots of books, and guests are encouraged to browse and borrow at will. Or you can relax by the fire in the living room with Daisy, the basset hound, at your feet, as you watch a classic film on the VCR. The Book and Blanket offers a home-cooked breakfast in its pleasant dining room.

VIEW AND FAR BETWEEN
Owners: Margo and Herb Glicksman.
518-946-1208.
www.lakeplacid.net/theview.
Rivers Rd.
Open: Year-round.
Price: Moderate to Expensive.
Credit Cards: Inquire.
Special Features: Therapeutic touch and reflexology practitioner on premises; no children; no pets.

As you'd guess, the sweeping vistas from this gorgeous, huge new log house are the star attraction. From every window and all the decks, you can see mountains, unbroken woods, and practically no other signs of civilization. Six rooms are available, including three with twin beds (which can be put together as king-size beds), two with queen beds, and the honeymoon suite, which has a fireplace and private bath. Whiteface Mountain (which dominates the view to the east) and trout fishing in the West Branch of the Ausable River are only eight miles away.

Keene

BARK EATER INN
Owner: Joe-Pete Wilson.
518-576-2221.
www.barkeater.com.
Alstead Hill Rd.
Open: Year-round.
Price: Moderate to Expensive.
Min. Stay: 2 nights on holiday weekends.

More than 150 years ago, the stagecoach carrying travelers from Lake Champlain to Lake Placid stopped overnight here; since the 1940s, members of the Wilson family have taken in guests. The main part of this country inn is a beautiful farmhouse with two stone fireplaces and wide board floors. There are seven rooms upstairs that share baths, plus four rooms in the new Carriage

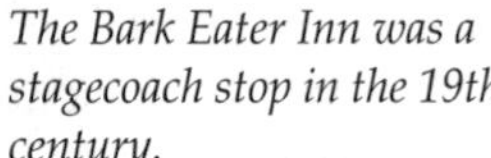

The Bark Eater Inn was a stagecoach stop in the 19th century.

James Swedberg

Credit Cards: AE, MC, V.
Special Features: Cross-country skiing; horseback riding; dinners available; children welcome; special packages.

House with private baths. The Log Cottage has two three-bedroom suites and two guest rooms with private baths. Breakfast is served family-style in the dining room; dinners are available by special arrangement.

Guests seek out the Bark Eater not just for the marvelous views of the High Peaks and the friendly staff, but for horseback riding, hiking, and cross-country skiing. The lodge has dozens of well-mannered English and Western mounts and many miles of woodland trails. Polo games are held in a nearby field on summer Sunday afternoons. In winter the bridle trails become groomed ski trails; Bark Eater's 20 kilometers connect with the Jackrabbit system, so you could ski for days and never cover the same territory.

Keene Valley

KEENE VALLEY LODGE
Innkeepers: George and Laurie Daniels.
518-576-2003.
www/keenevalleylodge.com.
Rte. 73
Open: Year-round.
Price: Moderate.
Min. Stay: 2 nights on summer weekends.
Credit Cards: MC, V.
Special Features: Fireplace, pool table; no smoking; children welcome.

From 1929 to 1949 this substantial Italianate home was known to travelers as Beede Cottage; now it's a cozy inn with all the modern comforts in eight guest rooms. On the first floor, there's a suite with queen-size bed, full bath, and its own entrance; a highlight upstairs is the room with queen-size bed, big picture windows framing mountain views, and a private bath. Some of the second-floor rooms have private baths and king-size beds. All are furnished with antiques and hand-stitched quilts. A full breakfast buffet is included in the rate.

Keene Valley Lodge is close to great High Peaks trails, but after all that exercise you can relax by the fire.

James Swedberg

MOUNTAIN MEADOWS
Owner: Patricia Quinn.
518-576-4771.
Rte. 73.
Open: Year-round.
Price: Inexpensive to Moderate.
Credit Cards: None.
Special Features: Children welcome.

The East Branch of the Ausable River curls through this property and the pointy peak of Noonmark Mtn. looms to the west. Mountain Meadows is a mecca for hikers, cross-country skiers, and climbers; Pat Quinn will help you plan an outing and drop you off at the trailhead.

The bed & breakfast is actually two comfortable Adirondack-style houses that share a sunny deck. The bedroom wing has three large rooms with king-size beds that convert to twins and which share two baths. There's another chamber with private bath and a southern exposure.

TRAIL'S END FAMILY INN & HIKER'S LODGE
Innkeepers: Jenny and Curt Borchardt.
518-576-9860 or 800-281-9860.
www.trailsendinn.com.
Trail's End Rd., off Rte. 73.
Open: Year-round.
Price: Moderate.
Credit Cards: MC, V.
Special Features: Fireplaces, hiking trails, children welcome.

A gambrel-roofed house with eyebrow windows on a quiet road, Trail's End calls itself a hikers' lodge, implying that the accommodations aren't so fancy that you need to worry about blow-drying your hair before you come to breakfast. Downstairs, the lodge has a large comfortable living room with a fireplace and VCR plus a winterized sun porch full of toys and games for kids.

Guest rooms upstairs include Catamount, which has a corner fireplace, a private porch, and full bath; Jay, the largest room, with a private bath; and Marcy Suite, a two-room suite with king-size bed, TV, bath, and futons on a sleeping porch. There are four double rooms that share baths, plus a newly refurbished two-bedroom cottage with complete kitchen, TV/VCR, washer/dryer, and stereo that accommodates up to six guests and even a pet. At times, hiking clubs or family groups take over the entire place, which can hold about 40 comfortably. Meals can be arranged for large groups.

You don't need a car to enjoy Trail's End and vicinity. The bus stops every day at the Noon Mark Diner, a five-minute walk away, and from the inn, there's easy access to numerous High Peaks hiking trails. Note that Jenny and Curt also rent fully equipped, newly renovated vacation houses along the Ausable River in Keene, and on Tupper Lake.

Lake Placid

ADIRONDAK LOJ
Manager: Rob Bond.
518-523-3441.
www.adk.org.
Adirondak Loj Rd., off Rte. 73, 3 mi. S. of Lake Placid village.
Open: Year-round.
Price: Inexpensive to Moderate.
Credit Cards: MC, V.
Special Features: Hiking; outdoor workshops; tent campground; backcountry cabins; High Peaks Information Center.

With its sweeping panorama of Mt. Marcy and Indian Pass, the drive in to Adirondak Loj sets you up for a visit to the Adirondack Mountain Club's (ADK) wilderness retreat. On Heart Lake in the midst of the High Peaks, the 1920s-era lodge is a rustic, comfortable place. In the living room, you can rock in an Old Hickory chair in front of the vast stone fireplace, and choose from the shelves practically any book that's ever been written on the Adirondacks. Breakfast — the wake-up bell rings bright and early — is served family-style at picnic tables in an adjoining room. Bag lunches are available, and plain, home-cooked dinners are served when the lodge is busy.

There are four private rooms, four bunkrooms, and a huge coed loft. The bunkrooms, which have four built-in log beds, are snug and cozy, like cabins on a ship; the loft can be a hard place to get a good night's sleep if there are any snorers in the crowd. The management refers to the bathrooms as "semi-private," but they're actually similar to facilities in a college dorm. You don't need to be a member of the ADK to stay at the Loj, but you must make advance reservations.

On Heart Lake are two cabins that accommodate four to 16 people during the fall, winter, and spring. For the intrepid traveler, ADK has three excellent backcountry cabins that are accessible by foot and available year-round: Johns Brook Lodge is a 3 ½-mile hike in from Keene Valley. Further still are Grace Camp and Camp Peggy O'Brien, which have tiers of bunks, gas lights, and wood heat; they're excellent bases for hiking, snowshoe, or ski weekends.

HIGHLAND HOUSE INN
Owners: Cathy and Ted Blazer.
518-523-2377.

Secluded but central, Highland House looks and feels like an authentic Adirondack inn, which it assuredly is. The main house, with antiques and rustic details, opened to guests in 1910. Downstairs,

3 Highland Place., off Hillcrest Ave. near the Holiday Inn.
Open: Year-round.
Price: Moderate.
Credit Cards: MC, V.
Min. Stay: 2 nights on weekends.
Special Features: Children welcome; mountain-bike rentals.

there's a large living room with a wood stove, a piano room, a dining room, and a deck with benches and a giant hot tub built around two big clumps of white birch trees. In nice weather, guests enjoy breakfast (which is included in the nightly rate) in a glass-enclosed garden room. It's only a two-minute walk from this residential neighborhood to Main Street.

The inn has seven rooms, all with private baths. Next door to the main lodge is Highland Cottage, a perky little spot complete with kitchen, fireplace, air conditioning, and deck; there's a two-night minimum reservation for the cottage.

THE INTERLAKEN INN
Owners: Carol and Roy Johnson.
518-523-3180 or 800-428-3269.
15 Interlaken Ave., around the corner from Mirror Lake Inn.
Open: Year-round; B&B only Apr. & Nov.
Price: Expensive, MAP; Moderate, B&B.
Credit Cards: AE, MC, V.
Min. Stay: 2 nights on fall and winter weekends.
Special Features: Fireplace; restaurant; children over 5 welcome.

Walnut-paneled walls, tin ceilings, a fireplace, a winding staircase, and all kinds of antiques make the Interlaken a true gem. Built in 1906 by one of the founders of the Bank of Lake Placid, the secluded spot has been operated as an inn for most of its existence. Downstairs, the dining room is elegant, yet casual; guests can eat on the porch during nice weather. Off the living room is a cozy little bar, with club chairs, a card table, and TV/VCR — the perfect place for reliving that golf match or discussing the fall foliage.

There are a dozen lovely guest rooms on the second and third floors, most with queen-size beds, all with private baths, and decorated with antiques. The Honeymoon Suite has a canopy bed and its own private balcony. The third-floor rooms are especially charming; even the bathrooms, with clawfoot tubs tucked under the eaves, are romantic. During most of the year, rooms are available on the modified American plan. On Sundays and Mondays, except for holiday weekends, no dinner is served and the bed and breakfast rate applies.

LAKE PLACID LODGE
Manager: Kathryn Kincannon.
518-523-2700.
www.lakeplacidlodge.com.
Whiteface Inn Rd.
Open: Year-round.
Price: Very Expensive.
Credit Cards: AE, MC, V.

First, a geography lesson: the village of Lake Placid is on tiny Mirror Lake; the lake named Placid is slightly west of town and it's a big body of water with a pair of islands and gorgeous views. Only a few lodgings are located on the secluded western banks of Lake Placid, with the Lodge in a particularly magical spot.

Built as a summer home at the turn of the cen-

Special Features: Boats and bikes for guests; fireplaces in rooms; well-behaved dogs and children welcome.

tury, the building has been enlarged over the years, adding a wing here and a porch there, changing the rooflines, and creating a dramatic staircase linking the guests' lodge with the dining room in 1994, but the heart of the building remains intact. In 1946, Mae and Teddy Frankel opened the place as a hotel, and for nearly 40 years ran it with a personal touch. Christie and David Garrett bought the Lodge in 1993 and transformed it into a stunningly beautiful resort that compares favorably to The Point, the Garretts' world-class hotel on Upper Saranac Lake. Actually, rates at the Lodge are a bit more within reach than The Point, and the restaurant (open to the public) offers marvelous selections for breakfast, lunch, and dinner.

Guests have 22 rooms from which to choose, such as Tamarac, with a king-size bed, cobblestone fireplace, and a cozy sitting alcove; St. Regis Suite, on the upper level of Lakeside Lodge, with two fireplaces, huge soaking tub, and porch overlooking the lake; and Pinnacle, which has the best views, king-size bed, and a stone fireplace. Fantastic rustic log cabins offer window seats, huge fireplaces, and the illusion of being all alone in the woods; you can even bring the family dog. There's a postage-stamp-size sandy beach, and canoes, sailboards, pedal boats, and bicycles are on hand for guests. The beautiful, challenging Whiteface Inn golf course is an easy walk from the Lodge.

Mirror Lake Inn spa was completely renovated in 1999, and the better suites have whirlpool tubs and fireplaces.

Mirror Lake Inn

MIRROR LAKE INN
Owner: Edwin Weibrecht.
518-523-2544.
www.mirrorlakeinn.com.
5 Mirror Lake Drive.
Open: year-round.

On a hillside overlooking Mirror Lake, this delightful resort hotel in the heart of town offers an inviting array of amenities and services. In 1999 the spa — offering everything from mud wraps and honey-almond exfoliation treatments to massage therapy, plus all kinds of exercise classes

Price: Moderate to Very Expensive.
Credit Cards: AE, D, MC, V.
Handicap Access: Yes, hotel rooms.
Special Features: Spa; tennis; heated pools; ice skating; restaurant; conference facilities; hair and skin-care salon; children welcome.

led by professionals — went through a major makeover. If your interest is relaxing, improving your skin, or launching a healthier lifestyle, there's someone on the staff who can help.

The best accommodations, "Placid Suites," are split-level rooms connected by an oak spiral staircase, with king-size beds, huge whirlpool baths, and private balconies overlooking the lake; suite guests receive champagne and flowers upon arrival, and nightly turn-down service. There are a full range of private rooms, from country-furnished doubles with private balconies, to the comfortable "Colonial Bedrooms," which give guests a chance to enjoy all that the inn offers at an economical price. Even the least expensive rooms have refrigerators, hair dryers, clock radios, cable TV, and magnifying make-up mirrors.

Mirror Lake Inn has a nice restaurant (with an extensive menu that includes low-fat choices), a cozy bar, and various nooks and crannies for guests to relax in. The inn is an exceptional facility for conferences, with plenty of attractive meeting rooms for large or small groups. Packages are available for early-season downhill skiing, midweek visits, and golf.

MT. VAN HOEVENBERG BED & BREAKFAST
Innkeepers: Katie Wolf and Seth Patterson.
518-523-9572.
www.adirondackrafting.com/bandb.
Rte. 73, near the Mt. Van Hoevenberg Recreational Complex.
Open: Year-round.
Price: Moderate.
Min. Stay: 2 nights on busy weekends.
Credit Cards: MC, V.
Special Features: Guide service; hiking trails; sauna; children welcome.

Tiny but immaculate four-season housekeeping cabins plus a three-bedroom, two-bath bed & breakfast would make Katie and Seth's facilities for guests appealing in any Adirondack setting, but the great attraction here is the place's proximity to excellent cross-country skiing and hiking. The B&B is next to the 50 km of groomed tracks at the Olympic cross-country complex and connects with the Cascade Ski-Touring Center and Jackrabbit trails. You can head into the High Peaks Wilderness Area without parking your car at a trailhead and afterwards enjoy an invigorating wood-fired sauna.

PARADOX LODGE
Innkeepers: Nan and Moses (Red) LaFountaine.
518-523-9078.
www.paradoxlodge.com.
76 Saranac Ave., near Howard Johnson's Motor Lodge.

In August 1999, a century after Paradox Lodge was built, the property reopened as a cozy inn. Though the place has been scrubbed, rewired, replumbed, painted, and decorated with an eclectic mix of antiques and art (clearly the LaFountaines have a sense of humor combined with a knack for finding cool stuff), the house's underlying charac-

Open: Year-round.
Price: Expensive.
Credit Cards: AE, MC, V.
Special Features: Dinner by request; no children; no pets; access to Paradox Bay of Lake Placid.

ter — wainscoting, woodwork, angles, and windows is handsomely intact. Four rooms, all with private baths, are upstairs. The Treetop Suite is especially nice, with lots of windows and a sunporch sitting area, clawfoot tub, and queen-size bed. Duvets are provided for chilly nights.

A parlor for guests is downstairs, along with two dining rooms that seat sixteen people. The food is terrific, featuring fresh seafood, excellent fish, *poussin*, and prime beef with whatever's in season for fruits, vegetables, and herbs. If you stay at Paradox Lodge, don't miss the opportunity to eat here too.

SOUTH MEADOW FARM LODGE
Owners: Nancy and Tony Corwin.
518-523-9369 or 800-523-9369.
Rte. 73.
Open: Year-round.
Price: Moderate.
Credit Cards: MC, V.
Min. Stay: 2 nights on holiday weekends; inquire.
Special Features: Farm animals; cross-country ski trails; fireplace; meals available; working maple sugarhouse; children welcome; no smoking.

Also near Mt. Van Hoevenberg's cross-country ski and biathlon facilities is a small family farm that operates as a homey bed & breakfast. The Corwins produce much of the food that appears on the table, including maple syrup. The lodge property contains ski trails that are part of the 50-km Olympic complex and is close to hiking trails up Cascade and Pitchoff mountains, making this is an ideal spot for outdoorspeople.

Accommodations include five rooms with half baths, rooms in the loft with shared baths, and four mountain cabins for the "soft camper," which have sleeping lofts, woodstoves, and candlelight, with running water and privies nearby. The lodge's living room is quite handsome and centers around a massive fireplace. Breakfast is included in the nightly rate; family-style dinners and trail lunches are available.

STAGECOACH INN
Owner: Peter Moreau.
518-523-9474.
370 Old Military Rd.
Closed: April.
Price: Moderate.
Credit Cards: MC, V.
Min. Stay: 2 nights, inquire.
Special Features: Fireplaces; children over 10; inquire about pets.

The first guests at this North Elba landmark checked in when Andrew Jackson was president. In the last 165 years, much care has gone into keeping this venerable lodge (located on the edge of town) handsome and inviting. Beaded-pine paneling gleams, rustic yellow birch trims the stairs and balcony, and a huge fireplace beckons.

There are nine guest rooms, five with private baths; two rooms have their own fireplaces. Four rooms share baths. A full country breakfast is included in the rate.

Newcomb

AUNT POLLY'S INN
Owners: Maggie and Doug Alitz.
518-582-2260.
Rte. 28N.
Open: Year-round.
Price: Inexpensive to Moderate
Credit Cards: MC, V.
Special Features: Hiking trails; dinners available by prior arrangement.

Before the Civil War, Aunt Polly Bissell took in travelers at her home on the edge of the High Peaks, and in August 1995, Maggie and Doug Alitz opened the doors once again. Their house is lovely, packed with eclectic antiques; four nice guest rooms share two modern baths.

The 70-acre property includes hiking and cross-country ski trails that lead back to a wild pond, and recreational opportunities abound in and around Newcomb. You can take the 10-mile trek into Santanoni Preserve on foot, bikes, skis, or by horse-drawn wagon, head off to climb in the High Peaks, or tour the Visitor Interpretive Center.

Guest room at Lake Harris Bay, a new bed and breakfast in Newcomb.

James Swedberg

LAKE HARRIS BAY BED AND BREAKFAST
Hosts: Brian and Diane Britt.
518-582-2184.
Rte. 28N.
Open: Year-round.
Price: Inexpensive to moderate.
Credit Cards: No.

Lakefront lodging in Newcomb was hard to come by, until the Britts turned their spacious home into a bed and breakfast in 1999. Two bedrooms in the main house plus a rustic cottage (no running water) right on the waterfront can accommodate couples or families. The place is well equipped for recreation, rain or shine, with a pool table, library room, and TV/VCR inside, and a sailboat, kayak, and fishing boat available to guests.

In summer, a full breakfast is served on the deck. As you sip your coffee, you can see the slides on Santanoni Peak, with Mount Marcy in the distance

Saranac Lake

AMPERSAND BAY BOAT CLUB
Hosts: Keti and John Zuliani.
518-891-3001.
12 Ampersand Bay Rd., off Rte. 3.
Open: Year-round.
Price: Moderate to Expensive.
Credit Cards: None.
Min. Stay: 1 week during summer for suites & cottages.
Special Features: Private beach; canoes; boat launch; children welcome; no pets.

A short distance from downtown Saranac Lake, but directly on beautiful Lower Saranac Lake, Ampersand Bay has several nice two-bedroom log cabins with screen porches and complete kitchens; studio apartments; two boathouse suites each with two bedrooms and overlooking the water; and assorted other cottages and rooms. If you're traveling with your own boat, you can handily launch and dock here; there's a fee for slips. The Zulianis' 40-acre retreat includes a private sandy beach and free canoes and sailboats, so guests can explore the many state-owned islands in the lake. From Lower Saranac you can travel through the locks to Middle Saranac Lake, or Oseetah, Kiwassa, and Lake Flower, with great fishing throughout.

THE DOCTOR'S INN
Innkeeper: Susan Moody.
518-891-3464.
Trudeau Rd., off Rte. 3.
Open: Year-round.
Price: Inexpensive to Moderate.
Credit Cards: MC, V.
Special Features: Guide service; children and pets welcome.

At the foot of Mt. Pisgah, on five quiet acres at the edge of the village, is this bed & breakfast that opened in 1994. The Doctor's Inn — named for its historic connection to a renowned sanitarium — has been renovated throughout with polished hardwood floors and big stone fireplaces, and offers two spacious suites with lovely mountain vistas and two double rooms. Ask about hiring a licensed guide if you're interested in backcountry exploring. Five golf courses are within 15 miles of the place; cross-country skiing on backcountry or groomed trails is just moments away, and two alpine areas (Whiteface and Mt. Pisgah) are close by.

FOGARTY'S BED & BREAKFAST
Owners: Emily and Jack Fogarty.
518-891-3755 or 800-525-3755.
37 Riverside Dr.
Open: Year-round.
Price: Inexpensive.
Credit Cards: None.
Special Features: Boat dock for guests; swimming; children welcome.

Built in 1910 as a cure cottage for tuberculosis patients, this attractive home overlooking Lake Flower has handsome woodwork, leaded-glass windows, wonderful porches, and five bedrooms sharing three baths. Although Fogarty's is a quick walk from Saranac Lake's business district and restaurants, it's in a very peaceful neighborhood and even has a dock on the lake for swimmers and boaters. Winter guests note that cross-country skiing at Dewey Mtn. is about a mile away, and in early February, when the winter carnival is in full swing, you can look over to the fabulous ice palace on the opposite shore of the lake. One point to keep in mind about Fogarty's: because the house is set on a steep hillside, you've got to climb a lot of steps (73 to be exact, says Emily) to get to the entrance.

HARBOR HILL COTTAGES
Hosts: Denise and Wayne Bujold.
518-891-2784.
www.adirondackvacations.com.
104 Riverside Dr.
Open: Year-round.
Price: Moderate.
Special Features: Sandy beach; fireplaces; boats for guests; dockage; children welcome.

A cluster of cabins on Lake Flower, Harbor Hill provides waterfront tranquillity within a residential neighborhood. On a July or August Friday night, guests sitting on the docks can enjoy the outdoor folk music concerts from across the water, or they can canoe over to the bandshell. In the winter, you can ice skate right from the front door.

Four of the five winterized housekeeping cabins have fireplaces; they range in size from one to three bedrooms, and all have picture windows and decks overlooking the water. There's a private beach for swimming; dock space for visiting motorboats; and rowboats, pedal boats, bikes, and canoes for guests.

Hotel Saranac offers excellent service, traditional hotel amenities, and is easily accessible by public transportation.

James Swedberg

THE HOTEL SARANAC OF PAUL SMITH'S COLLEGE
518-891-2200 or 800-937-0211.
www.hotelsaranac.com.
101 Main St.
Open: Year-round.
Price: Inexpensive to Moderate.
Credit Cards: AE, DC, MC, V.
Handicap Access: Elevators; most rooms.

For more than four decades, hospitality-management students of Paul Smith's College have gotten on-the-job training at this landmark downtown hotel. As a result, the staff here is friendly and helpful at all hours of the day or night. There are 91 air-conditioned guest rooms, all with private baths; rooms are spotless and comfortable. The second-floor grand hall, with beautiful painted wood beams, a grand piano, and potted plants, is elegantly welcoming and true to architect William Scopes's vision of how a fine hotel should greet its

Special Features: Restaurants; cocktail lounge; children welcome; inexpensive golf and ski packages.

guests. A.P. Smith's Restaurant, named after the famed North Country hotelier and college founder Paul Smith, is open from breakfast to dinner, while the Boathouse Lounge — a quiet, congenial pub — serves light meals as well. On the ground floor is a gift shop featuring quality crafts and a full-service travel agency.

The Hotel Saranac offers numerous packages for golf or skiing; tour groups or conferences are cheerfully accommodated; and Canadian money is accepted at par. Travelers wishing to see the Adirondacks via public transportation should note that the Adirondack Trailways bus stops here, and it's quite easy to see Saranac Lake on foot and take a cab to Lake Placid.

THE POINT
Owners: Christie and David Garrett.
518-891-5674 or 800-255-3530.
www.pointny.com.
Mail: Star Rte. Box 65.
Closed: Mar. 15–Apr. 15.
Price: Very Expensive.
Credit Cards: AE.
Min. Stay: 2 nights on weekends.
Special Features: Great Camp; gourmet meals; boats for guests; member *Relais et Chateaux*; no children under 18.

William Avery Rockefeller built a drop-dead gorgeous Great Camp named Wonundra on an Upper Saranac Lake peninsula in the thirties, and if you've read any recent articles about the Adirondacks, chances are you've seen The Point, that Rockefeller place that's now open to guests. A roundup of comments from the press gives you a glimpse of what's so special here: "Absolutely, but absolutely, lovely, a place in which everything you see is total perfection," wrote Rene Lecler in *The 300 Best Hotels in the World.* "A private estate that sweeps all honors as the most enchanting lakefront sanctuary of its kind in America," stated *The Hideaway Report*. "It's rather like those European castles where one can arrange to spend a week as the guest of the duke and duchess," commented the *Yale University Alumni Magazine*; "The Point: the wilderness at its most luxurious," summarized *Vogue Magazine*. In 1999, the readers of *Conde Nast Traveler* voted The Point their favorite hotel of all.

The 11 rooms, in four different buildings, each have vast beds, lake views, and fireplaces, and are filled with an astutely planned mixture of antiques, Adirondack furniture, Oriental rugs, old prints, and stuffed beasts. The Boathouse is a special gem, with its own private dining alcove and wraparound balcony, but all the rooms are divine.

In the Main Lodge, the Great Hall measures 30 by 50 feet; fireplaces of astonishing proportions blaze away. The atmosphere here is that of a truly elegant house party, with black tie suggested for dinner on Wednesday and Saturday nights. The food warrants that treatment too, with menus deftly combining native bounty, fine herbs, exquisite seafood, and imported ingredients in an imaginative kaleidoscope of flavors. The wine list is unsurpassed, the bar is always open.

All this elegance and hedonism comes at a price, with two nights for a couple at The Point costing about as much as a week for two at Elk Lake Lodge. But *Forbes* magazine sums it up well: "There are no telephones, no newspapers, and no menu choice. You partake of what is prepared each day and sit down to dine at the appointed hour. If you don't like the hosts, the food, the guests or the digs, tough luck . . . [yet] for those in search of sybaritic creature comforts, there is only one destination — The Point."

A final note: don't expect to be able to drive in for just a look at the place. No signs mark the way to The Point, and only registered guests get the secret directions.

Michael Kahn

A former Rockefeller family getaway, The Point has been voted one of the world's best hotels.

THE PORCUPINE
Owners: Barbara and Jerry Connolly.
518-891-5160.
www.theporcupine.com.
147 Park Ave.
Open: Year-round.
Price: Expensive.
Credit Cards: MC, V.

Architect William Coulter built this massive six-gabled, gambrel-roofed house for Thomas Bailey Aldrich, *Atlantic Monthly* editor, author of *The Story of a Bad Boy*, and friend of Mark Twain. The name "Porcupine" isn't some cute modern affectation: the place acquired that title in the early 1900s because "it had so many good points and because it was occupied by a quill driver" — the

Min. Stay: 2 nights on summer weekends.
Special Features: Fireplaces; vintage jukebox; porches.

quill driver being Aldrich. He brought his wife and children to Saranac Lake not on some vacation whim, but because one of his twin sons had tuberculosis, and the family hoped that the fresh mountain air and good doctors at nearby Trudeau Sanatorium could cure him. Sadly, the young man died.

In 1998, another, happier, chapter unfolded for this grand home. With some furniture wax, window cleaner, plenty of elbow grease, and lots of enthusiasm, the Connollys opened a five-room bed-and-breakfast. Downstairs is a comfortable, large living room with fireplace, as well as a smaller sitting room with fireplace, and antiques (including baseball memorabilia) are scattered artfully throughout.

Guest rooms — quite spacious and nicely separate from each other — are on the second floor, up the beautiful Jacobean-style staircase. All have private baths; most have glassed-in "cure porches," an architectural element dating back to the days when TB patients were made to sleep in unheated rooms, swaddled in blankets. Charles's Room, at the top of the stairs, has a working fireplace, a comfortable sitting area, and a porch with wicker chairs overlooking the garden. The Lake Mohawk Room, also with a fireplace, has a king-size rustic-frame bed. The Saranac Room is quite large, with a big cure porch, and has two double beds.

Breakfast is served on the downstairs porch in summer, and in a large, bright dining area during cold weather. Eggs Florentine with apple crisp, raisin-bread French toast, and mushroom soufflé are some of the possibilities.

Wilmington

WILKOMMEN HOF
Owners: Heike and Bert Yost.
518-946-7626 or 800-541-9119.
Closed: Apr. 15–May 15; Oct. 15–Nov. 15.
Price: Inexpensive to Moderate.
Credit Cards: MC, V.
Special Features: Meals available; sauna; hot tub; children and pets welcome; midweek ski packages.

A newly renovated European-style guesthouse, Wilkommen Hof has three rooms with private baths, a three-room suite, and three rooms that share baths, to house a maximum of 24 guests. Full breakfasts and after-ski treats are included in the room rate; hearty dinners may be arranged.

The fabled Ausable River trout waters are nearby, as are numerous state-marked trails for cross-country skiing and hiking. (Heike and Bert can suggest trips off the beaten path on foot or by bike.) Wilkommen Hof is quite popular with Whiteface Mtn. downhill skiers since it's just minutes away from the slopes. After all that exertion, guests can wind down in either the outdoor hot tub or indoor sauna.

NORTHWEST LAKES

Cranberry Lake Lodge — under new management — has been renovated throughout.

James Swedberg

Cranberry Lake

CRANBERRY LAKE LODGE
Owners: Cranberry Lake Lodging and Hospitality LLC
315-848-3301.
www.members.aol.com/burn 708/cranlake
Rte. 3.
Open: Year-round.
Price: Moderate.
Credit Cards: MC, V.
Handicap Access: Some units; inquire.
Special Features: Children and well-behaved pets welcome; lakefront.

Look down the lake from the motel/restaurant complex and you get a feel for just how wild and vast the Adirondacks are. This place is a good jumping-off spot for exploring Cranberry Lake or the Five Ponds Wilderness Area several miles to the southwest, or heading out on the network of nearby snowmobile trails.

In 1998 new owners took over. They completely gutted the old two-story hotel and upgraded the motel rooms, adding new carpeting, new plumbing, new beds, TVs, and so forth. The restaurant here (three meals a day) is one of the best in the area, and the antiques, stuffed animals, and old photographs give a good introduction to this uncrowded part of the park.

WILDCLIFFE LODGE
Owners: Barb and Vern Peterson.
315-848-2140.
Mail: Box 526.
Closed: Nov. 15–June 1.
Price: Inexpensive to Moderate; lodge rooms are MAP.
Credit Cards: None.
Special Features: Remote location; access by boat only; children welcome.

Unless you want to hike 13 miles, the only access to the Wildcliffe Lodge is across the lake by boat, a distance of about six miles. As a matter of fact, everything comes to this remote hostelry over the water, from steak to beer and the mail. Guests catch the water taxi from the Emporium, in Cranberry Lake. Forget about phones or TV; electricity is supplied by a generator, and the phone number listed above is off-island.

The main lodge is a big log building, with the dining room, a bar that's open to the public, and a long porch. There are four rooms upstairs in the lodge, sharing baths; rates include breakfast and dinner. Two log cabins are in the woods, which have full kitchens, baths, and gas heat. (For the cabins, guests need to supply all bed linens, blankets, towels, and even some cooking gear.) The Petersons serve plain, honest fare such as steaks, pork chops, and ham; the annual Fourth of July chicken barbecue and the September pig roast are jolly affairs.

From Wildcliffe, there are miles of wilderness hiking trails. Fishing and canoeing are good in Cranberry Lake, and the lodge is open during the first couple weeks of big game season if you'd like to hunt deep in the backcountry.

Lake Clear

THE LODGE AT LAKE CLEAR
Innkeepers: Cathy and Ernest Hohmeyer.
518-891-1489.
www.lodgeonlakeclear.com.
Rtes. 30 & 186; Box 46.
Open: Year-round.
Price: Moderate to Expensive.
Min. Stay: 2 nights in chalets; 2 nights on holiday weekends.
Credit Cards: MC, V.
Special Features: Fireplaces; restaurant; children welcome; pets allowed in chalets — deposit required.

The Hohmeyers have made the Lodge at Lake Clear highly acclaimed for home-style German cuisine, and overnight guests have enjoyed the family's gracious hospitality for more than four decades. On 25 secluded lakeshore acres, accommodations here combine modern conveniences with Old World charm.

There are four upstairs rooms in the inn, each with private bath. Lakeview suites have fireplaces, sitting rooms, and lovely sunset views; one has a double Jacuzzi. Two fully equipped houses can accommodate six to twelve people, or be divided into suites. And there are new winterized chalets. All of these buildings are located away from each other so that families can enjoy woodsy privacy.

Guests have use of canoes, rowboats, a picnic area, and beach, and Cathy is happy to arrange mountain-bike rentals, guide service, or overnight canoe trips for visitors. The lodge also offers packages ranging from wellness weekends to romantic getaways.

Paul Smiths

NORTHBROOK LODGE
Manager: Laura-Jean Schwartau.
518-327-3379.
Osgood Lake, off Rte. 86.
Closed: Sept. 15–June 15.
Price: Expensive. MAP; special rates for families.

Set on a magnificent secluded pine-shaded peninsula on Osgood Lake, Northbrook Lodge was constructed as a millionaire's retreat in the 1920s by the same builder as the magnificent Adirondack Great Camp, Topridge, a few miles away.

Sixteen rooms for guests are in appealing cottages connected by covered walkways and porches; all have

Min. Stay: 3 nights.
Credit Cards: None.
Special Features: Fireplaces; lakefront; sandy beach; children welcome.

private baths, refrigerators, and separate entrances.

Breakfast and dinner are included in the room rate, and meals — made completely from scratch — are served in the dining hall. The boathouse has a bar/lounge with a classic Brunswick Balke billiard table; canoes and rowboats are available for guests at no extra charge.

B. Folwell

A short walk from White Pine Camp's cabins is the lovely Japanese teahouse.

WHITE PINE CAMP
Manager: Lynn Witte.
518-327-3030.
www.whitepinecamp.com.
Osgood Lake, off Rte. 86.
Closed: Late Oct.–early May; inquire about winterized units.
Price: Expensive.
Min. Stay: 1 week in July and August. 2 nights in spring and fall.
Credit Cards: MC, V.
Special Features: Historic site; fireplaces; children welcome.

Imagine a week spent at a real Great Camp, once the summer White House of President Coolidge. Four of the cabins along Osgood Lake are available to guests by the week in July and August and for shorter visits in spring and fall; a couple of units will be available for winter rentals as well. All the cabins — furnished with an eclectic assortment of rustic and Mission-style antiques — have porches, fieldstone fireplaces, kitchens, and separate bedrooms that accommodate two to four people; one unit in the main lodge offers more flexibility. Guests can use the beach, boathouse, Japanese teahouse, croquet lawn, bowling alley, canoes, and rowboats, and enjoy the extensive grove of wild rhododendrons that covers the hillside.

White Pine Camp also operates as a historic site, with guided tours in the morning and evening, but tours avoid the cabins' private spaces.

Saranac Inn

SUNDAY POND BED & BREAKFAST
Owners: Lesley and Dick Lyon.
518-891-1531.
www.sundaypond.com.
Rte. 30 (Saranac Inn); Star Rte., Box 150 (Saranac Lake NY 12983).
Open: Year-round.
Price: Inexpensive.
Credit Cards: None.
Special Features: Guide service available; children welcome.

Say you're a canoeist or hiker and you want to explore the St. Regis Canoe Area with its dozens of lakes and ponds, but you hate the thought of camping out. Look no further: Sunday Pond is located smack where you can start all those adventures right from the front door.

The Lyons' home — one of a very few in this corner of the park — is quite nice, with a long porch, skylights, a fireplace, and a big family room. Guests can choose from two rooms that share a bath, a room with a private bath, or a spacious sleeping loft with its own bath. Breakfasts are ample and healthy; hearty trail lunches and dinners (pasta primavera, sautéed chicken breast with wild rice, London broil, vegetarian lasagna, etc.) are available to guests by request.

Tupper Lake

COLD RIVER RANCH
Hosts: Marie and John Fontana.
518-359-7559.
Rte. 3, Coreys; mail: Coreys, Tupper Lake NY 12986.
Open: Year-round.
Price: Moderate, B&B; MAP available.
Credit Cards: MC, V.
Special Features: Horseback riding; cross-country ski trails; children welcome.

Cold River Ranch is famous for wilderness trail rides and overnight pack trips into remote areas of the High Peaks, and the huge old farmhouse is a very comfortable B&B as well. Nine guests are accommodated in four rooms with shared baths. Breakfast, which John describes as "fancy home cooking," can include cheesecake still warm from the oven. Full board is an option, too. In the winter, the horse trails are endless backcountry ski trails. Guides, instructors, and rental equipment are available, and the Fontanas are happy to arrange custom ski tours for guests.

THREE PILLARS
Owners: Bob and Neil Shofi.
518-359-3093;
winter: 914-835-2900.
Moody Rd.; winter mail: 231 Halstead Ave., Harrison NY 10528.
Closed: Nov. 15–June 25.
Price: Moderate.
Min. Stay: 1 week in summer; 3 days in fall.

With about a quarter mile of shoreline on Big Tupper Lake, the secluded cabins at Three Pillars have a great view. The location, on the southern end of Big Tupper Lake and close to Bog River Falls, is one of the best you'll find on this large lake.

There are three pine-paneled, comfortably furnished housekeeping cottages with complete kitchens, fireplaces (wood is supplied), and screen porches, plus a three-bedroom apartment above

Credit Cards: None.
Special Features: Private beach; lakefront; children welcome.

the boathouse that offers the wonderful sensation of being right on the water. There's a nice sandy beach and a long dock for guests' boats. Ask about where to find the walleyes.

THE WAWBEEK RESORT
Managers: Nancy and Norman Howard.
518-359-2656 or 800-953-2656.
www.wawbeek.com.
553 Panther Mtn. Rd., off Rte. 30.
Open: Year-round.
Price: Moderate to Expensive; MAP available.
Min. Stay: 1 week in some accommodations in summer; inquire.
Credit Cards: All major.
Special Features: Lakefront; sandy beach; boats; boat launch and dockage for guests; tennis; restaurant.

Sharing the same Upper Saranac bay as the classic Great Camps Wenonah Lodge and Sekon Lodge, the Wawbeek Resort has an authentic Adirondack style. The original Wawbeek, itself a Great Camp, burned in 1980, and new owners consolidated that property with a former boys' camp next door. One of the buildings, Mountain House Lodge, is a wonderful turn-of-century structure with double-deck porches, stone fireplace, and great room; it's the kind of place that would be ideal for several couples or an extended family to share for a week in any season. Scattered under the trees are comfortable one-bedroom log cabins, larger cottages, and a three-bedroom carriage house.

Guests have all of gorgeous Upper Saranac Lake to explore by sailboat, rowboat, or canoe. There's a beach, tennis court, game room, basketball court, and boat launch on the premises. In the winter, cross-country skiers can try the Deer Pond cross-country trails just a short distance away.

The Wawbeek's restaurant is in one of the most attractive settings — with a first-rate menu, to boot — in the Adirondack Park.

CENTRAL ADIRONDACKS

Benson

LAPLAND LAKE CROSS-COUNTRY SKI & VACATION CENTER
Owners: Ann and Olavi Hirvonen.
518-863-4974 or 800-453-SNOW.
www.laplandlake.com.
Storer Rd. (Benson); RD 2, Box 2053 (Northville NY 12134).
Open: Year-round.
Price: Moderate.

Just when you think that you got the directions wrong to this rather remote spot, you see road signs in . . . *Finnish*? Quickly, the view opens up to a brand new ski shop and a bunch of neat little cottages. Readers of *Snow Country* magazine recently rated the Lapland Lake — with 35 km of groomed trails, a restaurant, and a full ski shop — among the top ten Nordic ski centers in the East.

Summertime is nice at Lapland Lake, too. There's a small spring-fed lake on the 300-acre property where guests can swim, canoe, and fish. Trails here connect with state-owned hiking trails;

Min. Stay: 2 nights on winter weekends; 1 week in high summer.
Credit Cards:D, MC, V.
Special Features: Cross-country ski trails; sauna, ski-rental shop; ski lessons; snack bar; live reindeer, children welcome; no pets.

you can pick up the Northville–Lake Placid Trail less than a mile away, or climb Cathead Mtn.

Ten housekeeping cottages range in size from two to four bedrooms, and are called *tupas*, which means "cabin" in Finnish. They're spotless and comfortable; most have wood stoves or screen porches. The biggest place, *Lapin Tupa*, is the property's original farmhouse. It has a formal dining room with a nice view of the pond, a big eat-in kitchen, living room with piano, four bedrooms, and two full baths.

TRAILHEAD LODGE
Owner: John Washburn.
518-863-2198.
Washburn Rd. (Benson); RD 2, Box 2047A (Northville NY 12134).
Open: Year-round.
Price: Inexpensive to Moderate.
Min. Stay: 2 nights winter weekends; 3 nights holiday weekends.
Credit Cards: MC, V.
Special Features: Guide service; canoe rentals; fireplace; outdoor-skill workshops; children over 6 welcome.

John Washburn's great-grandfather took in hunters and fishermen here more than a century ago, and guided them to the big ones; nowadays you can do much the same thing in a bit more comfort at Trailhead Lodge. On the outside, the building looks like a typical farmhouse; inside, the walls are finished off with new pine boards and Adirondack décor — snowshoes, pack baskets, and such. Four guest rooms share baths; visitors may choose bed and breakfast or modified American plan arrangements.

John, a licensed Adirondack guide, is very knowledgeable about the woods and wildlife; he leads map-and-compass workshops for groups, or takes folks on hikes, canoe trips, backcountry ski adventures, and snowshoeing trips. By the roaring fire on a chill night, you might coax him to recite Robert Service poems or tall tales.

Big Moose Lake

BIG MOOSE INN
Innkeepers: Bonnie and Doug Bennett.
314-357-2042.
www.bigmooseinn.com.
Big Moose Rd.; mail: Eagle Bay NY 13331.
Closed: Apr., Nov.
Price: Inexpensive to Moderate; MAP available.
Min. Stay: 2 nights on weekends.
Credit Cards: AE, MC, V.

Mud season is about the only time you can't enjoy Big Moose Inn. In late spring, you can canoe and fish on Big Moose Lake; summertime you can hike around Pigeon Lake Wilderness Area or visit nearby towns like Inlet and Old Forge; in the fall you can see beautiful foliage or hunt; when the snows arrive, there's snowmobiling or cross-country skiing practically right to the front door.

There are 16 rooms upstairs in the inn, all recently refurbished and with private baths. Most chambers have a nice view of the lake; one includes a fireplace, king-size bed, and Jacuzzi tub. Big Moose Inn's

Special Features: Canoes; restaurant; snowmobile trails; lakefront; children welcome.

restaurant is one of the best in the neighborhood, worth a detour.

COVEWOOD LODGE
Owner: C.V. Bowes, Jr.
315-357-3041.
Off Big Moose Rd.
Open: Year-round.
Price: Moderate to Expensive; depends on cottage size.
Credit Cards: None.
Special Features: Sandy beach; lakefront; cross-country ski trails; children welcome.

One of the all-time great woodsy Adirondack retreats, Covewood was built as a hotel back in the days when guests stayed all summer long. Even in today's busy world, you'd probably wish you could stay from Independence Day to Labor Day, the place is so peaceful. Major Bowes keeps it that way.

There are 17 housekeeping cabins along the lake and under the pines, ranging in size from one room to seven bedrooms plus kitchen, living room, and porches. All the cabins have fireplaces and furnaces. There's a big rustic lodge with a stone fireplace for guests to enjoy after they've explored the wild woods nearby.

THE WALDHEIM
Owners: Nancy and Roger Pratt.
315-357-2353.
Big Moose Rd.; mail: Eagle Bay NY 13331.
Closed: Columbus Day–Mid-June.
Price: Expensive, but includes 3 meals.
Credit Cards: None.
Special Features: Sandy beach; boats for guests; children welcome; rustic buildings; fireplaces.

The Waldheim was built in 1904 by E.J. Martin from trees cut on the property, and there's a wonderful old-time feel to the place. ("No phone, no TV, no clocks," says Nancy Pratt, the third generation of her family to run the place.) Many of the 15 cabins are made of vertical half logs and have twig-work railings on the porches. The places are aptly named "Cozy," "Comfort," "Heart's Content," and every one has a fireplace. Rates include three full meals a day, which are served in a gracious dining room furnished with antique chairs and tables.

Just about when the cottages open, lovely wild azaleas bloom along the pathways. Guests can hike, canoe, swim, and fish; arrangements can be made to have a seaplane pick you up at the dock for a scenic flight. There are no planned activities except the weekly camp picnic, a moveable feast taken to a remote part of the lake by boat. The 300-acre property is adjacent to state land so the location is secluded indeed.

Blue Mountain Lake

CURRY'S COTTAGES
Owners: Mike and Bob Curry.
518-352-7354,
winter: 518-352-7355.

These charming barn-red housekeeping cottages are a familiar sight to Blue Mtn. Lake visitors; photographs of the chorus line of white Adirondack chairs along the beach have appeared

Curry's Cottages once had a restaurant serving such delicacies as sardine sandwiches, as well as housekeeping units.

Courtesy Edward Comstock Jr.

Rte. 28.
Closed: Nov.–Apr.
Price: Moderate.
Credit Cards: None.
Min. Stay: 1 week in July–Aug.; weekends May–June, Sept.
Special Features: Boat launch; children welcome.

in numerous national magazines. Three generations of Currys have operated the cottages, and Bob, the current Curry, is always at work making improvements.

Nine cottages accommodate couples to families of six; four cottages are on the water, and the remainder are on the edge of the woods across the road. The beach at Curry's is a favorite with families; it's safe and shallow for kids.

FOREST HOUSE LODGE
Innkeeper: Anne LaForest.
518-352-7030.
Rtes. 28/30.
Open: Year-round.
Price: Inexpensive.
Credit Cards: None.

Year-round lodging near Blue Mtn. Lake has been hard to find — that is until recently, when Anne LaForest opened her restored Craftsman-style home to guests. The place is located on the state highway between Blue Mtn. and Indian lakes, next door to the Forest House restaurant (serving dinners on weekends fall through spring and daily in summer). Two good-sized bedrooms with antique or twig bedsteads share a bath upstairs, with plans to create a larger suite from a corner room.

Breakfast — homemade everything — is served on Portmeirion china at a table set with fresh flowers, with music from a huge collection of CDs that ranges from bluesman Delbert McClinton to classical music.

THE HEDGES
Owners: The Benton Family.
518-352-7325 or 518-352-7672.
Closed: Mid-Oct.–late May.
Price: Expensive; MAP.
Credit Cards: None.

Colonel Hiram Duryea, a Civil War veteran and millionaire industrialist, began building the Hedges in 1880. The main house, with four wonderful guest rooms all with private baths, has an unusual mansard roof line that sweeps onto a wraparound porch.The lovely Stone Lodge, built about 1890, has a three-bedroom suite with

Handicap Access: 2 cottages.
Special Features: Private sandy beach; boats for guests; tennis; meals; children welcome; no pets.

fireplace on the first floor, and six rooms with private baths upstairs. Antiques and fine woodworking are found throughout these two lodges.

There are a dozen one- to four-bedroom sleeping cottages along the secluded lakeshore. All accommodations are offered modified American plan; picnic lunches are available at a small charge. Guests have use of canoes, rowboats, a clay tennis court, and the library; the game room, a museum-quality gem of rustic detail, is worth a visit even if you don't play Ping-Pong.

Meals are served in the dining room lodge, another appealing old building, which has stamped-tin walls and ceilings and a stone fireplace. New owners acquired the property in 2000, so details on dining (an updated menu, for instance) were unknown as this edition was prepared.

Blue Mtn. Lake is a very beautiful, quiet lake; the Hedges is in a particularly lovely, private spot. Generations of families have returned since the hotel opened to guests more than 75 years ago.

Castle Rock, with its fantastic view of Blue Mtn Lake and its islands, is a short hike from Hemlock Hall.

James Swedberg

HEMLOCK HALL
Owners: Susan and Paul Provost.
518-352-7706.
www.hemlockhall.com.
Maple Lodge Rd.
Closed: Mid-Oct.–mid-May.
Price: Moderate to Expensive; MAP.
Min. Stay: 3 nights in summer; as available spring and fall.
Credit Cards: None.

On Maple Lodge Road, a mile off the main highway, is another stunning Adirondack hostelry. Hemlock Hall was carefully restored by Eleanor and Monty Webb in the 1950s, and their hard work still shows. The woodwork in the main lodge — a complicated pattern of wainscoting on the walls and ceilings — still gleams, and there are numerous antiques throughout. The stone fireplace has hearths on two sides, opening onto part of the living room and a wing of the dining room. There's even a fireplace in an upstairs hallway.

Special Features: Private beach; boats for guests; meals; children welcome; no pets.

There are 23 rooms for guests in accommodations ranging from lodge rooms with shared baths to motel units to two- or three-bedroom cottages. The tower suite in the main lodge has its own private screen porch and charming window seats; several of the lodge rooms have nice lake views; you can even rent the top floor of the boathouse. Breakfast and dinner are included in the room charges.

The dining room serves wholesome, plentiful food in a family-style arrangement. There's one entrée offered each evening, with chicken and biscuits on Wednesdays a great favorite. (Non-guests can dine with prior reservations.) Folks are seated at different tables each night so they get to mingle with the other visitors; alcoholic beverages, which might make all this mingling a bit easier, are not permitted in the dining room.

LAPRAIRIE'S LAKESIDE COTTAGES
Owners: Kim and Ernie LaPrairie.
518-352-7675.
Rte. 28/30.
Closed: Columbus Day–May 15.
Price: Moderate to Expensive.
Min. Stay: 1 week in summer; 3 nights spring and fall.
Credit Cards: No.
Special feature: Private beach and docks.

These two attractively renovated housekeeping cabins are so close to the shore of Blue Mtn. Lake that you can hear the waves washing up on the private beach. The Shanty can hold up to nine guests in three bedrooms and has a lakeside porch, fireplace, bath and a half, and complete kitchen; Crooked Cottage has a loft bedroom overlooking the lake and is comfortable for a couple or a small family. Traveling with teenagers? LaPrairie's cabins are among the only places in Blue Mtn. Lake with cable TV.

Rental canoes are available next door at Blue Mtn. Outfitters and there's swimming right out the front door.

POTTER'S RESORT
Owners: Laura and Ralph Faxon.
518-352-7331.
Rtes. 28 & 30.
Closed: Sept. 30–May 1.
Price: Inexpensive to Moderate.
Min. Stay: 1 week for housekeeping cottages July–Aug.
Credit Cards: MC, V.
Special Features: 1 year-round fully equipped house; private beach; dockage for guests' boats; tennis; restaurant; children welcome; no pets.

As you enter the hamlet of Blue Mtn. Lake, Potter's Resort is one of the first places you'll see. Ten housekeeping cottages are available: most have porches; several have fireplaces; some are huge old log cabins with cathedral ceilings. There are 10 motel units near the road that all have porches, and four motel rooms with fireplaces.

Potter's has a great beach, dock space for visitors' boats, and a tennis court. The classic Adirondack dining room is open for breakfast, lunch, and dinner from late June through Labor Day, with an American-style menu and liquor license.

PROSPECT POINT COTTAGES
Manager: Bob Webb.
518-352-7378.
Edison Rd., off Rte. 28.
Closed: Oct. 10–May 10.
Price: Moderate.
Min. Stay: 1 week July–Aug.; 3 nights spring and fall.
Credit Cards: None.
Special Features: Private sandy beach; wheelchair ramps on most cabins; children and pets welcome.

This beautiful peninsula on Blue Mtn. Lake was once the site of the mammoth 100-room Prospect House, the first hotel in the world to have electricity. (Never mind that technology went only so far; guests trudged off to outhouses when nature called.) Now a dozen two-bedroom housekeeping cottages occupy the point; completely rebuilt in 1999 and 2000, they line the curving shore. If you were turned off by the way this property looked a few years ago, try again. The cabins have skylights, new porches, new appliances, sliding glass doors, handicap-accessible bathrooms, TVs, and even phones.

The view of Blue Mtn. is simply magnificent. From Prospect Point, which is close to town, but off the highway, it's an easy walk to the arts center for a concert, the boat livery for a tour of the chain of lakes, or the post office to mail those picture postcards saying "Wish you were here."

Indian Lake/Sabael

CAMP DRIFTWOOD
Owners: Doris, Jon, and A.E. Voorhees.
518-648-5111, winter: 941-355-3535.
199 Sabael Rd., Indian Lake; winter mail: 2712 59th St., Sarasota FL 34243.
Open: Year-round.
Price: Inexpensive to Moderate.
Min. Stay: 1 week July–Aug.
Credit Cards: None.
Special Features: Private beach; boats for guests; children and well-behaved pets welcome.

Indian Lake is about 13 miles long, with numerous bays and publicly owned islands to explore, and Camp Driftwood is a good base from which to plan day trips, or simply to relax in a secluded spot. Nick, Jon, and Doris Voorhees rent 10 housekeeping cabins all along the shore and tucked back in the woods. Maple Cabin is an old lodge, with three bedrooms, a fireplace, screen porch, and deck; Birch also has three bedrooms, and you can practically roll out of bed in the morning for a dip in the lake. All cottages have full kitchens and wood stoves for cool mornings, plus outdoor fireplaces for barbecues. Guests need to bring bed linens and towels.

There's a sandy beach for wading, a float for advanced swimmers, canoes and rowboats for guests, and genuine hospitality from the Voorhees family. This is the kind of place where families settle in for two weeks or more and pretend they're at home.

CHIMNEY MTN. WILDERNESS LODGE
201-852-1912.
Off Big Brook Rd., Kings Flow.

King's Flow is a quiet, mile-long pond near the western border of Siamese Ponds Wilderness Area, with craggy, cave-riddled Chimney Mtn. looming above the valley. The "wilderness lodge"

Open: Year round.
Price: Inexpensive to Moderate.
Min. Stay: 1 week in cottages July–Aug.
Credit Cards: None.
Special Features: Private sandy beach; access to Chimney Mtn.; children and pets welcome.

isn't one building but a cluster of fully equipped, all-season two- and three-bedroom cabins set around the shore. Most cabins have fireplaces and screen porches.

Bring a canoe for exploring King's Flow, right out your front door, and Round Pond, about a half-mile hike away. Trails to Chimney Mtn. start from these cabins, and you can also walk or cross-country ski to Puffer Pond, John Pond, or the old garnet mine at Humphrey Mtn.

1870 BED & BREAKFAST
Host: Bill Zullo.
518-648-5377.
Main St.
Open: Year-round.
Price: Inexpensive.
Credit Cards: None.
Special Features: Fireplace; cable TV; children welcome; no pets.

Guestbooks from decades ago capture the flavor of this place: "Our stay here was wonderful as usual. In the past 16 years, nothing has changed," commented one repeat visitor 25 years ago. You'll still find real braided rugs on the floors, tatted spreads on the antique beds, ruffled curtains in the windows, family pictures dating back to the turn of the century on the walls, and a homey, quiet atmosphere.

There is one bedroom with a private bath on the first floor, and four nice rooms upstairs that share a bath and a sitting room. The living room has comfortable Grandma's-house-type furniture, a fireplace, cable TV, plus shelves of board games and puzzles. From the shady front porch, you can look out over the garden, and further back on the old 40-acre farm, there's a big raspberry patch that's open for grazing. Tennis courts (at the school) are kitty-corner; there are couple of new bikes in the barn that guests can use, and there's a private right-of-way to Lake Adirondack for fishing or canoeing about a half mile away.

GEANDREAU'S CABINS
Owner: Dotty Geandreau.
518-648-5500.
Rte. 28, Indian Lake.
Open: Year-round.
Price: Inexpensive.
Min. Stay: 2 nights.
Credit Cards: None.
Special Features: Children welcome; pets must be leashed at all times.

When you enter the hamlet of Indian Lake from the east, one of the first places that comes into view is Geandreau's cluster of well-kept cabins on Route 28 across from Lake Adirondack. In the summer, the border of bright red dahlias in the front yard might catch your eye. For more than 30 years Dot and her late husband, Bob, have built up a year-round business, accommodating everyone from adventure-seekers to folks looking for a peaceful place to rest.

The cabins sleep up to five people, and are fully outfitted with kitchen equipment, linens, towels, and so on. There are screen porches on all the cottages, making them particularly enjoyable during bug season. Rowboats and canoes for exploring the nearby lake are provided; there's a nice swimming beach about 200 yards away.

TIMBERLOCK
Owner: Richard Catlin.
518-648-5494,
winter: 802-457-1621.
On Indian Lake.
Closed: Sept. 20–June 23.
Price: Expensive; full American plan; special rates for families.
Min. Stay: 1 week.
Credit Cards: None.
Special Features: Private beach; boats; horseback riding; tennis; children welcome; no pets.

Timberlock welcomed its first guests in 1898. Not much has changed since those early days: all the common buildings and the guests' log cabins are still equipped with gaslights and wood stoves, so don't expect to find outlets for laptop computers. The atmosphere here is rustic, relaxed, peaceful, yet the resort offers a surprising variety of activities and amenities.

There are four Hartru tennis courts; gentle horses for guided trail rides; an excellent sandy beach; numerous boats to sail, paddle, or row on Indian Lake; and trails on the property for hiking and birding. Timberlock is home to fall Elderhostel seminars on Adirondack history and nature; there are adventure-camp sessions for teens and other outdoor-educational programs offered from year to year. If you'd prefer to discover the Adirondacks on your own, the Catlins have assembled a 120-page book outlining car trips, picnic spots, mountain climbs, museums, and other sites to explore.

"Timberlock is not for everyone," says Dick Catlin. "We are not a luxury place and have not paved away the wildlife." There are a dozen "family cottages," that have full baths, screen porches, and lake views, plus some small cabins without baths. Rates include three hearty meals a day and use of all the facilities and activities except horseback riding. There are no neighbors within miles of Timberlock, and your wake-up call in the morning may well be a loon's yodel from the lake.

Inlet

THE CROSSWINDS
Owner: Jan Burwell.
315-357-4500.
Rte. 28.
Closed: Oct. 15–May 15.
Price: Inexpensive to Moderate.
Min. Stay: 1 week July–Aug.; overnights welcome in off-season.
Credit Cards: None.
Special Features: Private beach; children welcome; no pets.

Located right on Fourth Lake are the Crosswinds' cabins, five attractive two-bedroom housekeeping units. All the places have completely equipped, knotty-pine-paneled kitchens; guests need to supply their own linens and towels. There's a 200-foot private sandy beach, and a large dock for boats (small extra charge for dock space). It's a short walk from the Crosswinds to downtown Inlet, which has a movie theater, restaurants, tennis courts, outfitters, liquor store, and shops.

DEER MEADOWS
Owners: Linda and Robert Gordon.
315-357-3274.
Rte. 28.
Open: Year-round.
Price: Inexpensive.
Min. Stay: 2 nights on holiday weekends; cottages rent by the week July–Aug.
Credit Cards: D, MC, V.
Special Features: Private beach; children welcome.

At Deer Meadows, there's a 10-unit motel on Route 28 with queen-size beds, cable TV, and in-room coffee; and on a private drive across the highway, there are six pleasant housekeeping cottages ranging in size from one to three bedrooms. All the cottages have fireplaces and complete kitchens; guests need to bring bed linens and towels.

There's a nice little beach and picnic area on Seventh Lake, free rowboats for guests, and plenty of friendly mallard ducks to feed in the summer. The accommodations are open year-round, and snowmobilers appreciate Deer Meadows because the Gordons have a heated garage available for minor repairs.

HOLL'S INN
Innkeeper: Rosemary Holl.
315-357-2941, winter: 315-733-2748.
www.hollsinn.com.
South Shore Rd.; winter mail: 615 Ravine Dr., Utica NY 13502.
Closed: Sept.–June.
Price: Moderate to Expensive; full American plan.
Min. Stay: 2 nights.
Credit Cards: None.
Handicap Access: 25 rooms have ramps.
Special Features: Private beach; restaurant and bar; library.

Rosemary Holl says, "The way we were is the way we still are!" This spacious resort — 150 beautiful acres on the shore of Fourth Lake — dates back to the 1920s, and the Holl family has been in charge since 1935. The buildings and grounds are meticulously maintained and quite secluded; whitetail deer often cross the lawn to drink from the lake.

There are numerous rooms with private baths in the original hotel building; 25 rooms with private baths in the Annex, and two apartments in the Alpine House. Guests get three hearty meals a day in the dining room, which is also open to the public with advance reservations. An especially charming nook of the inn is the Tyrolean Bar, done up in Dresden blue, yellow, and red, with cozy booths and hand-decorated plates commemorating all the honeymooners who have stayed at Holl's over the years. After all that food and drink, there are plenty of ways to work off the extra calories: swimming, tennis, rowing, or canoeing. Holl's also rents larger homes on adjacent properties if your family wants its own space.

ROCKY POINT TOWNHOUSES
315-357-3751 or 800-442-2251.
Rte. 28.
Open: Year-round.
Price: Expensive.
Min. Stay: 1 week July–Aug.

The original Rocky Point, an enormous old lodge, was razed to make room for lakeside three-bedroom townhouses. Each one is nicely appointed and has a fireplace, three full baths, and cable TV; kitchens have microwaves, dishwashers, washer/dryers and new appliances. The beach is excellent, nearly a quarter-mile long, but if the

Credit Cards: MC, V.
Special Features: Docks for guests' boats; children and pets welcome.

water's too chilly there's a indoor pool and spa. Four tennis courts are on the property, and two excellent golf courses are within a 10-minute drive.

Long Lake

The dining room at Long Lake's Adirondack Hotel still has old-fashioned charm.

James Swedberg

ADIRONDACK HOTEL
Owner: Carol Young.
518-624-4700 or 800-877-9247.
Rtes. 28/30.
Open: Year-round.
Price: Inexpensive to Moderate.
Credit Cards: AE, MC, V.
Special Features: Bar and restaurant; fireplace.

There's been a lodge at this spot overlooking Long Lake since before the Civil War, and portions of the current Adirondack Hotel date to the 1870s. Public spaces include a nice parlor and two dining rooms; the lobby includes a museum-quality turned-spindle cashier's booth. Taxidermy specimens (full-size black bear, giant moose head, and a goodly assortment of Adirondack mammals) add to the old-time feel.

Nineteen guest rooms are located on the second and third floors. Many have been renovated and have modern bathrooms, but some rooms share baths.

GREEN HARBOR
Owners: Ellen and Ken Schaeffer.
518-624-4133 or 800-845-5253.
Rte. 28/30.
Closed: Late fall–early spring.
Price: Moderate.

Six well-maintained housekeeping cottages and a small motel are set on a private sandy beach at Green Harbor; cabins have cable TV and decks or porches with views of the water. Winter visitors can stay in three bed and breakfast rooms in the main house and venture out on Long Lake's miles of cross-country skiing or snowmobiling trails.

Min. Stay: 1 week in July–Aug.
Credit Cards: None.

There's a game room with ping-pong table, library, and large color TV.

LONG VIEW LODGE
Owners: Angela and Fred Fink.
518-624-2862.
Deerland Rd.
Open: Year-round.
Price: Moderate.
Min. Stay: 2 nights on weekends; 3 nights holiday weekends.
Credit Cards: MC, V.
Special Features: Private beach; children welcome.

A Long Lake landmark since 1929, the Long View remains comfortably true to its roots. The inn has 14 bedrooms, most of which have private baths; the adjoining rooms with shared baths are ideal for families. There are two sleeping cottages on the property as well.

Public spaces are airy and comfortable, with chairs, books, and cozy nooks. The restaurant serves breakfast, lunch, and dinner daily all year-round; the new Ice House Tavern, built in 1994, is a great spot for enjoying a light meal. There's a shady veranda overlooking the lake and a nice beach.

WHISPERING WOODS
Owners: Margaret and Bob Sauerhafer.
518-624-5121 or 800-822-2814.
Walker Rd.
Closed: Nov. 1–Apr. 30.
Price: Inexpensive to Moderate.
Min. Stay: 2 nights; cottages rent by the week July–Aug.
Credit Cards: MC, V.
Special Features: Private beach; children welcome; leashed pets welcome.

The large sandy beach on a quiet shore of Long Lake is one of the major attractions at Whispering Woods, but the campground/cottage complex also has a well-stocked grocery store, game room, playground, and canoes and rowboats to rent. There are numerous options for lodging, from the five-bedroom Farmhouse and assorted cabins to apartments in the Main Lodge. All of the cottages have kitchens equipped with the basics; guests need to bring bed linens and towels. For recreational vehicles and travel trailers, there are wooded and lakeside sites with complete hookups available from May through October.

Minerva

MORNINGSIDE CAMPS AND COTTAGES
Owners: Sandy and Frank LaBar.
518-251-2694.
Minerva Lake.
Closed: Mid-Oct.–mid-May.
Price: Inexpensive to Moderate.
Min. Stay: 1 week in summer; 2 nights spring and fall.
Credit Cards: None.

Set on 80 acres of land accessible by a private road, Morningside Camps offer waterfront seclusion on Minerva Lake. There are 10 nice log cabins with stone fireplaces and five chalets, all of which have complete kitchens, bathrooms, and decks or screen porches. The property features a private beach, a play area with a treehouse for the kids, a tennis court, docks for canoes and rowboats, and hiking trails through the woods that lead you to the general store, the town beach, or around the shoreline. Each cabin comes with its own boat.

Special Features: Private beach; children welcome; pets may stay in spring and fall.

Understandably, there's a waiting list for the LaBar's cabins in July and August, but places are available before the Fourth of July and after Labor Day. Don't be afraid to ask.

North Creek

THE COPPERFIELD INN
Manager: Laura Hollenbeck.
518-251-2500 or 800-424-9910.
www.copperfieldinn.com.
Main St.
Closed: Nov.
Price: Moderate to Expensive.
Credit Cards: AE, D, DC, MC, V.
Special Features: Heated pool; health club; hair salon; midweek packages; children welcome; no pets.

An elegant, tasteful motor inn that comes as quite a surprise after you've driven down North Creek's modest Main Street, the Copperfield has all the amenities you'd expect at a real ski resort: heated pool, hot tub, tennis court, fancy restaurant, sports bar, conference facilities, shuttle bus to the slopes. Work completed in summer 1997 created the Trappers Tavern, a beauty salon, and a state-of-the-art health club. All kinds of interesting package deals for whitewater paddlers (lodging, breakfast, dinner, and Hudson River raft adventure for less than a hundred dollars more than you'd pay for the raft trip alone), golfers, senior citizens, and midweek guests are available. The 24 huge, luxurious rooms come with queen- or king-size beds, terrycloth bathrobes, and grand marble bathrooms.

GOOSE POND INN
Innkeepers: Beverly and Jim Englert.
518-251-3434 or 800-806-2601.
www.goosepondinn.com.
Main St. 1 block from the library.
Open: Year-round.
Price: Moderate.
Credit Cards: None.
Special Features: Fireplace; wood-fired sauna; children over 10 welcome; midweek ski packages; no pets.

A beautifully restored Victorian home set back on a shady lawn off Main Street, Goose Pond Inn has four lovely bedrooms, each with its own bath. Antiques, old prints, and amusing details are found throughout. Jim cooks up superb breakfasts, such as brandied French toast with sautéed apples, crêpes with rhubarb sauce, or Belgian waffles with flambéed bananas. From the inn, it's a five-minute drive to downhill skiing at Gore Mtn., or to any of the whitewater rafting headquarters for trips down the Hudson Gorge. If adventure isn't your thing, you can always commune with the resident geese at their pond here, or curl up by the fire with a good book.

North River

GARNET HILL LODGE
Owners: Mary and George Heim.
518-251-2444.

Cross-country skiers flock to Garnet Hill: there are some 35 miles of groomed trails, a full shop, and reliable snow cover. In fact, readers of

www.garnet-hill.com.
Thirteenth Lake Rd.
Closed: Thanksgiving week.
Price: Expensive; MAP.
Credit Cards: MC, V.
Special Features: Cross-country ski trails; ski shop; restaurant; fireplaces; private lakefront; children welcome; no pets.

Snow Country magazine honored the place as one of the 10 best Nordic centers in the country.

But you don't have to ski to enjoy this country inn, and you don't have to wait for winter, either. In the early spring, you can observe maple syrup making at the sugarbush. Later on, you can mountain bike or hike on the trails, plan a trip into Siamese Ponds Wilderness Area, or you can just watch the days pass in a beautiful setting from a comfortable chair near Thirteenth Lake.

The Log House, built in 1936, has 16 upstairs guest rooms, all with private baths. Downstairs is the restaurant, a game room, a massive fireplace made of local garnet, and two lounges for guests. Guests can also stay in Big Shanty, which was the home of Frank Hooper, developer of the original garnet mines in the area; this traditional Adirondack lodge has seven guest rooms, a stone fireplace, many rustic details, and overlooks Thirteenth Lake. A new building on the property, the Tea House, has just two luxurious rooms, with king-size beds and whirlpool baths, and its own private lounge.

Garnet Hill visitors can swim at the private beach, play tennis on the inn's courts, and rent canoes, rowboats, and sailboats for exploring Thirteenth Lake. Numerous packages are available for whitewater rafters, fishermen, inn-to-inn skiers, and groups.

Highwinds Inn has a cozy living room with a garnet fireplace; from the glassed-in dining room there's a panorama of Siamese Ponds Wilderness Area.

James Swedberg

HIGHWINDS INN
Innkeeper: Holly Currier.
518-251-3760 or 800-251-3760.
www.adirondack.net/tour/highwindsinn.

The former home of the president of Barton Mines, Highwinds Inn is a surprisingly civilized place in a very out-of-the-way spot, some five miles off the main highway. The house is lovely, with a beautifully furnished living room centered

Barton Mines Rd.
Closed: Apr. 1–June 30; Oct. 15–Dec. 24.
Price: Moderate, B&B; Expensive, MAP.
Min. Stay: 2 nights on winter weekends.
Credit Cards: MC, V.
Special Features: Cross-country ski trails; gourmet restaurant; wilderness cabin; children over 4 and pets welcome.

around a rough-hewn garnet fireplace. Four guest rooms, each with private bath, are upstairs, and rooms all look out on a sweeping vista of the ponds and hills in the Siamese Ponds Wilderness Area. The elevation here is 2500 feet above sea level, so Highwinds is probably the highest accommodations you can find anywhere in the state.

There are 1600 acres that guests can explore on foot over 25 km of cross-country trails, on mountain bike along old woods roads, or by canoe on small private ponds stocked with trout. Hikers are welcome to tour the old garnet mines with guides in the summer. On Pete Gay Mtn., which looks across at the downhill runs of Gore Mtn., there's a wilderness log cabin that's available for two-night stays.

One word summarizes the food at Highwinds: excellent (see Chapter Five, *Restaurants*). Breakfast is often whole-grain blueberry pancakes, sour cream waffles with maple syrup, or fresh-baked pastries.

Note: Closed at press time.

Northville

INN AT THE BRIDGE
Owners: Lee and Dot Brenn.
518-863-2240.
641 Bridge St.
Open: Year-round.
Price: Moderate.
Credit Cards: AE, D, MC, V.
Special Features: Fireplace; lakefront; well-behaved children welcome; no pets.

A grand Queen Anne–style cottage with porches, gables, and a tower, the Inn at the Bridge is a stylish place. All six bedrooms are furnished with Victorian antiques and have new private baths; one room is accessible to the mobility impaired. There's a lovely fireplace in the parlor, which also has comfortable couches, television, and books galore. Breakfast includes an assortment of homemade breads, muffins, bagels, fruit, and so forth; the inn serves full dinners on weekends and by private arrangement on other days for parties of four or more. (Some diners cruise over in their boats.) There's a gazebo on the lawn overlooking Great Sacandaga Lake, docks for guests, and visitors can stroll through town to the Adirondack Country Store and other shops along Main Street.

Old Forge/Thendara

THE KENMORE
Owners: Joyce and Ron Leszyk, Dave Harradine.
315-357-5285.
Fourth Lake, Old Forge.

A cottage colony off the main highway on the north shore of Fourth Lake, the Kenmore welcomed its first guests in 1901. Fourteen modern housekeeping cottages ranging in size from one to

Off Rte. 28.
Closed: Apr.
Price: Moderate.
Min. Stay: 1 week July–Aug.; 3 nights in winter.
Credit Cards: None.
Special Features: Canoes and rowboats for guests; children welcome; no pets.

three bedrooms are available by the week in summer and for three-night stays in spring and fall; four of the three-bedroom cabins are completely winterized and conveniently located for snowmobilers and cross-country skiers. Most of the cottages have lake views; many have fireplaces.

There's a shallow sandy beach and play area for the kids, free canoes and rowboats, picnic tables and outdoor grills, a volleyball court, and a campfire area. If the urge hits to explore farther afield, Old Forge's numerous attractions — from the Strand Theater to the Enchanted Forest/Water Safari park to the Fulton Chain of Lakes tour boats — are nearby.

VAN AUKEN'S INNE
Innkeepers: Kathleen and Paul Rivet.
315-369-3033.
Forge St., Thendara, off Rte. 28 by the Adirondack Railroad station.
Open: Year-round.
Price: Inexpensive to Moderate; B&B.
Min. Stay: 2 nights on weekends in high season.
Credit Cards: MC, V.
Special Features: Restaurant and bar; children welcome; no pets.

This grand old inn was a year old when the Adirondack branch of the New York Central made its first stop in Thendara station in 1892. Since then, the trains have come and gone (and are back again for scenic excursions from Thendara to Minnehaha and Rondaxe), while Van Auken's has remained a constant presence across the way.

The second floor — where 20 bedrooms used to share two baths — has been made into 12 nice guest rooms, each with private bath. Original details and antique furniture have been incorporated into these modern accommodations, and some rooms open onto the huge second-floor veranda. The public areas downstairs, like the taproom and the lobby, once again have polished wood floors, stamped-tin ceilings, and other elegant touches. The restaurant is open for breakfast, lunch, and dinner; see Chapter Five, *Restaurants* for a review.

Piseco

IRONDEQUOIT INN
518-548-5500 or 888-497-0350.
www.irondequoitinn.com.
Old Piseco Rd.
Closed: Apr., mid-Nov.–Dec. 26.
Price: Inexpensive to Moderate.
Credit Cards: MC, V.

The Irondequoit Inn was founded in 1892 by a group of upstate New York businessmen as an outdoor getaway. Now the property covers 650 acres and spans nearly two miles of shoreline on Piseco Lake. From the front porches of the two main buildings, you can look down the lawns to see Oxbow, Rogers, and Piseco mountains. There's even a private undeveloped island in the lake that

Special Features: Private beach; private island; tent campsites; canoes, kayaks, and fishing boats to rent; children welcome; no pets.

guests can canoe to for picnics, swimming, or sleeping out under the stars. Visitors have described a stay here as like summer camp for families.

There are nine rooms which share three baths, one-bedroom efficiencies, and housekeeping cabins. There's also a campground by the lake with tree-shaded sites.

Room rates for the main lodge include full breakfast. Dinners — good, simple family-style fare — are available to guests and the public by reservation.

Raquette Lake

RISLEY'S RUSH POINT
Owner: Barbara Risley Allen.
315-354-5211, school year: 315-429-9239.
Rte. 28, Raquette Lake; winter mail: 3 E. Spofford Ave., Dolgeville NY 13329.
Closed: During the school year.
Price: Moderate.
Min. Stay: 1 week; advance reservations only.
Credit Cards: None.
Special Features: Children welcome; no pets.

Several of the cottages here — part of the original 19th-century Adirondack camp — are rustic gems with stockade-style log siding, stone fireplaces, and long spacious porches under big pines and spruces. There are also three newer three-bedroom cottages, with eight cabins altogether on the 27-acre property. Each has a complete kitchen and bathroom; guests need to supply bed linens and towels.

A special attraction at Risley's is a natural sand beach that slopes gradually for a 100 yards into deep water. There's a dock for guests' boats, outdoor fireplaces, picnic tables, a playground, and two lean-tos.

Speculator

ALPINE MEADOW CHALETS
Owners: Chari and Chuck Smith.
518-548-5615.
Old Indian Lake Rd.
Open: Year-round.
Price: Moderate.
Min. Stay: 2 nights; inquire.

Just off the highway between Speculator and Indian Lake are a cluster of pleasant, winterized one- and two-bedroom chalets. They feature all the comforts of home: grills, picnic tables, microwaves, TVs, and have easy access to snowmobile trails, Lake Pleasant's waterfront, and the shops, restaurants, and activities to be found in "Sparkle City," as some call downtown Speculator.

BEARHURST
Owners: Helen and Dick Armstrong.
518-548-6427, winter: 518-842-6609.
South Shore Rd.
Closed: Oct.–May.

Most folks associate Great Camps with Raquette Lake or the St. Regis lakes, but in other parts of the park, there are some smaller estates that are equally nice. One of these is Bearhurst, which was built in 1894 by Herman Meyrowitz (fashionable optical shops in Paris, Geneva, and Milan still carry

A rustic gazebo looks out over Lake Pleasant at Bearhurst.

B. Folwell

Price: Moderate to Expensive.
Min. Stay: 1 week July–Aug.; 2 nights June, Sept.
Credit Cards: None.
Special Features: Private lakefront; dockage for guests' boats; children welcome; no pets.

his name), and it occupies a quarter-mile of lakefront on Lake Pleasant.

Guests stay in five of the original outbuildings including the icehouse, pumphouse, summer kitchen, and boathouse, all of which have been converted into delightful modern accommodations while still maintaining historical details and charm. The living rooms in each have fireplaces, and the fully outfitted kitchens have dishwashers.

The centerpiece of the property is the main lodge, a stunning log building with lovely leaded-glass windows and gracious porches; the stonework is intricate, with spiral stone staircases leading down from the front porch. One second floor fireplace has an inset oval leaded-glass window. The Armstrongs live in the main lodge, but guests can certainly enjoy the building from the outside.

There's a private beach, dock space for guests' boats, and a pretty little rustic gazebo for watching the sunset over the lake. If you visit in June, the grounds are covered with pinksters, the graceful wild azaleas.

Stillwater Reservoir

THE NORRIDGEWOCK III
Manager: Pat Thompson.
315-376-6200.
Beaver River, on Stillwater Reservoir; Box 232 (Eagle Bay NY 13331).
Open: Year-round.
Price: Moderate to Expensive; MAP.
Min. Stay: 2 days in cabins.
Credit Cards: None.
Special Features: Remote location; water taxi; children welcome; no pets.

Beaver River is a settlement on Stillwater Reservoir that's way off the beaten path — you can't drive here, although you can hike, cross-country ski, snowmobile, or canoe nine miles to reach the cabins and rooms at the Norridgewock. The Thompson family, who have run this unique lodge for three generations, also operate a water taxi that will pick up and deliver guests.

The place is quite self-sufficient, generating its own power and offering a modified American plan for overnighters. It accommodates between 25 to 35 people, "depending on how friendly you are," according to Pat Thompson.

STILLWATER
Owners: Marian and Joe Romano.
315-376-6470.
Stillwater Rd., Stillwater Reservoir; Star Rte., Box 258M (Lowville NY 13367).
Closed: Apr.
Price: Inexpensive.
Min. Stay: 2 nights in winter.
Credit Cards: AE, D, MC, V.
Special Features: Boat launch; restaurant; children welcome; no pets.

Stillwater Reservoir, which is several miles back from the main highways via a winding gravel road, has 117 miles of shoreline, 45 islands, and thousands of acres of public land for you to explore. There are more loons here than anywhere else in the Adirondacks, and the fishing's not too bad, either. Stillwater Hotel is understandably popular with snowmobilers since the snow cover is generally excellent and several trail systems are accessible right from the property.

Located at the western end of the lake is the Romano's hotel/restaurant complex, the only accommodations that you can drive to on the reservoir. There are seven winterized motel rooms, plus a restaurant and bar that are open to the public.

MOTELS & CAMPGROUNDS

For a list of public campgrounds, see "Camping" in Chapter Six, *Recreation.*

LAKE GEORGE AND SOUTHEASTERN ADIRONDACKS

For a complete list of accommodations in the Lake George–Chestertown–Warrensburg area, contact Warren County Tourism (800-95VISIT). A sampling of motel and campground accommodations is listed below.

Bolton Landing

Adirondack Park Motel (518-644-9800; Rte. 9N, Bolton Landing NY 12814) Price: Moderate. Pleasant, family-run motel with single and double rooms, efficiencies, two-bedroom cottages, and five-bedroom house on Lake George. Playground, pool, private beach. Closed: Columbus Day–Memorial Day.

Melody Manor (518-644-9750; Rte. 9N) Price: Moderate to Expensive. 40 rooms. Private beach; pool; boats; tennis; no pets. Closed Oct. 31–Apr. 30.

Victorian Village (518-644-9201; Rte. 9N) Price: Moderate. 30 units. Private beach; boats; tennis; no pets. Closed: Oct. 31–Apr. 30.

Diamond Point

Chelka Lodge (518-668-4677; Rte. 9N, Diamond Point NY 12824) Price: Moderate. Nice motel and efficiency units; private sand beach; continental breakfast included July and Aug. Min. stay 3 nights in summer. Closed: Nov.–Apr.

Sand 'n' Surf Motel (518-668-4622 or 800-903-4622; Rte. 9N) Price: Inexpensive to Moderate. Motel rooms, some with water bed and hot tubs. Lake George charter fishing operation on premises. Closed: Nov. 1–Apr. 15.

Lake George

Balsam Motel (518-668-3865; 430 Canada St., Lake George NY 12845) Price: Moderate. Quiet family-run motel with non-glitzy housekeeping cottages. Heated pool; beach; no pets. Closed: Oct. 15–May 15.

Colonial Manor (518-668-4884; Rte. 9N) Price: Moderate to Expensive. Motel and cottages. Heated pool; playground; no pets. Closed: Oct. 15–May 1.

The Georgian (518-668-5401; Canada St.) Price: Moderate to Expensive. Huge, modern motor inn. Heated pool; private beach; docks for guests' boats; restaurants. Open: Year-round.

Rock Castle Resort (518-668-3011; www.gate.net/~rcastle; 3229 Lake Shore Dr.) Price: Inexpensive to moderate. Rooms (six with private bath) in a stucco-and-stone mansion; housekeeping units and cabins. Pool, lakefront; trolley to downtown Lake George. Closed: Late fall–early spring.

Tea Island (518-668-2776; Lake Shore Dr.) Price: Moderate. Motel, efficiencies, and cottages. Private beach; cafe. Closed: Oct. 15–Apr. 15.

Paradox

Sunder Land (518-585-3520; Letsonville Rd., off Rte. 74; on Paradox Lake) Price: Inexpensive to moderate; one-week minimum. 7 housekeeping cabins, some with fireplaces, decks, or screened porches. No pets, no motorboats; canoes, kayaks, and rowboats available for extra charge. Bring your own bed linens.

Schroon Lake

Dun Roamin' Cabins (518-532-7277; www.webway.com/dunroamin; Rte. 9 one mile north of downtown Schroon Lake) Price: Inexpensive to moderate. 9 cabins, some with full kitchens, Vermont Castings gas fireplace, TV, screen porch. Pets welcome; open all year.

Warrensburg

Lake George/Schroon Valley Resort (518-494-2451 or 800-958-CAMP; www.campgrounds.com/lakegeorge.; Schroon River Rd.) 140 sites with full or partial hookups, heated pool, fishing, game room, laundry.

CHAMPLAIN VALLEY

For a complete list of accommodations in the area, contact Essex County Tourism (518-597-4646; Crown Point NY 12928).

Keeseville

Ausable Chasm KOA Campground (518-834-9990; Rte. 9, Keeseville NY 12944) 89 tent and RV sites; some full hook-ups. Short walk to Ausable Chasm. Closed: Mid-Oct.–mid-May.

Port Henry

Crag Harbor Canyon Campsite (518-546-7457 or 877-546-7457; 177 Main St., Port Henry NY 12974) Tent and RV sites; log cabins with composting toilets. Pets welcome; lake access. Closed: Mid-Oct.–mid-May.

Port Kent

Yogi Bear's Jellystone Park Camp Resorts (518-834-9011; Rte. 373, Port Kent NY 12975) Numerous RV hookups and tent sites, overlooking Lake Champlain at the Port Kent Ferry. Pool; nature trails; activities for kids; camping cabins; playground; laundromat. Closed: Mid-Oct.–mid-May.

Ticonderoga

Ranchouse at Baldwin on Northern Lake George (518-585-6596; 79 Baldwin Rd., Ticonderoga NY 12883) Price: Moderate. Eight units, some with complete kitchens. Lakefront; near hiking trails to Rogers Rock; canoe and fishing boat for guests. Closed: Mid-Oct.–May 1.

HIGH PEAKS AND NORTHERN ADIRONDACKS

Lake Placid has lodging information available at 800-44PLACI, or you can contact the Visitors Bureau (518-523-2445; Main St., Lake Placid NY 12946).

A sampling of motels in the area is listed below.

Lake Placid

Best Western Golden Arrow (518-523-3353; www.golden-arrow.com; 150 Main St.) Price: Moderate to Expensive. Modern motor inn on the lakefront in the heart of downtown. Health club; heated pool; private beach; shopping arcade. Open: Year-round.

High Peaks Hostel (518-523-3764; 337 Main St., next to High Peaks Cyclery) The cheapest lodging to be found in town, and within walking distance to restaurants, the Olympic arena, and pubs. Groups of 20 or fewer can rent the whole house, including kitchen privileges, for $250 a night; a bunk is less than 20 bucks.

Holiday Inn Lake Placid Resort (518-523-2556; 1 Olympic Dr.) Price: Moderate to Very Expensive. 200+ nicely appointed suites and rooms. Overlooking the Olympic Arena. Heated pool; access to Jackrabbit cross-country ski trails; 2 championship golf courses; health club; lake view; restaurant and lounge. Open: Year-round.

Howard Johnson Lodge (518-523-9555; Saranac Ave.) Price: Moderate to Expensive. Tennis; indoor pool; near Peninsula hiking trails and Paradox Bay of Lake Placid. Open: Year-round.

Lake Placid Hilton (518-523-1120; 1 Mirror Lake Dr.) Price: Moderate to Expensive. Large, downtown motor inn complex across from the lake. Extensive upgrades are planned for 2000. Indoor and outdoor pools; restaurant and lounge; shops. Ask about packages for family vacations: kids may stay and eat for free. Open: Year-round.

Lakeshore Motel (518-523-523-2261; 54 Saranac Ave.) Price: Inexpensive to Moderate. Nice family-run place with eight double rooms and eight efficiencies on Lake Placid. Private beach; rowboats and canoes; picnic tables and grill for guests. Open: Year-round.

Northwoods Inn (518-523-1818; 122 Main St.) Price: Moderate to Expensive. Extensively renovated in 1994–95 with 89 suites. Try the restaurant downstairs for steaks and pub fare; the selection of microbrews is the best in town. Breakfast in the Northern Lights Pavilion is quite good. Open: Year-round.

Prague Motor Inn (518-523-2587; 25 Sentinel Rd.) Price: Inexpensive to Moderate. Quiet, folksy Mom-and-Pop place with an amusing Queen Anne house in front of the motel units.

North Hudson

Blue Ridge Falls Campground (518-532-7863; Blue Ridge Rd., North Hudson NY 12855) Off the main highway; pool; walk to waterfalls. Closed: Winter.

Ray Brook

Sherwood Forest Motor Inn (518-891-4400; Rte. 86 near Tail o' the Pup, Ray Brook, 12977) Price: Inexpensive to Moderate. Not a motel at all but nice one- and two-bedroom housekeeping cabins, just off the busy highway. Most cabins have wood-burning fireplaces and views of a pretty little pond.

Saranac Lake

Comfort Inn (518-891-1970; 148 Lake Flower Ave., Saranac Lake NY 12983) Price: Inexpensive to Moderate. Nice, new motel with pleasant grounds and a decent restaurant, McKenzie's Grill. Open: year-round.

Wilmington

Hungry Trout Motor Lodge (518-946-2217; Rte. 86, Wilmington NY 12997) Price: Moderate to Expensive. 20 rooms. Great view; nice restaurant and R. F. McDougal's Tavern; excellent fishing on private stretch of river; fly-fishing guide service, lessons, and tackle shop. Closed: Mid-Apr.–late June; Nov.–Dec.

NORTHWEST LAKES

For a complete list of lodgings in the immediate area, contact the Tupper Lake Chamber of Commerce (518-359-3328 or 800-640-6785; 60 Park St., Tupper Lake NY 12986).

Tupper Lake

Pine Terrace Resort (518-359-9258; Rte. 30) Price: Inexpensive to Moderate. Housekeeping units and motel rooms. Pool; clay tennis courts; private beach across the road; picnic area. Closed: Nov.–Apr.

Red Top Inn (518-359-9209; Rte. 30) Price: Inexpensive. 18 rooms. Lake view; private beach across the road; fishing dock. Open: Year-round.

Shaheen's Motel (518-359-3384; 310 Park St.) Price: Inexpensive to Moderate. 33 motel rooms; heated pool; copier and fax service; continental breakfast. Open: Year-round.

CENTRAL ADIRONDACKS

See Chapter Eight, *Information*, for individual town chambers of commerce; the Central Adirondacks is cottage country, with lots of housekeeping cabins on lakes available. A sampling of motels, campgrounds, condos, and other options is listed below.

Inlet

Nelson's Cottages (315-357-4111; Rte. 28 near the state boat launch, Inlet) Price: Inexpensive. Old-fashioned cabins named after the 50 states set along a sandy circular drive. The accommodations aren't deluxe, but they're clean and quiet; most cabins have refrigerators, grills, and picnic tables. There is a tiny beach, fine for launching a canoe or kayak, but better swimming is at the town beach, about a quarter-mile away.

Parquet Hotel (315-357-6294; Rte. 28 near Arrowhead Park, Inlet NY 13360) Price: Inexpensive. A funny little hotel (six rooms or so), nicely redone in 1999, set amidst the splendors of downtown Inlet. The public beach and tennis courts are a two-minute walk away, as is the Tamarack Moviehouse, the bakery, Ara-Ho Outfitters, and so forth.

Long Lake

Sandy Point Motel (518-624-3871; Rte. 28/30, Long Lake NY 12847) Price: Inexpensive to Moderate. Motel units and efficiencies. Private beach; docks; cable TV; rental boats for guests; cross-country skiing and snowmobiling. Open: Year-round.

Shamrock Motel (518-624-3861; Rte. 28/30) Price: Inexpensive to Moderate. Motel and neat-as-a-pin housekeeping cottages. Private beach; picnic area. Closed: Mid-Oct.–Memorial Day.

North Creek

Broderick Real Estate (518-251-0103 or 800-309-0577; www.goremountainskiresorts.com; Rte. 28 near Peaceful Valley Rd.) Rental agent for nicely equipped one- to four-bedroom townhomes (fireplaces, Jacuzzis, dishwashers, TV/VCR) at Pine Ridge and the Summit, both only a few minutes away from Gore Mountain Ski Center. Open: Year-round.

Campers at Old Forge KOA.

James Swedberg

<u>*Old Forge*</u>

Best Western Motel (315-369-6836; Rte. 30, Thendara NY 13472) Price: Moderate. 50 renovated rooms. Indoor pool; tennis; Jacuzzis; putting green. Open: Year-round.

Clark's Beach Motel (315-369-3026; Main St., Old Forge NY 13420) Price: Moderate. 42 units. Lake view; next to public beach; indoor pool. Open: Year-round.

The Forge Motel (315-369-3313; Main St., Old Forge) Price: Moderate. 61 units. Lake view, the best from Room 13; pool; next to public beach; walk to restaurants. Open: Year-round.

Old Forge KOA (315-369-6011; Rte. 28, Old Forge) Campground. 200 sites on 101 acres. Private lake; Laundromat; showers; convenience store; dumping station; canoes; movies. Open: Year-round.

Water's Edge Inn and Conference Center (315-369-2484; Rte. 30, Old Forge) Price: Moderate. 42 rooms. Lakefront; indoor pool; sauna; dock; family restaurant; across from Enchanted Forest/Water Safari park. Open: Year-round.

Hollywood Hills, in Old Forge, was once the largest log hotel in the world.

Courtesy *Adirondack Life* magazine

CHAPTER FOUR
From Folkways to Fine Arts
CULTURE

Private collection

From 1918 to 1934 Georgia O'Keeffe spent summers at Alfred Stieglitz's family estate in Bolton Landing, where she painted wildflowers, barns, clouds, and the wild moods of Lake George.

Culture, if regarded as the noble endeavors in human society — fine arts, literature, classical music, theater, ballet — may have been out of reach of the old-time Adirondack woodsman and his family, but the wild landscape inspired many a visiting painter, writer, and composer. It could be argued, too, that because of popular fiction, weekly national magazines like *Harper's* and *Every Saturday*, and Currier & Ives prints, the Adirondacks were much better known as a particular place a hundred years ago than they are today.

Consider *The Last of the Mohicans*, for example. The harrowing trip from what's now called Cooper's Cave, in Glens Falls, to the fort at Ticonderoga went along the Hudson River, crossed over the Tongue Mountain range, skirted the west side of Lake George and reached Lake Champlain at its narrowest spot. The adventure is now firmly etched in American letters, but few of us connect the journey with actual sites located in the Adirondacks. James Fenimore Cooper visited Warrensburg and Lake George in 1824 to research his story and observe the landscape. Many of his landmarks are inaccessible today, but you may catch a few glimpses if you follow in his tracks, on modern-day Rte. 9.

Visual artists recorded the region in a state of bucolic grace, before the iron industry's charcoal kilns darkened the skies and lumbermen cut the forests; beginning in 1830, and on up through the turn of the 19th century, the countryside practically swarmed with painters. Thomas Cole, Frederic Church, and other Hudson River School artists depicted perfect scenes of glowing mountains, shimmering lakes, and tiny villages. Frederic Remington, who was born just north of the Adirondacks, in Canton, New York, sketched trappers' cabins and lumber camps. The English painter A.F. Tait also showed the manly side of the wilderness, in oil paintings of groups of hunters and fishermen and portraits of their prey. Many of Tait's images were used for Currier & Ives lithographs, but the popularity of those Adirondack prints also created demand for Tait imitators; more than 100 different Currier & Ives images illustrate scenes of the region, from maple-sugaring parties to ice fishing to humble log farmsteads.

Winslow Homer painted woodsmen in Keene Valley and at the North Woods Club, near Minerva, in a luminous, impressionistic style that helped cinch his career as America's premier watercolorist. His illustrations of hunters and lumberjacks that appeared in weeklies brought the backwoods to urban homes. Harold Weston, who lived most of his life in Keene Valley, made bold, burly oils of the High Peaks that were exhibited widely from the 1920s to 1970s, and now reside in major collections throughout the world. Rockwell Kent spent his last decades at his farm near Au Sable Forks, painting the Ausable River valley and designing houses; major exhibitions showing his works (many donated to museums in the former Soviet Union) are on the schedule at the Adirondack Museum, in Blue Mtn. Lake, 1999–2000, and at the State University of New York–Plattsburgh. David Smith, one of the best-known sculptors of the modern age, lived in Bolton Landing; today, in a field overlooking Lake George, many of his abstract sculptures remain, but unfortunately, the property is rarely open to the public.

Composers found their muse in the woods and waters too. A few parlor ditties made the rounds in the late 19th century, like "Floating for Deer" and "The Adirondacks: A Gallop," and the immense popularity of canoeing at the turn of the century created a whole new genre of songs celebrating the sport, such as "Paddlin' Madeline Home." But, more importantly, two of the finest modern composers, Charles Ives and Béla Bartók, both spent extended periods of time working in the Adirondacks. Ives composed the *Concord* piano sonata while visiting Elk Lake, and began the *Universe Symphony*, one of his last major works, while at his wife's family's summer home in Keene Valley. Bartók wrote the *Concerto for Orchestra* at a modest cottage in Saranac Lake, where he was taking the "cure" for tuberculosis.

With only a few exceptions, women are notably absent from this list of resident and visiting artists. Jeanne Robert Foster grew up in grinding poverty in Johnsburg, and went on to be an editor of the *Transatlantic Review*. Her circle of friends included Ezra Pound, T.S. Eliot, and John Butler Yeats, father of the Irish poet. Her poetry-and-prose memories of her youth were published in *Adirondack Portraits* (Syracuse University Press, 1989).

Folk arts from the 19th-century Adirondacks reflect the lumbering days, in songs and tall tales, and the Gilded Age, in rustic furniture and decorative items local carpenters and blacksmiths created for the Great Camps. Traditional music can be heard at many of the arts centers listed elsewhere in this chapter; the best place to see rustic furniture in quantity and quality is at the Adirondack Museum, in Blue Mtn. Lake. Throughout the park the icons of North Country material culture are ubiquitous: the guideboat, pack basket, lean-to, and Adirondack chair. The art of storytelling is also alive and well in informal gathering places and on stage.

With the dawn of a new millennium, the cultural scene in the Adirondacks is remarkably diverse, showcasing native skills and crafts, and honoring the fine artists who visited the region. There's real community pride in libraries, arts centers, theater companies, historic-preservation groups, museums, and musical ensembles. But beyond the good feelings and active schedules, there's also a level of excellence that rises above sometimes humble settings. The following descriptions will tell you where to go in search of history and the arts throughout the park, but you'll have to call or write to get a current schedule of events. Local radio stations and weekly papers offer calendars of events for communities within the park; the *Adirondack Daily Enterprise* has a weekly calendar that extends from Blue Mtn. Lake to Keene, and *The Chronicle,* based in Glens Falls, lists numerous southern Adirondack happenings. *Adirondack Life* has a bimonthly calendar in each issue, "Inside & Out," which does cover the entire Adirondack Park, but it's always a good idea to call ahead to confirm ticket availability or location of an event. Websites for tourism offices listed in Chapter 8, *Information,* usually contain schedules of cultural events.

ARCHITECTURE

Michael Kahn

Camp Eagle Island, on Upper Saranac Lake, is a wonderful example of Adirondack Great Camp architecture.

Compared to touring Vermont, with its many postcard-pretty villages, old-house hunting in the Adirondack Park may be disappointing to the historic-preservation buff. Bear in mind that settlements in the North Country, especially in the central Adirondacks, are considerably newer than New

England towns, and that the communities which date back to the 1700s along Lakes George and Champlain were destroyed during the French and Indian and Revolutionary wars. Devastating fires before the turn of the century in towns such as Tupper Lake and Indian Lake obliterated hundreds of prosperous businesses and homes. However, along the eastern edge of the park, there are several lovely towns with fine buildings dating back two centuries.

The celebrated Adirondack rustic style of architecture, which borrowed designs from Swiss chalets, English half-timber buildings, pioneer cabins, and even Japanese pagodas, isn't easy to view from the comfort of an automobile. You'll find rustic lodges and boathouses in all their twiggy glory mainly on remote lakeshores: **Sagamore Great Camp** (315-354-5311), the former Vanderbilt summer estate near ***Raquette Lake***, and **White Pine Camp** (518-327-3030), the summer White House of Calvin Coolidge, on ***Osgood Pond***, are two Great Camps you can easily see. Visiting **Santanoni Preserve**, near ***Newcomb***, requires a 10-mile round trip without a car, but it's well worth the effort. You can reach the impressive rustic complex by walking, cross-country skiing, biking, or riding a horse-drawn wagon, and you get a real sense of its woodland isolation.

Adirondack Architectural Heritage (518-834-9328; 1759 Main St., Keeseville) is a parkwide non-profit organization founded in 1990 devoted to historic preservation. Tours of public and private sites in summer and fall, lectures, workshops, and technical assistance to building owners are just a few of the programs and services offered by AARCH.

LAKE GEORGE AND SOUTHEASTERN ADIRONDACKS

For many travelers, ***Warrensburg*** is the gateway to the Adirondacks. Along Main Street (Rte. 9), there are stately 19th-century homes, from Greek Revival and Gothic cottages to Italianate villas and Queen Anne mansions. The oldest building in Warrensburg, across from the Ford dealership on Rte. 9, is a former blacksmith shop, dating back to 1814. Along the Schroon River (Rte. 418 west), you can see remnants of the village's industrial center in several old mill buildings; the Grist Mill, now an excellent restaurant, still has grindstones, chutes, grain-grinding apparatus, and a small exhibit that describes the building's past. Also on Rte. 9, ***Chestertown*** has a historic district with colorful Greek Revival houses and restored storefronts.

CHAMPLAIN VALLEY

Essex County is especially rich in architectural sights. Beginning in the south, the town of ***Ticonderoga*** is a major destination for history lovers. **Fort Ticonderoga** is about 2.5 miles south of the village on Rte. 22, but you can find the tumble-down walls and rusting cannons of **Fort Mount Hope** by exploring near the old cemetery on Burgoyne St., not far from the village waterworks. At the head of Montcalm St. is a replica of John Hancock's Boston home, built by Horace Moses in 1926. Moses made his fortune with the Strathmore Paper Company and funded many town beautification projects, including the **Liberty Monument**, a bronze statue by Charles Keck that's in the center of the traffic circle across from Hancock House. A walking tour that highlights Ticonderoga's bustling 19th-century industrial history is available (518-585-6366).

The Town of Moriah offices, in Port Henry, were the headquarters of a prosperous mining concern.

James Swedberg

At ***Crown Point***, there were several fortifications along the lake harkening back to the French occupation of the Champlain Valley in the early 18th century; near the bridge to Vermont, off Rte. 22, is **Fort Crown Point**. West of Crown Point is **Ironville**, a well-preserved gem of an early 19th-century community, with several white clapboard homes, a lovely church, numerous farm buildings, and peaceful, tree-shaded roads. On the way to Ironville, in **Factoryville**, you'll see the only octagonal house in the Adirondacks.

Historic markers erected by New York State abound along Rte. 22 as you approach ***Port Henry***. The original settlement here supplied lumber for the forts at Crown Point and for Benedict Arnold's naval fleet. Later, the discovery of abundant iron ore shaped the town. Evidence of this prosperity shows up in an ornate downtown block, elaborate churches, and the exuberant high Victorian **Moriah Town Office** building, formerly the headquarters of the Witherbee-Sherman Iron Company, near the Amtrak station. In the carriage house next to the town offices the **Iron History Center** opened in 1999 as a museum dedicated to local mining and railroads (518-546-3341).

The Essex County seat is ***Elizabethtown***, founded in the 1790s. The county courthouse complex is impressive, and about half a mile away are brick buildings built by the illustrious Hand family, which produced a dynasty of civic leaders and lawyers. The well-preserved Greek Revival Hand House and the Hands' free-standing law office are on Rte. 9 near the flashing light. About eight miles east of E'town, along Champlain's shore, is ***Westport***, which was first settled in 1770. Buildings from that era have all disappeared, but a few homes near the lake on Washington St., off Rtes. 9N and 22, were built in the 1820s. Westport was a vital port shipping out iron, lumber, wool, and other farm products before the Civil War, and a thriving summer community afterwards. Following Rte. 22, you pass Gothic cottages and impressive stone houses overlooking the lake. Between Westport and Essex, on Rte. 22, is the tiny farm community of ***Boquet***, with its odd little octagonal schoolhouse, recently restored and occasionally open to the public.

The Adirondack community richest in architectural treasures is undoubtedly ***Essex***; it's as if the clock stopped here in 1856. There are wonderful Dutch Colonial, Georgian, Federal, and Greek Revival buildings in excellent repair throughout the town: check under "Historic Buildings and Districts" for more information. Continuing on Rte. 22, ***Willsboro*** and ***Keeseville*** contain many historic buildings. Keeseville has several homes made of buff-pink native sandstone which date back to the 1830s, and buildings in the full range of 19th-century styles from Dutch Colonial to Federal and Greek Revival to Gothic Revival and Romanesque. The **Stone Arch Bridge** over the Ausable River, built in 1842, is the largest single-span arch bridge in the country. From the bridge you can see the huge factory buildings that made horseshoe nails, an indispensable product of the 19th century.

The monograph *Crossing the River*, published by the Friends of North Country (518-834-9606), highlights historic bridges in Essex County, and makes an excellent driving tour. Another interesting driving tour for the historic **Boquet River** is published by the Boquet River Association (518-962-8296); the loop begins just off the Northway and follows the river through Elizabethtown, Wadhams, Whallonsburg, Boquet, and Essex to its northernmost point, at Willsboro, and then goes south to Reber and Lewis. A map with interpretive signs along the route has been published by the Champlain Valley Heritage Network (518-597-4646; Rte. 1, Box 220, Crown Point) and highlights historic sites, farmsteads, local industries, and vistas from Keeseville to Ticonderoga.

HIGH PEAKS AND NORTHERN ADIRONDACKS

The Ausable River valley holds many historic buildings that are visible along roadways. South of Keene Valley, it's worth a quick detour off Rte. 73 at ***St. Hubert's*** to see the massive Victorian inn, the **Ausable Club**. It's "members only" inside the building, but you can get a rare glimpse of the kind of hostelry that visitors once enjoyed throughout the Adirondacks. North on Rte. 9, between ***Upper Jay***, ***Jay***, and ***Au Sable Forks***, there are fine Federal-style stone and brick houses and churches; in Jay, the sole remaining covered bridge in the Adirondacks was dismantled in 1997. You can see its three sections (Mill Hill Rd., 1/4 mi. off Rte. 9), but it's anyone's guess if and when the structure will once again span the Ausable River.

The Olympic Village — ***Lake Placid***, that is — has only a few buildings left from its earliest days, when the settlement of **North Elba**, near the ski jumps, was a iron-mining center: one that's easy to spot on **Old Military Road** is the **Stagecoach Inn**.

In ***Saranac Lake***, which was incorporated in 1892, the tuberculosis industry inspired its own architecture, manifested in "cure porches" and "cure cottages." The group **Historic Saranac Lake** sponsors lectures and tours from time to time highlighting buildings of note (518-891-0971); a current project is restoring a cure cottage used by Béla Bartók.

Tucked back in the woods at ***Loon Lake***, partly visible from County Rd. 99, is a surprising collection of cottages and other elaborate buildings designed by Stanford White. The best way to see these haunting structures is by playing a round of golf at the Loon Lake course.

North of ***Newcomb*** on CR 25, en route to the Upper Works trailhead for the High Peaks, is the **Adirondac blast furnace**, an immense stone monolith built in 1854 that produced high-quality iron. Continuing on the road, you'll pass a faded white farmhouse that was the office of an early iron-mining concern. (The other deserted buildings nearby belonged to the Tahawus Club.)

On ***Upper Saranac Lake***, which straddles the High Peaks and Northwest Lakes regions of this book, there are fine examples of rustic architecture, but you'll need a canoe to paddle by **Wenonah Lodge**, **Prospect Point** (now a Christian summer camp), **Camp Wonundra** (now "The Point," a sumptuous inn), **Pinebrook**, **Eagle Island** (now a Girl Scout camp), and **Sekon Lodge**. Don't expect more than a tantalizing peek at these places hidden by the trees, and for heaven's sake, don't go ashore on private lands. Another vehicle for touring the lake may be the summer mail boat; check at the Saranac Lake post office to learn if the mail-delivery person is taking passengers.

NORTHWEST LAKES

For boathouse fans, ***Upper St. Regis Lake***, near Paul Smiths, has many lovely waterfront buildings, in high rustic, cobblestone, and shingle style. You'll need a boat to make this tour, and you'll have to paddle several miles from the public put-in on Keese Mill Rd., west of Paul Smith's College. Also, a reminder — respect landowners' privacy by staying away from docks and shore.

CENTRAL ADIRONDACKS

The heart of the Adirondacks has few buildings dating from before the Civil War, but it's home to a vernacular architectural style that honors French-Canadian and Yankee traditions in steep-roofed, simple homes. ***Olmstedville***, off Rte. 28N, has a cluster of Greek Revival storefronts and houses from the 1840s. Farther south, on Rte. 30, ***Wells*** has several nicely restored Victorian-era homes along the Sacandaga River. For rustic architecture, a boat tour of

Raquette Lake, either on Bird's mail boat (315-354-4441), or the *W.W. Durant*, a replica of an old steamboat (315-354-5532), allows glimpses of the Great Camps like **Pine Knot** (the first rustic camp designed by William West Durant), **Camp Echo**, and **Bluff Point** (the former Collier estate). **Great Camp Sagamore** (315-354-5301) occasionally offers tours of nearby rustic estates.

ARTS CENTERS & ARTS COUNCILS

The arts scene is surprisingly lively in this, New York's most rural area, thanks in part to the long-time leadership of the New York State Council on the Arts. Through grants from the state council to arts presenters, producers, and non-profit galleries, and a re-grant program to fledgling and volunteer organizations, all kinds of arts programs can be found in all kinds of towns.

ADIRONDACK ART ASSOCIATION
518-963-7270.
Schoolhouse Gallery, Essex.
Season: Spring–fall.
Open: Daily.

This 30-year-old community gallery showcases regional professional artists in solo and group exhibitions, from quilts to photography and watercolor paintings to designer crafts.

ADIRONDACK LAKES CENTER FOR THE ARTS
518-352-7715.
www.netheaven.com/~alca.
Rte. 28, next to the post office, Blue Mtn. Lake.
Mail: Box 101, Blue Mtn. Lake NY 12812.
Season: Year-round.
Price: Concert, film, and theater tickets $5–$12. Discounts for seniors, children. Workshop fees vary.

Since 1967 this multi-arts center has brought a full palette of programs to Blue Mtn. Lake, population 150 (give or take). The Adirondack Lakes Center for the Arts, a former garage, has presented hundreds of concerts, including performances by the Tokyo String Quartet, Doc Watson, the Dixie Hummingbirds, Paul Taylor, the Seldom Scene, Odetta, Livingston Taylor, and more.

Exhibitions include contemporary paintings, sculpture, photography, and crafts; Adirondack furniture; children's art; and traveling shows. Complementing the shows are intensive workshops for adults, on weekends in fall and winter and weekdays in summer. Programs for kids range from crafts, dance, and music workshops to films and family presentations of storytelling, New Vaudeville, and magic.

ARTS CENTER/OLD FORGE
315-369-6411.
Rte. 28, Old Forge.
Season: Year-round.

The Arts Center/Old Forge is the oldest community-arts organization in the region, and the organization continues to grow, change, and pursue new directions. The facility is a former boat-storage barn, but it's truly transformed by annual

The annual fall quilt show at the Arts Center/Old Forge attracts visitors from across New York State.

James Swedberg

Price: Concert & theater tickets $5–$12. Donations suggested for special exhibitions.
Gift Shop: Open 7 days in July & Aug.; during exhibitions rest of year.

events such as the Adirondacks National Exhibition of Watercolors (Aug.–Sept.) and the October quilt show. The same space hosts theater by Pendragon, a touring company from Saranac Lake, and excellent children's performances. Classical concerts are often held in the Niccols Memorial Church, a few miles away, while bluegrass, folk, or jazz programs may be on stage at McCauley Mtn. Ski Area, at the Old Forge beach front, or in the center's black box theater.

In the summer, there are local history outings and lectures and presentations by artists and writers. Throughout the year, the arts center shows contemporary American and foreign films in different venues and offers crafts workshops for adults from boatbuilding to basketry. There are numerous kids' programs for ages five and up. The center also has a cooperative crafts shop on Main Street, one block past Old Forge Hardware.

ARTS COUNCIL FOR THE NORTHERN ADIRONDACKS
518-962-8778.
www.artsnorth.org/html/acna.
Rte. 22, Westport.
Season: Year-round.

Launched as an advocacy group for local artists and craftspeople, the Arts Council for the Northern Adirondacks publishes a comprehensive summer events calendar for exhibitions; lectures; fairs; music, theater, and dance performances; and children's programs. The organization also offers grants to working artists, presents traditional and contemporary musicians from the region in different towns, and sponsors traveling juried art shows.

FULTON CHAIN OF LAKES PERFORMING ARTS COUNCIL
315-357-5501.
Rte. 28, Inlet.
Season: Summer.
Price: Varies.

New in summer 1999, the Fulton Chain group brings professional musicians to small central Adirondack communities that may never have seen the likes of piccolo or timpani: the council's first event was a concert featuring the entire Syracuse Symphony Orchestra in a tent overlooking Fourth Lake. That initial show was a huge risk that's paid off, and plans are to offer programs on a regular basis in 2000.

LAKE GEORGE ARTS PROJECT
518-668-2616.
Canada St., Lake George.
Season: Year-round.
Price: Concerts are free.

Of all the Adirondack arts institutions, the Lake George Arts Project (LGAP) is decidedly the hippest. Over the years, LGAP has organized contemporary sculpture shows on the frozen lake, in tree-shaded Shepard Park, and alongside the scenic highway up Prospect Mtn. The offices and gallery are on the ground floor of the old courthouse in the center of town; special exhibitions featuring regional artists with national renown are scheduled monthly. Ongoing programs are fiction and poetry workshops, weekly summer concerts in the park (including Tony Trischka and Skyline in 1999), the hot Lake George Jazz Festival (Sept.), and the Black Velvet Art Party, a celebration of terminal tackiness, usually slated for early November. If you've been waiting for the right venue in which to debut your Elvis schtick, seek no further.

LAKE PLACID CENTER FOR THE ARTS
518-523-2512.
www.lpartscenter.org.
Saranac Ave., Lake Placid.
Season: Year-round.
Tickets: Concert & theater $6–$12. Discounts for seniors, students.

The Lake Placid Center for the Arts (LPCA) has metamorphosed through different identities, beginning as the Center for Music, Drama, and Art; then as an accredited two-year arts school; and next as the summer campus for the Parsons School of Design. Now a multi-arts center with a community-service focus, the facility is topnotch, with a beautiful theater that seats about 300, well-equipped studios, and a bright, airy gallery. Exhibitions are slated throughout the year, with two juried shows for regional artists and craftspeople.

Presentations include visiting theater groups; contemporary American and foreign films; folk music; dance-company residencies; gala programs by soloists of the New York City Ballet; and excellent classical and chamber performances during the summer. The summer Lake Placid Chamber Music Festival highlights many acclaimed ensembles, including the Amadeus Trio.

The LPCA also is home to the Community Theater Players, who offer three or four shows annually. For kids, in July and August, there's the free "Young and Fun" performance series on weekday mornings.

SACANDAGA VALLEY ARTS NETWORK
518-863-8797.
Box 660, Northville NY 12134.
Season: Year-round.

New in 1997, the Sacandaga Valley Arts Network is an active group of visual artists eager to share their knowledge and philosophy through programs ranging from group shows of internationally acclaimed sculptors to guided canoe trips exploring the social history of the southern Adirondacks. Acoustic concerts are occasionally held at the old Adirondack Lumber Company, in Wells, or in downtown Northville. A two-week-long festival in August celebrates "life, the ultimate art form."

CINEMA

During the silent-film era, the Adirondacks provided a backdrop for popular films including *The Shooting of Dan McGrew, The Wilderness Woman, Glorious Youth,* and dozens more; the movie industry thrived for more than a decade in unlikely places such as Saranac Lake, Plattsburgh, and Port Henry. There were cowboy scenes at Ausable Chasm, "Alaskan" trapper cabins in Essex County farmyards, and adventures supposedly set in South America, Siberia, Switzerland. As the cameras rolled, Washington crossed the frozen Delaware — somewhere on the Saranac River.

In 1941, Alfred Hitchcock's only comedy, *Mr. and Mrs. Smith,* was set at the Lake Placid Club. A few years later, *Lake Placid Serenade,* which featured dizzying reels of figure skating and Roy Rogers as king of the Placid winter carnival, was a commercial success. In 1958, scenes of *Marjorie Morningstar* were shot in Schroon Lake; local extras were paid the princely sum of $125 per day. (*The Sweet Hereafter,* from the Adirondack novel by Russell Banks, was filmed in Canada, alas.) Today there are many places where you can catch foreign, classic, and first-run films. Several vintage theaters have been lovingly restored since 1997.

The **Lake Placid Film Forum** (518-576-2063; Box 489, Lake Placid) launched a very successful silent film series in 1999, using the Palace Theater and its magnificent Robert Morton theater organ. Plans are underway to continue showing silent films in the fall and add a conference for screenwriters, directors, and cinematographers in springtime.

LAKE GEORGE AND SOUTHEASTERN ADIRONDACKS

Carol Theater (518-494-0006; Main St., Chestertown) Open Memorial Day–fall. First-run films; children's matinees.

Strand Theater (518-532-9300; Main St. Schroon Lake) Open May–Oct., plus some off-season weekends. Recently restored art deco setting, with state-of-the-art sound system.

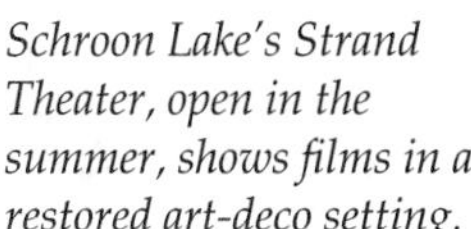

Schroon Lake's Strand Theater, open in the summer, shows films in a restored art-deco setting.

James Swedberg

HIGH PEAKS AND NORTHERN ADIRONDACKS

Berkeley Theater (518-891-5470; Broadway & Berkeley Square, Saranac Lake) Cozy new theater, first-run films.

Lake Placid Center for the Arts (518-523-2512; Saranac Ave., Lake Placid) Foreign and contemporary American film series in fall, winter, and spring.

Palace Theater (518-523-9271; Main St., Lake Placid) Recently restored Art Deco stenciling in the lobby and displays of Lake Placid movie memorabilia. Current American releases, 3 screens, open daily year-round. On summer nights, an organist plays the awesome theater organ before 7pm features; in October, the Lake Placid Film Forum holds a silent film festival with live accompaniment.

NORTHWEST LAKES

State Theater (518-359-3593; Park St., Tupper Lake) Recent releases.

CENTRAL ADIRONDACKS

Adirondack Picture Show (518-548-6199; Rte. 8, Speculator) A huge, funky barn, probably the oldest movie theater in the park still operating. First-run films in the summer.

Lake Theater (518-648-5950; Main St., Indian Lake) Recent films nightly from late May–fall; occasional foreign films on fall weekends in conjunction with the Adirondack Lakes Center for the Arts; films during Indian Lake's Winter Festival, in February.

Strand Theater (315-369-6703; Main St., Old Forge) Carefully restored vintage cinema. Two or three shows nightly; children's matinees; occasional foreign films in cooperation with the Arts Center/Old Forge. Plans for 2000 or 2001 are to add two theaters in an adjacent lot.

Tamarack Moviehouse (315-357-2001; Rte. 28, Inlet) Recent films nightly Memorial Day–Labor Day; weekends in fall and winter. Check out the ice-cream parlor next door. Closed in winter.

CRAFTS INSTRUCTION

Weave a traditional Adirondack pack basket, spin a skein of wool, tie a dry fly, build a guideboat — you can learn these old-time skills, as well as contemporary crafts, in several centers across the park. Classes for adults range from one or two-day intensive programs to week-long sessions; prices vary. Always call ahead to register for these workshops.

HIGH PEAKS AND NORTHERN ADIRONDACKS

Adirondack Mountain Club (518-523-3441; Adirondak Loj Rd., Lake Placid) Painting, photography, and traditional craft classes that make use of a spectacular natural setting for both materials and inspiration.

Lake Placid Center for the Arts (518-523-2512; Saranac Ave., Lake Placid) Watercolor painting, photography, basketry, figure drawing, and other classes for adults, year-round.

Newcomb Visitor Interpretive Center (518-582-2000; Rte. 28N, Newcomb) Weekend classes year-round in Adirondack basketry, fly tying, watercolor painting, and nature photography. Also children's programs on most Saturdays.

NORTHWEST LAKES

Paul Smiths Visitor Interpretive Center (518-327-3000; Rte. 30, Paul Smiths) Workshops similar to the Newcomb center, above.

CENTRAL ADIRONDACKS

Adirondack Lakes Center for the Arts (518-352-7715; Rte. 28, Blue Mtn. Lake) Painting, photography, guideboat building, woodcarving, rug-hooking, rustic furniture-making, basketry, and other crafts, year-round.

Arts Center/Old Forge (315-369-6411; Rte. 28, Old Forge) Watercolor painting, wooden boatbuilding, quilting, pottery, rug making, lampshade making, basketry, and more, year-round.

Sagamore (315-354-5311; Sagamore Rd., Raquette Lake) Weekend courses in traditional music and dance, basketry, woodcarving, rustic furniture building, quilting, nature illustration, paper-making and so forth. Fees include room and board.

DANCE

The **Lake Placid Center for the Arts** (518-523-2512) sponsors a modern dance company in residence each year: in 1999, Rebecca Kelly's group was in residence for two weeks. The program always includes classes for adults and children; usually several evening performances and a children's daytime program are scheduled. The LPCA also presents modern dance concerts, including stars of the New York City Ballet, throughout the year.

Courtesy of *Adirondack Life* magazine

Stepping lively at Camp Santanoni, 1890s.

Square, round, line, and altogether shapeless dancing to the fiddle and banjo is a North Country tradition. Neophytes are welcome at community square dances, and callers usually explain each dance. During the summer, there are weekly dances on the tennis courts in **Schroon Lake** (518-532-7650). In Stony Creek, **Stony Creek Mountain Days** (518-696-2332) also feature old-time dancing.

BEYOND THE BLUE LINE

You'll have to venture outside the Adirondack Park for a full calendar of professional dance, but by traveling not too far afield you can catch rehearsals and performances of the New York City Ballet at the **Saratoga Performing Arts Center** (518-587-3330; www.spac.org; Saratoga Spa State Park) in ***Saratoga Springs***. At rehearsals, seating is usually open so you can get up close, to really get a sense of the sheer physical strength of the dancers. At the other end of the spectrum, the annual ballet gala, in July, is an elegant, magical evening.

ELDERHOSTEL

The Adirondack Park is a favorite learning laboratory for Elderhostel, the international educational organization for people over age 60. Generally, these inexpensive, informal, non-credit courses last five or six days and cover history, nature, folklore, and even culinary arts, in sessions led by local experts. Some recent Elderhostel programs have included maple-sugar traditions, Lake George shipwrecks, canoeing, ethnic groups in the Adirondacks, historic preservation, and the region's role in the American Revolution.

Adirondack sites for Elderhostel programs include **Sagamore Great Camp**, in ***Raquette Lake*** (315-354-5311); Adirondack Mountain Club, at **Adirondak Loj**, outside ***Lake Placid*** (518-523-3441); **Silver Bay Association**, on the northern end of Lake George (518-543-8833); and **Fort Ticonderoga** (518-585-2821). For more information write to Elderhostel, 75 Federal St., Boston MA 02110; the web address is www.elderhostel.org.

HISTORIC BUILDINGS AND DISTRICTS

More than two dozen sites in the Adirondack Park are on the National Register of Historic Places; oddly enough, all of the state land — the Adirondack Forest Preserve — is a historic district, although there are very few important buildings left on these lands for reasons too complicated to explain fully here. Suffice it to say that once private land becomes public property, the terrain is to be returned to a natural condition, and structures must be destroyed. At least, that's the usual scenario. **Santanoni Preserve**, a hundred-year-old rustic enclave described earlier in this chapter, is slowly being stabilized thanks in large part of the efforts of Adirondack Architectural Heritage and the Town of Newcomb. Plans are in the works to continue restoration in 2000 and beyond.

Listed below is a selection of architecturally significant places, forts, interesting homes, and local preservation organizations.

LAKE GEORGE AND SOUTHEASTERN ADIRONDACKS

MARCELLA SEMBRICH MEMORIAL STUDIO
518-644-2492.
Lakeshore Dr./Rte. 9N, Bolton Landing.
Season: Mid-June–Labor Day; daily 10–5.
Small admission fee.

During the early decades of the 20th century, Bolton Landing was a Mecca for opera stars and composers, such as Samuel Barber and Gian Carlo Menotti. From 1921–1935, Marcella Sembrich, a Polish soprano, made her home here. Born Marcella Kochanska, she was a European sensation, and in 1898, she joined New York's Metropolitan Opera. Sembrich founded the vocal departments of the Juilliard School, in Manhattan, and the Curtis Institute, in Philadelphia; during the summers, a select group of students came to her cottage studio under the pines. The charming little museum now houses a collection of music, furniture, costumes, and opera ephemera related to Sembrich's brilliant career, including tributes from the leading composers of the day; stroll around the lakeside trail for a peaceful moment. Music lectures and concerts by young composers are held on summer afternoons and evenings; curator Richard Wargo is a highly regarded opera composer.

CHAMPLAIN VALLEY

CROWN POINT STATE HISTORIC SITE
518-597-3666.
www.fiwar.virtualave.net/forts.
Rte. 17, off Rtes. 9N & 22, Crown Point.
Season: May–Oct.; Weds.–Sat. 10–5, Sun. 1–5.
Handicap Access: Yes.

Poking into Lake Champlain, there's a thumb-shaped point that parts the waters, with Bulwagga Bay to the west and the long reach of the lake on the east. The sweeping view to the north once provided an ideal spot for guarding the territory. The French built a gargantuan stone octagon here in 1734, Fort St. Frederic, which was attacked repeatedly by the British in 1755–58 and finally captured by them in 1759. Colonial forces launched their assault on the British ships in Lake Champlain from Crown Point in 1775.

In 1910, the ruins of the French, British, and colonial forts were given to the state of New York. There's an excellent visitor center that explains the archaeology and political history of this haunting promontory through exhibits and audiovisual programs, and several miles of interpretive trails winding around stone walls and redoubts. If you're curious about a multitude of French and Indian War sites in New York, Vermont, and Canada, look up the excellent website noted above. Also, at geocities.com, there's historical site homepage for Lake Champlain and Lake George.

ESSEX COMMUNITY HERITAGE ORGANIZATION
518-963-7088.
Rte. 22, Essex.

During the brief peaceful period between the French and Indian War and the American Revolution, William Gilliland, an Irish immigrant, bought up huge tracts of land along Lake Champlain. He envisioned a string of prosperous communities, and by 1770, had established Essex. Unfortunately the town lay smack in the path of General Burgoyne as British troops marched from Canada to Saratoga and, just a decade after the settlers arrived, their town was destroyed.

By 1800, Essex was again thriving thanks to iron mining, stone quarrying, a tannery, shipbuilding, and other commerce. By 1850, the population of the town was 2,351, but when railroads came to eastern New York, in the 1870s, fortunes changed for Essex and other lakeside towns. That era was the peak of the town's prosperity.

Then the population dwindled steadily to its current level of about a thousand residents. Because of this decline, and the lack of economic opportunities, there was little need for new housing; old buildings were preserved out of necessity. Today Essex contains one of the most intact collections of pre-Civil War buildings in the Northeast. The Essex Community Heritage Organization has published an excellent booklet describing the dozens of fine homes, inns, and commercial buildings in town ($3), and a self-guided walk through town in summer or fall is a delightful way to spend a day.

PENFIELD HOMESTEAD MUSEUM
518-597-3804.
Old Furnace Rd., off Rte. 74, Ironville.
Season: Mid-May–Columbus Day, daily 9–4.
Fee: Nominal.
Handicap Access: Partial.

A sign in the front yard of the homestead makes an astonishing claim: the site is the birthplace of the Electrical Age. In 1831 Allen Penfield used a crude electromagnet to separate iron ore from its base rock, thus testing electricity in an industrial application for the first time.

Ironville today is a lovely, quiet spot so different from its heyday as the center of a major iron industry during 1830–80, when smoke from the smelters filled the skies and the clatter of rock crushers ceased only after dark. The complex is an open-air museum dedicated to the local mines, forges, and old railroads, with an eclectic historical collection in the homestead itself, a white-clapboard Federal building circa 1826. The other buildings along the lane in town are mainly Greek Revival, in excellent condition; there's a self-guided walking tour of the 550-acre grounds that takes you for a nice hike in the woods to find remnants of the days of iron. In mid-August, Heritage Day is a festival of traditional crafts and skills, with wagon rides and a chicken barbecue, and there's a harvest festival in the fall.

HIGH PEAKS

HISTORIC SARANAC LAKE
518-891-0971.
132 River St., North Elba Town Hall, Saranac Lake.
Season: Year-round.

The health care history of Saranac Lake is unique, and in 1980, Historic Saranac Lake was founded to commemorate the special architecture that evolved to help tuberculosis patients get more fresh air and sunlight. Numerous cure cottages and sanatorium-related buildings have now been recognized on the National Register of Historic Places. The group has published a walking tour of selected structures, presents lectures and conferences, and is a key player in restoring the village's railroad station, which may once again see passenger service in 2000 when the tracks between Saranac and Lake Placid are repaired.

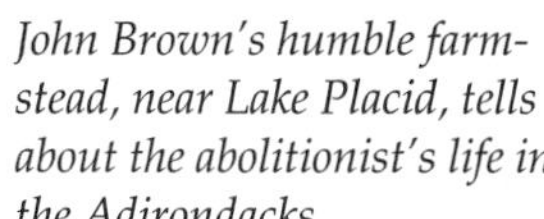

John Brown's humble farmstead, near Lake Placid, tells about the abolitionist's life in the Adirondacks.

James Swedberg

JOHN BROWN FARM
518-523-3900.
John Brown Rd., off Old Military Rd., Lake Placid.
Season: Mid-May–Oct. (exc. Mon. & Tues.) 10–5.
Handicap Access: Yes.

In 1849, abolitionist John Brown came to North Elba, near Lake Placid, to help Gerrit Smith launch a self-sufficient enclave for free blacks. Smith owned more than 100,000 acres across northern New York, and his plan was to give 40 acres to each would-be black homesteader. The idea may have been doomed from the start since the families — many of them from northern cities — were not prepared to farm in the harsh climate or work the rugged, unprepared ground. Most of the residents of "Timbuctoo," as it became known, left within a few years of their arrival. Brown himself lived only a few years at the farm, leaving his family for months at a time in order to pursue a failing wool business and antislavery concerns. After his final adventure in Harper's Ferry, Brown was executed on December 2, 1859, in Charlestown, Virginia.

In 1870 the property was acquired by a group of the abolitionist's admirers. Today the farmhouse and outbuildings, managed by New York as a state historic site, contain exhibits related to John Brown's life, and his "body lies a-mouldering in the grave" nearby. Civil War re-enactors occasionally camp at the farm, and John Brown's birthday, May 1, brings a major gathering of New Abolitionists to the site. For an Internet sketch of John Brown's life, go to www.lakeplacid.com/lphs/jbf.

ROBERT LOUIS STEVENSON MEMORIAL COTTAGE
518-891-4480.
11 Stevenson Ln., Saranac Lake.

In 1887–88, Robert Louis Stevenson took the "cure" for tuberculosis in Saranac Lake, sleeping in an unheated porch all winter, and taking in plenty of fresh air while hiking and skating. During his Adirondack stint, Stevenson wrote a

Season: July 1–Sept. 15 (exc. Mon.) 10–4.
Fee: Nominal.

dozen essays for *Scribners*, started *The Master of Ballantrae*, and worked on *The Wrong Box*, a collaborative effort with Lloyd Osbourne. In a letter to Henry James, the Scotsman described his tiny cottage: "Our house . . . is on a hill, and has sight of a stream turning a corner in the valley — bless the face of running water! — and sees some hills too, and the paganly prosaic roofs of Saranac itself; the Lake it does not see, nor do I regret that; I like water (fresh water, I mean) either running swiftly among stones, or else largely qualified with whiskey."

The Stevenson Society was founded in 1916 to commemorate the writer's life and works; one of the group's original projects was to interest Gutzon Borglum, the sculptor best known for creating Mt. Rushmore, in designing a bronze bas-relief depicting Stevenson — now next to the front door. The society still manages the cottage, which has displays of Stevenson letters, photographs, memorabilia, and first editions, and sponsors readings and lectures.

NORTHWEST LAKES

BETH JOSEPH SYNAGOGUE
518-359-7229.
Lake St., Tupper Lake.
Season: July–Aug.

Built in 1905, Tupper Lake's temple is a elegant structure made of simple pine boards and tall arched windows. Beth Joseph once served an active congregation, but after the 1930s, attendance declined. Scout troops met in the basement, and for a time, a group of Baptists even worshipped there as they didn't have a church of their own. In 1959, the synagogue closed, and stood vacant for 25 years.

Community interest in the historic building was rekindled by a summer resident, who encouraged former temple members to get the structure listed on the National Register of Historic Places and begin restoration work. Local people of all religions pitched in with donated labor, materials, and funds; the ornate embroidered velvet Torah covers were painstakingly restored by a local weaver. In 1991, work was completed, and now the facility hosts art exhibitions, concerts, Adirondack Discovery lectures, and other events.

CENTRAL ADIRONDACKS

SAGAMORE GREAT CAMP
315-354-5311.
www.sagamore.org.
Sagamore Rd., off Rte. 28, Raquette Lake.
Season: July 4–fall.
Tours: Call for schedule.
Fee: $6; $3 children.

Adirondack entrepreneur William West Durant built Sagamore, a massive rustic lodge, along the lines of a Swiss chalet, in 1897, and sold it to Alfred G. Vanderbilt, Sr., in 1901. Even though the Vanderbilts spent much of their time elsewhere, Sagamore was a self-sufficient village in the heart of the wilderness, with its own farm and a crew of

James Swedberg

Great Camp Sagamore, built by William West Durant, is open for conferences and tours May–October.

craftsmen to supply furniture, hardware, and boats. Today, the millionaires' complex — main lodge, dining hall, rustic guest cottages, casino playhouse, open-air bowling alley, and boathouse — and the artisans' barns, carriage house, workshops, and blacksmith shop are open to the public. Two-hour tours are presented by college interns; a highlight is sending a vintage ball down the lane toward the pins in order to demonstrate the loop-de-loop ball return.

Sagamore is in a gorgeous setting on the shore of Sagamore Lake, four miles off the main road on a rough dirt road. Beside tours for the public, the Great Camp sponsors workshops and conferences, is available for overnight accommodations, has a small gift shop and cafe, and can be hired for special events like wedding receptions and family reunions.

LECTURE SERIES

An Adirondack education is possible through numerous public lectures at libraries, museums, town halls and other sites. The **Atmospheric Science Research Center** (518-946-2142) on ***Whiteface Mtn.*** presents natural history and environmental science lectures on Tuesdays in July and August. At the **Visitor Interpretive Centers** in ***Paul Smiths*** (518-327-3000) and ***Newcomb*** (518-582-2000) there are nature, history, and arts presentations year-round. The **Huntington Lecture Series**, presented in July and August by the Adirondack Ecological Center (a major research facility associated with the State University of New York's College of Environmental Science and Forestry), at the Newcomb visitor center, is an excellent assortment of programs on current environmental topics, as well as fishing, landscape photography, and natural history.

Since 1978, **Adirondack Discovery,** based in ***Inlet*** (315-357-3598; mail: Box 545, Inlet NY 13360), has become a sort of mobile Chatauqua, offering guided canoe trips and hikes to historic sites and along old railroad routes, evening lectures ranging from aerial photography tips to old postcard collections, hands-on workshops by local craftspeople, and folk music performances in Inlet, Indian Lake, Raquette Lake, Speculator, Old Forge, Minerva, Silver Bay, North Creek, Ticonderoga, and Saranac Lake. In 1999, for example, Adirondack Discovery presented more than 110 different programs from July through September.

LIBRARIES

There are 30-some public libraries inside the Adirondack Park, and visitors are always welcome, rain or shine. In this wired age, what used to be hallowed halls for books and reading have evolved into key places for visitors and residents to check their e-mail, surf the Internet, and catch up with the cyberworld; many libraries offer free or very inexpensive on-line time.

Several libraries are known for their special collections of books of regional interest, classic and children's videos, and even mini-museums. Most libraries offer children's programs, readings by regional writers, films, travel lectures, how-to sessions, concerts and even good used books for sale; pick up a schedule locally for details. A brief sampling of libraries with noteworthy collections, exemplary programs, or fine buildings follows.

LAKE GEORGE AND SOUTHEASTERN ADIRONDACKS

Caldwell Lake George Library (518-668-2528; 340 Canada St., Lake George) Films, lectures, workshops. Catch a performance by Shirley McPherson, the librarian, if you can — she's an expert on local ghost stories, known as "Sweet Mama Stringbean."

Horicon Free Library (No phone; Rte. 8, Brant Lake) Tiny, picturesque cobblestone building perched over the lake.

CHAMPLAIN VALLEY

Black Watch Library (518-585-7380; Montcalm St., Ticonderoga) Designed as a medieval-looking "shrine to literacy" in 1905, and named after the 42nd Highland Regiment, which fought at Ticonderoga in 1758.

Paine Memorial Free Library (518-963-4478; 1 School St., Willsboro) Lovely brick building overlooking the Boquet River. The Paine Jordan bird-skin collection is here for ornithologists to study; there's also a good local history selection. Numerous summer programs, from art exhibitions to traditional craft demonstrations.

Westport Library Association (518-962-8219; Washington St., Westport) Look for the clock tower. Great old building with fireplaces, antique woodwork, natural lighting, high ceilings, comfy couches, and several computers for Internet access. Lecture series and occasional concerts on the library lawn.

HIGH PEAKS

Keene Valley Library (518-576-4335; Main St., Keene Valley) Excellent local history and mountaineering collection with monographs, maps, photographs, and rare books. Lectures, readings, special exhibitions on local history.

Lake Placid Library (518-523-3200; 67 Main St., Lake Placid) Story hours for children; good general collection.

Saranac Lake Free Library (518-891-4190; 100 Main St., Saranac Lake) Extensive Adirondack collection in the William Chapman White Room, open by appointment. Brown-bag luncheon lecture series, evening lectures; gallery featuring local artists; Charles Dickert Wildlife Museum open in July and August.

NORTHWEST LAKES

Cubley Library (518-327-6313; Paul Smith's College, Paul Smiths) College reference library, with fall and winter concert series open to the public.

Goff Nelson Memorial Library (518-359-9421; 41 Lake St., Tupper Lake) Good Adirondack collection available to readers whenever the library is open; crafts and local history exhibits; lectures.

CENTRAL ADIRONDACKS

Indian Lake Public Library (518-648-5444; Pelon Rd., Indian Lake) New facility. General collection, with lectures and special programs year-round.

Johnsburg Library (518-251-4343; Main St., North Creek) New town library with general collection and computer stations.

Old Forge Library (315-369-6008; Crosby Blvd., Old Forge) Adirondack collection, lecture series, writers' workshops, children's programs, performances by Adirondack storytellers.

Raquette Lake Library (315-354-4005; Dillon Rd., Raquette Lake) Charming turn-of-the-century building with window seats and fireplace; lectures and special programs.

MUSEUMS

Children's programs — with plenty of hands-on activity — are scheduled year-round at the Adirondack Museum.

Courtesy of Adirondack Museum

THE ADIRONDACK MUSEUM
518-352-7311.
www.adkmuseum.org.
Rtes. 28 & 30, Blue Mtn. Lake.
Season: May 23–Oct. 15, daily 9:30–5:30. Call ahead for 2000 season information!
Fee: $10 adults; discounts for children, seniors, groups.
Handicap Access: Yes.
Book and gift shop; snack bar.

If your last trip to the Adirondack Museum was on a rainy day ten years ago, it's high time you went back. Major construction — scheduled to be completed by summer 2000 — will add new introductory exhibits, a new shop with a great selection of books and gifts, and new classrooms for the education program.

Simply put, no visit to the Adirondacks is complete without seeing the Adirondack Museum. Perched on the side of Blue Mtn., and overlooking the island-studded lake, is a major outdoor museum that is user-friendly, scholarly, beautiful, amusing, and superlative in every way. Not surprisingly, the place has been described by the *New York Times* as "the best museum of its kind in the world."

The museum's theme is interpreting man's relationship to the Adirondacks, and it does so in 20-plus exhibit buildings. Adjacent to the entrance is a theater showing "The Adirondacks: The Lives and Times of an American Wilderness," an award-winning film. In the galleries of the main building, there are changing exhibits of paintings; in 1999–2000 the centerpiece show is Rockwell Kent landscapes, including Adirondack scenes on loan from Armenia.

There are scores of wooden boats, including fine Adirondack guideboats and a Gold Cup racer; there are dozens of carriages, sleighs, and wagons. You can glide through August Belmont's private railroad car and imagine yourself en route to your very own Great Camp, or you can picture the other extreme of Adirondack life, in buildings devoted to logging and mining. In "Woods and Waters: Outdoor Recreation in the Adirondacks," you'll find hunting and fishing paraphernalia. On Merwin Hill, Bull Cottage — a nice example of everyday rustic architecture — showcases rooms of rustic furniture.

The museum is a great place for children who can read and understand historical ideas; there are audio- and videotape stations that add depth to the displays. One suggestion, though: parents should keep a close eye on young ones who may be tempted to touch fragile artifacts. The Marion River Carry locomotive, in the center of the campus, is a good place to let active kids be themselves.

The museum comes alive with craft demonstrations, music, and storytelling on selected days. The Rustic Furniture Makers' Fair, in September, showcases 40 or so builders so that visitors can decide how to begin their own Adirondack collections.

It's probably a natural response to plan a visit to the Adirondack Museum on a rainy day, but thousands of other folks think along the same lines, and the place can get crowded. Far better to pick a gorgeous day when you can savor the view and the many outdoor displays, and see the exhibits without having to jockey for position.

ADIRONDACK HISTORY CENTER
518-873-6466.
Court St./Rte. 9, Elizabethtown.
Season: Mid-May–mid-Oct.; Mon.–Sat. 9–5, Sun. 1–5.
Fee: $3; $2 seniors, $1 children 6–16.
Handicap Access: Yes.

If all the military skirmishes along Lake Champlain have blurred into one confusing cloud of cannon smoke, the Essex County Historical Society's museum has a nifty sound-and-light show that puts the battles into a geographical and chronological context. That's not the only reason to visit: the Adirondack History Center interprets local pioneer life — mining, farming, trapping, logging — through its permanent exhibits, and showcases contemporary local artists during the summer.

There's a stagecoach that once carried passengers from Elizabethtown to Keene, a fire tower that you don't have to climb a mountain to enjoy, a roomful of dolls, and the wonderful Colonial Garden of perennials and herbs. For Adirondack and genealogical scholars, there's an excellent library open by appointment year-round.

Canoe-camping, 1890s: sailing canoe with canvas tent hung from its spars, at the Adirondack Museum.

Courtesy of Adirondack Museum

Vintage Watercraft

In 1843 John Todd visited the lonely settlers in Long Lake and wrote, "Their little boats were their horses, and the lake their only path." Traditional wooden boats, especially the guideboat, performed a major role in 19th-century work and play. At several gatherings across the park, you can get a taste of this era, and enjoy beautifully restored guideboats, canoes, sailboats, and classic powerboats.

The **No-Octane Regatta** (518-352-7311) held in ***Blue Mtn. Lake*** in June attracts a glorious array of muscle- and wind-powered watercraft. There are builders' displays at the Adirondack Lakes Center for the Arts and lectures and toy-boat races at the Adirondack Museum, but the main attraction is on the waterfront, off Rte. 28, where boats are displayed. There are old-fashioned contests, including canoe jousting, where standing contestants try to knock each other out of canoes with long, padded poles, and the hurry-scurry race, where participants' boats are anchored out in the lake: the competitors run from the beach, swim to the boats, clamber in, then paddle or row to the finish line. You won't believe your eyes when you see a war canoe — propelled by eight or ten paddlers, including the author — pull a water skier off the town beach.

The **Maritime Festival** in *Essex* (518-963-7504) features antique boats on Lake Champlain, plus races, a parade, music, and house tours, in July.

The **Wooden Canoe Heritage Association Assembly** (no phone; Box 226, Blue Mtn. Lake) is a four-day canoe confabulation held at Paul Smith's

College, in ***Paul Smiths***, in late July. There are demonstrations and workshops by boatbuilders, lectures on historic voyages and techniques, and opportunities for the public to paddle and sail traditional canoes.

The **Adirondack Chapter of the Antique and Classic Boat Society** (315-369-3552) holds its annual show and rendezvous on the ***Fulton Chain of Lakes*** in July; visitors can get a good look at all that mahogany and brass when the boats are at the public docks, or watch the parade through the lakes in the afternoon. Woody cars are also displayed near the Old Forge beach.

Late summer and early fall bring **Boats and Autos of Yesterday** and **A Northern Exposure** to ***Bolton Landing***, sponsored by the fledgling Lake George Antique Boat and Auto Museum (518-644-2127). The website www.hagueticonderoga.com has news about these events.

In ***Cleverdale***, on the eastern side of Lake George, Castaway Marina hosts its annual **Antique and Classic Boat Show** (518-585-6472) in late August. This is another place to see gleaming old Fay & Bowens, Chris-Crafts, HackerCrafts, and Garwoods.

At Willsboro's 1812 Homestead, sheep, pigs, chickens, and oxen live in a pioneer setting.

James Swedberg

1812 HOMESTEAD
518-963-4071.
Rte. 22, Willsboro.
Season: July–Oct. 15, daily 1–4:30.
Fee: Nominal.

History comes alive at this early farm complex, with an original homestead, barn, and schoolhouse. Families can try making candles, cooking in an open hearth, or gathering eggs, and can meet the farm's resident oxen, sheep, and pigs. Demonstrations include blacksmithing, spinning, shingle-making, quilting, and other old-time skills. In season, the farm makes apple cider and maple sugar; call ahead to learn about special events. Recommended for kids ages six to twelve.

FORT TICONDEROGA
518-585-2821.
www.fort-ticonderoga.org.
Fort Rd., off Rte. 22, Ticonderoga.
Season: Mid-May–mid-Oct., daily 9–5.
Fee: $6; children 10–13 $5; under 10 free.
Handicap Access: Yes.
Museum shop; snack bar; picnic grove.

High above Lake Champlain is a must-see for Adirondack visitors: Fort Ticonderoga. In 1755, the French built a fort, *Carillon*, on the site, and for the next quarter century, the stone fortification was a key location in the struggle to claim North America. The Marquis de Montcalm defended the site against numerous British invaders until 1758, when Lord Jeffery Amherst captured the fort. Ticonderoga was British territory until Ethan Allen and the Green Mountain Boys took the fort "in the name of Jehovah and the great Continental Congress," during the American Revolution.

In the early 1800s, the Pell family acquired the ruins and fields where the soldiers once camped. Work was begun in 1908 to rebuild the barracks and parade grounds, making Fort Ticonderoga the nation's first restored historic site (in contrast, Colonial Williamsburg's restoration dates back to the 1930s).

Inside the barracks are exhibits on the French and Indian War and the American Revolution, from intricately inscribed powderhorns to blunderbusses, cannons, and swords. The grim side of winter warfare is clear (some youngsters love the gory stuff), and there's little glorification of the ordeal of battle. Below the barracks is the subterranean kitchen, which once supplied thousands of loaves of bread every day to the standing army. Beneath the walls, on a broad plain facing the lake, is the King's Garden, a beautiful spot that's been cultivated for hundreds of years and is open for tours. The walled English-style garden dates back to the 1920s and is one of a handful of American places recognized by the Garden Conservancy.

There's plenty of action at the fort in the summer, from demonstrations of black-powder shooting and cannon firing to fife-and-drum drills; many of the demonstrators are local teenagers who are happy to explain what they're up to. On some weekends, there are encampments of regiments reenacting battles, or bagpipe-band concerts. And, every day in July and August (additional fee), there's also a boat tour on the *Carillon*, which goes from Fort Ticonderoga to Crown Point and back.

The fort is set in a spectacular spot with a magnificent view of the lake, but don't end your visit there. It's worth a side trip up Mt. Defiance, near town, to get an even higher perspective. From the top of that hill, a show of British cannons so intimidated the officers at Ticonderoga and Mt. Independence, a fort across the lake in Vermont, that colonial troops fled both strongholds. (Shots were never fired.) Bring a pair of binoculars and a picnic lunch.

SIX NATIONS INDIAN MUSEUM
518-891-0769.

Native people did travel to the Adirondacks for spring fishing, summer gathering, and fall hunting: the mountains, forests, and lakes offered

Buck Pond Campsite Rd., Onchiota.
Season: July 1–Labor Day, Tues.–Sun. 10am–6pm; May–June, Sept.–Oct. by appointment.
Fee: $2; $1 children.

abundant resources. At many local institutions this information is overshadowed by all the other stories those museums have to tell, but at Six Nations, the kaleidoscopic collection of baskets, beadwork, quill work, tools, weapons, paintings, drums, cradle boards, hats, pottery, and clothing all celebrate the Iroquois tribes' lives and times. Artifacts fill cases, line the walls, hang from the ceilings; take the time to look closely and you'll be rewarded.

In 1999 museum founder Ray Fadden died, but his family intends to carry on his work. A call ahead is advised before you make the trip.

LAKE GEORGE AND SOUTHEAST ADIRONDACKS

In Warren County you'll find numerous small museums to visit. The **Bolton Historical Museum** in ***Bolton Landing*** (518-644-9960; Rte. 9N) is housed in a former Catholic church. Nineteenth-century photos of Lake George hotels by Seneca Ray Stoddard give a taste of the Gilded Age; more contemporary photos show sculptor David Smith at work in his Bolton Landing studio. There's an assortment of furniture, clothing, agricultural implements, and items relating to the town's days as a summer retreat for musical superstars.

In ***Brant Lake***, the **Horicon Museum** (518-494-7286; Rte. 8) is a well-kept nine-room farmhouse full of antiques, agricultural implements, prints, photos, toys, and dolls open from Memorial Day through Labor Day. The **Frances Kinnear Museum**, open year-round in a historic ***Lake Luzerne*** home (518-696-4520; 2144 Main St.), is similarly chock-full of local memorabilia; the town is also home to two summer museums: the **Mill Museum**, set in a park near the lake (no phone; Mill St.), and the **Schoolhouse Museum** (518-696-3500; Main St., near the Norstar Bank). In ***Chestertown***, local history comes alive from July to Aug. at the **Town of Chester Museum of Local History** (518-494-3758; Town Hall, Main St.), with neat displays on village life. Ask about photographer "Its" Sumy, a Japanese bachelor who took endearing pictures of people and events from the late 1930s to the 1960s.

In ***Lake George***, in the old courthouse, the **Lake George Historical Museum** (518-668-5044; Canada St.) is three floors of exhibits, from the 1845-vintage jail cells in the basement to "the church that cheated the hangman." The detailed folk-art model was carved in 1881 by a convicted murderer. He sold it, hired a new lawyer, appealed his conviction, and was acquitted. Also in Lake George is **Fort William Henry** (518-668-5471; www.adirondack.net/history; Canada St.), a restored log fortress dedicated to French and Indian War history, with life-size dioramas, assorted armaments, and lots of action: military drills, musket and cannon firing, fife and drum bands. The fort is open daily spring–fall, and you can even get college credit at the annual archaeology field school.

In ***Schroon Lake***, the **Schroon–North Hudson Historical Society** (518-532-7798; Olden Dr.) is open Thurs.–Sun. in July and Aug.; there's also the 1840

Stowell Homestead (518-532-7456; Stowell Rd.), a private house museum open Thursday–Saturday in summer. In ***Warrensburg***, the **Warrensburg Museum of Local History** (518-623-9826; 47 Main St.) highlights the town's early industries, from garment factories to sawmills.

CHAMPLAIN VALLEY

Hague, home port of the Lake George monster, is also home to Stan Burdick's **Cartoon Museum** (518-543-8824; www.hagueticonderoga.com; Main St.), which is packed with old political cartoons, comic book characters, and animation art. It's open Saturdays, Sundays, and Thursday evenings, and offers occasional workshops for adults and children.

James Swedberg

Hancock House, now the Ticonderoga Historical Society, is a replica of John Hancock's Boston home.

Nearby ***Ticonderoga*** has two local-history museums right in town: the **Heritage Museum** (518-585-6366; Bicentennial Park), and the **Historical Society** (518-585-7868; Hancock House), located in a replica of John Hancock's Boston home. The Heritage Museum depicts local 19th-century industries including paper- and pencil-making, in a Victorian office building that's open daily in July and Aug. and on fall weekends. Hancock House was the first home of the New York State Historical Association (which is now based in Cooperstown), and the house has several period rooms illustrating social history from the 1700s to the turn of the century, including some fine antiques. There's an extensive research library open by appointment year-round. Pick up the brochure "Marker and Monument Tour Guide" when you're in Ticonderoga for connect-the-dots historical trivia, and you'll learn about such figures as the Jesuit martyr Isaac Jogues (died by torture), Lord George Howe (died by musket ball), and Horace Moses, (died a millionaire).

In ***Essex***, just a minute's walk from the ferry landing, **Greystone Mansion** (518-963-8058; Rte. 22) is open daily (except Tuesdays) in July and August and weekends in May–June and the fall. The 1853 house is packed with the Empire-style antiques and decorative arts that a wealthy Essex family of the time would cherish, providing a real contrast to the rustic and Victorian embellishment usually associated with the Adirondacks.

HIGH PEAKS AND NORTHERN ADIRONDACKS

In ***Lake Placid***, the train station for the Adirondack Division of the New York Central is home to the **Lake Placid–North Elba Historical Society Museum** (518-523-1608; Averyville Rd.). There's a nostalgic country store display, sporting gear and memorabilia from the 1932 Olympics, and a music room honoring residents Victor Herbert and Kate Smith; the place is pretty lively in the summer with lectures and concerts. Open June–Sept., Tues.–Sun. afternoons.

In the Olympic Center is the **Lake Placid Winter Olympic Museum** (518-523-1655; www.orda.org), open daily year-round. Photographs, vintage films, equipment, trophies, clothing, and memorabilia illustrate the two sets of Olympic competitions that have come to town.

Tucked away in the basement of the ***Saranac Lake*** Free Library, the **Charles Dickert Memorial Wildlife Museum** (518-891-4190; 100 Main St.) is open some weekday mornings in July and Aug., with displays of hundreds of stuffed mammals, birds, and fish native to the Adirondacks.

NORTHWEST LAKES

Under development in ***Tupper Lake*** is the **Natural History Museum of the Adirondacks** (www.adknature.org; Box 897, Tupper Lake, NY 12986), envisioned as a huge, high-tech showcase for learning about flora, fauna, geology, and weather. No opening date has yet been set, but watch for programs in advance of the physical space.

CENTRAL ADIRONDACKS

Riley's Tavern in ***Piseco*** is home to the **Piseco Lake Historical Society** (518-548-6401; Piseco Lake Rd.), a local collection of antiques and ephemera open in the summer; in ***Edinburg***, the **Nellie Tyrell Edinburg Museum** (no phone; RD 1) is an old schoolhouse with displays showing life before the creation of the Great Sacandaga Reservoir. ***Northville*** is home to two museums right on South Main Street: the **Gifford Valley Schoolhouse**, behind the municipal offices, and the **Paul Bradt Museum**, which is filled with North American wildlife and housed inside the village office complex. The outdoor museum complex near ***Caroga Lake***, the **Caroga Historical Museum** (518-835-6335; London Bridge Rd.) recreates pioneer life in the southern Adirondacks in a farmstead, schoolhouse, and country store, and hosts changing exhibits.

In ***Olmstedville***, the **Minerva Historical Society** (518-251-2229; Main St.) is open July and Aug.; its displays honor artists who visited the area, such as Winslow Homer. In ***Old Forge***, the **Town of Webb Historical Association** (315-369-3838; Main St.) has exhibits on railroads, resorts, rustic furniture, and early industries; the museum is open year-round. Just east of Old Forge is the **Forest Industries Exhibit Hall** (315-369-3078; Rte. 28), with displays on forest management, logging history, and dioramas, open Memorial Day–Labor Day.

BEYOND THE BLUE LINE

In ***Glens Falls***, the **Hyde Collection** (518-792-1761; 161 Warren St.) contains an exceptional private art collection including works by da Vinci, Botticelli, El Greco, Rembrandt, Rubens, Degas, Renoir, Cezanne, and Picasso, along with famous American artists, and 16th- through 19th-century antique furnishings, all in a handsomely restored villa. There's a new wing with changing exhibits, and many participatory programs. Also in Glens Falls, the **Chapman Historical Museum** (518-793-2826; 348 Glen St.) is a historic house with a modern gallery highlighting photographs by Seneca Ray Stoddard and interesting exhibits on regional social history.

Southeast of the Adirondacks, in ***Granville***, the **Pember Museum of Natural History** (518-642-1515; 33 W. Main St.) is a wonderfully preserved Victorian gentleman's collection of hundreds of birds, butterflies, and trophy heads in polished wood cases. Also located in Granville, the **Slate Valley Museum** (518-642-1717; www.slatevalleymuseum.org; 17 Water St.) opened in fall 1995; it depicts the social history and folk art of the area's quarries. In ***Saratoga Springs***, next door to Lincoln Baths, a public spa, is the **National Museum of Dance** (518-584-2225; Rte. 9). Open from Memorial Day through the fall, the museum's collection includes costumes, films, and sets, hundreds of photographs, and special exhibitions highlighting international dance history.

North of the park, in ***Chazy***, is another private museum, the **Alice T. Miner Colonial Collection** (518-846-7336; Main St.), in a three-story mansion with a fine textile collection, china and glass, rare books, colonial furniture, and strange curiosities from around the world. In ***Plattsburgh***, the **Kent-DeLord House Museum** (518-561-1035; 17 Cumberland Ave.) is a nicely restored late 18th-century home. Near ***Malone*** is the **Farmer Boy's Home** (518-483-1207; Stacy Rd., Burke), the setting for *Farmer Boy*, by Laura Ingalls Wilder. The farmstead, which is gradually being restored, was the home of Almanzo Wilder in the mid-19th century.

South of the park, in ***Johnstown***, but pertinent to Adirondack studies is **Johnson Hall State Historic Site** (518-762-8712; Hall Ave.). The restored 1763 Georgian mansion was the home of Sir William Johnson, who served as superintendent of Indian affairs for the northern colonies; the Adirondack fur trade was a mainstay of his wealth. The Colonial Market Fair is a popular event, and the site hosts reenacted encampments of frontiersmen, Canadian fur traders, and native people.

The guidebook *Adirondack Odysseys* (Adirondack Museum and Berkshire House Publishers, 1997) details a hundred historic sites from the Mohawk Valley to the St. Lawrence River, with entertaining capsule histories of the region and information useful to traveling families.

MUSIC

African-American musicians entertain a group of canoeists, Lake George.

Seneca Ray Stoddard photograph, private collection

Traditional North Country music is represented by dance and fiddle tunes that have roots in French-Canadian and Irish music, and by ballads of the lumber woods, like "Blue Mountain Lake," "The Jam on Gerry's Rocks," "The Wild Mustard River," and "Once More A-Lumbering Go."

To hear authentic old-time instrumental music, look for the occasional fiddle jamborees or square dances, sponsored by arts groups and towns: the **Forest, Field, and Stream Festival** in September at the **Adirondack History Center** (518-873-6466) features traditional music and the **Adirondack Museum** (518-352-7311), in Blue Mtn. Lake, occasionally presents music within exhibit settings, like songs about lumbering performed in the logging buildings. The **Adirondack Fiddlers Association** meets once a month at the Schuylerville American Legion Hall (518-695-3011).

Nearly every town with a summer tourist draw presents outdoor or indoor musical programs. A few examples include: In the Champlain Valley, ***Port Henry's*** **Concerts in the Park**, featuring jazz, classical, and folk music, are held in the bandshell overlooking Lake Champlain. In *Essex*, the **Organ Concert Series** (518-963-7766) at the Essex Community United Methodist Church features some of the best organists in New York and Vermont, plus midday programs in summer featuring vocal and classical music. If you're traveling to the High Peaks, in *Keene*, the new **East Branch Friends of the Arts** (518-576-4769; Box 768, Keene) presents music and children's arts programs in sites around town. New in the Northwest Lakes is the **Tupper Lake Center for the Arts** (518-359-7986), presenting music and drama. In the central Adirondacks, *Long Lake* **Parks and Recreation** (518-624-3077) sponsors fiddlers' gatherings in spring and fall, plus occasional other concerts. To hear folk songs and ballads, jazz riffs and recitatives, check with music presenters listed below:

LAKE GEORGE AND SOUTHEASTERN ADIRONDACKS

LAKE GEORGE ARTS PROJECT
518-668-2616.
Canada St., Lake George.

During the second weekend in September, the Lake George Jazz Festival, in Shepard Park, is the place to be. The bands — often Latin or Afro-Caribbean stars — are topnotch, the vibe is cool, and the price is free. The arts project also sponsors music in the village park on summer nights, from reggae to new blues.

LUZERNE CHAMBER MUSIC FESTIVAL
518-696-2771.
Luzerne Music Center, Lake Tour Rd., 1.3 mi. off Rte. 9N, Lake Luzerne.
Season: July–Aug.
Tickets: $10.

Members of the Philadelphia Orchestra (who also perform at the Saratoga Performing Arts Center in July and Aug.) present a superb chamber-music concert series on Monday nights. Artistic directors of the center are Toby Blumenthal, piano, and Bert Phillips, cello, and they pride themselves on bringing internationally acclaimed soloists to join the resident ensembles. The music center is also a summer camp for gifted young musicians, and the free student/faculty recitals held Fridays, Saturdays, and Sundays are definitely worth a listen.

SCHROON LAKE ARTS COUNCIL
518-532-7675.
Boat House Theater, Schroon Lake.
Mail: Box 668, Schroon Lake NY 12870.
Season: July–Aug.
Tickets: $5; $3 children.

On the lakeshore, yet within walking distance of downtown Schroon Lake, the Boat House Theater is a fitting spot to hear traditional Adirondack music. The arts council presents evening concerts and dance performances in summer in the historic building, and a festival of folk music, storytelling, and rustic crafts each August. Featured regional folk artists have included Chris Shaw, Peggy Eyres, Dan Berggren, Roy Hurd, and storyteller Bill Smith.

SEAGLE COLONY
518-532-7875.
www.seaglecolony.com.
Charley Hill Rd., Schroon Lake.
Season: July–Aug.
Tickets: Prices vary.

Oscar Seagle, famed tenor and voice teacher, established this country retreat in 1915. Vocal music is still the primary program, with coaching and master classes in opera and musical theater for conservatory students and aspiring performers. Every Sunday evening in the summer, the nondenominational Vespers concerts feature exceptional choral singing; public concerts featuring scenes from opera and musical theater are held in July. In 1999 Johann Strauss's *Die Fledermaus* attracted sell-out crowds.

CHAMPLAIN VALLEY

MEADOWMOUNT SCHOOL OF MUSIC
518-873-2063.
www.meadowmount.com.
Lewis-Wadhams Rd., Lewis.
Mail: 1240 Barrister Rd. Ann Arbor MI 48105
Season: July–Aug.
Tickets: Prices vary.

A short list of Meadowmount's alumni gives a hint of the talent that has rusticated in the hills of the Boquet Valley: Yo-Yo Ma, Itzhak Perlman, Pinchas Zukerman, Michael Rabin, Lynn Harrell, Jaime Laredo. Distinguished faculty, visiting artists, and promising students give free concerts at the camp on Wednesdays, Fridays, and Sundays, while the annual scholarship-benefit concert features world-famous string players in a cozy, informal setting. Meadowmount is a rare treasure, and if you're visiting the eastern Adirondacks, the programs are certainly worth a half-hour drive. Events for 2000 include a concert commemorating cellist Gregor Piatigorsky, who lived in nearby New Russia in the 1940s.

TICONDEROGA FESTIVAL GUILD
518-585-6716.
Montcalm St., Ticonderoga.
Mail: Box 125, Ticonderoga NY 12883.
Season: July–Aug.
Tickets: Prices vary.

An enormous striped tent in the center of town is the festival guild's summer home; under the big top there are weekly performances of music, dance, and theater, with concerts on Tuesday nights, and "Arts Trek" kids' shows on Wednesday mornings. Guests in past seasons were have been Banjo Dan and the Midnight Plowboys, the Burns Sisters, kids' troubador Bill Shontz, magicians, puppets, and other participatory programs.

HIGH PEAKS AND NORTHERN ADIRONDACKS

ADIRONDACK FESTIVAL OF AMERICAN MUSIC
518-891-1057.
Various locations, Saranac Lake.

Since 1973, Gregg Smith, one of the country's leading choral directors, and the Grammy-award-winning Gregg Smith Singers have called Saranac Lake their summer home. Their gift to the

Mail: Box 562, Saranac Lake NY 12983.
Season: July.
Tickets: Prices vary.

community is music, music, music. The month-long festival includes workshops for music teachers, composers, and schoolkids, and there are dozens of choral, chamber, jazz, cabaret, and pops concerts sprinkled throughout Saranac Lake in churches, parks, and the town hall. Resident ensembles are the Adirondack Festival Chorus, the Adirondack Chamber Orchestra, among others; guest artists have included the Dave Brubeck Quintet.

HILL AND HOLLOW MUSIC
518-298-7633.
Church in the Hollow, Rte. 3, Saranac.
Mail: Weatherwatch Farm, 550 #37 Rd.
Saranac NY 12981.
Season: Year-round.
Tickets: $5 for adults.

Angela Brown and Kellum Smith bring fine chamber music to an off-the-beaten-path corner of the northeastern Adirondacks, offering six or more concerts a year in an old Methodist church that happens to have excellent acoustics. Past performers have included Japanese pianist Rieko Aizawa, the Canadian string quartet Quatuor Redpath, the baroque Four Nations Ensemble, and the Meliora Winds.

LAKE PLACID INSTITUTE FOR THE ARTS AND HUMANITIES
518-523-1312 or 800-226-0728.
www.lakeplacidinstitute.org.
Various locations, Lake Placid.
Mail: Box 988, Lake Placid NY 12946.
Season: Year-round.
Tickets: Prices vary.

Take a walk on a summer evening in downtown Lake Placid and you'll likely hear the sound of French horn, flute, or trumpet as jazz and classical musicians and composers practice new works. The Lake Placid Institute offers leading performers a place to learn and play, with concerts at the Olympic ski jumps, the North Elba Bandshell, and the Lake Placid Center for the Arts, all part of the International Music Seminars.

The Institute is far more than just music, however. There are residencies for cutting-edge playwrights (New Dramatists program), poetry and nonfiction events for children, ongoing workshops in ethics, and other events.

LAKE PLACID SINFONIETTA
518-523-2051.
Various locations, Lake Placid.
Mail: Box 1303, Lake Placid NY 12946.
Season: July–Aug.
Tickets: Prices vary.

In 1917, the Sinfonietta was established to be the house orchestra at the Lake Placid Club, playing for the guests at the exclusive resort. Now the 18-member chamber orchestra is a valued community resource, presenting free Wednesday night concerts in the band shell overlooking Mirror Lake in the center of town (7pm; bring a cushion), children's programs at the Lake Placid Center for the Arts, the Pops and Picnic at the Horseshoe Grounds on Old Military Rd., and the annual Train Station Concert at the Lake Placid–North Elba Historical Society in August. On Sunday nights, the Sinfonietta performs in the art center's theater with selected guest artists; the programs range from newly commissioned works by American composers to Mozart, Haydn, Bach, and Schubert. Vienna Night is a Strauss celebration usually held in early August; the gala features dinner, dancing, and music through the night.

LOON LAKE LIVE
518-891-0757.
Jewish Center, Loon Lake.
Mail: Sara Fierer, General Delivery, Vermontville NY 12989.
Season: July–Aug.
Tickets: Prices vary.

Launched in 1994, Loon Lake Live presents small classical ensembles in cozy spaces like the Saranac Lake United Methodist Church and Loon Lake's Jewish Center. Each concert is preceded by a workshop (suitable for children and adults) with the performers; programs are delightfully informal.

CENTRAL ADIRONDACKS

ADIRONDACK ENSEMBLE
518-251-5811.
Mail: Box 123, Johnsburg NY 12843.
Season: Year-round.
Tickets: Prices vary.

In 1995, violinist Michael Dabroskie and his wife, pianist Lisa Spilde, left Philadelphia for that hotbed of chamber music, downtown Wevertown. Entirely from scratch, they've created a popular music series in the Wevertown Methodist Church, where audience members come from miles around to hear duos, trios, and quartets playing everything from Mozart to Medelssohn to Miles Davis. The Adirondack Ensemble spends a fair amount of time on the road, performing in Keene Valley, Old Forge, and local schools all year. The ensemble began a small but excellent music camp in summer 1998 for teenagers; write to them for admission information.

BEYOND THE BLUE LINE

It's confusing, but the **Lake George Opera Festival** (518-793-3866; Box 2172, Glens Falls), isn't in Lake George. From its original home in a tin-roofed barn in Diamond Point, the summer opera festival has moved (to ***Glens Falls***, a few miles down the road), and matured to become one of the country's most prestigious series. Performances — always in English — are staged at the Queensbury High School Auditorium, and the organization is actively seeking a permanent home.

Saratoga Springs isn't too far beyond the Adirondack Park, and the **Saratoga Performing Arts Center** (518-587-3300; www.spac.org; Saratoga Springs) is a wonderful outdoor setting for the New York City Opera, the Philadelphia Orchestra, the Newport Jazz Festival-Saratoga, and the new Saratoga Chamber Music Festival. From mid-June through Labor Day, SPAC is busy practically every night.

Washington County, east of Lake George and just this side of the Vermont border, is home to two fine chamber groups in ***Cambridge***: **Music from Salem** (518-677-2495; Hubbard Hall, Cambridge NY 12816), with the Lydian String Quartet in residence, and **L'Ensemble** (518-677-5455; Content Farm Rd., Cambridge).

NATURE CENTERS

Mark Kurtz

Trails at the Adirondack Park Visitor Interpretive Center, Paul Smiths, are open year-round for skiing, snowshoeing, and hiking.

The Adirondack Park has two excellent state-funded facilities that explain the region's natural history through permanent exhibits, public programs, workshops for children and adults, and extensive trails for hiking, snowshoeing, and cross-country skiing. In the lobbies, interactive computer stations allow visitors to get detailed information about specific towns, great canoeing and hiking destinations, and services for tourists. Works by regional artists are featured in rotating exhibitions. The **Visitor Interpretive Center** in ***Paul Smiths*** (518-327-3000) has a wonderful butterfly house with flowers, plants, and indigenous insects, and also sponsors a wildflower festival in July. The VIC in ***Newcomb*** (518-582-2000) is home to the Huntington Lecture Series, with talks by ecological experts; you can also try snowshoeing for free on their trails through old-growth forest. Both centers are active year-round and can be previewed on their website, www.northnet.org/adirondackvic.

Up Yonda Farm (518-644-9767; Rte. 9N, Bolton Landing) is a lovely lake-view property that opened in 1997 as an environmental education center. The site, operated by Warren County, is busiest during warm weather, with guided trail walks, after-dark tours, and programs on birds, bats, butterflies, and other beasts.

NIGHTLIFE

Compared to a half century ago, when Duke Ellington's and Count Basie's bands played in local hotels, nightlife here in the new millennium is pretty sedate. For live music, check out the offerings at arts centers listed above, and more than a dozen free concerts on Thursday and Friday nights in ***Saranac Lake*** sponsored by the **Saranac Lake Chamber of Commerce** (518-891-1990). Most of the tour boats described in Chapter 6, *Recreation*, schedule moonlight cruises with live music.

Stony Creek Inn (518-696-2394), across from Floyd's Mall in ***Stony Creek***, has rock, country, and blues every weekend from spring through fall. In ***Lake George***, **John Barleycorn's Pub** (518-668-9348; Canada St.) books good local bands for dancing into the wee hours. **Kindred Spirits** in ***Olmstedville*** (518-251-5131; at the Four Corners) is an outfitter's shop that presents Adirondack singers and songwriters in summer and fall in a coffeehouse setting. **Waterhole #3** in ***Saranac Lake*** (518-891-9502/6215, Main St.) is the liveliest source for music in the High Peaks, presenting big names like Leon Russell and local rockers on Fridays and Saturdays.

SEASONAL EVENTS

Throughout the Adirondack Park, special occasions celebrate local traditions and old-time North Country culture. The events listed below *(in chronological order by region)* emphasize history, music, storytelling, crafts and skills, or a combination of the arts. You'll also find annual athletic contests, such as the White Water Derby and the Whiteface Mtn. Uphill Footrace listed in Chapter Six, *Recreation;* craft fairs and antique shows are noted in Chapter Seven, *Shopping*, while affairs with a gustatory focus, like the Newcomb Steak Roast, are outlined in Chapter Five, *Restaurants and Food Purveyors*.

LAKE GEORGE AND SOUTHEASTERN ADIRONDACKS

Lake George Winter Carnival spans several weekends beginning in February, with kid-oriented activities, fireworks, races, and contests (518-668-2233).

Hague Winter Carnival is slated for the second full weekend in February, starting off with a torch-light parade on Friday evening. Daytime action includes the National Ice Auger and Chisel Contest, which involves boring through frozen Lake George, and plenty of other competitions for adults and children, from broom hockey to ice fishing and cross-country skiing (518-543-6161).

Americade is reportedly the world's largest motorcycle-touring rally. Held in and around Lake George in early June, there are guided rides on Adirondack back roads, seminars, swap meets, and banquets. Bikes range from tasteful special-edition Harleys worth tens of thousands of dollars, to rusty "rat bikes" that look like found-object sculptures. The participants aren't scary; they're just ordinary folks who love motorcycles (518-656-9367).

Hoaxfest celebrates Georgie, the Lake George Monster, in July (518-543-6353).

Summerfest features music, arts and crafts, and games for kids in Shepard Park in Lake George, on the last weekend in June (518-668-5755).

Stony Creek Mountain Days highlight Adirondack skills and pastimes in lumberjack contests, craft demonstrations, square dancing, and wagon rides, followed by fireworks, held the first weekend in August (518-696-2332).

Adirondack Folk Music Festival is an all-day affair in Schroon Lake that also includes rustic furniture and crafts, in mid-August (518-532-9259).

Warren County Country Fair is a family-oriented fair, with the usual 4-H and agricultural exhibits, a horse show, historical displays, traditional music, a pony pull, carnival rides, and fish-and-wildlife exhibits, held in mid-August at the fairground on Horicon Ave. outside Warrensburg (518-623-3291).

Barbershop Quartet and Chorus Festival in Bolton Landing features singers from around the country, on Labor Day Weekend (518-644-3831).

CHAMPLAIN VALLEY

Grand Encampment of the French and Indian War at Fort Ticonderoga features hundreds of make-believe French, Scottish, and colonial troops, Native American scouts, and camp followers in authentic costumes, in late June (518-585-2821).

Essex Maritime Festival highlights the town's lakefront heritage through an antique boat show, music performances, parades, rowing races, and other events, in Essex, in mid-July (518-963-7501).

Celebrate the Lake highlights the environment and heritage of Lake Champlain for two weeks in July, in both Vermont and New York. Guided hikes, lectures, and programs for children are sponsored by the Lake Champlain Basin Program. (800-468-5227).

Old-Time Folkcraft Fair, on the lawn of the Paine Memorial Library in Willsboro, is a showcase for local artisans and a chance to learn traditional North Country skills in late July (518-963-4478).

Essex County Fair, in Westport, features harness racing, livestock and agricultural displays, a midway, educational programs by Cooperative Extension, and lots of cotton candy. The fair runs for five days in mid-August (518-962-4810).

Forest, Field and Stream Festival, at the Adirondack History Center in Elizabethtown, happens during the height of fall color, in September, with a full slate of storytelling, old-time music, craft demonstrations, black-powder shooting, and participatory programs for children (518-873-6466).

Apple Folkfest at the Penfield Museum, Ironville, features traditional crafts, music, animals, and activities for children, in early October (518-597-3804).

Haunted Fort at Fort Ticonderoga, in late October, turns the historic site into a gallery of ghoulish mysteries (518-585-2821).

HIGH PEAKS

Mark Kurtz

Every year, a new ice palace is the centerpiece of Saranac Lake's winter carnival.

Saranac Lake Winter Carnival, in February, is reputedly the oldest winter carnival in the country. On the shore of Lake Flower, there's an awesome ice palace, dramatically lit by colored spotlights each evening; events include ski races, a parade, concerts, and special activities for kids (518-891-1990).

Round the Mountain Festival in Saranac Lake is a spring celebration with an afternoon of bluegrass bands, a barbecue, and a canoe race, all on the second Saturday in May (518-891-1990).

Native American Festival at Whiteface Mtn., in Wilmington, celebrates music, dance, crafts, and skills of Northeastern tribes, on the first weekend of August (518-946-2233).

Festival of the Lakes runs for three weekends in September, primarily in Saranac Lake, featuring live theater, plenty of music, programs for kids, artists' gallery and studio tours, and workshops. Contact Pendragon Theatre for information (518-891-1854).

Bull Moose Days in Newcomb, Minerva, and North Creek celebrate Teddy Roosevelt's wild ride to the presidency with historical programs, train rides, and sports contests, in mid-September (518-582-2811).

NORTHWEST LAKES

Woodsmen's Field Days in Tupper Lake highlight old-time lumber skills and underline the importance of logging in the Adirondack economy today. There's a parade with sparkling log trucks hauling the year's biggest, best logs; contests for man (ax-throwing, log-rolling, and speed-chopping), beast (skidding logs with draft horses), and heavy equipment (precision drills for skidders and loaders); clowns and games for kids. It's all on the second weekend in July, in the municipal park on the lakefront in Tupper Lake (518-359-3328).

Adirondack Wildlife Festival at the Visitor Interpretive Center in Paul Smiths offers guided wildflower walks, wildflower craft workshops, wildflower cooking demonstrations, and art programs for kids, in late July (518-327-3000).

CENTRAL ADIRONDACKS

Indian Lake Winter Festival on Presidents' Weekend in February mixes local history programs with outdoor events such as cross-country ski treks, downhill races at the town ski area, snowmobile poker runs, and snowshoe events throughout Indian Lake and Blue Mtn. Lake. There's music and sometimes square dancing in the evenings, plus community suppers (518-648-5112).

Old Home Days in Wells are held the first full weekend in August, with a parade featuring horse-drawn wagons, antique cars, floats, and marching bands. There's all kinds of music, plus a carnival and a craft fair (518-924-7912).

Fox Family Bluegrass Festival at Old Forge's McCauley Mtn. presents the town's own bluegrass stars plus other national bands, in early August (410-267-0432).

Adirondack Authors' Fair at Hoss's Country Corner (518-624-2481), in Long

Lake, is a great opportunity to meet and greet dozens of regional writers, held under a huge tent in mid-August.

Gore Mountain Oktoberfest is the last weekend in September in North Creek, with plenty of oom-pah-pah and *gemütlichkeit*. There's live music and German-style dancing, a crafts fair, ethnic food and beer booths, children's activities, and rides on the ski area's chairlift to view the fall foliage (518-251-2612).

Apple Festival, in Long Lake's Sabattis Park, serves up family fun with performances and games for kids, apple-cider making, a craft show, and apple pies galore, usually on the Saturday before Columbus Day (518-624-3077).

THEATER

LAKE GEORGE AND SOUTHEASTERN ADIRONDACKS

ADIRONDACK THEATRE FESTIVAL
518-798-7479.
www.atfestival.org.
French Mountain Playhouse, Lake George.
Season: Summer; occasional winter shows in other venues.

The Adirondack Theatre Festival, a young, ambitious professional group, was launched in June 1995. Founders of the company were involved with the production of the Broadway hit *Rent*, and bring real sophistication to their shows. The season begins in June, with three or four shows, children's workshops, and new play readings; the late-night solo artist cabaret performances are decidedly more hip than typical summer stock.

LAKE GEORGE DINNER THEATER
518-761-1092, year-round information.
518-668-5781, summer reservations.
Holiday Inn, Lake George.
Season: Mid-June–mid-Oct.
Tickets: Varies
Handicap Access: Yes.

This Actors Equity company presents one show a season in a semi-proscenium setting; a sample from past playbills includes *Oil City Symphony*, *Dames at Sea*, *Over the River and Through the Woods*, and *On Golden Pond*. Productions are thoroughly competent, as is the food at the Holiday Inn's banquet room.

CHAMPLAIN VALLEY

DEPOT THEATER
518-962-4449.
Delaware & Hudson Depot, Rte. 9N, Westport.
Mail: Box 414, Westport NY 12993.

Westport's D&H depot has found a surprising new life as home to a fine professional equity acting company directed by Westport native Shami McCormick. The former freight room comes alive with four or five plays each summer:

Season: June–Sept.
Tickets: $15–18; $13–14 students, seniors.
Handicap Access: Yes.

1999's smash hits were *The Pajama Game* by Adirondack summer resident Richard Adler and Jerry Ross, and Garson Kanin's *Born Yesterday*. Each year, a new musical debuts, and performance-art pieces by visiting artists are scheduled midweek. Depot Theater offers matinees for each of its shows — a nice option on a rainy day — but be sure to call ahead for tickets.

The region is also home to two good community theater organizations. The **Essex Theatre Company** (518-963-7442; Box 295, Essex) was formed in 1993 to showcase local talent. Productions in recent summers were held at the Masonic Lodge and included *The Fantasticks*, *On Golden Pond*, and musical cabarets. The **Boquet River Theatre Festival** (no phone; Box 701, Willsboro) performs in the Whallonsburg Church, on Rte. 22; programs are geared toward young audiences and performers.

HIGH PEAKS AND NORTHERN ADIRONDACKS

COMMUNITY THEATRE PLAYERS, INC.
Mail: Box 12, Lake Placid NY 12946.

An amateur group founded in 1972, CTP usually mounts four shows a year at the Lake Placid Center for the Arts and other venues. Productions — consistently good — have included such mainstays as *Peter Pan*, *Brigadoon*, *Babes in Toyland* (written by Lake Placid summer resident, Victor Herbert), *Li'l Abner*, and so forth.

PENDRAGON THEATRE
518-891-1854.
www.northnet.org/pendragon.
148 River St., Saranac Lake.
Season: Year-round.
Tickets: $12; $10 students, seniors.
Handicap Access: Yes.

This highly successful local troupe was awarded the prestigious Governor's Art Award in spring 1995, and has received acclaim for performances at the Edinburgh International Arts Festival, the Dublin Theatre Festival, and in Stockholm at the English-Speaking Theater. During the summer, Pendragon puts on three or four shows in repertory format; in 1999 shows included *Amber Patches* with the incomparable Julie Harris, *The Baltimore Waltz* by Pamela Vogel, and *Communicating Doors* by Alan Ayckbourn. In the fall, there's typically a classic show like *Macbeth*, and during the school year, actors form the Prop Trunk Players and tour local classrooms. In fall 1999, the Prop Trunk play was *Quilters*, which wowed even the most blasé teenage boys.

Pendragon, anchored by husband-and-wife team Bob Pettee and Susan Neal, was founded in 1981. The group's performances are worth a special trip.

Julie Harris and Alan Toy in Amber Patches, *a Pendragon Theatre production.*

Brantley Carroll

CENTRAL ADIRONDACKS

Community theater has grown exponentially in this part of the park, drawing from the talents of skilled amateurs and retired professionals. Indian Lake's **Cabin Fever Players** (518-648-5112) stages musicals and dramas in the 300-seat Lake Theater; Long Lake's **Bear Foot Players** (518-624-3077) puts on a couple of comedies a year in the town hall. In North Creek, Lyle Dye's **Our Town Theatre Group** (518-251-2422) is active all year in various venues, presenting classic plays as well as works written for specific events like the Teddy Roosevelt Days. Dye's *Radiorama*, with sketches from the heydays of radio was a local smash hit in 1999. Old Forge's **ACT, INC**. (315-369-6411) operates out of the Arts Center, putting together a couple of high-energy musicals each year.

WRITERS' PROGRAMS

The **Writer's Voice**, a nationwide program of the YMCA, has a center at Silver Bay Association (518-543-8833), on the northern end of Lake George. Workshops and readings (funded by the Lila Wallace-Reader's Digest Fund and the National Endowment for the Arts) by highly regarded poets, travel writers, novelists, and essayists are slated for spring and summer. Featured authors recently have included Terry Tempest Williams, two-time National Book Award winner Katherine Patterson, and mystery writer Archer Mayor.

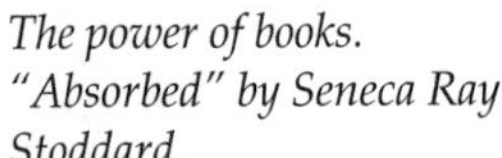

The power of books. "Absorbed" by Seneca Ray Stoddard.

Private collection.

The **Lake George Arts Project** (518-668-2616) offers fall and spring workshops in poetry, creative nonfiction, and fiction led by regional writers with national reputations.

At Paul Smith's College, the new **Adirondack Center for Writing** (518-327-6278; www.paulsmiths.edu/acw; Box 265, Paul Smiths, NY 12970) schedules workshops, readings, in-school programs, and has a comprehensive listing of opportunities for writers for the Adirondacks and beyond.

The **Old Forge Library** (315-369-6008) offers summer writing workshops, readings, and a regional authors' fair with dozens of Adirondack writers.

CHAPTER FIVE

Always in Good Taste

RESTAURANTS & FOOD PURVEYORS

A food revolution — maybe a couple of decades behind the rest of the country, but happening all the same — crept into the Adirondack Park as the 1990s came to a close. A few talented chefs spurned the iceberg lettuce and anemic tomatoes, chucked their old Fry-o-Laters, and turned their backs on frozen portion-control entrées covered with very thick, unconvincing sauces. They began taking risks: finding fresh local vegetables and fruits, introducing foreign cuisines, and developing their menus into individual expressions. They were bucking a tough trend, since the tradition of Adirondack restaurant cuisine teetered somewhere between hearty and heavy as lead, and years of complacency had produced a widespread reliance on a handful of so-so suppliers selling the same tired, generic stuff.

Katherine McClellan, courtesy of Smith College Archives

The quintessential Adirondack table, circa 1900.

Other regions of the Northeast — with access to the ocean, longer growing seasons, and an eclectic ethnic mix — spawned more distinctive cuisines. At the dawn of North Country tourism, Yankee-owned taverns offered travelers what grew from their own ground (apples, berries, beans, cabbage, onions, turnips, and potatoes), along with a bit of salt pork, perhaps a haunch of venison, or maybe, if the guests were particularly blessed, a freshly caught speckled trout. The all-purpose sweetener was maple sugar or maybe wild honey. Food was food; you ate it because you were hungry, and that was that.

The arrival of railroad service to many Adirondack towns enlivened dining options considerably by bringing in fresh seafood, warm-weather fruits, and exotic vegetables. By the 1880s, as humble woodsmen's lodges gave way to grand hotels, there was an elite clientele to please. Menus evolved into elaborate affairs listing *quenelles, duxelles,* and *mirepois,* alongside the caviar, fresh figs, sweetbreads, and lobster.

The grand hotels and their elaborate style fell out of favor by the 1920s. Vacations became family car trips, and a new kind of restaurant specializing in unadorned, filling, eat-and-run chow sprang up along the highways. Diners proliferated at the crossroads. Resorts with individual sleeping cabins and dining buildings where guests could gather for breakfast and supper became the standard for lodgings.

James Swedberg

The William West Durant offers a fine meal with great views as it cruises Raquette Lake.

Today many towns still have a diner, where local news is discussed and the coffee's always hot. Nowadays, diners take considerable pride in homemade baked goods and wonderful soups. The original screen-door, roadside tourist stops are rarer: Tail O' the Pup, on Route 86 in Ray Brook, which hasn't changed much from when it began in 1946, and Burke-Towne, a breakfast-and-lunch place in Raquette Lake, come to mind as examples. (Resorts which still offer meals to guests under full or modified American plans are listed in Chapter 3, *Lodging*.)

When the restaurant scene in the Adirondack Park underwent its recent revival, this was a real response to improve basic food, not a trendy spin on made-up tradition. (In other words, don't look for landlocked salmon steamed in maple syrup.) Competition created a number of establishments that could hold their own anywhere in the country, with clusters of exceptional restaurants in Lake Placid and a few stars — like The Owl at Twilight, in downtown Olmstedville — in truly out-of-the-way places.

Today, there's a surprising variety of eateries for what remains basically a rural area. Across the park there are old-timey ice cream parlors, a couple of barbecue joints, lots of decent family restaurants, plus many places with spotless linen tablecloths, fresh flowers, and color-coordinated candles on the tables, staffed by waiters and waitresses who can adroitly pronounce the names of foreign foods. A couple of options are literally moving experiences: the cruise-and-dine ship William West Durant (315-354-5532; Raquette Lake), which provides an excellent lunch, dinner, or Sunday brunch from May through Columbus Day during its Raquette Lake excursions, and the Norridgewock III (315-376-6200), which features a 10-mile water-taxi ride into Beaver River, the most remote community in New York State, for meals at a rustic lodge. Another interesting local fad is the sudden appearance of outdoor dining patios; the best have lake or mountain views, while some just overlook parking lots.

In preparation for this chapter, the author and nine other Adirondack residents took to the byways, looking for restaurants that operate with a clear sense of what they are trying to do; demonstrating their purpose through good service, quality food, and fair prices. So, you'll find listed here some very inexpensive places as well as some fancy places, and all kinds of choices in between. We hope that the descriptions give you an impression of what to expect once you walk in the door of any given eatery, or lead you to explore a new part of the region. Near the end of the chapter is a selection of informal places (taverns, diners, and similar joints) that are worth a quick stop.

The list that follows is long, but it's by no means exhaustive. The Lake George area alone has scores of restaurants, including nearly two dozen eateries that tout home-cooked Italian food. Thus, in these pages, if you're a veteran Adirondack eater, you may not find your favorite place. Maybe we didn't get a chance to eat there during the months this research was going on, or maybe we did try the place and felt that other places in the neighborhood were more noteworthy. In the years since the first edition of this book was released, many favorite places have undergone changes in management and kitchen staff; if you've got the original Adirondack Book and a highlighted place is missing, it's either closed or has — in our opinion — diminished in quality.

We present here everything from neighborhood joints where five bucks gets you a satisfying bellyful, and the company's good to boot, to thoroughly elegant restaurants with well-deserved renown. Each restaurant is designated with a price code that summarizes the cost of one meal (appetizer, entrée, and dessert), but does not include wine, cocktails, sales tax, and tip. (Nouvelle cuisine — tiny portions marooned on enormous plates — never really got a foothold in the Adirondacks. If you're not prepared for a large serving, order an appetizer for your main course.)

The restaurants are grouped by region, starting with Lake George and the southeastern portion of the Adirondack Park. Within the regions you'll find the towns in alphabetical order, with restaurants described alphabetically under each town. At the end of the chapter, you'll find a sampling of bakeries, brew pubs, candy makers, delicatessens, farmstands, maple-syrup makers, and so on. You'll also find a short calendar of community suppers that offer great chow at low prices. All these places are listed in the index, too. Finally, note that few Adirondack restaurants have websites, so searching on-line for menus and specials can be fruitless. A nationwide site called www.the-restaurant-guide.com, which in most regions links to jazzy, informative restaurant home pages, isn't particularly useful for the Adirondack Park. Material is organized by county, but phone numbers and street addresses are about all you'll learn.

Dining Price Codes	Inexpensive: Up to $15 Moderate: $15–$20 Expensive: $20–$35 Very Expensive: Over $35
Credit Cards	AE: American Express CB: Carte Blanche D: Discover DC: Diners Club MC: MasterCard V: Visa
Meals	B: Breakfast L: Lunch SB: Sunday Brunch D: Dinner

ADIRONDACK RESTAURANTS

LAKE GEORGE AND SOUTHEASTERN ADIRONDACKS

Bolton Landing

THE ALGONQUIN
518-644-9442.
www.thealgonquin.com.

Located on Lake George's Huddle Bay, this bustling lakeside institution continues to attract waterfront diners all summer long. Most guests

Route 9N, Lake Shore Drive, Bolton Landing (about 1/2 mile south of town in Huddle Bay).
Open: Daily at noon, mid-April through Columbus Day.
Serving: L, D.
Cuisine: Continental, American.
Price: Moderate to Expensive.
Credit Cards: AE, D, DC, MC, V.
Reservations: Suggested (only for upstairs dining room Friday, Saturday, and Sunday nights).
Handicap Access: Yes.
Special features: Live music on the deck weekends in summer; boat docks.

prefer to arrive by boat, leaving their craft to be valet-parked by eager young dockhands.

There are some drawbacks to the Algonquin: in high summer, an hour wait is normal for seating on the deck and the background rock music takes away from the beautiful vistas seen through large picture windows in the upstairs and downstairs dining rooms. Be aware that service upstairs begins at 5pm, for full entrées only (no burgers or sandwiches); this dining room prohibits smoking and children under ten.

The menu's "beginnings" range from chicken wings and nachos to duchess paté and escargot bourguinonne. Salads include chef, shrimp Caesar, and Tuscan — fresh mozzarella, tomato, roasted red pepper, and roasted garlic on a bed of greens. Dinner entrées (served with a house salad) include veal piccata or marsala, herbed salmon, steak au poivre, and vegetable stir fry. The Greek shrimp with feta cheese, tomatoes, and herbs in a sherry sauce over linguini is quite tasty. Burgers and club sandwiches are available on the deck and in the downstairs dining room.

MISTER BROWN'S PUB
518-644-9400.
www.sagamore.com.
Sagamore Hotel, Sagamore Road, off Rte. 9N.
Open: Daily year round.
Serving: L, D.
Cuisine: American.
Price: Moderate.
Credit Cards: AE, DC, Entertainment, MC, V.
Reservations: No.
Handicap Access: Yes.
Entertainment: Guitar player nightly during the summer season starting at 9pm.

Mister Brown's Pub is a great opportunity to enjoy a moderately priced meal at the grand Sagamore Hotel. The pub — with Adirondack cedar posts, antler chandeliers, twig trim, and cozy fireplace set off by oversized armchairs — is considerably less formal than the other hotel dining rooms. The place is named for one of the Sagamore's founding fathers, Myron Brown, born in the town of Bolton in 1837. An early developer on Lake George, he was the first manager of the Sagamore when it opened in 1893. Severely damaged by fire a decade later, the hotel was rebuilt and Brown continued as manager, helping to popularize Bolton as a summer resort.

At the ground-floor tavern, diners are greeted with a birch-bark basket filled with hot biscuits. The menu ranges from cheddar-ale soup and campfire chili to a host of club sandwiches and traditional American pub fare like nachos, buffalo wings, and cheeseburgers. Daily specials include a pasta creation, "mom's favorite" (updated comfort food), and a catch of the day. Dinner entrées include pecan-crusted chicken, rainbow trout, and barbecue pork rib platter. Be sure to save room for dessert; the menu includes key lime pie and dark chocolate bread pudding. Lunch is an abridged dinner menu with starters, fresh salads, and stacked sandwiches.

We offer two words of advice about the pub and dining at the Sagamore. At Mister Brown's Pub in the early evening, your fellow diners may include several tables of children accompanied by their baby-sitters. Parents send youngsters to this moderately priced option while they enjoy the fancier, quieter dining rooms upstairs. Also, the Sagamore adds a 17 percent gratuity to all services, including dining checks, regardless of party size. Often the wait staff does not mention the added gratuity and an additional tip is left by unknowing customers.

PUMPERNICKEL'S
518-644-2106.
Lake Shore Dr.
Closed: Mar.; Mon.–Wed. in winter.
Serving: L, D summer; D winter.
Cuisine: German.
Price: Moderate.
Credit Cards: AE, MC, V.
Reservations: Yes.
Handicap Access: Yes.

It's almost too bad that Pumpernickel's boasts America's largest cuckoo clock, an eleven-foot tall timepiece that hung for many years in Times Square. It makes the place appear like a German theme park, and it might distract you from the food, which is very good.

German cooking has a bad reputation — heavy, greasy, inert. But in the capable hands of chef Hans Winter, the wursts and the schnitzels and virtually everything on Pumpernickel's menu tastes vivid, intense, almost light. Don't miss the potato pancakes with applesauce; they're deftly fried, a crisp treat. Dinner comes with hearty soup and a decent salad bar as well as plenty of side dishes, plus a fresh loaf of pumpernickel on every table.

It's a great place to take children, of course. And it's a great place to come without children, because families with kids have been neatly corralled into a loft where they can watch the cuckoo clock without bothering other diners. The service is swift and pleasant. And it's the only place in the southern Adirondacks with a wide selection of the finest German beers on draft.

VILLA NAPOLI
518-644-9047.
www.melodymanor.com.
Route 9N, Lake Shore Drive (about 1 mile south of town on 9N).
Open: Daily July and August; 5pm weekends only May–June and September–October.
Serving: D.

Naples meets the Adirondacks in this lakeside restaurant: frescos and paintings of quaint towns and Lake Como adorn the dark green dining room walls. With heavy drapes and shelves filled with wine bottles and cascading plastic grapes, the atmosphere is unmistakably Old Country but the view is pure North Country.

Like a foreign film, the menu is written in Italian with English subtitles. Warm rolls are served with rosemary-infused olive oil. Appetizers include

Cuisine: Italian.
Price: Moderate.
Credit Cards: AE, MC, V.
Reservations: Suggested.
Handicap Access: Yes.

sauteed artichoke hearts, stuffed little-neck clams, and a large antipasto with Italian meats, vegetables, cheeses, and olives. Traditional pasta, veal, chicken, steak, and fish entrées offer many delicious, bountiful choices. Try the pesce al griglia — the catch of the day grilled and topped with a warm salad of roasted peppers, tomatoes, onions, and basil, or the ravioli parma rossa, fresh cheese ravioli in a tomato-pesto-cream sauce. If you're stumped how to complement your choices with the proper beverage, the menu includes wine suggestions for each entrée from the restaurant's generous wine list. Be sure to leave room for tiramisu, a cannoli, or cappuccino to conclude your Villa Napoli experience.

Chestertown

FRIENDS LAKE INN
518-494-4751.
Friends Lake Rd.
Open: Year-round.
Serving: B, L (winter only), D.
Cuisine: Contemporary American.
Price: Expensive in dining room; inexpensive in Bistro.
Credit Cards: AE, DC, MC, V.
Reservations: Recommended.
Handicap Access: Yes.

This handsomely restored inn began serving the public before the Civil War, and was a hot spot during Prohibition. Friends Lake Inn today is a rewarding destination for a romantic getaway or a fine meal. The wine list is longer than the local phone book, and there's an impressive selection of American craft and imported beers. If the choices have you confused, innkeepers Sharon and Greg Taylor sponsor occasional beer- and wine-tasting events that pair imaginative cuisine with interesting beverages.

In the main dining room, there's a distinct difference between the summer and winter menus, with seasonal fruits and vegetables and lighter presentations favored during warm weather. For appetizers try peppered bison carpaccio, lobster risotto, or cilantro-corn fried shrimp with papaya salsa. Entrées range from roast chicken with braised leeks and soft polenta to rack of lamb rubbed with Moroccan spices served with ratatouille, plus halibut and shrimp served in saffron herb broth accompanied by pear tomatoes and spinach. New since 1998 is the Bistro, which doubles as a bar and restaurant serving lunch and dinner, as well as wine and cheese. If you're searching for interesting food on a budget, the Bistro (open 2 to 10pm) is a good choice. Recommended are the crab and salmon cakes, duck spring rolls with curried coconut dipping sauce, and pizza rustica. Desserts are all made on the premises and match the seasons admirably, from fresh fruit tarts in summer to grand chocolate concoctions for the holidays.

MAIN STREET ICE CREAM PARLOR
518-494-7940.
Main St.
Open: Daily.
Serving: L, D.
Cuisine: Deli, ice cream parlor.
Price: Inexpensive.
Handicap Access: Yes.

Antiques, advertising art, old photographs, farm implements, and the telephone switchboard that once served all of the southern Adirondacks fill the walls charmingly here, and the food's fun, too. Sandwiches, soups, and chili are excellent; go for the thick, complicated sandwiches layered on rye and stuffed with bacon, tomatoes, Russian dressing, cheese, and meat. The ice cream concoctions are definitely worth saving room for, whether it's a sundae topped with local maple syrup or a coffee or chocolate malted made with lots of real malt powder. If you're in the vicinity looking for an inexpensive place to take the family for dinner, the ice cream parlor is a good bet.

RENE'S MOUNTAIN VIEW HOUSE
518-494-2904.
White Schoolhouse Rd., 1 mi. E. of Rte. 8.
Open: Year-round.
Serving: D.
Cuisine: Swiss, Continental.
Price: Expensive.
Credit Cards: AE, DC, MC, V.
Reservations: Recommended.
Handicap Access: Yes.

Swiss-born chef Rene Plattner and his wife, Barbara, came to Chestertown in the 1980s to revitalize an old inn and have run the Mountain View House since 1989. Their attention to detail is evident everywhere in the restaurant: from the vintage china with its leaping-deer motif (made in the 1930s for a another resort in town), to the tangy vinaigrette on the house salad, to the plump spaetzel beneath the meat entrées, to an award-winning creation called Chocolate Trilogy, a zillion-calorie affair that proceeds from a dense, rich torte to a clouds of mousse.

The Swiss potato soup alone is worth the drive. Other signature dishes include lobster ravioli in basil cream sauce; filet mignon topped with shrimp and morel mushrooms in a Madeira sauce; and the Mountaintop, combining beef, pork, and veal with that heavenly spaetzel. Fresh fish, like braised salmon with ginger and citrus confit, is well prepared in simple sauces that allow the fish's true flavor to shine. Think ahead when ordering so you'll be sure to have room for dessert. Even the ice cream is made in Rene and Barbara's kitchen, and you can get it in a cookie basket sauced with raspberry coulis.

Hadley

SARATOGA ROSE INN AND RESTAURANT
518-696-2861 or 800-942-5025.
Closed: Mon.–Wed. fall and spring; open daily in summer.

High above town like a great pink wedding cake is this lovingly restored Victorian inn. Owners Nancy and Anthony Merlino have pulled out all the stops in their effort to invoke the high-living yet homey Gilded Age, with chandeliers,

Serving: L, D.
Cuisine: Italian, Continental.
Price: Moderate to Expensive.
Credit Cards: D, MC, V.
Reservations: Recommended.
Handicap Access: Ramp in rear.

mock-faded wallpaper, hardwood floors, and marble hearths. Dining rooms occupy what used to be the parlor, library, and living room of the old mansion, and the picture lacks only a player piano in the corner cranking out a ghostly tune.

Semi-formal Italian and European cuisine perhaps best describes Tony Merlino's ambitious efforts in the kitchen. His selection of classic continental fare — richly sauced, comfortably seasoned, and often generously stuffed — includes shrimp scampi, veal marsala, ravioli, tortelloni, rolled sole, pork tenderloin, salmon, and duckling in orange sauce. Small but tasty salads come with the meal, and desserts range from homemade rice pudding to old-time ice cream parfait.

If all this serious eating makes a full bottle of wine too much to manage, the restaurant offers a welcome array of wines by the glass. Also, check local papers for off-season promotions, like half-price entrées.

Hague

DOCKSIDE LANDING
9130 Lakeshore Drive (Rte. 9N about a mile from Hague proper).
518-543-8888.
Open: Summer.
Serving: L, D.
Price: Expensive.
Reservations: Recommended.
Credit Cards: All major.
Handicap Access: Yes.

Situated on a remote stretch of northern Lake George and seemingly miles from any town, Dockside Landing was a destination restaurant. Its dining area featured elegant cloth-covered tables arranged in a V-pattern on a deck right on the water's edge, and naturally the fine view and good food attracted a dedicated clientele. Although the restaurant was partially destroyed by a fire in September 1999, just as it was preparing to close for the season, the owners have announced their intentions to rebuild in 2000.

Though the setting may change a bit, the menu is expected to remain the same, highlighting fresh seafood and pasta. Sauteed scallops and fettucine alfredo are just two recommended entrées, available at lunch and dinner; pasta portions are big enough for two to share. Desserts include delicious cheesecake, also in generous servings.

ISLAND VIEW CAFE
Lakeshore Drive (Rte. 9N).
518-543-6367.
Open: Memorial Day–Labor Day.
Serving: B, L, D.

Charmingly located on Lake George in the hamlet of Hague, the Island View Cafe has tables inside and tables on a little brick patio next to a dock. Not only can you can sit outside but you can even arrive by boat.

Reservations: No.
Credit Cards: Inquire.
Handicap Access: Street-level entry.

Food can be categorized as summertime casual, with big, juicy (and pricey — six bucks for a burger without fries) hamburgers a main attraction. Homemade hard-packed ice cream is another reason to visit the cafe; strawberry cheesecake is an excellent choice among the many flavors.

Lake George

THE BARNSIDER
518-668-5268.
www.barnsider.com.
Rte. 9.
Closed: Columbus Day–May 1.
Serving: L, D.
Cuisine: American, barbecue.
Price: Inexpensive to Moderate.
Credit Cards: All major.
Handicap Access: Yes.
Special features: Blues on Thursdays, jazz on Sundays.

The Adirondack Park is not what anyone would call ribs country, but as folks keep on discovering the family-run Barnsider, this could change. Owner-chef Ed Pagnotta's rack of pork is as scrumptious as it gets. Pagnotta's parents ran a produce market on this roadside spot, so he comes by his food savvy naturally. The method, says the chef, is called "Memphis style," and involves "a process using dry rub which kind of marinates the ribs, then I throw 'em in a water smoker, and use hickory and oak for wood, which filters up through the oven and heats up the water, which I think keeps a moister flavor."

The only trouble with the Barnsider is the on-site competition. Generous halves of barbecue chicken are every bit as tender and savory with smoke as the ribs, and there's smoked baked beans and brisket, too. What's an omnivore to do? Our suggestion: get the chicken 'n' ribs combo. It comes with good corn on the cob and onion rings as stiff and round as hula hoops. Prompt, cheerful service and outdoor decks make a summer dinner at this congenial spot a real Adirondack find.

EAST COVE
518-668-5265.
Rte. 9L and Beach Rd.
Open: Daily May–Oct.; Wed.–Sat. Nov.–Apr.
Serving: D, SB.
Cuisine: American, seafood.
Price: Moderate to Expensive.
Credit Cards: AE, DC, MC, V.
Handicap Access: Ramp in rear.

Just a city block or so from Lake George's Million Dollar Beach, but psychologically miles away from the T-shirts and souvenir jive of Canada St., is this cozy, overgrown log cabin decked out with ship's-wheel chandeliers, old hand-colored engravings, and flags. East Cove is a spot that locals cherish, and they come early — the place opens for dinner at 5pm — to unwind after a long day.

The moment you sit down, your server arrives with a bowl of tasty homemade cole slaw, some carrot and celery sticks, and a basket of rolls. There's a good selection of American wines available by the glass; you might want to sample some as you decide what to order from the extensive menu, which includes usually half a dozen specials. Shrimp scampi is what regulars rave about. The generous entrée is perfectly cooked and finished off with a velvety garlic-and-cream sauce. Occasionally sauteed soft-shell crab is offered, and it, too, comes with a rich garlicky sauce.

Meat eaters can choose from herb-crusted rack of lamb finished with Madeira demiglace (also a large portion), pork tenderloin, veal with artichokes and mushrooms, and big steaks. Chicken comes Santa Fe style, with sun-dried tomatoes, broccoli, and feta cheese, or à la Louise, with tarragon-cream sauce. Salads are forgettable, but desserts are delicious, over-the-top creations like raspberry rumble (raspberry-laced cheesecake with Oreo-cookie crust) and cappuccino silk pie.

GEORGE'S RESTAURANT
518-668-5482.
Route 9L, east side of Lake George.
Open: Daily June–September; Wednesday–Sunday in April–May, October–November.
Serving: D.
Cuisine: Steak and Seafood.
Price: Expensive.
Credit Cards: MC, V.
Reservations: Essential.
Handicap Access: Yes.

George's is the real deal, the place steak house chains aspire to become, set on the east side of Lake George, a short drive from busy Canada Street. Dozens of assorted Tiffany lamps hang from the rafters to illuminate the cozy log cabin interior. The large wooden bar is separated from the dining room by colorful stained glass windows and huge, heavy-framed mirrors cover the walls.

Clams casino, wine-sauced escargots, and stuffed mushrooms are good starters for a long list of main courses. All entrées include access to a generous salad bar stocked with typical offerings and more interesting salad combinations such as Mexican black bean, cold spaghetti, and chickpea-and-roasted-garlic. A tip: don't let the salad bar slow you down or fill you up.

You can't go wrong with the beef here — first-rate porterhouse, sirloin, or filet mignon. Rack of lamb and stuffed boneless pork chops are also good. Seafood entrées include broiled swordfish, salmon and lobster tails, and seafood marinara or alfredo; the poultry menu offers chicken alfredo, parmigiana, or Oscar. There's a children's menu too.

LEO'S LOBSTER
518-793-2654.
Route 9, Lake George (between exits 20 and 21 off the Northway, 1/4 mile north of the outlet shops).
Open: Daily May through October.

A roadside attraction between Lake George Village and Glens Falls, Leo's Lobster is difficult to miss: numerous Christmas lights and an illuminated fountain beckon the traveler. Once you pull up closer, it sure looks like an Maine coast lobster shack, with a log interior decorated with fishing nets, plastic crustaceans, conch shells, starfish, and even a red torpedo hanging over the bar.

Serving: D.
Cuisine: Seafood.
Price: Moderate.
Credit Cards: AE, D, DC, MC, V.
Reservations: Recommended.
Handicap Access: Yes.

If you're looking for seafood, Leo's is worth the short drive from downtown Lake George. Begin your meal with an appetizer of steamed clams, shrimp cocktail, mussels marinara, or deep-fried calamari. Lobster — naturally — tops the list of seafood entrées, with one-pound to pound-and-a-half boiled whole lobsters or broiled lobster tails. Snow and king crab legs, shrimp scampi, and a featured catch broiled, sauteed, or Cajun spiced are among the list of choices. Sole fillet stuffed with crabmeat and scallops is excellent. If you prefer a terrestrial meal, several beef, chicken, veal, and pasta dishes are available.

Entrées are served with an uninspired iceberg lettuce salad and choice of steak fries or baked potato. With a children's menu offering burgers, chicken tenders, hot dogs, or spaghetti, Leo's Lobster is a fun stop for the entire family. There's even entertainment, after a fashion: kids enjoy watching the action in two big fish tanks in the dining room.

Melody Thomas

Lucille's Restaurant, on Lake George's Canada Street, is a feast for the eyes.

LUCILLE'S RESTAURANT
518-668-9224.
www.menumart.com/lucilles.
259 Canada Street, Lake George Village.
Open: Daily May–October; Thursday–Sunday winter and spring; closed March and November.

In the raucous heart of Lake George Village, a flashing neon fish and four-foot carved lobster are displayed from the "deck" of this boat-shaped restaurant. The nautical theme of hanging fishnets and navigational instruments assures the hungry traveler that he should order fish from the wait staff — dressed as sailors, no less. If you're looking for a fun place to watch the people promenading

Serving: D.
Cuisine: Seafood.
Price: Moderate.
Credit Cards: AE, DC, MC, V.
Reservations: Recommended.
Handicap Access: Yes.
Entertainment: piano player Friday and Saturday nights during the summer.

down Canada Street, have a high tolerance for kitschy decor, and enjoy traditional seafood, Lucille's is a good choice.

A "how to eat lobster" placemat greets you at the table. The classic seafood menu offers lobster broiled or steamed or sauced as thermidor or newburg. Clams, oysters, shrimp, scallops, crabs, scrod, flounder, halibut, and salmon are likewise prepared in different ways. Lucille's also offers land-raised entrées, such as several chicken, veal, pork, beef, and pasta dishes. The wine selection is limited and there's only one beer on tap.

S.J. GARCIA'S
518-668-2190.
www.menumart.com.
192 Canada St.
Open: Daily 12pm–11pm, May through October.
Serving: L, D.
Cuisine: Mexican.
Price: Moderate.
Credit Cards: All major.
Reservations: No.
Handicap Access: Yes.

Although the colorful Mexican blankets, large sombreros, and cactus pinatas try to convince you otherwise, you're a long way from the border at Garcia's Restaurant. For good margaritas and homemade guacamole, you've come to the right spot — especially if you've snagged a seat on the outdoor deck in back. The menu offers Mexican fare including tacos and chimichangas as well as burgers and club sandwiches. The burritos and enchiladas are unmemorable and the red snapper vera cruz is, well, fishy. If you have your heart set on Mexican cuisine, this is the only place in town.

RIDGE TERRACE
518-656-9274.
Rte. 91.
Open: May–Oct.
Serving: D.
Cuisine: American.
Price: Moderate to Expensive.
Credit Cards: MC, V.
Handicap Access: Yes.

Chef Raymond Rios and his wife, Norma, have a winning place here on the east side of Lake George. A big rustic chalet set among tall evergreens, Ridge Terrace is quiet and comfortable, with a very extensive menu.

Folks come from as far away as Vermont for the succulent olive-oil-braised veal chop and seafood au gratin; an appetizer-size portion of the latter makes a lovely light meal. Among the more intriguing main courses are planked salmon served on wilted greens with sunflower seed/pumpkin vinaigrette, real chateaubriand with duchess potatoes piped around the platter, and seafood strudel made with crab legs, gulf shrimp, and bay scallops. If you're traveling with children, this is a good choice; while the atmosphere is mellow, kids are made welcome, and there's a menu just for them.

TAMARACK INN
518-668-5400.

The Tamarack Inn is on the northern end of Lake George's main drag — the Adirondack end.

440 Canada St.
Open: Daily.
Serving: B, L, D.
Cuisine: Regional American.
Price: Moderate.
Credit Cards: AE, DC, MC, V.
Reservations: Recommended in summer.
Handicap Access: Yes.

And the mood and decor reflect the location: the handsome cabinlike building is chock-a-block with Adirondack boats, trophy deer, stuffed mallards, and North Country prints. It prepares you for the drive north up into the mountains, or eases you back into the real world after a weekend at camp.

Like most Lake George restaurants, the Tamarack is usually crowded on summer nights, as vacationers sample the seafood dishes that make up much of the menu, or drink the daiquiris and other specialty drinks from the full-service bar. Among the entrées are low-cal specials for those worried about fitting into their bathing suits on nearby Million Dollar Beach. The breakfast menu focuses on flapjacks with real maple syrup. Dinner includes country favorites like Yankee pot roast, twin beef filets, and grilled honey chicken breast.

WAGAR'S SODA FOUNTAIN
518-668-3770.
327 Canada Street, Lake George (just north of the Gulf station).
Open: Daily 10am–11:30pm May through October, 10am–4pm daily during the rest of the year.
Serving: L, D.
Cuisine: confectionery, ice cream parlor, sandwiches.
Price: Inexpensive.
Credit Cards: AE, D, MC, V.
Reservations: No.
Handicap Access: Yes.

This turn-of-the-century ice cream parlor — with its marble soda fountain, heart-shaped wire chairs, and player piano — features good deli sandwiches and extravagant ice cream concoctions. Pick from a variety of flavors when you order a soda, egg cream, float, shake, or malt. For the more adventurous, the parlor's "colossal creations" include a one-pound ice cream cone (containing almost a quart of ice cream) or the magnificent Chicago Fire, a monstrous mess of 20 scoops of ice cream, toppings, bananas, nuts, and whipped cream. The shop also has a confectionery on site making fudge, fresh roasted nuts, and Adirondack Bear Claws (almonds topped with caramel and chocolate). Other specialties include rock candy, licorice ropes, cotton candy, and the world's largest jawbreakers, about the size of billiard balls. Yow!

Lake Luzerne

DEFINO'S HERITAGE RESTAURANT
518-696-3733.
Northwoods Rd., off Rte. 9N.
Open: Mid–May–mid–Oct.; Wed.–Sun.

Everything — from the creamy garlic salad dressing to the crusty, hot bread to the carrot cake — is made from scratch in the kitchen here, and the ambiance at DeFino's is as warm and comfortable as the food. The place used to be a dude ranch in the 1930s, but today the overgrown log

Serving: D.
Cuisine: Italian.
Price: Moderate.
Credit Cards: MC, V.
Reservations: Suggested for summer weekends.
Handicap Access: Yes.

cabin is a welcoming restaurant under quiet pines. Linguine with white clam sauce is a good pick, a huge serving with plenty of shellfish, and chicken cacciatore is authentic and hearty. For real home cooking, you can't go wrong with the baked chicken or stuffed cabbage. When you finally push your chair back from the table, you'll feel like you're one of the family — happily stuffed, but maybe you can find room for a smidgen of dessert.

Real ice cream sodas and fountain treats are Papa's specialty.

Melody Thomas

PAPA'S
518-696-3667.
Main St.
Closed: Oct.–late May.
Serving: B, L (until 8pm; ice cream until 10pm).
Cuisine: Ice cream parlor.
Price: Inexpensive.
Credit Cards: None.
Handicap Access: No.

Don't miss this landmark if you're anywhere in the vicinity. Papa's is the real thing — an ice cream parlor with roots stretching back to the 1930s. The decor here proves it, with old postcards and photographs of the Hudson Valley mill towns and glass milk bottles from the dairies that once thrived in this valley. You can certainly order a wonderful breakfast or a great burger or a peanut-butter-and-bacon sandwich, but really, you're here for the ice cream concoctions: floats, malts, sundaes, splits, shakes, and cones. They're all served in the right kind of tulip glass or boat; even the cones come in little twisted-wire holders. You can dine in one of the little booths or take your treat out on the deck overlooking the river. On Thursday nights in the summer, barbershop singers serenade you.

Schroon Lake

DRAKE'S RESTAURANT
518-532-9040.
Rte. 9.
Open: Memorial Day–Columbus Day.
Serving: L, D; B daily from late June to Labor Day, otherwise just weekends.
Cuisine: Italian/American.
Price: Moderate to Expensive.
Credit Cards: All major.
Handicap Access: yes.

No-nonsense Drake's, on the north side of Schroon Lake village and under the direction of Tony and Margo Bartolomeo, has been a popular spot for twenty-five years. There's a medium-sized dining room with a small bar and two-table solarium (the smoking section) off to the side. The cuisine is Italian/American, with an extensive array of seafood dishes.

Appetizers of note are steamed mussels, jumbo shrimp cocktail, and Italian-style roasted red peppers in fresh garlic and olive oil with garlic bread. For entrées, look for favorite Italian chicken dishes like cacciatore, parmigiana, and marsala, plus a handful of vegetarian selections like eggplant parmigiana and baked ziti. On the seafood side — all are served with garden salad, potato or rice, vegetable, and roll — try the Alaskan king crab legs, seafood newburgh, sauteed scallops, or have a big ol' New England lobster (check out your dinner victim in the tank on the way in). There are other traditional entrées as well, like grilled lemon pepper chicken and roast duckling. Tuesday through Sunday there is a different special each night, from surf-'n'-turf to roast prime rib of beef. The wine list is newly expanded, with bottle selections in the $12–$24 range.

Good desserts — Ticonderoga bread pudding, "Chocolate Beyond Reason," and New York cheesecake, among others — are made on premises.

PITKIN'S
518-532-7918.
Main St.
Open: Year-round.
Serving: B, L, D.
Cuisine: American.
Price: Inexpensive.
Credit Cards: None.
Handicap Access: Street-level entry.

If only every town had a spot as good as Pitkin's — where the homemade soups are thick with real stuff (not cornstarch), pies are heavenly, service is brisk — why, we'd never leave. The cole slaw and potato salad are the best around, and then there's the barbecue. Sure, Pitkin's looks like your average North Country diner with giant lake trout and panoramic color photos on the walls, but there's authentic Texas-style barbecue, beef brisket, pork ribs, and chicken. On Thursday nights in the summer, the lines of ribs fans snake down Main Street, and the wait for a table can be long. Happily, the restaurant is open all year, and you can get barbecue at lunch. Even in mud season.

The bar at Terrio's Carriage House is packed with eclectic antiques.

James Swedberg

TERRIO'S CARRIAGE HOUSE
518-532-7700.
Rte. 9.
Closed: Mon.–Wed. in fall–winter.
Serving: D.
Cuisine: American.
Price: Moderate.
Credit Cards: AE, D, MC.
Reservations: Recommended for summer weekends.
Handicap Access: Dining room but not bar.

This place really was a carriage house, once part of a stately Schroon Lake manor, and it's decorated with antiques. Eclectic antiques: a suit of armor in one corner, a brace of brass fondue pots in another, a luge, license plates, baskets. The menu is a little the same way, covering the waterfront of American resort cuisine with no special Adirondack emphasis: Alaskan king crab, Long Island roast duckling, fried calamari, Cajun chicken.

The cooking is straightforward and solid. The house special is the Crabarooney, two small pieces of filet mignon topped with Alaskan crabmeat and béarnaise sauce. Everything comes with soup or salad, the baked potatoes are good, and if you remember to ask the waitress, they even have Saranac Pale Ale with which to wash it all down. Desserts are unmemorable, but novelty coffees are fun.

The main room and the porch with a wood stove are usually bustling, and kids are welcome. The children's menu is a junior version of the abundant adult fare. On Tuesdays, the restaurant offers a twin-lobster special, and on Thursdays they grill steaks in different ways and offer them at special prices. After dinner, a visit to the bar — packed to the rafters with even more assorted antiques — offers lots of visual amusement and occasionally live music too.

Stony Creek

A rockin' roadhouse with good Mexican food and live music is Stony Creek Inn's ticket to success.

Melody Thomas

STONY CREEK INN
518-696-2394.
Corner Branch Rd. and Hadley Rd.
Closed: Mon. and Tues. Dec.–Mar.
Serving: L on weekends, D.
Cuisine: American.
Price: Inexpensive to Moderate.
Credit Cards: No.
Reservations: Accepted, but not necessary.
Handicap Access: Yes, but not rest rooms.
Special Features: Live music on Fri. and Sun.

The Inn is a southern Adirondack institution, one of the funkiest spots between Saratoga and Montreal. You can get a good solid dinner here during the week (a slab of decent prime rib on Friday for ten bucks), but it's on Sunday night that the joint really jumps, when there's great Mexican food and local bands.

Long a Mecca for square dancers, and the home stage for the regionally renowned Stony Creek Band, the Inn now presents everything from straight country to rhythm and blues, old-time fiddle to salsa. All this music -— a rarity in the area — attracts crowds from far and wide; owner Dot Bartel says her mailing list of 600 names includes regulars from New Jersey and Vermont. Along with hot tunes, the Stony Creek Inn offers some unbeatable specials: steamed clams and roast beef for ten bucks on Wednesdays and two prime rib or two steak dinners for $20 on Fridays.

TASTE OF POLAND
518-696-2868 or 800-449-6992.
1200 Harrisburg Road at the Harrisburg Lake Club,(follow Route 418 to

Eleven miles outside Stony Creek is a wonderful opportunity to visit Poland without leaving the Adirondacks. In 1999 the Oblaczywinski family took over management of the Harrisburg Lake Club, a backwoods resort that offers hiking, cross-country skiing, and even mushroom hunting.

Stony Creek, turn right onto Harrisburg Road and continue 11 miles).
Open: Daily June–September, open only by reservation in winter.
Serving: B, D.
Cuisine: Polish and American.
Price: Inexpensive to Moderate.
Credit Cards: MC, V.
Reservations: Recommended.
Handicap Access: Yes.

Catering to urban Polish-Americans (who arrive in groups from New York City) looking for a taste of the old country, this Bavarian-style lodge really feels like another world; you'll notice most guests aren't speaking English. The cozy front room, with a fieldstone fireplace and leather couches, welcomes diners and sets a pleasant tone.

The fixed-price menu (less than $15 in 1999) includes an appetizer such as Polish kebabs with cucumbers, pickles, kielbasa, olives and tomato, and a choice of homemade soups, like wild mushroom or sour cucumber. Six or seven entrées include house specialties like *bigos* (kielbasa, sauerkraut, and mushrooms), *pierogi* (pastry turnovers filled with meat, cheese, sauerkraut, or mashed potatoes) or *golombky* (cabbage stuffed with rice and beef or veal). The pork loin and kielbasa dishes are made from pigs raised on the property; the homemade sauerkraut is fantastic. (If this sounds too exotic, there are also American selections such as filet mignon and fried chicken.) Dinner concludes with coffee or tea and delicious homemade strudel or other traditional pastry. Bring a spirit of adventure and a big appetite — you won't be disappointed.

Warrensburg

BRUNETTO'S
518-623-1041.
Rte. 9, just south of Northway Exit 23.
Open: Tues.–Sun.
Serving: D.
Cuisine: Italian.
Price: Moderate to Expensive.
Credit Cards: MC, V.
Handicap Access: Yes.
Special Features: Bring your own wine or beer.

Granted, the setting isn't exactly inspiring: exterior repairs on this roadside restaurant and cabins never seem to be quite completed, but the full parking lot night after night is a sure tip-off. Brunetto's serves great food, and plenty of it.

As soon as you're seated, a waiter comes around with a corkscrew for the wine that you've remembered to bring, and toting a plate full of paté and crackers. The temptation is to fill up on the freebies, but show some restraint. Salads are served family-style with homemade dressings, another challenge to holding back for better things to come.

Seafood takes center stage here, in appetizers such as steamed mussels or clams casino (highly recommended), and lovely entrées like salmon in dill caper sauce or seared tuna loin. Brunetto's regulars, though, cheerfully put on their plastic bibs and plow through the awesome zuppa di mussels, which comes in a vast bowl containing about two pounds of pasta, five dozen mussels, and maybe a whole head of garlic. It's enough for a couple of meals.

If you're not in the mood for fish, the rack of lamb is very good, as are the chicken picatta and chicken marsala. If you're a devoted dessert eater, ask the wait staff for suggestions. In all our trips to this landmark, we've never even nibbled the sweets.

THE GRIST MILL
518-623-8005.
100 River St. (Rte. 418 just beyond the iron bridge).
Open: Daily Labor Day–Memorial Day; Closed, Jan–Mar.; Wed–Sun. rest of year.
Serving: D.
Cuisine: Contemporary American.
Price: Expensive.
Credit Cards: AE, MC, V.
Reservations: Recommended.
Handicap Access: Yes.
Special Features: Mill museum, screen porch overlooking the river.

Overhanging the rapids of the Schroon River, this authentic water-powered mill offers a rare opportunity to enjoy a truly fine meal in a historic setting. Built in 1824, the Warrensburg landmark serves contemporary American cuisine amidst a museum of old gears and turbines, chutes and pulleys. Closed for several months in early 1999, the restaurant was recently opened by new owners, a father-and-son team

The Grist Mill features a premium wine list and its own excellent Grist Mill American Wheat Beer. Meals begin with a tray offering slices from three different craft breads from Rock Hill, a superb bakery midway between Saratoga Springs and Glens Falls. Appetizers range from grilled eggplant ravioli filled with goat cheese to jumbo gulf prawns stuffed with pine nuts and fresh herbs over angelhair pasta. All entrées are served with a mixed organic greens salad and a choice of homemade dressings.

Dinner entrées expertly combine traditional American favorites with a noveau flair. Pan-roasted halibut is presented over shrimp fried rice; grilled, marinated boneless pork chops are served over a black bean sauce and pilaf; rack of lamb is paired with spinach and roasted garlic; and pan-roasted chicken breast is topped with spinach, prosciutto, fresh mozzarella, and wild mushroom sauce. Desserts are terrific.

MERRILL MAGEE HOUSE
518-623-2449.
2 Hudson St. (near the band shell off Rte. 9).
Closed: Mar.
Serving: L Tues.–Sat. May–Oct.; D daily.
Cuisine: Continental.
Price: Expensive.

Behind a prim white picket fence and across the street from Warrensburg's pocket-size band shell is the Merrill Magee House, a historic inn with charming dining rooms and a cozy wood-paneled pub. Meals begin with a basket of excellent homemade breads and proceed to good salads; entrées range from traditional rack of lamb to wiener schnitzel to Maryland crabcakes with basil tartar sauce, tournedos béarnaise, and fresh fish. A

Credit Cards: AE, DC, MC, V.
Handicap Access: Yes.

new generation of management took over in fall 1999 (son and daughter of the previous innkeepers), and they have great plans to update facilities, accommodate large groups, host weddings in a lovely garden, and tinker with the menu.

Authentic English ales and stouts are available in the cozy pub, and the wine list is quite complete. Merrill Magee House is a popular spot for dinner seminars, with a staff accustomed to entertaining groups.

CHAMPLAIN VALLEY

Crown Point

FRENCHMAN'S RESTAURANT
Route 9N/22, near the Champlain Bridge.
518-597-3545.
Open: Year-round.
Serving: B, L, D; breakfast and lunch only Mondays and Tuesdays.
Price: Inexpensive to moderate.
Credit cards: All major.

Under new — friendlier — management, Frenchman's Restaurant features good home-cooked fare at very reasonable prices. If you've stopped here after crossing the Champlain Bridge or touring the Crown Point State Historic Site and found the place wanting, you'll be glad to know the service and atmosphere have improved.

Locals come for the homemade lunch special, usually under $5, things like goulash over noodles, lasagna, and so on. Dinner continues in the same homey theme, with meatloaf, pastas, and steaks. Dessert is homemade pies and cakes, or in summer you can walk next door for soft ice cream or a sundae, at Frenchy's Ice Cream.

Elizabethtown

DEER'S HEAD INN
518-873-9903.
Court St.
Open: Year-round.
Serving: L, D.
Cuisine: American, Continental.
Price: Inexpensive to Moderate.
Credit Cards: AE, MC, V.
Handicap Access: Yes.

This rambling inn, built in 1808, has a pleasant ambiance in three adjoining dining rooms. The two front rooms — one outfitted with a stone fireplace — are decorated in blue and white, and the walls are hung with landscapes by a well-known Adirondack artist, Ruth Rumney. The cozy dining room in the back is wood-paneled and lined with shelves of old books.

Dinners at the Deer's Head start with mini corn fritters, pesto-lobster linguine, or venison ravioli.

Entrées — updated considerably in 1999 — include grilled quail, wild boar, rack of lamb, and a delicious seafood stew made with black beans, tomatoes, garlic, scallops, and shrimp. There's a bistro menu too, with less exotic, less expensive things like grilled sausages with homemade mashed potatoes, pork chops, and grilled chicken marina, served over linguine. Lunches include cold and grilled sandwiches (try the Jamaican chicken or tuna-artichoke melt), soups, and salads, all reasonably priced and done well.

THE RIVER RUN
518-873-3379.
Rte. 9, south of Elizabethtown.
Open: year round except January.
Serving: D.
Cuisine: American.
Price: Moderate to Expensive.
Credit Cards: AE, D, MC, V.
Handicap Access: Yes, and handicap bathroom.

This friendly, family-run tavern/restaurant is on the way to New Russia, a tiny hamlet bypassed by the Northway. Big buckets of steamed mussels are a River Run specialty; wash them down with a good draft beer.

Dinners are prepared with care and served with delicious homemade soup, good rolls, and mixed-greens salad. Avoid the chicken marsala, we suggest, but don't be afraid of the lobster, which can be fabulous. There aren't many vegetarian selections except for eggplant parmigiana — which never looks exactly the same from meal to meal but usually tastes just fine. New York strip steaks are good quality too.

Essex

THE ESSEX INN
518-963-8821.
16 Main St.
Open: Year-round.
Serving: B, L, D, SB.
Cuisine: American.
Price: Moderate to Expensive.
Credit Cards: AE, MC, V.
Handicap Access: Through the rear courtyard.

The owners of this landmark, Trish and John Walker, have created bright, welcoming surroundings in an 1810 inn in the center of the small, historic village of Essex. Tables are placed by the windows in the two front dining rooms, and meals are also served on the columned veranda, a great place to sip a glass of wine (the wine list is surprisingly extensive) and watch the summer people amble by.

Though the menu has plenty of intriguing choices, dinner always includes two entrée and one appetizer specials, offering the chef's interpretations of seasonal fresh foods. Soup and dessert offerings change also change along with the harvest. Potato-leek soup is very good, especially accompanied by the inn's crusty homemade bread. Red-meat options, like steak, are more reliable than, say, the vegetarian stir fry; pasta and chicken are typically good.

Lunches are simpler, but quite good: turkey club sandwich, Reuben, grilled cheese, burger. On Sundays, the champagne brunch offers hearty selections such as lasagna, baked ziti, and chicken, along with the usual eggs and pancakes.

OLD DOCK RESTAURANT
518-963-4232.
Lake Shore Rd.
Open: Mid-May–Columbus Day.
Serving: L, D.
Cuisine: American.
Price: Moderate to Expensive.
Credit Cards: AE, D, MC, V.
Handicap Access: Inside dining room only.
Special features: Boat dockage for diners.

Like many of the commercial establishments in Champlain Valley villages, the Old Dock house is located in a handsome stone building dating back to the early 19th century. It was converted to a restaurant in the 1930s, and overlooks the landing of the popular ferry to Vermont.

The current owners, Eric and Jeff Lipkin and Jim Glatz, have several restaurants in Burlington, but this one in Essex is probably the most fun. The setting is great — in good weather, everyone sits outdoors to watch the seagulls spiraling overhead and the clouds racing above Vermont's Green Mountains — and the extensive and eclectic menu looks promising, but in truth, not everything lives up to the copy written about it.

The lunch offerings are nearly as varied as are dinner's, with options like Cajun chicken wrap, quiche of the day, pastas, and our favorite, the pork tenderloin sandwich. At dinner, there are plenty of appetizer choices, from pork dim sum to buffalo wings; our recommendations are sweet potato chips and pesto cornmeal pizza. The chef clearly likes Thai peanut sauce and bruschetta (topped with green olive tapenade), and has a good hand with salads, especially peanut noodle salad and the Mediterranean summer salad, with white beans, kalamata olives, and artichoke hearts.

Entrées include herb-crusted pork tenderloin, blackjack chicken with bourbon-honey mustard sauce, coconut shrimp, cedar plank salmon, lobster and shellfish pie topped with mashed potatoes, and shrimp and crab strudel with spinach and mushrooms. Fish in a bag (crab-stuffed haddock) is tasty, as is the Cuban marinated swordfish. Vegetarians have more possibilities here than at most Adirondack eateries.

SUNBURST TEA GARDEN
618-963-7482.
Main St.
Open: Mid-June–mid-Sept.
Serving: Wed.–Sun. 2–5pm.
Cuisine: English cream teas.
Price: Inexpensive.
Credit Cards: No.
Handicap Access: Yes; park in adjacent lot.

True bliss on a summer afternoon is sitting at a shady table set on the rolling green lawn at the Sunburst Tea Garden, nibbling on a cucumber sandwich, and gazing at Lake Champlain. You enter this bit of heaven through a flower-covered trellis next to a white-painted cottage. The grass is dotted with tables and chairs, some with umbrellas and some set under a broad maple tree. Elsa Sorley, the charming woman who runs this lovely place, hands you a small menu that, along with the offerings, contains a quote from Henry James: "There are few hours in life more agreeable than the hour dedicated to the ceremony known as afternoon tea." A visit to Sunburst proves this sentiment.

For tea, you can order scones with clotted cream and jam, cucumber sandwiches, a plate of assorted tea sandwiches and cookies, or a slice of sponge cake with strawberries or chocolate mud pie. Hot teas include orange pekoe, Darjeeling, Earl Grey, or caffeine-free herb tea.

If you truly love it here, you can spend the night. Sunburst is also a bed and breakfast with a couple of sweet little rooms.

Port Henry

Views of Lake Champlain are framed by windows at the King's Inn.

James Swedberg

THE KING'S INN
518-546-7633 or 800-600-7633.
109 Broad St., off Rtes. 9/22, just west of downtown.
Open: Year-round.
Serving: D.
Cuisine: American.
Price: Moderate.
Credit Cards: All major.
Reservations: Recommended.
Handicap Access: Yes.

Restoring this rambling stone mansion from foundation stone to chimney cap, and creating a good restaurant in a town that has lacked such things since the heydays of iron mining ended, has been a labor of love. The efforts have paid off: the King's Inn now has such a regional following that reservations are essential in summer.

One big, airy dining room with a stone fireplace occupies the long side of the building; across the front, with windows facing the lake, is a smaller dining room generally reserved for smokers. (We prefer this space, especially if there aren't any smokers, but the other dining room is fine.)

Meals begin when your server presents you with a salad checklist; it looks like a multiple-choice quiz, which it is. Choose which things you'd like on your salad — sunflower seeds, green peppers, and black olives, say, or tomatoes, cucumbers, and red onions — and write your name on top. This approach works like a salad bar, but with considerably less waste. That done, order appetizers and entrées. Beef is generally quite good, as is broiled salmon; seafood fra diavolo, with lots of big, juicy shrimp, scallops, and clams over pasta, is abundant and excellent. Note that the King's Inn generally does not have off-menu specials.

Between the two dining rooms is a nice little bar, fine for lingering before dinner in cool weather. The inn has a old-fashioned porch with comfortable wicker furniture and a deck with a view down the hill to the lake; that's where you want to enjoy a glass of wine, dessert, or after-dinner drink on a summer night.

MISS PORT HENRY DINER
518-546-3663.
3 Church St.
Open: Year-round.
Serving: B, L, D.
Cuisine: American.
Price: Inexpensive.
Credit Cards: No.
Handicap Access: Yes.

Day or night, the liveliest scene in this settlement is undoubtedly the Miss Port Henry, which began its working life as a horse-drawn lunch wagon. The diner has been a permanent fixture in downtown Port Henry since the Depression. For many years, though, it lingered doomed and decrepit, but energetic new owners brought the eatery back to life in 1996. Today, decked out in shades of green and cream, it's nostalgic but not gimmicky, and the chow is dandy.

Chicken and biscuits are a hit, as is meatloaf and gravy. Italian night, with lasagna, spaghetti, manicotti, and more, is every Wednesday. Be sure to save room for pie — or have it for breakfast.

<u>Ticonderoga</u>

THE CARILLON
518-585-7657.
61 Hague Rd.
Closed: Wed.
Serving: L, D.
Cuisine: Seafood.
Price: Expensive.
Credit Cards: AE, MC, V.
Handicap Access: No.

Carillon is the original French name of Fort Ticonderoga, the historic site three miles from this restaurant, which is a modest red-painted wooden building close by Rte. 9.

Seafood is always very fresh, and the catch of the day lives up to its name. Soups, especially the creamy seafood bisque, are excellent. Lean fish fillets, shrimp, and bay scallops are competently prepared without fuss and their succulent flavor shines through; the seafood potpie is delicious. Homemade desserts are a cut above the usual.

FORT VIEW INN
518-585-7767.
Rte. 22, 1 mile south of town.

The Fort View Inn was remodeled in 1999 and now features dining on an enclosed porch overlooking Lake Champlain and Fort Ticonderoga. The

Open: daily.
Serving: L, D.
Cuisine: American.
Credit Cards: MC, V.
Handicap Access: Yes.

view is outstanding, with rock cliffs in the foreground, the lake in middle distance, and the stone walls of the fort beyond. The inn's interior wood motif is charming and bright, and service is fast and efficient. There's an extensive sandwich menu for lunch, with sandwiches named after historical figures who visited Fort Ticonderoga. For instance, the General Burgoyne is a lot of turkey piled on a kaiser roll (what, you thought colonial hero Ethan Allen would be represented by turkey?), topped with a tasty sauce and veggies. Sweet-potato fries or fresh, thick homemade French fries are recommended side orders.

Seafood, steaks, and pasta are the featured dinner fare. Desserts include cheesecake and very good homemade pies; this is orchard country, with luscious apple pie a fall favorite.

HOT BISCUIT DINER
518-585-3483.
428 Montcalm St.
Open: Year-round.
Serving: B, L, D.
Cuisine: American.
Price: Inexpensive.
Credit Cards: None.
Handicap Access: Yes.

A few years back, a fire nearly destroyed this cheery, checked-tablecloth place, but thank heavens owners Bonnie and Orley Dixon decided to build up from the ashes. The Hot Biscuit's worth a stop for any meal or if you've got a sudden hankering for hot made-from-scratch gingerbread dolloped with whipped cream or genuine slow-cooked tapioca pudding. Everything's homemade, from blueberry muffins to the trademark biscuits; chili and soup are tasty and a real bargain. For breakfast, go for the plump, puffy Belgian waffles topped with whipped cream and strawberries.

The country dinner plates — less than five bucks and one special per day — feature stuffed peppers, knockwurst and kraut, pot roast, meatloaf, gravy-slathered hamburg, or chicken and biscuits, and come with real cornbread, vegetables, and potatoes. It's true comfort food at a reasonable price. Besides the chow, the place is a mini-museum, decorated with old photos, sheet music, tools, advertising art, and local mementos.

O'LEARY'S
O'Leary's Restaurant at Ticonderoga Country Club.
518-585-7435.
Hague Road (Rte 9N).
Open: Summers only.
Serving: L, D.
Cuisine: American.
Credit Cards: All major.
Handicap Access: Yes.

Located in the clubhouse at Ticonderoga Country Club, O'Leary's offers dining on a sun porch or in a spacious dining room. The course is unquestionably one of the most beautiful in the Adirondacks; the views of the green fairways and nearby mountains from the porch windows are breathtaking. Service is quick and polite, and the menu is more inventive than most other places in town.

At lunch, O'Leary's serves very good salads (grilled chicken Caesar, among others), seafood (broiled scallops are delicious) and great big sandwiches on crusty French bread. Dinner includes aged steaks, sauced chicken dishes, quality seafood, accompanied by nice salads, rolls, and seasonal vegetables.

Westport

LE BISTRO AT THE YACHT CLUB
518-962-8777.
On Lake Champlain, off Rte. 22.
Open: Mid-June–mid-Sept.
Serving: L, D.
Cuisine: French.
Price: Expensive.
Credit Cards: AE, MC, V.
Handicap Access: Yes.

Bernard Perillat, former chef-owner of Le Bistro in Essex, has moved his signature French flair to one of the finest waterfront settings on either side of Lake Champlain. Guests arrive by car — or they sail right up to the concrete dock that forms the front of the outdoor dining area. Le Bistro is without a doubt one of the top ten restaurants in the Adirondacks: simple, fresh ingredients combine in inventive, but not gimmicky, ways.

Start with ciabatta bread. Proceed to wonderful appetizers like escargot on puff pastry, moules marinieres (mussels and shallots in white wine cream sauce), a fine country pâté, or smoked bluefish bruschetta, offered as a special. Then endive salad, or salad with bits of duck or lobster. Entrées are presented elegantly, in perfect (not gluttonous) portions.

The rack of lamb with rosemary and garlic sauce, filet of beef with béarnaise sauce, and duck with green peppercorns are all winners. Le Bistro may be the only spot between Montreal and Manhattan with true filet tartare on the menu. The bouillabaisse provencal is highly recommended, and the lovely broth overflows with succulent lobster, mussels, scallops, shrimp, and clams; chicken is prepared in a different way each day. The wine list is excellent, and Continental desserts feature seasonal fruits and top-quality chocolate.

Lunch offers an excellent, reasonably priced, way to sample the menu and enjoy an alfresco meal in the sun. Choices include half a lobster with tarragon mayonnaise, spinach quiche, an excellent burger, and many specials.

Willsboro

UPPER DECK AT WILLSBORO BAY MARINA
518-963-8271.
Klein Dr., on Lake Champlain, off Point Rd.
Open: Mid-June–Labor Day.
Serving: D.

The Upper Deck's two airy dining rooms — with walls of windows that are kept open in warm weather — overlook Willsboro Bay and the wooded cliffs beyond. To complement the ambiance, chef Laurie Anne Foster has created menus that meld American dishes with world flavors. For example, enticing lunch selections include sun-dried-tomato

On warm summer days, these garage doors roll up to provide open-air dining at the Upper Deck.

James Swedberg

Cuisine: American, Continental.
Price: Moderate to Expensive.
Credit Cards: MC, V.
Handicap Access: Yes.

tortillas rolled around grilled onion, zucchini, and shrimp or a grilled ham, cheese, and artichoke sandwich on a crusty roll. Soups are very good, especially the gazpacho with homegrown herbs.

For dinner, appetizers include eggplant and red pepper terrine, gravlax, and Boursin-stuffed mushrooms, which make nice transitions to rack of veal with fresh sage, rotisserie chicken with maple-mustard sauce, or red sky ravioli, which are colorful striped ravioli served with roasted red pepper cream sauce. Three to five specials are offered each night, and vegetarians should be quite happy here. (If you can't eat milk products or wheat, call ahead; the chef will make something delicious just for you.) There's a scaled-down menu for children, an extensive wine list, and good desserts, like strawberry torte and chocolate pecan pie.

HIGH PEAKS AND NORTHERN ADIRONDACKS

Keene

BAXTER MOUNTAIN TAVERN
518-576-9990.
Rte. 9 (Spruce Hill) about a mile east of Rte. 73.
Open: Year-round.
Serving: L, D.
Price: Moderate.
Cuisine: American.
Credit Cards: MC, V.
Handicap Access: Yes.

Purchased by siblings David and Christie Deyo in 1999, Baxter Mountain Tavern is casual and comfortable, with an overstuffed couch facing a stone fireplace, a big bar, and a dining room with a view of Hurricane Mountain. Settle in with a good draft beer, like Sierra Nevada or Sam Adams pale ale. If you're traveling through the High Peaks with a family, this place is very kid-friendly too.

The Deyos are trying hard to please, responding to customer suggestions that have already helped them improve. Every day there's a ravioli special; the portabella ravioli (ask for marinara sauce; the cream sauce is awfully rich) is quite good, as are the pork chops. Save room for dessert, which is always made by Christie and always good.

ELM TREE INN
518-576-9769.
Rtes. 9N and 73.
Closed: Tues.
Serving: L, D.
Cuisine: American.
Price: Inexpensive to Moderate.
Credit Cards: None.
Handicap Access: Yes.

Renovations on this 19th-century landmark tavern were recently completed, and Purdy's — as it's locally known — looks terrific. There are tables on the spacious porch (although this intersection is noisy during the summer months), and the two indoor dining rooms are nicely finished off with gleaming wainscoting.

The food is absolutely no-nonsense, reasonably priced, and delivered to your table with cheerful efficiency. Soups, like cream of mushroom or cream of spinach, are delicious; the cole slaw is probably the best in Essex County. Sandwiches and hand-patted hamburgers are huge, juicy, and worth, say, a half-hour drive. Dinners are fairly simple, with your best choice the center-cut pork chops or rib eye platter, or you can always fall back on the classic Purdy burger, topped with a thick slice of Bermuda onion and melted cheese. There's a full bar and a small selection of American wines. Vegetarians may find this place a challenge, but the baked potatoes are excellent.

Keene Valley

AUSABLE INN
518-576-9986.
Rte. 73/Main St.
Closed: Mon.
Serving: D.
Cuisine: American.
Price: Moderate.
Credit Cards: MC, V.
Handicap Access: Yes.

What distinguishes the Ausable Inn from other typical Adirondack restaurants (dim, but cozy, with pine-paneled walls and a bar off to one side) are its margaritas, Mexican night, and lobster night — and the greatest of these is the margarita. Tiny, the bartender, knows tequila.

Lobster night (Wednesdays in winter; call to check) is usually surprisingly good; when Mexican fare is featured, it tends to be the same four or five ingredients arranged in six or seven ways. The vegetable burrito is tasty, as is the homemade salsa. For regular dinners, the open-faced steak sandwich is both a bargain and a treat; hunter's chicken, sautéed in white wine with tarragon, tomatoes, and mushrooms, is also worthwhile.

CLIFFHANGER CAFE
518-576-2009.
Main St. (Rte. 73), across from the library.
Open: Year-round.
Serving: B, L summer; D on fall weekends.

People told Brooklynite Karen Trank she was crazy to open a vegetarian restaurant in the carnivorous Adirondacks, but a successful first summer in 1999 proves otherwise. Because of the variety of offerings, folks don't miss the hamburgs or pastrami sandwiches.

Cuisine: Vegetarian.
Price: Inexpensive to Moderate.
Credit Cards: MC, V.
Handicap Access: Yes, but tables are quite close together.

Belgian waffles are huge, popular, even hugely popular, served with blueberries, strawberries, or bananas, maple syrup, and whipped cream. A specialty of the house is *panini*, a pressed Italian sandwich available at breakfast or lunch, with combinations like the Sierra (egg, avocado, sprouts, tomatoes, onion, and cheddar) or the Dolomite (portabella mushrooms, spinach, pesto, and tomato). Homemade soups often use produce from Keene's own Rivermede farm, and include sage, potato, and kale; acorn squash; and Senegalese seafood stew. Salads are also recommended, with smoked tofu a best-seller. The coffee — from Cold River, a local roaster — is excellent. Dunk your homemade biscotti in it, or sip as you enjoy a chocolate pecan oatmeal cookie or a lemon-ginger scone.

A word here: don't wait for a server to take your order. Walk up to the counter, tell the person at the cash register what you want, pay, take a number, and sit down. Your food will be delivered to your table. This system adds to a crowded feeling on a summer day, but most of the time it works.

NOON MARK DINER
518-576-4499.
Rte. 73/Main St.
Open: Year-round.
Serving: B, L, D.
Cuisine: Diner.
Price: Inexpensive.
Credit Cards: None.
Handicap Access: Yes.

Everybody from High Peaks backpackers to investment bankers to local kids on bikes converges at the Noon Mark at some point during a typical week, to stoke up on great homemade doughnuts, cinnamon buns, pies, muffins, banana bread, soups, French fries, and whatever else is on the menu. You can order breakfast any time, if you're not up for excellent chili made with chunks of beef round, or the trail blazer, a steak sandwich with sautéed mushrooms, onions, and peppers on a hard roll. The BLTs are good, but request your bacon extra crisp.

Dinners lean toward frozen things popped into the deep fryer, like clams or shrimp, but soup, salad, and potatoes or rice come with any choice, and nothing on the menu is more than $8. After a long day in the outdoors, try turkey or lasagna, and then order some heavenly pie (worth a visit for coconut cream alone) to have for breakfast the next day. An ice cream stand is off to one side of the huge front porch, if you want some walk-around dessert. Note that the Noon Mark can be jammed on summer weekends, with sometimes a half-hour wait for a table and another half hour before your meal is served.

Lake Placid

CHARCOAL PIT
518-523-3050.

The menu announces that this family-run place goes through "10,000 pounds of charcoal a

Saranac Ave. near the Grand Union.
Open: Daily in summer; closed midweek off-season.
Serving: D.
Cuisine: American.
Price: Expensive.
Credit Cards: AE, DC, MC, V.
Reservations: Suggested.
Handicap Access: Yes.

year," which should put steak stalkers on alert. The Charcoal Pit is a big place, but not overwhelmingly so, and it's got a dedicated following among older Placidians who want good American food without gimmicks. On summer evenings, especially during big events like the horse show, this restaurant can be jammed, but the quiet bar is a nice place to wait for your table.

Dinners come with homemade soup and salad, plus rice or potato, so think twice before you order an appetizer (stuffed mushrooms, escargot, and Caesar salad are among the choices). Lamb chops are good; steaks are quite good, and come in sizes from a six-ounce petite filet with bearnaise sauce to Chateaubriand for two. Chicken Eric, with spinach, pine nuts, and sun-dried tomatoes, finished in a wine-butter sauce is delicious and rich. Some subtle Greek touches are evident in the plaki sauce (tomato, garlic, black olives, feta, and olive oil) offered for shrimp and broiled halibut.

Desserts come to your table on a gold-painted two-tiered cart. It's tough to resist the chocolate-banana cake and various toffee-crunch tortes and fruit pies, although you can always take dessert home for a midnight snack.

INTERLAKEN INN
518-523-3180.
15 Interlaken Ave.
Closed: Tues.–Wed.
Price: Expensive to Very Expensive.
Cuisine: Contemporary American.
Serving: D.
Credit Cards: AE, MC, V.
Reservations: Recommended.
Handicap Access: No.
Special Features: Lovely old inn.

One of Lake Placid's fine old homes has been transformed into a Victorian inn by its present owners, the Johnson family. Only a limited number of outside diners are accepted beyond the house count; typically six to nine can be accommodated on a given evening. Chef Kevin Gregg and his staff lavish care upon the food they prepare, and individual attention is given to the serving as well. The small dining room is lovely, with tall windows and high ceilings.

The Interlaken features a full menu with appetizers that include crab cakes, lobster crepes, wild mushroom cannelloni, and roasted corn and tomato soup; a different house salad is created each night. Main course highlights include orange-glazed duck breast; sautéed veal medallions; black angus filet mignon accompanied by shiitake potato gallette and roasted pear-tomato sauce; homemade wild mushroom pasta; rack of lamb provencal with ratatouille and nicoise olive tapenade; and scampi risotto with grilled shrimp. For dessert try the Grand Marnier creme brulée, homemade ice cream, or warm truffle cake. Gregg prefers to call the Interlaken's style American, but enjoys trying different combinations and subtle flavorings that add unique touches his dishes.

The Lake Placid Lodge combines wonderful ambiance with innovative cuisine.

Ben Stechschulte

LAKE PLACID LODGE
518-523-2700.
Whiteface Inn Rd.
Open: Daily.
Serving: B, L, D.
Cuisine: Continental.
Price: Very Expensive.
Credit Cards: AE, DC, MC, V.
Reservations: Suggested.
Handicap Access: No.

Fabulously restored, the Lake Placid Lodge is a genuine destination resort. The building is a wonderful old Adirondack camp, with a sweet little bar decorated with deep green walls and yellow-birch-log trim, wraparound porches with sweeping lake views, and a sitting room with a huge cobblestone fireplace. The dining room deftly combines austere elegance with rustic twig-work, in dark walls and delicate peeled branches extending from the floor to the ceiling.

Chef Robert Breyette's dinner menu is fantastic, with a long list of appetizers that reflect what's in season, such as venison on creamy polenta, homemade tortellini, lobster risotto, and terrine of smoked salmon. Salads are very good, and panzanella (Tuscan bread salad) makes an excellent entrée in the summer. Main courses run from whole Dover sole, to cider and peppercorn glazed venison loin, to superb lamb chops, prepared with imaginative sauces and presented beautifully. Each meat or fish is combined with its own complementary potato, rice, or grain pilaf, and seasonal vegetable. Desserts are all made on the premises; the outstanding Ménage à Trois is three different crème brûlées.

The wine list contains thoughtfully chosen domestic, French, and Australian wines. The service is consummately professional and well informed.

If you'd like to try the Lodge, but with a more modest budget, breakfast and lunch are wonderful, and there's a bistro menu (soups, salads, appetizers) available in the bar. Sunday brunch costs more than lunch but less than dinner; for the holidays, the prix fixe dinners are divine.

LE BISTRO LALIBERTÉ
518-523-3680.
51 Main St., underneath Eastern Mountain Sports.
Open: Year-round.
Serving: D.
Cuisine: Contemporary American, Continental.
Price: Expensive to Very Expensive.
Credit Cards: MC, V.
Reservations: Recommended in summer.
Handicap Access: No.

Two lovely, small dining rooms in shades of almond, peach, and forest green offer an intimate atmosphere at this upscale bistro, but the best place to eat in summer or fall is on the deck overlooking Mirror Lake. From several tables, you get a clear view of Whiteface, and trees screen the setting beautifully from the adjacent park. On Wednesdays in the summer, you can listen to the Lake Placid Sinfonietta as you dine.

Chef Robert Borden learned about pastries during a stint at Le Cirq, but the entire menu is as imaginative as you'll find anywhere in northern New York. For starters, try the mussels steamed in vermouth, salmon with Thai peanut sauce, or shrimp and andouille sausage brochette. Although the list of entrées is brief, the choices are intriguing and delicious: real cassoulet, with smoked duck, lamb sausage, and white beans; crisp lemon-rosemary chicken with potato-celery root puree; or shrimp and scallops provençal. Desserts are presented with a flourish. The Napoleon *pallaison* — an over-the-top creation — comes with polka dots of fruit puree, layers of shredded phyllo, fresh berries, and crème fraîche, while La Grand Opera is deep chocolate cake with the kind of sumptuous butter cream that few dare to make anymore. The chocolate soufflé is pure heaven.

MIRROR LAKE INN
518-523-2544.
5 Mirror Lake Dr.
Open: Daily.
Serving: B, D, afternoon tea.
Cuisine: American, Continental.
Price: Expensive to Very Expensive.
Credit Cards: AE, CB, DC, MC, V.
Reservations: Suggested.
Handicap Access: Yes.

For years it seemed that the lovely Mirror Lake Inn was stuck in a time warp, with a stuffy, formal dining room serving unmemorable food. The good news is that the dress code has lightened up (no more jackets and ties required, but men should wear shirts with collars and women should avoid shorts). The menu's been livened up too, with plenty of interesting things from starters to desserts. Mirror Lake Inn deserves to be considered one of Lake Placid's top five restaurants.

This new approach shows a real understanding of what diners want. The wine list contains dozens of wines available as half bottles, perfect for couples. The dining room is huge, but corners and crannies and luxuriant Boston ferns divide the space into more intimate nooks. The wait staff is thoroughly professional —friendly, but not too friendly.

For appetizers, start with the delicious home-smoked prawns; Montrachet cheese, red pepper, and grilled eggplant terrine; or the three-onion tart: leeks, shallots, and sweet onions with gorgonzola cheese and lemon sage cream. For a nice vegetarian entrée, try Pasta Algonquin, orechiette with pine nuts,

Mirror Lake Inn's dining room is one of the best in Lake Placid, with excellent contemporary American food and comfortable ambiance.

Mirror Lake Inn

roasted peppers, spinach, and whole roasted garlic. There's a spa menu with things like braised sea bass with polenta or wild mushroom pasta. Steak lovers can find excellent beef here; the grilled duck breast with apple, apricot, and ginger conserve is quite good, but ask for the duck to be served rare to get the best flavor.

If you have remembered not to gorge utterly (it's tempting, especially when your server casually mentions seconds are available), desserts run from homey banana bread pudding and maple crème brûlée to white chocolate cappuccino cheesecake or chocolate bourbon pecan tart. This is one of the few places in northern New York where you can find true ice wine to accompany that dessert, or select from ten dessert coffees.

Just across Mirror Lake Drive is the **Cottage**, a breezy little bar right on the lake. It's a fine spot for enjoying a glass of wine or a featured draft beer and some nachos; though there is a menu showing a variety of sandwiches and salads, the kitchen is limited.

NICOLA'S OVER MAIN
518-523-4430.
90 Main St., upstairs.
Open: Daily.
Serving: D.
Cuisine: Mediterranean.
Price: Moderate to Very Expensive.
Credit Cards: MC, V.
Reservations: Recommended in summer or for large parties.
Handicap Access: Yes.

Lake Placid natives remember this site as the former NAPA store, but under the assiduous care of Mike and Nia Nicola, the place has been transformed into one of the Olympic Village's top restaurants. (The Nicolas also own Mr. Mike's Pizza, Mr. Mike's Pizza Express, and the Main Street Diner; success at those restaurants has contributed to the polished presentation and wonderful menu here.)

The list of appetizers is long and tempting, with two calamari dishes, fritto misto, basilla torta (a layer cake of basil, soft cheese, and garlic to spread on bruschetta), and pikilia (assorted Greek dishes including tiropetes) at the top of the list. Salad lovers have plenty of great options, including niçoise, Caesar, spinach, Mediterranean, and unique combinations of greens, fruits, and nuts, available in small and large sizes. Entrées range from a dozen kinds of excellent wood-fired pizza (try the gorgonzola, rosemary, and black olive) and fresh pasta dishes to grilled seafood, veal, pork, and chicken served with crusty hearth-baked bread. The dessert list often includes homemade tiramisu; there's a small wine list with appropriate selections and full-service bar.

TASTE OF INDIA
518-523-8298.
97 Saranac Ave.
Open: Year-round.
Serving: L, D, SB.
Cuisine: Indian.
Price: Inexpensive to Moderate.
Credit Cards: AE, MC, V.
Reservations: No.
Handicap Access: Yes.
Special Features: Take-out and catering available.

Ethnic food in Lake Placid, a town that prides itself on international sports, has been pedestrian (Mexican and Italian) at best — until Taste of India opened in summer 1997. Planted next door to a mini-mart, it's a surprisingly attractive, friendly place.

There are scores of provocative choices for vegetarians and carnivores alike, in a full range of spiciness; if anything, the kitchen could turn up the heat just a little. Start your meal with vegetable pakoras, some poppadums, or shrimp pakoras. Take your next cue from the menu, which firmly states "an Indian meal, without bread, is not complete," and order naan with garlic or the house special bread, stuffed with cauliflower, cheese, morsels of chicken tikka, and spices.

Tandoor items, especially the mixed grill Bombay, tend to be too dry; better choices are saagwala curries (garlicky, creamy spinach sauce for lamb, chicken, or shrimp), delectable chicken Jalferezi, bhuna lamb, shrimp masala, or the house vegetarian thali, with dal, chana masala (gingery chickpeas), roti bread, mattar paneer (yogurt cheese with peas), and rice. The house special biryani, packed with vegetables, lamb, and shrimp, is also quite good, and take-out portions are positively enormous.

THE THIRSTY MOOSE
518-523-3222.
Main St., across from the Olympic Arena.
Open: Year-round.
Serving: L, D.
Cuisine: American.
Price: Inexpensive to Moderate.
Credit Cards: MC, V.
Reservations: No.
Handicap Access: Yes.

Family dining in Lake Placid can be a challenge: at one end of the spectrum is McDonald's, and at the other, places that cost $40 per person. Thankfully, the Thirsty Moose rises to the occasion with a menu that has plenty for kids to enjoy (burgers, chicken fingers, spaghetti), plus good options for the grown-ups. The dining room — booths ringing a big open space with a fireplace in the center — is child-friendly, but not generic looking. The beer selection is a treat, featuring Red Hook, Sam Adams, Saranac Pale Ale, and other quality brews, and the homemade nachos with chunky salsa offer the perfect starting point.

For entrées, try shrimp tequila served over pasta, excellent beef or turkey potpies, roast pork loin, or Mount Whitney chicken, with raspberry sauce.

VERANDA
518-523-2556.
1 Olympic Dr. (across from the Holiday Inn).
Closed: Mon.
Serving: D.
Cuisine: French.
Price: Expensive to Very Expensive.
Credit Cards: AE, CB, DC, MC, V.
Reservations: Recommended.
Handicap Access: Yes.

Where to start with the superlatives when describing the Veranda? The list begins with an amazing view, an elegant old mansion, and a classic French menu. This place is worth a special trip, and eating on the deck is heavenly. A stunning panorama of the Sentinel Range marches across your field of view, with a bit of Mirror Lake showing in the foreground.

Downstairs are two dining rooms of comfortable size, each with cobblestone fireplaces; upstairs are three private dining rooms accommodating from six to 40 or so guests. All are finished with handsome woodwork, wallpapers, and drapes.

Don't look for evidence of the latest dining fad when you pick up the menu; the choices are tried and true examples of French country cuisine. Appetizers are all delectable, with the escargot, jumbo shrimp amandine, and vegetable terrine at the top of our list. The house salad (note that everything is à la carte) covers a dinner plate with artfully arranged shredded vegetables and greens; the Caesar salad is also good.

The many entrée options include duck breast with a duet of sauces (green peppercorn and raspberry), salmon quenelles, grilled rosemary lamb (terrific), aged steaks, and superb bouillabaisse (summer only). Desserts, all made in the Veranda's kitchen, show real finesse, such as apple tart, peach Melba, and Paris-Brest (puff paste with hazelnut cream). The wine list is extensive, although house wines available by the glass are limited.

Ray Brook

TAIL O' THE PUP
518-891-5092.
Rte. 86, next to the Evergreens cabins.
Closed: Mid-Oct.–mid-May.
Serving: L, D.
Cuisine: Barbecue.
Price: Inexpensive.
Credit Cards: None.
Handicap Access: Yes.
Special Features: Folk music in summer.

For more than half a century, Tail O' the Pup has served happy travelers with its winning combination of great, cheap food, and come-as-you-are atmosphere. You can eat at a picnic table under the stars or beneath a huge tent, inside at a booth, or even beep for a carhop. Bring the kids: they'll love the place, especially on the nights when "Dr. Y," the owner, is dressed up and dancing around in his lobster outfit.

The ribs and chicken are terrific, smoked and smothered with tangy, not-too-sweet sauce, and come with waffle fries, corn on the cob, and a minuscule dab of pretty good cole slaw. On Wednesday, Thursday, and Friday nights, you can also get steamed clams or whole lobster for bargain prices. Onion rings are just the way they should be, crunchy and sweet; better order a couple of portions for the table. About half a dozen good imported and domestic beers are on tap. Oddly, the hot-dogs — for which this landmark is named — aren't so terrific.

Saranac Lake

THE BELVEDERE RESTAURANT
518-891-9873.
57 Bloomingdale Ave.
Open: Year-round.
Serving: D.
Cuisine: American, Italian.
Price: Moderate.
Credit Cards: None.
Handicap Access: Yes.

Since 1933, there's been a member of the Cavallo family in the Belvedere's kitchen, and the restaurant is known for consistently good Italian home cooking. If you've been to a Midwestern supper club, you'll recognize the ambiance: the rambling dining room, a dim and smoky bar, a crew of regulars who have their own special tables. The staff is competent and treats you like a member of the community; if you don't want to feel like a tourist, this is the place. The drinks are reasonably priced, including a good selection of Italian and California wines.

Hot sausage is made right here, and provides zip to thick tomato sauces; recommended entrées include veal and peppers, chicken cacciatore, and lasagna with homemade noodles. Appetizers are few and downright quaint — celery and olives, for instance. For dessert, try spumoni or save room for cheesecake.

CASA DEL SOL
518-891-0977.
154 Lake Flower Ave.
Open: Year-round.
Serving: L, D.
Cuisine: Mexican.
Price: Inexpensive to Moderate.
Credit Cards: None.
Reservations: No.
Handicap Access: Yes, but rest rooms are not accessible.

Suspicious about just how good Mexican food could be this far from the border? Cast those doubts aside: Casa del Sol offers ample fire and spice in its authentic dishes. The place has been wildly successful since it began in the late seventies, so much so that sometimes the staff forgets the necessary niceties in dealing with the public. Leave your credit cards at home; don't ask about reservations (Tom Brokaw tried and failed); and you won't be seated — even if there are empty places — if your party isn't complete. Expect to wait for a table in the summer and on weekends, but you can certainly spend a little time on the patio sipping an outstanding margarita made with designer tequila.

Recently the menu underwent a long overdue update, and low-fat black bean selections were added to offset the heavier *frijoles refritos.* Chimichangas (shrimp, beef, or chicken), flautas (chili verde, chorizo, or beef), enchiladas with red or green sauce, tostadas, tacos, quesadillas, burritos, and combination plates are all consistent and as good as you might find in the Southwest. Salads and soups, especially the tortilla soup, are delicious. Desserts — well, who lusts for dessert in a Mexican restaurant? Have a cup of steaming hot chocolate with a shot of Kahlua.

LA BELLA RISTORANTE
518-891-1551.
175 Lake Flower Ave.
Open: Year-round.
Serving: D.
Cuisine: Italian.
Price: Moderate to Expensive.
Credit Cards: MC, V.
Handicap Access: Yes.

Walls made of peeled cedar logs, white tablecloths, and fresh flowers make this Saranac Lake eatery appealing, and the unending sounds of Frank Sinatra on the CD player hammer home the fact this is an Italian restaurant. Well, actually, the owners escaped from war-torn Bosnia, but they've definitely got a way with Mediterranean cooking.

Hot antipasto, which includes clams casino, eggplant parmesan, and calamari, is a great starter for two to share or a nice light meal. You can order sauces with your choice of pasta (ziti, linguine, fettuccini, or cappelini), or try more elaborate presentations, like gnocchi bolognese, mussels fra diavolo, or seafood Neapolitan over tortellini. Pasta à la guesta, with scallops, shrimp, and half a lobster, occasionally offered as a special, is definitely recommended. For dessert, spumoni.

The same extended family operates **Corvo**, across from the Hotel Saranac, and **Jimmy's**, in downtown Lake Placid. The menus are similar, and the dining room at Jimmy's is smaller (but with a view of Mirror Lake and a few tables outside). Parking in downtown Lake Placid can be a challenge, though, on summer nights.

A.P. SMITH'S
Hotel Saranac of Paul Smith's College.
518-891-2200.
101 Main St.
Open: Year-round.
Serving: B, L, D.
Cuisine: American, Continental.
Price: Moderate.
Credit Cards: AE, DC, MC, V.
Reservations: Required for theme buffet.
Handicap Access: Yes.
Special Features: Bakery in lobby.

This comfortable, spacious dining room has at least two important roles: to offer reliable fare to travelers and to train future restaurateurs who are students of nearby Paul Smith's College. The hosts, bartenders, wait staff, bakers, and "cheffies" are all anxious to please.

A. P. Smith's presents the best sit-down lunch in Saranac Lake, with good grilled chicken sandwiches, salads, burgers, soups, and specials like the cold lamb sandwich with chutney. At dinner appetizers range from baked brie with raspberry coulis to crisp calamari, plus specials. Typical entrées include Cornish game hen with a warm potato-portabella mushroom salad, shrimp and pesto over fettucine, chicken manicotti with braised spinach, barbecued ribs, and vegetarian lasagna.

Looking over the menu, you may start to wonder just what the kitchen is trying to prove. The offerings are eclectic, yes, but with good reason: to allow students to master a wide range of cuisines. On Thursday nights during the school year, the budding culinary artists prepare multi-course buffets on ethnic themes (Cajun, Polynesian, German), which are served in the lovely second-floor lobby.

Wilmington

THE HUNGRY TROUT
518-946-2217.
Rte. 86, at the Ausable River bridge.
Closed: Mid-Mar.–mid-May, Nov.
Serving: D.
Cuisine: Continental.
Price: Expensive.
Credit Cards: AE, MC, V.
Handicap Access: Yes.

A mile-long section of the legendary West Branch of the Ausable River wraps around this motel/restaurant/fly shop complex, and fine views of Whiteface Mountain and a foaming waterfall can be seen from the dining room. Arrive before dark, as the setting sun puts a golden glow on the hillside; the scenery is awesome, and upstages the food.

The menu is extensive, with numerous trout (farm-raised) dishes, plus quality lamb, steaks, pasta, chicken, and excellent mesquite-grilled Norwegian salmon. The combination plate "American Bounty" includes venison medallions, pan-fried trout, and whiskey-peppercorn steak. The house salad, dressed with balsamic vinaigrette, is quite good, and desserts range from premium ice creams to fruit pies.

If you'd like to sample this spot, but prefer not to spend a bundle, try the tavern on the ground floor, **R.F.** (as in Rat Face McDougall, a trout fly) **McDougall's.** It's casual, with antique woodsy/sporty decor, comfortable booths, a lighter menu (excellent char-broiled burgers) and lots of good beers on hand. It's such a nice setting, you've got to wonder what the karaoke machine is doing there.

MEL'S DINER
518-946-2654.
Rte. 86 near the Whiteface Memorial Highway intersection.
Open: Daily, year-round.
Serving: B, L, D.
Cuisine: American.
Price: Inexpensive.
Credit Cards: MC, V.
Handicap Access: Yes.

Brand-new in 1999, but looking inside like a classic fifties diner, Mel's tries pretty hard. The successes come from the soda fountain (really great malts and milk shakes) and the grill (good burgers). What doesn't always work are the sides like bland macaroni or potato salad, bowls of soup or chili, or dinner entrées that appear to have gone from the freezer to the microwave without much actual human contact.

That said, Mel's is a fine place to bring the kids. They'll think the setting is way cool (including the life-size cut-outs of movie stars in the bathrooms), and they'll love the Sabrett hot dogs, spicy fries, grilled cheese sandwiches, and hamburgs. Adults can sit back and enjoy a beer or wine while the kids check out the historic displays.

PINETREE PASTA COMPANY
518-946-2262.
Rte. 86 near the Wilmington post office, in the Mountain Brook Motel.
Open: Thurs.–Sun., year-round.
Serving: D.
Cuisine: Italian.
Price: Moderate.
Credit Cards: MC, V.
Handicap Access: Yes.

Leery of restaurants at small motels? Most of the time you have good reason to be. But the Pinetree Pasta Company, part of the Mountain Brook Motel, is really a nice little place with good homemade Italian food.

For appetizers, try the broiled eggplant packages or tomato, mozzarella, and basil foccacia; for salads, try the Greek, the Caesar, or the corkscrew pasta salad with asparagus. Homemade lasagna — a thick, cheesy, delicious slab — is what Wilmingtonians come here for, but the tortellini with artichoke hearts is pretty good too. Save room for lovely pie.

NORTHWEST LAKES

Cranberry Lake

CRANBERRY LAKE LODGE
315-848-3301.
www.cranberrylake lodge. com.
Rte. 3.
Closed: Apr.
Serving: B, L, D.
Cuisine: American.
Price: Moderate.
Credit Cards: MC, V.
Handicap Access: Yes.
Special Features: Picnic tables overlooking the lake.

Stanley Kolonko, a graduate of the Culinary Institute of America, took over the kitchen here in 1998, and developed great menus for breakfast, lunch, and dinner — no easy task anywhere, but a particular challenge so far from farmstands and meat purveyors. At breakfast, something called Brandy Brook (named after a local stream) features cornbread-crumbed trout with two eggs, a new spin on the classic guides' breakfast. At lunch, the crab-cakes with chipotle mayonnaise, taco salad with black beans, chicken Caesar wrap, and chicken quesadilla are all winners. Vegetarians can't beat the California Cruiser, a kaiser roll topped with guacamole, grilled Bermuda onion, and tomato.

For dinner, you can start with crab-stuffed portabella mushrooms or a table of four could split an order of the tangy house-smoked baby back ribs. Entrées include fifteen-layer lasagna (with plenty left for lunch the next day); chicken provencal, with tomato, basil, and garlic; lobster with spinach fettucini; and many specials. One favorite: smoked pork tenderloin with chipotle sour cream plus roasted-garlic mashed potatoes on the side. Hog heaven.

Lake Clear

THE LODGE AT LAKE CLEAR
518-891-1489.
Rtes. 30 and 186.
Closed: Mon.–Tues.
Serving: D.
Cuisine: German.
Price: Expensive to Very Expensive.
Credit Cards: MC, V.
Reservations: Recommended.
Handicap Access: No.

This charming Adirondack inn, built in 1886, was the area's first post office and an early stagecoach stop; the decor today is a pleasant European/ Adirondack fusion. Bring a small group of friends for dinner so you can sample many of the interesting appetizers (marinated herring, smoked oysters, and pate, for example) and homemade desserts. Soups, especially oxtail, are wonderful. All meals come with a combination of German potato pancakes, wild rice, potato dumplings, fresh vegetables, and a bowl of sweet red cabbage and green apples.

Entrée choices — usually six to eight options each night — are heirloom German recipes that showcase farm-raised venison, rabbit, duckling, pork, and veal in traditional sauces, plus sauerbraten, rouladen, and schnitzels. Also look for regional dishes like Adirondack rainbow trout or salmon. Desserts can include blueberry strudel (right from the oven if your timing's good), Black Forest cake, and a brownie a la mode.

After dinner, take your party down to the rathskeller to sit by the fire and digest, or play pool, Ping-Pong, or backgammon. There is an extensive variety of beers and a good list of German, French, and California wines.

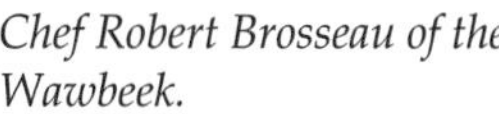
Chef Robert Brosseau of the Wawbeek.

Ben Stechschulte

Tupper Lake

THE WAWBEEK
518-359-2656.

On a summer visit to the Wawbeek, head to the second-story deck to enjoy a cocktail over-

Panther Mtn. Rd., off Rte. 30.
Closed: Nov.; Mon. and Tues. in off season.
Serving: D, year-round.
Cuisine: Contemporary American, Continental.
Price: Very Expensive.
Credit Cards: AE, DC, MC, V.
Reservations: Recommended for weekends.
Handicap Access: Side door.

looking gorgeous Upper Saranac Lake. You'll see sailboats and canoes gliding down the waters, between pretty little islands. The Wawbeek is simply one of the most delightful dining destinations around. The building — with two magnificent fireplaces and two screen porches, an architectural gem — is worth the trip, and the setting is simply wonderful. Arrive before dark!

Chef Richard Brosseau took the helm in 1997, adding real creativity to the menu along with a dedication to finding local suppliers for wild mushrooms, first-rate vegetables, interesting cheeses, maple syrup, excellent farm-raised game. His inventiveness shows — from appetizers like leek and gruyere tart to his signature dessert, wintergreen ice cream, subtle and refreshing. And his eye to detail means that the baguettes on the table have perfect crusts and absorbent crumbs for dunking in infused olive oil.

Entrées include top-quality beef, occasionally ostrich or quail, consistently good fish, shellfish, and venison. A winter favorite is authentic cassoulet laden with chunks of duck and garlicky sausage; beef with Moroccan spices is likewise terrific. The wine list is extensive, as you would expect.

Wanakena

THE PINE CONE
315-848-2121.
Ranger School Rd.
Closed: Mon.
Serving: L, D.
Cuisine: American.
Price: Moderate.
Credit Cards: None.
Handicap Access: Street-level entry.

A classic north woods tavern with respectable fare, the Pine Cone is worth a visit just to check out the ceiling — it's plastered with caps of all descriptions, somewhere in the vicinity of a thousand chapeaux. Come by boat from Cranberry Lake for one of the pig roasts or barbecues; there's plenty of dock space.

The Friday fish fry (beer-batter haddock) is fine, and try the prime rib, which is quite popular. You'll find the service to be quick and friendly.

CENTRAL ADIRONDACKS

Big Moose

BIG MOOSE INN
315-357-2042.

Overlooking Big Moose Lake is this old-time lodge, a favorite destination for year-round

Big Moose Rd., 6 mi. N. of Rte. 28.
Closed: Apr. and Nov.
Serving: L, D.
Cuisine: American, Continental.
Price: Moderate to Expensive.
Credit Cards: AE, MC, V.
Reservations: Recommended.
Handicap Access: Yes.

residents who want to go someplace special on birthdays, anniversaries, and other occasions; some people even come by seaplane for dinner. In the summer, eating on the lakeside deck is a treat; ask for a table by the windows in the winter. The Bennetts—Doug and Bonnie, with son Scott and his wife Robbie — go out of their way to make guests feel welcome, adding a homey touch to this popular place.

In the fall of 1999 chef Jon Wright, former owner of Eckerson's in Eagle Bay, moved north and took over the kitchen at the Big Moose Inn. His menu is hearty and interesting — one of the most extensive in the area. There's fine aged beef, fresh seafood, chicken, veal, and a personal favorite, tasty, crisp duck. The dessert tray is full of excellent, tempting choices, so save room.

Courtesy of Edward Comstock Jr.

Big Moose Station, back when the New York Central came to town.

BIG MOOSE STATION
315-357-3525.
Big Moose Rd.
Closed: Mon.–Wed. in winter.
Serving: B, L, D.
Cuisine: American.

This attractively restored depot for the Adirondack Railroad hasn't seen regular passenger service for years (that could change by 2002, when the line from Thendara is extended), but it's still a fine destination for hungry travelers. The down-home fare is tasty, presented in ample portions,

Price: Moderate.
Credit Cards: AE, MC, V.
Handicap Access: Yes.

and the setting is charming. For breakfast, try waffles or thick French toast; at lunch, hearty soups and a grilled burger or club sandwich. The daily dinner specials are always "special," even the popular Friday night fish fry.

Forestport Station

BUFFALO HEAD
315-392-2632.
Off Rte. 28 in Forestport Station on North Lake Rd.
Open: Year-round.
Serving: L, D.
Cuisine: American.
Price: Moderate.
Credit Cards: AE, DC, MC, V.
Reservations: Yes.
Handicap Access: Yes.

As you drive north on Rtes. 8, 12, and 28 from Utica you pass billboards emblazoned with a huge buffalo head, proclaiming that this restaurant is "famous for fine food." This statement isn't merely advertising hype, it's the Buffalo Head's well-earned reputation. Large dining rooms accommodate crowds easily, the service is excellent, the menu has a varied list of steaks and fish, and the place is deservedly popular in all seasons.

The Buffalo Head name traces back to logging days, when immigrant work crews came by train to Forestport Station. For some reason now lost in the mists of time, a worker brought a buffalo head along with him, which the loggers nailed to the side of the railroad depot. The nickname stuck for that particular stop on the old Adirondack Division of the New York Central, and the restaurant, across the street from the station, carries on the bison motif.

Indian Lake

CHILI NIGHTS
518-648-5832.
Main St., at Marty's Tavern.
Closed: Mon.–Wed.
Serving: L, D.
Cuisine: Mexican.
Price: Moderate.
Credit Cards: MC, V.
Reservations: Suggested for parties of six or more.
Handicap Access: Yes.

In 1997 an unlikely place took over the front room of a local watering hole and surprised everyone by offering authentic Mexican food and even real south-of-the-border crooners on the jukebox. There's Mexican beer on draft, fried ice cream for dessert, and an upbeat, earnest ambiance that's hard to resist.

Appetizers include the usual suspects — nachos, guacamole, and such — but the entrée list is every bit as complete and tasty as any of the other Mexican eateries in the Adirondacks. If a chimichanga or chiles rellenos isn't for you, then try the steaming chili served in a bowl made of bread, or perhaps a mildly hot vegetarian fajita. Specials often include delicious fresh seafood enchiladas.

Inlet

SEVENTH LAKE HOUSE
315-357-6028.
Rte. 28.
Closed: Nov.
Serving: D.
Cuisine: Contemporary American.
Price: Expensive.
Credit Cards: MC, V.
Reservations: Suggested.
Handicap Access: Yes.

Hamilton County, which stretches from Long Lake to Hope Falls, covers nearly as much territory as Rhode Island, and without a doubt, Seventh Lake House is the best restaurant in the whole county. Chef/owner Jim Holt has presided here since 1989, and his varied seasonal menus continue to offer innovative new dishes made from the best ingredients.

The place is elegantly simple, with white tablecloths, an imposing fireplace, and lots of picture windows facing toward the lake. There's a comfortable bar off to one side, and a big canopied deck stretching across the back trimmed with tiny Christmas lights. Seventh Lake House is totally child friendly, especially in the summer, when the deck is open. Last time we ate on the deck, a toy kitchen was set up in one corner for junior chefs.

Appetizers are delicious, ranging from smoked venison ravioli or smoked trout with Dijon-horseradish sauce to "turkey toes," spicy deep-fried morsels wrapped in tortillas. Soups are heavenly, especially the black bean. You can't beat the Caesar salad. Entrées run the gamut of fresh seafood on angel-hair pasta to triple meatloaf made with beef, veal, and pork — a combination that relegates all other recipes to shame. Steak, lamb, chicken, and fresh fish are generally good. Desserts made on the premises include a flourless chocolate gateau and the Adirondack, a warm pastry made with fresh apples, walnuts, and maple syrup.

For mud season, Seventh Lake House sponsors a day of goofy races and a Bavarian buffet, and just before the blackflies hatch, on the first Sunday in May, is the Fire and Spice competition. That event is definitely worth a trip so that you can savor Indian, Tex-Mex, Caribbean, and Thai dishes from dozens of amateur and professional kitchens.

Long Lake

LONG LAKE DINER
518-624-3941.
Rte. 30.
Closed: Holidays.
Serving: B, L.
Cuisine: American.
Price: Inexpensive.
Credit Cards: MC, V.
Handicap Access: Yes.

Under new management and totally refurbished, this spotless, bright restaurant is hard to beat. The staff is friendly and fast, and it's impossible to find a clunker on the menu. In the morning, go for the eggs Benedict or Belgian waffles with real maple syrup; at lunch, homemade soups, chargrilled burgers, club sandwiches, and huge Caesar salads are all good. The clam roll is the best you'll find this far from the Atlantic. In the off season (after Columbus Day and before Mother's Day), the diner's open Wednesdays for prime rib or chicken dinners. Whatever you choose, save room for one of Chuck Frost's scrumptious sticky buns.

LONG VIEW LODGE
518-624-2862.
Rte. 28/30.
Open: Year-round.
Serving: B, L, D.
Cuisine: American.
Price: Moderate to Expensive.
Credit Cards: MC, V.
Reservations: Not necessary.
Handicap Access: Yes.

Extensive renovations have made the Long View Lodge into one of the area's most attractive restaurants. The main dining room is cozy and bright, with a huge fireplace; the airy pine-paneled bar offers nearly every table a view toward the lake, and you can catch summer breezes from a sheltered deck that's well away from the road.

Breakfasts are hearty stuff like pancakes and bacon and eggs. The lunch menu includes burgers, club sandwiches, and excellent homemade quiche. For dinner, try the shrimp-and-scallop kebab, grilled chicken on a spear of rosemary, or cheese ravioli. Entrées include meatless pastas, old-fashioned roast turkey with all the trimmings, chicken breast with white zinfandel sauce, pork loin with applesauce, and swordfish with ginger-leek butter. (Simpler dishes are more successful, though.) For dessert, there's tiramisu, homemade pies, good fruit crisps (in season), and ice cream sundaes.

Mayfield

LANZI'S ON THE LAKE
518-661-7711.
Rte. 30.
Open: Daily Memorial Day–Columbus Day.
Serving: L, D.
Cuisine: American.
Price: Moderate to Expensive.
Credit Cards: All major.
Reservations: Yes.
Handicap Access: Yes.

On the western shore of Great Sacandaga Lake, this spacious, attractive modern restaurant is deservedly popular. Ample docks and a long outdoor deck invite boaters. No need to dress up — the mood here is vacation casual.

Dinner portions are large and often provide leftovers for meals the next day. Fresh fish and quality steaks are carefully prepared; vegetables, salads, and desserts are tasty, too. Lanzi's can become crowded on weekends, so reservations are recommended

North Creek

GARDENS
518-251-2500.
Main St., at the Copperfield Inn.
Open: Jan.–Mar., May–Oct.

With its marble foyer, sparkling chandeliers, and opulent decor, the Copperfield Inn offers a distinctly out-of-the-Adirondacks dining experience: the place seems to have been conjured out of a pattern book for 18th-century reproduc-

Serving: B, L, D.
Cuisine: Contemporary American.
Price: Moderate to Expensive.
Credit Cards: All major.
Reservations: Recommended for weekends.
Handicap Access: Yes.

tions, which would be unsettling if the fare weren't in keeping with the illusion. Thankfully, the food at Gardens, the inn's elegant dining room, is good.

The whole complex — less than ten years old — underwent another round of building and renovations that were completed in summer 1997. Gardens is tucked away from the lobby, in a series of horseshoe-shaped raised platforms with floral carpet, swooping drapes, and arched windows overlooking a patio. Breakfast at an umbrella table on the patio is very civilized. Lunch is another fine way to get acquainted with this spot, and salads really shine.

For dinner, you can start with steamed clams, baked brie, or hearty French onion soup. Entrées range from simple roast half chicken or stuffed shrimp; meat eaters won't be disappointed with the prime rib, rack of lamb, or filet brochette. Pies are all made on the premises, with mud pie — a vast slab of coffee ice cream with fudgy layers — a specialty of the house.

Also at the Copperfield, there's **Trapper's Tavern**, which serves thin-crust pizza, good chili, and sandwiches. A sports bar with rustic decor that is *the* jumping joint in town during rafting and ski season, Trapper's can be very loud or very lively, depending on your point of view.

SMITH'S RESTAURANT
518-251-9965.
Main St., across from the Copperfield Inn.
Open: Year-round.
Serving: B, L, D.
Cuisine: American, German.
Price: Inexpensive.
Credit Cards: AE, MC, V.
Handicap Access: Yes.

Not to be outdone by its glamorous across-the-street neighbor, Smith's had a makeover in 1997 too. With the new look came a new attitude, a move away from the Adirondacky diner this place used to be; you can't get an early-morning breakfast here anymore.

Some things haven't changed, though, like the chunky, creamy New England clam chowder; roast pork or turkey dinners (served with a mountain of stuffing, real mashed potatoes, and excellent gravy); sauerbraten or knockwurst plates (with buttery spaetzel). Don't miss a piece of pie; although we'd place the coconut cream at the head of the class, all are good. Beer and wine are available.

North River

GARNET HILL LODGE
518-251-2444.
Thirteenth Lake Rd. (5 mi. off Rte. 28.)
Open: Year-round.

Come here for the view, a sweeping vista of pristine Thirteenth Lake and Peaked Mountain to the west; save room for dessert, which is definitely the highlight of a Garnet Hill meal. Breakfast

Serving: B, L, D.
Cuisine: Country American.
Price: Moderate to Expensive.
Credit Cards: MC, V.
Handicap Access: Portable ramp.

and lunch are hearty, but not memorable, although real maple syrup from the lodge's sugarbush is included with your flapjacks or French toast.

The quality of dinner entrées is uneven. Herb-crusted trout is delicious; salmon in different sauces can also be very good. Simpler chicken dishes are fine; steer clear of the steaks. Locals flock to the lodge for the occasional dinner buffets, with real roast turkey, steamship round, stuffing, mashed potatoes, pasta, and mountains more. There's a service bar and a serviceable wine list.

Mary Jane Freebern, the Garnet Hill baker, is a Zen master of pie: light, crisp crust with succulent fresh fruit fillings. Berry shortcake is likewise excellent.

Becky Luigart-Stayner

Highwinds Inn's dining room has wonderful light and great views — plus fine food.

HIGHWINDS INN
518-251-3760.
Top of Barton Mines Rd., off Rte. 28.
Closed: 2 weeks in Nov.

North River is a very small settlement and the fact that the town's only two restaurants have remarkable views is particularly noteworthy. The scene from the Highwinds dining room, of Siamese

Serving: D daily in summer; Fri.–Sun. fall and winter.
Cuisine: Regional American.
Price: Moderate to Expensive.
Credit Cards: D, MC, V.
Reservations: Recommended.
Special Features: BYOB, fireplace.

Ponds Wilderness Area, is spectacular. And the food is too.

Be sure to make reservations. Make sure to stop in North Creek or Indian Lake for a bottle of wine. And, make sure you've checked the almanac before you book your table: what you want is to be here at sunset, which means right at the opening hour in midwinter.

The friendly, low-key staff will take care of everything else, often pointing you to a particularly delicious appetizer — spinach-goat cheese terrine or plump cold prawns or silky butternut squash-pumpkin bisque, for example. The salads — straight from nearby gardens in summer — are impeccable. Come winter, there's a fire in the garnet-boulder fireplace to warm you up after a trip around the cross-country trails that they reserve for their guests. Once you've stepped out of your ski boots and into comfortable shoes, settle into one of chef Mark Trietley's innovative entrées like seared venison loin with homemade chutney, ginger-glazed salmon, beef fillet with chipotle chili; there's always something good, something interesting, for vegetarians too.

Desserts are made on the premises. Our favorites are "Barton's Mine" (chocolate mouse triangles with nuggets of "garnet" — walnuts and fruit), bread pudding, and pumpkin log, although you really can't go wrong ordering anything featuring chocolate, maple syrup, fresh fruit, or heavy cream.

Note: Closed at press time.

Old Forge

Breakfast or lunch, the Farm Restaurant serves abundant home-style chow.

James Swedberg

THE FARM RESTAURANT

This big, fun, eatery, packed with fascinating antiques from floor to ceiling, runs like clock-

315-369-6199.
Rte. 28.
Closed: Spring and late fall.
Serving: B, L.
Cuisine: American.
Price: Inexpensive.
Credit Cards: None.
Handicap Access: Yes.

work, presenting great service and very good food. Longtime owners Bev and Frank Burnap have turned over the management of the restaurant to their daughter Hilary, and her enthusiasm and charm only make the place better than ever.

For breakfast — which is available all day — try blueberry pancakes, eggs Benedict, or cinnamon French toast. For lunch, homemade chili (topped with sharp cheddar cheese) and soups are tasty; also recommended are bacon cheeseburgers and Reubens. There's a children's menu, and beer and wine can be ordered with lunch.

FRANKIE'S TASTE OF ITALY
315-369-2400.
Main St., at the Ferns Building.
Open: Year-round, Wed.–Sun.
Serving: D.
Price: Inexpensive.
Cuisine: Italian.
Credit Cards: D, MC, V.
Reservations: Not in summer; yes rest of year.
Handicap Access: Yes.

Frankie and Tina Zammiello — who had a very successful Italian restaurant in Utica, a city known for great ethnic food — have brought a new, authentic flavor to Old Forge. In the back of the Ferns complex, behind Walt's Diner, they've earned a faithful year-round following.

It's easy to see why. The pasta couldn't be fresher or the hospitality warmer. Be prepared to wait for a table in high summer. Frankie checks every plate thoroughly, and he refuses to rush diners through a meal. If you have to wait, rest assured you'll get the same personal attention as those ahead of you.

Frankie's Italian approach to a New York strip steak is inspired. Veal and chicken dishes are exceptional. But be sure someone at the table tries Riggies Anna, rigatoni with a light sauce and morsels of homemade sausage. Greens — spinach sautéed in olive oil — spiked with garlic and topped with cheese are the signature appetizer. Salad comes to the table in a huge bowl for family-style serving, accompanied by the house balsamic vinaigrette (a secret Zammiello recipe, so don't even ask). Bread — hot, crusty — comes right from the oven to your table. For dessert, there's spumoni, cannelloni, and other traditional Italian sweets. One more note: Frankie's place is so popular with locals that you might find it crowded on a Wednesday night — even in mud season.

THE KNOTTY PINE
315-369-6859.
Rte. 28, Thendara.
Open: Year-round.
Serving: D.
Cuisine: American.
Price: Moderate.
Credit Cards: AE, MC, V.
Handicap Access: Yes.

A treasured local place, especially for the Friday fish fry, the Knotty Pine is known for its friendly atmosphere. Cindy and Gary Isensee make everyone feel welcome. The popcorn (help yourself) is always hot in the machine on the corner of the bar; a real log fire glows in the dining room fireplace.

The menu includes prime rib, sirloin, beef fillets,

chicken marsala, and tender beef en brochette; Cajun shrimp on angel-hair pasta is listed as an appetizer but makes a nice light meal. Children are welcome, and there's a special menu for them. A private dining room accommodates large parties (call to reserve).

THE OLD MILL
315-369-3662.
Rte. 28.
Open: Year-round.
Serving: D.
Cuisine: American.
Price: Moderate to Expensive.
Credit Cards: MC, V.
Handicap Access: Yes.

Come early to the Old Mill to relax in the new bar, which is a bright, soaring space with exposed beams, couches clustered by the fireplace, and lots of windows. There's also a porch for alfresco dining, but unfortunately it faces the highway rather than the Moose River, which is just beyond the parking lot.

Meals start off with a big tureen of delicious homemade soup, to be dished out family-style. Salads are reliably good and similarly generous. Entrées include steaks, chops, roast duckling, and chicken; some recommended dishes include the steamed-shrimp-in-the-rough platter, char-grilled rack of lamb (nicely marinated with red wine and rosemary), and stuffed pork chops. The service is competent and congenial.

VAN AUKEN'S INNE
315-369-3033.
Rte. 28, Thendara, behind the Adirondack Railroad depot.
Open: Year-round.
Serving: L, D.
Price: Moderate.
Cuisine: American.
Credit Cards: MC, V.
Reservations: Suggested for dinner on weekends.
Handicap Access: Yes.

Since June 1996, Kathy and Paul Rivet have taken loving care of this century-old inn, renovating guest rooms and public areas and compiling one of the most innovative menus around. Chef Paul changes his menu with the seasons, always taking advantage of what's fresh. He's also very attentive to the interactions among different elements on a dinner plate: don't expect to be offered a choice of starch once you've ordered your main course. Not to worry, though, because side dishes are very bit as wonderful as the headliners.

For the perfect summer lunch, sample a steak salad, with slivers of rare sirloin, kalamata olives, blue cheese, and red onions over greens, or order the shrimp and andouille sausage sandwich, served on a crusty French roll. Turkey hash with zingy mustard sauce occasionally surfaces as a special; it's wonderful.

For dinner, start with almond-crusted goat cheese or satay-style beef skewers with peanut sauce. Main course selections include grilled veal chop in blood orange sauce, scallops with lime cilantro mayonnaise, grilled vegetables with polenta, and pasta puttanesca. Aged beef and pork medallions with apple ginger chutney are also very good, and desserts are all homemade.

Olmstedville

Olmstedville's the Owl at Twilight has become a popular spot for Southwestern/Spanish fare.

James Swedberg

THE OWL AT TWILIGHT
518-251-4696.
Main St., next to O'Connor's Bed and Breakfast.
Closed: Wed., year-round.
Serving: D.
Cuisine: New American, Southwestern.
Price: Moderate to Expensive.
Credit Cards: MC, V.
Reservations: Suggested.
Handicap Access: Yes.

Olmstedville, about eight miles from North Creek, is in the town of Minerva, and Minerva's companion in Greek mythology was an owl . . . hence the name of this restaurant. With that background out of the way, on to the food: in a word, superb, and the service, likewise.

The Owl opened in winter 1999, and people wondered how the place could survive since it's off the beaten track — unless, that is, you live in Olmstedville. But word of mouth about the restaurant's great menu and lovely co-owner/maitre d'/waitress/bartender (Joanne Dwyer does it all and makes it look easy) brought in a dedicated clientele. Her husband, Rich, is in the kitchen, creating Spanish/Southwestern/Italian dishes with flair.

Start with risotto of the day (billed as an appetizer, but big enough for an entrée), the mussels steamed in tequila and habanero chiles, or littleneck clams with orzo. Proceed to cioppino, seafood stew in fennel and saffron broth; ropa viejo (Cuban pot roast); paella; or guava-glazed baby back ribs. Linger over chocolate mousse or crème brûlée, or head to the bar for an after-dinner glass of fine sherry or port. The wine list here is excellent, with delicious but obscure wines you won't find elsewhere.

Speculator

MELODY LODGE
518-548-6562.
Rte. 30.
Closed: Mon.–Tues. in winter.
Serving: L, D.
Cuisine: American.
Price: Moderate to Expensive.
Credit Cards: AE, MC, V.
Reservations: Suggested.
Handicap Access: Yes.

Melody Lodge feels almost like an Adirondack Great Camp, with its assorted antiques, massive stone fireplaces, and lovely view down Page Hill toward Lake Pleasant. The rambling inn (there are 10 guest rooms with shared baths upstairs) was built in 1912 as a singing school for young girls, and first opened to the public as a restaurant and hotel in 1937.

If you visited a few years back and were disappointed by the food, try again. The new chef has revamped the menu and takes great pride in unexpected combinations, like spinach-stuffed salmon on avgolemono sauce or sesame chicken and shrimp with rice and peas. Seafood fans will be happy with the numerous fresh offerings; the only purely vegetarian entrée is eggplant parmesan, although a call ahead would yield something special. Steaks are good, with a delicious portabella mushroom and sirloin combination occasionally presented. There's a small, very reasonably priced wine list, and likewise a small, but well-chosen selection of desserts, with homemade rice pudding at the top of the list.

ROAD FOOD AND QUICK BITES

LAKE GEORGE AND SOUTHEASTERN ADIRONDACKS

In ***Chestertown***, **The Place** (518-494-3390; Rte. 8) looks nondescript, but it has inexpensive, tasty, homemade Italian food and a pleasant family atmosphere. In ***Warrensburg***, **Bill's Restaurant** (518-623-2669; 190 Main St.) makes a fine roast-turkey sandwich and serves breakfast all day. **Dragon Lee** (518-623-3796; 35 Main St., next to Stewart's) has a huge Chinese menu with great carry-out options; sauces tend to be on the syrupy side, so ask for spicy, not sweet.

CHAMPLAIN VALLEY

In ***Elizabethtown***, **Arsenal Inn** (518-873-6863; Rte. 9) makes a good breakfast, especially if you like griddle-toasted biscuits and crisp bacon. It's a real local hangout, made distinctive by 40-some wind chimes hanging from the ceiling. **Evelyn's** (518-873-222; Court St., in rear, across from the county courthouse) is a good deli with excellent baked goods; sandwiches on homemade bread are recommended, as are the pizzas, with all fresh ingredients.

HIGH PEAKS AND NORTHERN ADIRONDACKS

In ***Ausable Forks***, the **D&H Freighthouse** (518-647-8800; Rte. 9N) is open from late spring through fall, serving decent pizza, good sandwiches and burgers, and homemade pies, cakes, and muffins in the front office of an old-time railroad warehouse. In ***Lake Placid***, **Aromaround** (518-523-3818; Saranac Ave. near the synagogue) has a very hip breakfast and lunch menu and great atmosphere in the former Austrian Olympic building, but the wait staff can be utterly clueless. **Desperadoes** (518-523-1507; Cold Brook Plaza, near the Grand Union) is open for dinner every night and lunch Thurs–Sat., serving fajitas, quesadillas, flautas, and chiles rellenos, along with good margaritas. Likewise, the **Down Hill Grill** (518-523-9510; 434 Main St.) is a good choice for lunch or a no-jive dinner; burgers, sandwiches (try the chipotle chicken sandwich), and Mexican food; start off with the Mexican layer dip, with black beans, sour cream, guacamole, tomatoes, jalapenos, and cheese, if you've got a hungry crew in tow. For takeout wraps, deli sandwiches, and vegetarian options, **Main Street Marketplace** (518-523-8224; 300 Main St., across from Stewart's Shop) is the best all-around choice. **Mr. Mike's Pizza** (518-523-9770; 332 Main St.) has great pizza with all kinds of exotic toppings, good eggplant parmesan, and big, delicious salads for eat-in or carry-out; they deliver, too. Across from the Olympic Speed-Skating Oval, the **Woodshed** (518-523-3436; 237 Main St.) is under new management, serves lunch and dinner, and has a huge, inexpensive Italian menu, with more than a dozen seafood pastas and some good choices for vegans, like penne with sautéed greens and broccoli.In ***Wilmington***, the **Country Bear** (518-946-2691; Rte. 86) bakes good homemade bread for its sandwiches and dishes out really fine chili, with or without meat

NORTHWEST LAKES

In ***Cranberry Lake***, the **Stone Diner** (315-848-2678; Rte. 3) is cheerful place with good chow and ice cream. In ***Tupper Lake***, **Main Street Restaurant** (518-359-7449; 79 Main St., in "the Junction") is smoke-free, clean, and good, with terrific homemade soups and pies. In ***Star Lake***, **Mountain Gate Inn** (315-848-9992; Rte. 3) has a complete and reasonably priced menu for breakfast, lunch, and dinner, plus ice cream.

CENTRAL ADIRONDACKS

If you're entering the Adirondacks from Amsterdam or Gloversville, here are a couple of options for inexpensive food: in ***Rockwood***, at the very southern tip of the Adirondack Park, try the **Rockwood Tavern** (518-762-9602; Rtes. 29 and 10) for inexpensive lunches and dinners. Pizza, served all day, is the best around. In ***Wells***, stop at the **Country Kitchen** (518-924-3771; Rte. 30) for simple, low-priced fare brought to you with speedy service. The menu's long on fried foods, and desserts are huge. In ***Speculator***, **King of the Frosties** (518-548-3881; Rte. 30) has soft-serve ice cream, as well as good burgers, salads, and excellent Filipino noodle soup. Open breakfast, lunch, and dinner.

In ***Long Lake***, the **Island Snack Bar** (518-624-2160; Rtes. 28/30, by the bridge) is a tidy little diner serving hearty breakfasts and good homemade soups and sandwiches for lunch. It's open well before the crack of dawn if you need a hot meal before fishing or hiking. Although it doesn't look like much from the outside, the **Cellar** (518-624-5539; Walker Rd.) serves great pizza and has a friendly atmosphere. In ***North Creek***, **Charity's Outback** (518-251-3000; 302 Main St., near the train station) has Italian-style subs, Buffalo-style wings, good pizza, and eggplant parmesan for lunch or dinner. The deck in the rear of the building is a nice place to eat. New in December 1999 is **Casey's North** (518-251-5836; www.caseynorth.com; Rte. 28 across from Stewart's gas station), open from 11am to midnight, with a lengthy menu, great antique bar, and occasional live music.

In ***Inlet***, **Kirsty's Red Dog Tavern** (315-357-5502; South Shore Rd.) has good bar food, including chicken wings, quesadillas, and bruschetta. In ***Old Forge***, the **Muffin Patch** (315-369-6376; Rte. 28) serves breakfast, lunch, and dinner in July and August and breakfast and lunch the rest of the year. Some top picks there are Belgian waffles with pecans and strawberries, roast-pork club sandwich, spinach salad, chicken gumbo (with real okra, something most Adirondackers have yet to appreciate), and ice cream specialties like the pecan turtle sundae or the McCauley Mountain Volcano, multiple scoops of ice cream with multiple toppings, perfect for a foursome of teenage boys. The best burger in Old Forge can be found at **Slickers** (315-369-3002; Rte. 28, near the covered bridge); we also like the nachos with guacamole and salsa.

ADIRONDACK FOOD PURVEYORS

BAKERIES

The Adirondack Park used to be balloon-bread heaven, but as the century draws to a close, several great new bakeries have opened. Some are in extremely out-of-the-way places, like Gilmantown; call ahead and they'll send you a map. Bear in mind that some places are operating in former gas stations and might not look as cute as bake shops in the suburbs; the proof is in the pie crust — or the muffins, or the sticky buns. Also, bakeries that are open seven days a week in July and August usually cut back their hours when Labor Day rolls around. A call ahead is always best.

Albo's Just Desserts (315-369-6505; Main St., Old Forge) Rich cheesecake, down-home pies and cookies, and breads, year-round.

The Best Bakery by Farr (518-624-6941; Rte. 28N next to the Laundromat) New in summer 1999, making French bread, crusty rolls, croissants, sweet breads, and — as the highway sign proclaims, "Get your buns in here!" — sticky buns. Open summers, plus winter holiday weekends.

Bluesberries Bakery (518-523-4529; 26 Main St., next to the Palace Theatre, Lake Placid) Real European-style strudels, croissants, Napoleons, and tortes made by Rainer Schnarrs. Open year-round.

Borne and Bread (518-891-3333; Rte. 86, across from Tail O' the Pup, Ray Brook) Off to the side of a neat new Adirondack furniture store, the Ray Brook Frog, is a great bakery with olive bread, semolina bread, excellent rustic pizza, heavenly (but expensive) tortes and pies. Open summer–fall.

Crown Point Bread Company (518-597-4466; 90 Buck Mountain Rd., Crown Point) True French country bread made in a wood-fired oven; available at the Hap's Store in Crown Point or at the source, baker Yannig Tanguy's cabin in the forest. New in 1999 are rolls made from the same dough: unbeatable! If you're reluctant to make the trip to Crown Point, look for Yannig's bread at Keene Valley's Town and Country Gourmet (below) — they put a huge banner on the front of the store when it's in stock.

The Donut Shop (315-357-6421; Rte. 28, Eagle Bay) A giant doughnut-shaped sign looms high above this drive-in on the edge of Eagle Bay, home of the best doughnuts in the central Adirondacks. A couple of hot cinnamon-and-sugar-dipped sinkers and a steaming cup of black coffee makes a terrific cheap breakfast. Open May–Oct.; closed Tues.

Great American Bagel Factory (518-523-1874; 9 Main St., Lake Placid) Big, fat, delicious bagels, deli sandwiches (stuffed with anything from mortadella to avocado slices), good salads, and lots of rich, chocolatey desserts make this place an interesting stop for lunch or a take-out picnic. Allow plenty of time; unfortunately, the service can be inept.

Lake Flour Bakery (518-891-7194; 14 River St., Saranac Lake) The best baguettes around; chewy semolina bread; strawberry-cheese, chocolate, and plain croissants; bagels; homemade ice-cream sandwiches. Open Mon.–Sat. winter; daily in summer.

Leslie's Placid Baked Goods (518-523-4279; 99 Main St., Lake Placid) With the most interesting window on Lake Placid's Main Street, Leslie's is a treat for the eyes, nose, and tastebuds. The display changes often, showcasing vintage clothing and antique toys interspersed with the cookies, cakes, and pies; intriguing smells are broadcast outdoors by the ventilating fan; the giant snickerdoodles, molasses crinkles, and chocolate-chip cookies are great to munch on when you're strolling. Closed Apr.

Nathan's Adirondack Bakery (315-369-3933; Crosby Blvd., Old Forge, around the corner from Old Forge Hardware) Nathan's is *the* place for wonderful, chewy bagels and bialys; the dense, crusty 8-grain bread is good, too. Cinnamon buns, sour-cream doughnuts (heaven!), bran muffins, pizza

Bona fide bagels and bialys are Alan Nathan's specialty.

James Swedberg

slices, and special-occasion cakes are highly recommended. Open weekends during the school year; daily in July and Aug.

A Piece of Cake (518-576-9943; Rte. 73, Keene, next to Evergreen Trading) A full range of deli items and very good sandwiches on unusual, chewy home-made veggie or whole-wheat rolls. Rockhill bread is available, along with good cakes, tortes, and pies.

Seneca's Trading Post (518-597-4422; Rte 9N near the road to the bridge, Crown Point) New in 1999. Don't let the funky-looking exterior deter you: there's good baking going on here. Excellent coffee cakes with sweet fillings; nice round loaves of sunflower seed bread. Try whatever's fresh out of the oven.

Sherwood Forest Bakery (518-924-7825; Sunset Circle off Gilmantown Rd., Wells; call for directions) Hand-crafted breads like roasted garlic, cinnamon raisin, or honey whole wheat; muffins, cookies, rolls. New in 1999.

Spruce Mountain Bakery and Pizza (518-623-2911; Rte. 9, bet. Chestertown and Warrensburg) Seen from the highway, Spruce Mountain Bakery might not look too inviting, but do check it out. The Danishes and other gooey, sweet offerings are very good, and the light, buttery onion rolls are excellent. Real, crusty Italian bread is made every morning; the cannolis are first-rate.

BREWPUBS

Adirondack Trail Brewing Company (315-392-4008; Rte. 28, Alder Creek) Good light ales are made on the premises and the food is likable: barbecue ribs on Thurs. and fish fry on Fri.

Lake Placid Pub & Brewery (518-523-3813; 14 Shore Dr., across from the Mirror Lake beach) New in 1997, with a half dozen ales and beers, including very strong Ubu ale and a sweet amber brew. Lunch and light suppers are available; there's a deck overlooking Mirror Lake for summer sipping.

Madison Brewing Company (518-668-4259; Lake George Village Mall, 204 Canada St.; Lake George) New in summer 1999, with a half dozen handmade beers and a good view of the lake.

CANDY

The Candy Man (518-946-7270; Rte. 9, Jay; and Main St., Lake Placid) There are no shortcuts here, no high-tech approaches; the Candy Man even makes all the fillings in the Jay shop and covers them with a generous layer of chocolate. Dark chocolate, especially with coffee cream filling, is quite good. The sugar-free candies get high marks for tasting remarkably like the real thing. Open year-round; mail orders available.

Wagar's Confectionery (518-668-2693 or 800-292-4277; 327 Canada St., Lake George) Don't miss this landmark if you're anywhere near Lake George. Wagar's has a wonderful old-time soda fountain and excellent chocolates.

The Yum Yum Tree (518-891-1310; 46 Main St., Saranac Lake) Home of the Spirited Truffles, rich, buttery candies that come in Irish Coffee, Amaretto, Grand Marnier, Raspberry Schnapps, White Russian, and other flavors. The Yum Yum Tree also has a bakery counter offering croissants, breads, strudel, and rolls. For the truly chocoholic, there are chocolate-dipped chocolate chip cookies made on the premises. Open year-round; truffles can be shipped.

DELICATESSENS, CAFES, AND GOURMET SHOPS

Adirondack General Store (518-494-4408; 108 East Shore Dr., Adirondack) Some stores have little niches for reserved newspapers; the Adirondack General Store has slots for reserved pies. The pies are definitely worth asking for in advance, and they're practically no more expensive than the cardboard-box numbers at the Grand Union. Baker Joan Lomnitzer also makes dozens of different soups including tangy Reuben soup, excellent corn chowder, and spicy chili; the deli sandwiches are inexpensive and generous. In the summer, try the kielbasa-spiked potato salad. A couple of tables are for lunches or you can eat outside. Open year-round.

Blue Moon Cafe (518-891-1310; 46 Main St. near the town hall, Saranac Lake) Nice storefront cafe serving full breakfasts and lunches plus light evening meals. Homemade muffins and desserts. Open all year.

Common Corners (518-668-0339; 16 McGillis Ave., Lake George) Excellent coffees, plus homemade soups, salads, and sandwiches; stop here to build a great picnic for an outing on the lake. Open year-round; closed Tues.

Kalil's Grocery (315-357-3603; Rte. 28, Inlet) This independent grocery makes splendid tabouli, hummus, cole slaw, and potato salad in its deli, and has authentic pita bread sent up from a Lebanese bakery in Utica. You can buy other great local products here, too: Garlic Burst Salsa made by Seventh Lake House and some truly incendiary hot sauce from the Red Dog Tavern.

Lakeview Deli (518-891-2101; 102 River St., Saranac Lake) Exceptional sandwiches, fresh salads, gourmet treats like spinach-artichoke dip, Green Mountain coffees, Rockhill bread, and exotic sodas are on tap at the Lakeview, just across the street from Lake Flower. New in 1999: full meals to warm up at home. Open year-round.

Luna Java Coffeehouse (518-891-9426; 100 Lake Flower Ave., Saranac Lake) Great coffee, college-town ambience, fresh pastries. Open year-round.

Perfect Grinds (518-623-4149; Main St., Warrenburg) Coffee, latte, espresso, mochachino . . . plus deli-style sandwiches, homemade soups, and even live acoustic music some evenings; nice setting. Open year-round.

Saranac Sourdough (518-523-4897; Saranac Avenue, Lake Placid, near the Lake Placid Center for the Arts) Good sandwiches (Cuban pork, real roast turkey, etc.) on craft bread or hard rolls baked on the premises; interesting salads, including roast eggplant and antipasto; great big cookies, muffins, and sweets. Take home a loaf of the raisin brioche for great toast; leftovers make wonderful bread pudding. Sit at one of the half-dozen tables for breakfast, lunch, or dinner, or place your order to go. One drawback to an otherwise fine place: the service can be really slow no matter the time of day, or whether you wish to take out or eat in. Call ahead for best results.

Keene Valley's Town and Country Gourmet is a one-stop shop for gourmet goods.

James Swedberg

Town & Country Gourmet (518-576-9731; Rte. 73, Keene Valley) When the Country Gourmet closed in 1998, summer people especially missed the assortment of imported condiments, fine coffee, candy, bread, and frozen entrées perfect for feeding unexpected guests in style. If anything, the new gourmet shop is bigger, better, and brighter, with a remarkably extensive selection of Silver Palate sauces, designer chips, exotic cheeses, fancy soft drinks, and summer dinner fare to take home to cook. You can spend some serious cash here, but they take Visa and MasterCard.

Villa Vespa (518-523-9789; Saranac Avenue near the NAPA store, Lake Placid) When the restaurant of the same name closed a couple of years ago, folks for miles around were sad; the Rite-Aid drugstore occupies the site now. However, the great homemade Italian sauces, frozen and dry pastas, and ready-to-heat entrées are available in a bright, clean shop (the first floor of a Victorian home) open year-round. Salads are good, ample enough for two; risotto, lasagna, and eggplant parmigiana portions likewise. Entrées generally include chicken cacciatore, sole, and a meat-based special. The mushroom raviolis — about three inches in diameter — are wonderful. Open year-round.

Village Meat Market (518-963-8612; Rte. 22, Willsboro) Great sandwiches; homemade breads, rolls, and doughnuts. Open year-round.

FARM MARKETS AND ORCHARDS

The **Lake Placid–Essex County Visitors Bureau** (518-597-4646; Bridge Rd., Crown Point) has published a brochure that lists dozens of farmstands, including a place in North Hudson where you can buy buffalo meat (Adirondack Buffalo Company; 518-532-9466; Blue Ridge Rd.). Most of the roadside stands are near Crown Point and Ticonderoga, in the temperate Champlain Valley; look along Rte. 22 July–October for good local produce, including Silver Queen corn and heirloom tomatoes.

The **Adirondack Farmers' Market Cooperative** (518-298-3755; Box 136, Chazy) organizes several Adirondack Park locations for farmers' markets, which feature native-grown fruits and vegetables, honey, maple syrup, jams and jellies, herbs and herbal teas, and all kinds of flowers. Markets are held on a weekly basis in Elizabethtown, Port Henry, Ticonderoga, Westport, and other towns; check locally for the schedule.

Bessboro Orchards (518-962-8609; Rtes. 9N and 22, Westport) Lou Gibbs has worked hard to establish his small, high-quality orchard and offers many varieties of eating apples that he sells as they're picked. Open in fall.

Eagle Mills (518-883-8700; Rte. 29, Broadalbin, 5 miles east of intersection of Rtes. 29 and 30) Water-powered cider mill with bakery. Special events every fall weekend, including an antique tractor show in October. Open Wed.–Sun. in the fall.

Forrence Orchards (518-643-9527; Rte. 22, Peru) One of the best-known orchards for Macintosh apples, but also growing Honey Crisp, Gala, Cortland, Empire, Macoun, and Delicious. Open daily in the fall.

Gunnison's Orchards (518-597-3363; Rtes. 9N and 22, Crown Point) Honey from the bees that pollinate the trees, and all kinds of apples, including Honey Crisp, Gala, Empire, Jonagold, and MacIntosh, are available right up until springtime at this impressive roadside orchard. Of course, October is the best time for a visit, but even if you're traveling the highway in the winter, stop in. Gunnison's will ship gift packs to anywhere in the country, in late fall. Open Mon.–Sat. year-round.

Harris Hives (518-656-3420; Kattskill Bay, Lake George) Local honey, available from the source or from numerous outlets around the southeastern Adirondacks, including Common Corners and Oscar's Smoke House.

King's Apple Orchard (518-834-7943; Mace Chasm Rd., off Rte. 9, Keeseville) This orchard opens in August, offering Tydemans and other early apples; later on in the fall and through December, you can get Paula Red, MacIntosh, Cortland, Empire, and Red Delicious apples.

Lakeview Orchards (518-661-5017; Mountain Rd., Mayfield, look for the sign on Rte. 30) Pick-your-own blueberries and apples, plus cider, maple syrup, honey. Early apples include MacIntosh, Macoun, and Empire, followed by Red and gold Delicious, Cortland, Jonagold, Northern Spy, and Rhode Island Greening. Open daily in the fall.

Ledgetop Orchards (518-597-3420; Lake Rd., off Rte. 22, Crown Point) Not too far from the Crown Point bridge, you pick your own sour pie cherries in July, gather drops from the apple orchard in the late September, and select the perfect jack-o-lantern at the farm stand in October. The stand offers Cortland, Empire, Red Delicious, MacIntosh, and Kendall (think of a crunchier Mac) apples beginning in early September.

Pray's Family Farms (518-834-9130; Rte. 9N, Keeseville) People come from miles around when the strawberries ripen at Pray's, usually in mid-June. Beside the berries (there are blackberries and raspberries, too), the roadside stand sells home-grown vegetables of all kinds, right up to pumpkin season. Check out the jack-o-lantern display around Halloween.

Rivermede (518-576-4386; Beede Rd., Keene Valley) Brown eggs, maple syrup from the farm's sugarbush, and fresh beans, broccoli, herbs, leaf lettuce, new potatoes, scallions, squash, tomatoes, carrots, and more come from this High Peaks area farm. Valley Grocery, in Keene Valley, often has Rivermede produce in its cooler.

Rulf's Orchard (518-643-8087; Bear Swamp Rd., Peru, off Rte. 22) Excellent farmstand with vegetables, baked goods (great apple pies), and a variety of apples in the shop or to pick yourself: MacIntosh, Macoun, Cortland, Northern Spy, Mutsu, and Spartan.

Valley View Farms (518-585-9974/6502; Rte. 9N, Ticonderoga) Just south of the Ticonderoga Country Club you can enjoy another aspect of the country: pick-your-own strawberries mid- to late June, red raspberries in late July, and blueberries spanning both seasons. (Note that fruit ripening always depends on the weather; if spring is late and cold, it's best to call ahead to be sure the berries are ready for you.) There's also a farm stand with fresh vegetables open about June 20–late September.

HEALTH FOODS

Nori's Natural Foods (518-891-6079; 70 Broadway, Saranac Lake, near the post office) Recently expanded to encompass two storefronts, Nori's has a natural-food deli with daily lunch specials and excellent salads, plus all you'd expect from a good health-food store: bins of grains and flours; jugs of oil, honey, and maple syrup; and canisters of herbs line the walls. There's a selection of Kiss My Face lotions and insect repellents, plus a cooler full of North Country cheeses and organically grown vegetables. The bulletin board is a good source for checking out local alternative-lifestyle happenings. Open year-round.

MAPLE SYRUP

Upstate New York is a leading producer of high-quality maple syrup, and Adirondack syrup tastes no different from the Vermont stuff, which seems to get all the glory. Across the park, you can buy local syrup in craft shops, general stores, and farm stands; listed below you'll find a sampling of a few syrup processors who sell directly from their homes and sugarbushes. There are many more folks who make syrup, and they advertise that fact with a large lithographed tin sign showing a maple leaf.

If you'd like to learn about sap, taps, and boiling off, the *Uihlein-Cornell Maple Sugar Project* (518-523-9137; Bear Cub Rd., Lake Placid), a joint project of the New York State College of Agriculture at Cornell University and Henry Uihlein, is open most weekday afternoons from spring through fall. Admission is free; in Mar. and Apr., you can observe the entire process from the tree to the finished product. The Visitor Interpretive Center in Paul Smiths also has special maple-sugar season demonstrations.

Alstead Farms (Patrick Whitney; 518-576-4793; Alstead Hill Rd., Keene) Wholesale and retail Adirondack maple syrup, 1/2 pint to 5-gallon drums.

Frog Alley Farm (518-576-9835, Rte. 73, Keene Valley) Retail maple syrup.

Leadley's Adirondack Sugar Bush (Jack Leadley, Sr.; 518-548-7093; Rte. 30, Speculator) Retail maple syrup.

Toad Hill Maple Products (Randy Galusha; 518-623-2272; Athol) Syrup, sugar, and a complete line of maple-syrup-making supplies.

MEAT MARKETS

Doty's Country Road Beef House (518-891-3200; Lake Colby Dr., Saranac Lake) The folks at Doty's make excellent breakfast and Italian sausages, and offer a full variety of aged beef cuts, lamb, pork, and deli meats. Try their "Snappy Grillers" white-hots. Open year-round.

Jacobs & Toney (518-623-3850; 157 Main St., Warrensburg) The front of the building proclaims "Meat Store of the North," and the folks here pride themselves on prime beef cut to order, fresh pork, chicken, lamb, and homemade fresh sausage. Open year-round.

Oscar's, in Warrenburg, smokes ham, bacon, lamb, chicken, turkey, trout, and cheese.

James Swedberg

Oscar's Adirondack Mountain Smoke House (800-627-3431; 22 Raymond Lane, Warrensburg) For half a century, the Quintal family has been smoking up a storm — wonderful hams, sausages, cheese: in all, about 200 different smokehouse products — in a shop just off Warrensburg's main street. You can get smoked trout, boneless smoked chicken breast, smoked lamb, and eight kinds of bacon. Oscar's blends a variety of flavored cheese spreads, and the shop has gourmet crackers, condiments, and mixes. It's also a terrific butcher shop for fresh meat and bratwurst, weisswurst, knockwurst, all kinds of wieners and wursts. Open year-round; mail-order catalog available.

Shaheen's Super Market (518-359-9320; 252 Park St., Tupper Lake) A family-run store staffed by genuinely friendly folks who still carry grocery bags out to your car, Shaheen's is known for quality meats cut to order. Occasionally, homemade Lebanese specialties appear in the cooler; the kibbe is very popular and sells out within hours. Open year-round.

SPECIAL EVENTS: BARBECUES AND COMMUNITY SUPPERS

Throughout the Adirondacks, civic organizations, fire departments, historical societies, and church groups put on a variety of public suppers. Don't be shy! Visitors are welcome at these affairs, and furthermore, the food is generally cheap and delicious.

A North Country favorite is the chicken barbecue, with half chickens marinated in a tangy lemon-based sauce cooked outdoors over the coals. The trimmings are usually an ear of roasted sweet corn, potato salad, cole slaw or tossed salad, roll, watermelon wedge, and coffee; the price hovers around the $7 mark, less for kids' portions. There are also steak roasts, clambakes, pig roasts, and buffets. Listed below (*in chronological order*) are some of the annual feasts found in the Adirondacks; check local newspapers for more.

Secret Recipe Chicken

Chances are if you asked a local grillmeister for the chicken barbecue sauce recipe, you'd be told it was a family heirloom not to be shared with casual visitors. Actually most of the Adirondack barbecues rely on variations of the Cornell University recipe; since 1949, the Poultry Science Department of the school has distributed close to a million copies of it. Below you'll find that secret marinade so that you can replicate smoky, lemony chicken at home.

1 cup good cooking oil
1 pint cider vinegar (some folks use lemon juice and vinegar)
3 TB salt (or less, to taste)
1 TB Bell's poultry seasoning
1/2 tsp black pepper (or more, to taste)
1 egg

Beat the egg vigorously. Then add the oil and beat again to emulsify the sauce. Add other ingredients. Dunk chicken halves in the sauce and let marinate in the refrigerator for a few hours. While grilling over hot coals, baste each side.

The sauce will keep in the refrigerator for about a week. Enough for 8 to 10 half chickens. Leftover barbecued chicken makes superb chicken salad.

Newcomb Lions Club Chicken Barbecue (518-582-3211; Newcomb) At the Newcomb Town Beach, on Lake Harris, off Rte. 28N, first Sat. in July.

North Creek Fire Department Chicken Barbecue (518-251-2612; North Creek) At the North Creek Ski Bowl, off Rte. 28, first Sat. in July.

Keene Valley Fire Department Open House and Chicken Barbecue (518-576-4444; Keene Valley) At the firehall, on Market St., Keene Valley, fourth Sun. in July.

Newcomb Fire Department Steak Roast and Parade (518-582-3211; Newcomb) Rib-eye steaks, burgers, corn, hot dogs, and salads, at the Newcomb Town Beach, last Sun. in July.

Inlet Volunteer Hose Co. Chicken Barbecue (315-357-5501; Inlet) At the Fern Park pavilion, second Sat. in Aug.

Chilson Volunteer Fire Department Chicken Barbecue (518-585-6619; Ticonderoga) At Elks Field, Rte. 22, Ticonderoga, second Sun. in Aug.

Penfield Museum Heritage Day Chicken Barbecue (518-597-3804; Penfield Homestead Museum, Ironville) On the museum grounds, third Sat. in Aug.

Keene Fire Department Open House and Chicken Barbecue (518-576-4444; Keene) At the firehall, on East Hill Rd., last Sat. in Aug.

Plump Chicken Inn (518-251-2229; Minerva Historical Society, Olmstedville) Chicken and biscuits, homemade pickles and salads, real mashed potatoes, plus live music and costumed serving wenches, at Minerva Central School, in Olmstedville, last Sat. in Aug.

Lewis Volunteer Fire Co. Ox Roast (518-873-6777; Lewis) At the firehall on the last Sun. in Aug.

Indian Lake Pig Roast (518-648-5112; Indian Lake Volunteer Fire Dept., Indian Lake) Succulent roast pork and stuffing, steamed clams, homemade clam chowder, corn, and burgers, held at the Indian Lake firehall, on Rte. 28, Sat. before Labor Day.

Bloomingdale Fire Department Field Day (518-891-3189; Bloomingdale) Chicken barbecue and games, held at the firehall, off Rte. 3, Sun. before Labor Day.

Westport Marina Labor Day Lobsterfest (518-962-4356; Washington St., Westport) Lakeside feeding frenzy at the Westport Marina, on the Sun. before Labor Day. Advance tickets are necessary.

Fish & Game Club Lobster and Clam Bake (518-532-7675; Schroon Lake). At the Fish and Game Club headquarters, second Sun. in Sept.

Raquette Lake Fire Department Clambake (315-354-4228; Raquette Lake) Ever wonder how to remove grit and sand from steamers? At the Raquette Lake Fire Department's annual bash, they run the clams through a commercial dishwasher. Advance tickets necessary; held on the second Sun. in Sept.

WINE AND LIQUOR STORES

You can purchase wine and liquor in numerous shops throughout the park. Some of the smaller places are adjacent to taverns, or even the owners' homes; you may have to ring a buzzer to have them open up for you. Note that New York State liquor stores are closed on Sundays; beer and wine coolers are available in grocery stores, although you can't buy either until after noon on Sunday.

A handful of shops stand out for their good selection of domestic and imported wines and knowledgeable staff. In ***Lake Placid,*** **Terry Robards Wines and Spirits** (518-523-9072; 243 Main St.) is worth a visit; Robards was a columnist for the *Wine Spectator,* and occasionally sponsors amusing dinners with wine tasting. If you're looking for a summery wine to go with a picnic, or a particular pressing from an obscure vineyard, he's the one to ask. Further south in the Adirondacks, in ***Speculator,*** Elizabeth Gillespie at **Speculator Spirits** (518-548-7361; Rte. 30) knows her grapes, and her tiny shop offers an astonishing variety of wines. In ***Inlet,*** talk to Anna Schmid at the **Wine Shop** (315-357-6961; Rte. 28, near the hardware store), for advice about great German, French, Australian, and domestic wines.

CHAPTER SIX

A Land for All Seasons

RECREATION

Adirondack woods and waters beckoned to 19th-century visitors with promises of a primeval wilderness overflowing with fish and game. City "sports" relied on Adirondack guides to row them down lakes, lead them through forests in pursuit of deer or moose, cook them hearty meals, and finally tuck them into balsam-bough beds at night. The popular press swelled with accounts of these manly Adirondack adventures, and by the 1870s, the North Country was a great destination for thousands.

Katherine E. McClellan photograph courtesy of Smith College Archives

Hiking, camping, and sketching in fresh Adirondack air were deemed suitable recreation for the ladies.

In those rough-and-tumble days, hunting and fishing were the prime recreational pursuits. Hiking through the woods was something done as a last resort: "[I]f there is one kind of work which I detest more than another, it is *tramping*; . . . How the thorns lacerate you! How the brambles tear your clothes and pierce your flesh!" wrote William H.H. Murray in his 1869 best seller, *Adventures in the Wilderness*. Boating was simply a method of transportation, to row from one campsite to the next or a necessary component of a hunting or fishing trip. Later, near the turn of the 20th century, recreational canoeing swept the nation (the idea of using Native American watercraft for fun came across the Atlantic from England).

Despite Reverend Murray's opinion, hiking or mountain climbing for pleasure was a 19th-century notion that coincided with the growth of grand hotels across the Adirondacks. Walking in the woods — dressed in long skirts, shirtwaists, high boots, wool stockings, gloves, hats, and veils — was fine for ladies; they could hire their own guides, too, to take them up High Peaks or into pristine scenes. Hiking was healthful: breathing in pine-scented, ozone-laden air was regarded as a tonic for frail, dyspeptic, or consumptive patients.

Winter, however, was no time for fun. Getting around in the snow and cold was hard work; the idea of going outside to play when temperatures were below freezing was regarded as sheer folly — until Melvil Dewey created the Lake Placid Club in the early 1900s and thereby launched America's first full-service winter resort, complete with skiing, skating, sleigh riding, snowshoeing, and backcountry bonfires to ward off the chill.

With the advent of the automobile, recreation in the Adirondack Park changed. No longer were the lake country and High Peaks inaccessible to the masses; no longer did the exodus north take long days and large sums. Vacations were within reach of almost every working person, and with the help of a reliable Ford or Chevy, so were the Adirondacks. In the wake of this new, more democratic summer vacation approach, the huge hotels closed one by one, to be replaced by motels and housekeeping cabins. The New York State Conservation Department responded by creating car-camping havens under the pines.

Today in the Adirondack Park, whether you come for health, adventure, solitude, or just plain fun, you'll find that outdoor recreation opportunities are limited only by your imagination. Nowhere else east of the Mississippi is there such a variety of sport: wilderness canoeing, backcountry hiking, rock climbing, downhill and cross-country skiing, fishing, big-game hunting . . . the list goes on. If you want to get away from civilization, this is indeed the place; there are nearly three million acres of public lands to explore. In that regard, the Adirondack Park compares favorably to the national parks, and there's an added bonus: there's no entry fee when you cross the Blue Line. You may hike or mountain bike, bird watch, canoe or kayak, rock-climb, ski tour or snowshoe in the forest preserve without having to buy a special permit.

If your taste runs to a round of golf, or watching a chukker of polo, you'll find those here, too. There are tour boats to ferry you around scenic lakes, and pilots to hire for flying high above the mountaintops. The Adirondacks might also be regarded as the birthplace of two of the cornerstones of American popular culture: theme parks and miniature golf.

In this chapter you'll find descriptions of myriad diversions, along with suggestions on how to find the requisite gear, who to call for further details. What you won't find in this chapter are specific instructions on where to begin or end a particular hike, climb, or canoe trip; it's important that you take the responsibility to read guidebooks and study maps. Each season a few unprepared outdoors-folk become unfortunate statistics due to errors in judgment. The Blue Line encircles a wonderful park, but if you get lost, we can't "just turn the lights on" (as one urban dweller suggested to forest rangers involved in a search) to find you.

ADIRONDACK GUIDES

An Adirondack woodsman "falls so to speak out of his log cradle into a pair of top boots, discards the bottle for a pipe, possesses himself of a boat and a jackknife and becomes forthwith a full-fledged experienced guide," wrote an observer in 1879. William H.H. Murray described guides thusly: "A more honest, cheerful, and patient class of men cannot be found the world over. Born and bred, as many were, in this wilderness, skilled in all the lore of woodcraft, handy with the rod, superb at the paddle, modest in demeanor and speech, honest to a proverb, they deserve the admiration of all who make their acquaintance." Of course, not everyone agreed with him — one 19th-century writer declared "a more impudent, lazy, extortionate, and generally offensive class . . . would be hard to find" — but Murray's view became the popular ideal.

The Adirondack Guides' Association was established in 1891 as a backwoods trade union to adopt uniform pay for a day's work (then about a dollar a day), and follow the state's new game-protection laws. Nowadays, the Department of Environmental Conservation (DEC) licenses hundreds of men and women as guides for rock climbing, hunting, fishing, and whitewater rafting. Guides pass a written exam that tests woods wisdom and responses to weather and safety situations; they must also know first-aid and CPR.

There are several hundred guides who are members of a select group within the DEC-licensees: the New York State Outdoor Guides Association (NYSOGA). These folks make a point of preserving wild resources as well as helping clients find the right places for hunting, fishing, camping, and climbing; many guides practice low-impact camping and offer outdoor education.

Under the separate sports headings in this chapter, you'll find a sampling of licensed guides for different outdoor activities.

BICYCLING

As the twenty-first century begins, promising all kinds of technological marvels, plain old bicycling is undergoing a renaissance in the region. New publications and maps plus new trail systems provide the information that visitors have been waiting for. Highways, byways, and skidways offer challenges, variety, and great scenery for road and mountain bikers; May through October are the best months. In April, road bikers might find that the snowbanks are gone, but a slippery residue of sand remains on the road shoulders. Likewise, springtime backcountry cyclists might discover patches of snow in shady stretches of woods or stretches of muddy soup on sunnier trails. At the other end of the year, note that big-game season begins in October, and some of the best mountain-biking destinations are also popular hunting spots.

The long-awaited guide for all-terrain cyclists was published in 1999: *25 Mountain Bike Tours in the Adirondacks* by Peter Kick (Backcountry Publications). Amusing and informative, the guide outlines really tough singletrack routes requiring map-and-compass and advanced riding skills as well as adventures suitable for families. Some of the trips combine rides on the Adirondack Scenic Railroad, in Thendara, to get to starting points. (See the Scenic Railroads section elsewhere in this chapter.) The most comprehensive book for road cyclists is *25 Bicycle Tours in the Adirondacks: Road Adventures in the East's Largest Wilderness* by Bill McKibben, Sue Halpern, Barbara Lemmel, and Mitchell Hay (Backcountry Publications). It describes loop trips in wonderful detail, with an eye toward scenic and historic destinations like Willsboro Point, a thumb of land sticking into Lake Champlain, with great views coming and going. Three free guides offer more riding options: **Historic Boquet River Bike Trails** (518-873-6301; Boquet River Association, Elizabethtown NY 12932) outlines excellent road trips with interesting historical stops; **Essex County Visitors Bureau** (518-523-2445; Olympic Center, Lake Placid NY 12946) has a selection of 25 backcountry bike trips of varying difficulty; and **Franklin County Tourism** (518-483-6788; Box 6, Malone NY 12953) publishes a brochure describing 15 off-the-beaten-path treks. Also, **Lake Champlain Bikeways** (518-597-4464; Visitor Center, Bridge Rd., Crown Point NY 12928) has identified a network of interconnected routes around the lake, with a map in progress. The Annual Guides published by *Adirondack Life* have listed dozens of bike trips; back issues are available (518-946-2191; www.Adirondacklife.com; Box 410, Jay NY 12941). For still more trip ideas, ask at regional bike shops; many of them sponsor guided rides or have their own maps of local trips.

If you'd like to join a group on a van-supported trip, **John and Jackie Mallery** (518-624-2056; Box 366, Long Lake) offer guided bike tours of selected North Country destinations. Here's another great concept: the folks at **Lake George Kayak Company** (518-644-9366; Main St., Bolton Landing) will drive you to the top of Tongue Mountain so you can coast miles and miles downhill.

As mountain biking continues to grow in popularity, the Inlet–Old Forge

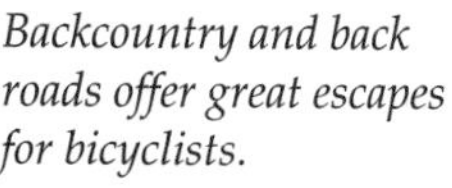

Backcountry and back roads offer great escapes for bicyclists.

James Swedberg

area has emerged as a center for the sport. Old Forge opened its extensive snowmobile trails to pedalers in 1996; call the **Central Adirondack Association** (315-369-6983, www.oldforgeny.com; Main St., Old Forge NY 13420) for a map. Inlet is perched on the edge of the Moose River Recreation Area, which is laced with old logging roads. In spring (the Blackfly Challenge) and fall the town hosts mountain-bike weekends that attract hundreds of cyclists, sponsored in part by **Mountain Man Outdoor Supply** (315-357-6672; www.mountainmanoutdoors.com; Rte. 28, Inlet NY 13360). Lift-serviced biking is available at both of the New York State-owned ski areas, **Gore Mtn.** (518-251-2441; www.goremountain.com; Peaceful Valley Rd., North Creek NY 12853) and **Whiteface Mtn.** (518-946-2233; www.whiteface.com; Rte. 86, Wilmington NY 12997); fat-tire festivals are on their agendas in July and August. Some ski trails — as you'd suspect — are gnarly, scary, bumpy rides, but both areas have traverse routes and woods roads too.

All-terrain bicycles are barred from wilderness and primitive areas in the Adirondack Park, but many wilderness hiking trails are inappropriate for bikes anyhow: too steep, too narrow, too wet, too rocky. In the state-land areas designated as wild forest, you'll find old logging roads that make excellent bike routes, and in most of these places, you'll find far fewer people.

Road cyclists will discover that many state highways have wide, smooth shoulders. You won't have to contend with much traffic in May and June or September and October except on weekends, but be aware that main roads become quite busy with all kinds of vehicles from log trucks to sight-seeing buses to RVs throughout the summer. Also, be prepared for any long trips: check topographical as well as highway maps for significant hills on your proposed route. Always carry plenty of water and a good tool kit. ***Wear a helmet!***

BICYCLE DEALERS AND OUTFITTERS

LAKE GEORGE AND SOUTHEASTERN ADIRONDACKS

Lake George Kayak Company (518-644-9366; Main St., Bolton Landing) Complete land and water outfitter, home of Bolton Downhill Bicycles: ride up Tongue Mtn. in a van, coast down on your bike. Good-quality bikes to rent too.

CHAMPLAIN VALLEY

High Peaks Cyclery & Touring (518-963-7028; below The Store at Essex, Essex) Bikes and kayaks to rent; guided road-bike tours on Wed. and Sun.; bike and boat combination tours midweek in summer, with cycling to Willsboro and kayaking back on Lake Champlain. Tours by reservation.

Westport Cycle and Sport (518-962-8988; 125 Pleasant St., Westport) New and used bikes and repairs.

Rules of the Trail

- **Ride on open trails only.** Respect trail and road closures and avoid trespassing on private lands. Wilderness areas are closed to cycling.
- **Leave no trace.** Even on open trails, you should not ride under conditions where you will leave evidence of your passing. Practice low-impact cycling by staying on the trail and not creating any new ones. Pack out at least as much as you pack in.
- **Control your bicycle.** There is no excuse for excessive speed.
- **Always yield the trail** to hikers and others. Make your approach known well in advance; a friendly greeting or a bell works well.
- **Never spook animals**. Give them extra room and time to adjust to your presence; use special care when passing horseback riders.
- **Plan ahead**. Know your equipment, your ability, and the area in which you are riding, and prepare accordingly. Be self-sufficient; carry the necessary supplies and tools you may need.

From the *International Mountain Bicycling Association*

HIGH PEAKS AND NORTHERN ADIRONDACKS

Barkeater Bicycles (518-891-5207; 15 Broadway, Saranac Lake) New and used bikes; repairs.

High Peaks Cyclery (518-523-3764; Saranac Ave., Lake Placid) Road and mountain bike sales, repairs, and rentals.

Placid Planet (518-523-4128; Saranac Ave., Lake Placid) New and used bikes and repairs; occasional group rides. Recommended.

CENTRAL ADIRONDACKS

Beaver Brook Outfitters (518-251-3394 or 888-45GUIDE; www.beaverbrook.com; Rte. 28 at the stoplight, Wevertown) Mountain bike rentals.

Garnet Hill Lodge (518-251-2821; Thirteenth Lake Rd., North River) Woods roads and singletrack routes; citizen races; shop; bike rentals for use on their trails only.

Mountain and Boardertown (518-251-3111; www.boardertown.com; Main St. in Grand Union plaza, North Creek) Excellent selection of top-of-the-line mountain bikes, helmets, and clothing, plus equipment for downhill biking. Open all year.

Mountainman Outdoor Supply Company (315-357-6672; www.mountainmanoutdoors.com; Rte. 28, Inlet) Mountain bikes and gear for sale and rent; maps, guidebooks, outdoor clothing. Sponsors mountain-bike weekend in early fall.

Pedals & Pedals (315-357-3281; Rte. 28, Inlet) Bikes for sale and rent; repairs. Sponsors major mountain-bike race in spring. Ask here for trip suggestions in the Moose River Plains.

Sporting Propositions (315-369-6188; Rte. 28, Old Forge) Bikes for sale and rent; group rates available.

BEYOND THE BLUE LINE

There are two excellent bike shops in ***Glens Falls***: **Inside Edge** (518-793-5676; 624 Upper Glen St.) and the **Bike Shop** (518-793-8986; Quaker Rd.). In ***Plattsburgh***, **Wooden Ski and Wheel** (518-561-2790; Rte. 9, Plattsburgh NY 12901) is a professional shop for new bikes, tune-ups, and equipment.

BOATING

Raquette Lake has plenty of territory for boaters to discover.

James Swedberg

Scores of lovely Adirondack lakes have public launches for motor- and sailboats, operated by the New York State Department of Environmental Conservation, villages, or individual businesses; you'll find these clearly marked on regional road maps. Many state campgrounds (listed under "Camping" later in this chapter) have boat ramps. If you have a reserved campsite, there's no extra charge to launch a boat, and if you'd like to visit Lake Eaton, Buck Pond, or Eighth Lake, for example, you pay the day-use fee. Note also that motorboats (over 10 hp) and sailboats (longer than 18 feet) used on Lake George must have a permit, available from local marinas or the Lake George Park Commission (518-668-9347; Box 749, Lake George).

Marinas and boat liveries offer yet another chance for folks with trailers to get their boats in the water. Many more options are open to canoeists and kayakers who can portage their boats a short distance, so look under "Canoeing" for further information.

The *New York State Boater's Guide* contains the rules and regulations for inland waters, and is available from offices of the Department of Transportation. Some statewide laws for pleasure craft:

- You must carry one personal-flotation device for every passenger in your boat. Children under 12 are *required* to wear life jackets while on board.
- Any boat powered by a motor (even canoes with auxiliary small motors) and operated mainly in New York State must be registered with the Department of Motor Vehicles.
- When traveling within 100 feet of shore, dock, pier, raft, float, or an anchored boat, the speed limit is 5 mph. (Maximum daytime speed limits are 45 mph, and night time, 25 mph, although on many lakes with rocky shoals, or on water bodies which are also popular with non-motorized craft, lower speeds are prudent).
- Powerboats give way to canoes, sailboats, rowboats, kayaks, and anchored boats.
- The boat on your right has the right-of-way when being passed.
- Running lights *must* be used after dark.
- Boaters under 16 must be accompanied by an adult, or, if between 10–16 and unaccompanied, they must have a safety certificate from a NYS course.
- Boating under the influence of alcohol carries heavy fines and/or jail sentences.
- Littering and discharging marine-toilet wastes into waterways is prohibited.

Zebra Mussels

A tiny, striped mollusk from the Caspian Sea was accidentally introduced into Michigan's Lake St. Clair in the 1980s when a European freighter discharged its ocean-water ballast. From there, zebra mussels (*Dreissena polymorpha*) have been spread by recreational boaters to Lake Erie, Lake Ontario, and in 1993, Lake Champlain. Some beaches there are now treacherous to barefoot waders and swimmers because the shells are razor-sharp.

Zebra mussels can clog water-intake pipes, attach themselves to navigational markers in such quantity that the buoys sink, and damage boat hulls. Beside affecting manmade objects, the non-native mussels have the potential to irrevocably change a lake's ecology. The mussels' free-swimming larvae are so small that thousands can be found in a boat's live well or cooling system and even bait buckets, and if these contaminated waters are released into lakes and rivers, the mussels may spread into new territory.

Canoes and car-top boats usually don't harbor the mussels because they're not left at anchor long enough for mussels to attach and because they don't carry water when transported from one lake to the next. Trailerable boats, especially inboards, pose a greater risk, but boat owners can minimize that by flushing the cooling system on land thoroughly before launching in a new lake, and rinsing the boat hull and trailer. To be doubly safe, you can use a mild bleach solution for the rinse, or let the boat and trailer dry out completely on a hot, sunny day.

Eurasian Milfoil

A new invasive species is spreading throughout Adirondack waters: Eurasian water milfoil. This leafy underwater plant grows luxuriantly in hundreds of lakes, creating a nearly impenetrable tangle that can stop a small outboard in its tracks. Paddling through a milfoil jungle is no fun either. Eurasian milfoil chokes out native plants that offer better food and cover to fish, and once established, it's very tough to eradicate.

It's clear that this milfoil, like zebra mussels, is brought into new habitat inadvertently by recreational boaters. If you've taken your boat through milfoil-infested waters, clear the weeds off the prop and trailer carefully when your boat is on land, pulling off leaves and stems. Even tiny fragments can grow quickly into ten-foot-long underwater vines.

Privately owned marinas and boat liveries offer a variety of services; complete listings are available from tourist-information booklets published by Warren, Essex, Clinton, Franklin, Fulton, Herkimer, and Hamilton counties (see Chapter Eight, *Information*).

BOAT TOURS

There are nearly 3,000 Adirondack lakes, ponds, and reservoirs to explore, but if you'd prefer not to be your own helmsman, practically every water body of significant size has a cruise vessel. Prices vary widely depending on the length of the tour, and what kind of frills come with it — music, dancing, and champagne, for example. Most boats can be chartered for special events like receptions and parties; some captains are licensed to perform weddings too.

The season generally runs from early May through October. Note that many of the boats are enclosed, so this is an activity you can try on a drizzly day. Regardless of whether you choose sunshine, clouds, or moonlight for your cruise, call ahead for a reservation. At this writing, a new ferry/excursion boat for Lake Champlain is in the works. Designed after a traditional working watercraft, this boat will travel from the Crown Point Historic Site to Vermont and back with room for pedestrians and bikes.

LAKE GEORGE AND SOUTHEASTERN ADIRONDACKS

Lake George Shoreline Cruises (518-668-4644; Kurosaka La., Lake George) Several boats to choose from, including the adorable *Horicon*; narrated daytime and dinner cruises. Several boats take school groups to Lake George's Underwater Classroom; the *Horicon* departs at dusk on Thursdays in the summer for fireworks cruises.

Lake George Steamboat Company (518-668-5777; www.lakegeorgesteamboat.com; Beach Rd., Lake George) Three enclosed boats, including the huge *Lac du Saint Sacrement* and the paddlewheeler *Minne-ha-ha*. The *Mohican* makes a 4 1/2-hour-long tour of the lake daily in the summer and navigates

Not your typical tour boat — Grace, *on Big Moose Lake.*

James Swedberg

through the Narrows, among the islands each afternoon. In addition to shorter narrated trips, boats have cocktail lounges and offer dinner, pizza, and moonlight cruises with live music.

CHAMPLAIN VALLEY

Fort Ticonderoga Ferry (802-897-7999; Rte. 74, Ticonderoga) Inexpensive scenic trip across Lake Champlain on a small car ferry.

Lake Champlain Ferries (518-963-7010; Rte. 22, Essex) Car ferry between Essex NY, and Charlotte VT, with hourly trips. Also, car ferry between Port Kent and Burlington with hourly trips. Passengers without cars are welcome (518-834-7960; Rte. 22, Port Kent).

Lake Champlain Scenic & Historic Cruises (802-897-5331; Fort Ticonderoga, Ticonderoga) Operates the *Carillon*, which offers narrated tours near Fort Ticonderoga and longer cruises to Whitehall NY, and Vergennes VT.

Philomena D. (518-962-4356 or 800-626-0342; www.shipstore.com or www.westport marina.com; Westport Marina, off Rte. 22, Westport) 50-foot wooden boat built in 1948. Historic cruises up to Lake Champlain's Palisades and Split Rock Friday-Monday afternoons; private charters; cocktail parties; trips from Westport to Basin Harbor VT to the Lake Champlain Maritime Museum.

HIGH PEAKS AND NORTHERN ADIRONDACKS

Lake Placid Marina Boat Tours (518-523-9704; Lake Dr., Lake Placid) Scenic trips on Lake Placid aboard the enclosed, classic wooden boats *Doris* (1950) and *Lady of the Lake* (ca. 1929).

CENTRAL ADIRONDACKS

Bird's Marina (315-354-4441; Rte. 28, Raquette Lake) Daily (except Sunday) rides on the mail-delivery boat.

Blue Mountain Lake Boat Livery (518-352-7351; Rte. 28, Blue Mtn. Lake) Narrated rides through the Eckford Chain of Lakes aboard two restored wooden launches, the *Neenykin* and the *Osprey*.

Dunn's Boat Service (315-357-3532; Big Moose Rd., Big Moose Lake) Tours of the setting of *An American Tragedy* aboard *Grace*, a beautiful inboard.

Norridgewock II (315-376-6200; Number Four Rd., Stillwater Reservoir) Tours and water taxi service on Stillwater Reservoir; access to Beaver River, the most isolated community in the park.

Old Forge Lake Cruises (315-369-6473; www.oldforgecruises.com; Rte. 28, Old Forge) Narrated 28-mile cruise on the Fulton Chain of Lakes aboard the *Uncas* or the *Clearwater*. Also offers weekend shuttles to Inlet from Old Forge for lunch or exploring town.

Raquette Lake Navigation Co. (315-354-5532; www.raquettelakenavigation.com; Pier I, Raquette Lake) Lunch, brunch, and dinner cruises — by reservation only — aboard the posh *W.W. Durant*.

CAMPS

Famous folks spent their summers at Adirondack camps: Vincent Price was a counselor at Camp Riverdale, on Long Lake; Bonnie Raitt is an alum of Camp Regis, on Upper St. Regis Lake; G. Gordon Liddy went to Brant Lake Camp; Arlo Guthrie and his mother, a dance instructor, enjoyed many seasons at a Raquette Lake camp.

Throughout the Adirondacks summer camps offer a wide range of programs. There are high-adventure canoeing, backpacking, and rock-climbing camps, with emphasis on self-reliance in the wilderness. There are also very comfortable camps that offer nice cabins, good food, and fine arts or technology programs. Some camps are truly Great Camps — in the architectural sense

Learning to swim is part of any Adirondack camp experience.

Rick Godin

— housed in impressive vintage estates. And several camps offer family sessions so that everyone can share in the fun.

The following list is a sampling of summer camps with winter and summer addresses, Web addresses and phone numbers. Note that camps owned by the Boy Scouts of America are generally open only to members of certain troops; Girl Scout camps are usually open to all girls, with a modest fee to join as a scout (for insurance coverage). Likewise, YMCA camps are open to youngsters once they pay their dues.

If you're in the Adirondacks during July or August, and would like to visit a particular camp with your prospective happy camper, you should call ahead; also, many camps will send videos to give you a taste of the action. If you want to let your fingers do the walking, check out these websites: www.acacamps.org for American Camping Association accredited camps; www.nycamps.org, which has online descriptions of camps without web pages as well as links to those that do; or www.camppage.com/newyork, with similar links to camp websites.

LAKE GEORGE AND SOUTHEASTERN ADIRONDACKS

Adirondack Camp: Director Matthew Basinet; 518-547-8261; www.Adirondackcamp.com; Box 97, Putnam Station NY 12861. Coed. Established in 1904 on the east side of Lake George. Wilderness trips, team sports, culinary arts, crafts, drama. Ages 7–15; 4-week session.

Brant Lake Camp: (Boys). Directors, Karen G. Meltzer, Robert Gersten, Richard Gersten; summer phone: 518-494-2406; Brant Lake NY 12815. Winter office: 212-734-6216; www.brantlake.com; 1202 Lexington Ave., New York NY 10028. Established in 1917 and still run by the same family. Programs include a full range of team sports; water sports (canoeing, waterskiing, fishing, swimming, sailing); computers; crafts, music, photography, theater. Ages 7–15 in different divisions; 8-week session. Also, **Brant Lake Dance and Tennis Center for Teenage Girls** for ages 12–16; 4 weeks; and **Brant Lake Sports Center for Teenage Girls** highlighting basketball, soccer, softball, volleyball and tennis for ages 12–16; 2 weeks.

Camp Echo Lake: 518-623-9635; www.campecholake.com; Off Hudson St., Warrensburg NY 12885. Winter office: 914-345-9099; 3 W. Main St., Elmsford NY 10528. Established 1946. Coed; on private lake. Swimming, riding, backcountry adventures, arts, crafts, canoeing. Ages 7–17. See Echo Lake Southwoods, below.

Camp Somerhill: Director, Lawrence Singer; summer phone: 518-623-9914; High St., Athol NY 12810. Winter office: 914-793-1303; 20 Huntley Rd., Box 295, Eastchester NY 10709. Coed; on private lake. Programs in athletics, science, horseback riding, creative arts, water sports; overnight backpack and canoe trips; flying lessons; trips to Boston, Montreal, and museums. Ages 7–17; 2–8 weeks.

Camp Walden: Directors, Amy and Wayne Gould. 518-644-9441; www.camppage.com/walden; Trout Lake Rd., Diamond Point NY 12824. Winter office: Box 57, Leetsdale, PA 15056; 412-429-5111. Established in 1931. Coed; four- and eight-week sessions with sailing, canoeing, kayaking, tennis, hockey, soccer, horseback riding, golf, lacrosse, gymnastics, and martial arts.

Chingachgook on Lake George: Director, George W. Painter; summer phone: 518-656-9462; Pilot Knob Rd., Pilot Knob NY 12844. Winter office: 518-373-0160. Established in 1913 on the east side of Lake George; affiliated with the Capital District YMCA. Coed; program includes sailing, waterskiing, canoeing, hiking, arts, drama, team sports, ropes course. Ages 7–adult; 1–2 weeks. Also operates the **Lake George Family Sailing School**.

Double "H" Hole in the Woods Ranch: Executive Director, Max Yurenda; 518-696-5676; www.holeinthewallgang.org/camp-support; RR 2, Box 288, Lake Luzerne NY 12846. Established in 1993 on Lake Vanare. Coed; supported by Paul Newman's Hole in the Wall Gang fund, for children with cancer or blood-related diseases and/or neuromuscular impairments that preclude attending other camps. Horseback riding, ropes course, water sports; creative arts; children's farm; winter sessions with downhill skiing. Ages 6–16; 7–10 days.

Echo Lake Southwoods 800-44-WEEKS; www.southwoods.com; Rte. 74, Paradox NY 12858. winter: 3 W. Main St., Elmsford NY 10523. Recently refurbished complex. Coed; two four-week sessions on Paradox Lake highlighting water sports, crafts, canoeing, cricket, archery, gymnastics, team sports, backcountry adventures, tennis, performing arts.

Forest Lake Camp: Director, Garry Confer; 518-623-4771; Box 67, Warrensburg NY 12885; winter office: 908-534-9809; Box 648, Oldwick NJ 08858. Established in 1926. Horseback riding, water and team sports, theater, creative arts, wilderness trips. Sessions for boys and girls. Ages 8–16; 4 weeks.

Luzerne Music Center: Directors, Bert Phillips and Toby Blumenthal; 518-696-2771; Lake Tour Rd., Lake Luzerne NY 12846. Winter office: 800-874-3202; 7648 Ponte Verde Way, Naples FL 33942. Established in 1980. Coed; excellent chamber music program led by members of the Philadelphia Orchestra; recreation includes canoeing, whitewater rafting, team sports. Ages 10–18; 4 weeks. Also 1-week session for adults.

Point O' Pines Girls Camp: Directors, Sue and Jim Himoff; 518-494-3213; RR 1, Box 191A, Brant Lake NY 12815. Girls; on Brant Lake; 8-week session; team sports, gymnastics; dance, horseback riding, drama, fine arts. Ages 7–15; 8 weeks.

Skye Farm Camp and Retreat Center: Director, Debi Paterson; 518-494-3432; Sherman Lake, Bolton Landing NY 12814. Winter office: 518-494-7170; HCR 2, Box 103, Warrensburg NY 12885. Boys; girls; adults. Operated by United Methodist Church; full summer program for children; special fall hiking and canoeing weekends for adults; winter cross-country skiing and snowshoeing days. Ages 6–adult; 1 week.

Sonrise: Directors, Larry and Ruth McReynolds; 518-494-2620; PO Box 51, Pottersville NY 12860. Boys; girls; coed; adults. Lutheran; affiliated with Atlantic District Missouri Synod. On Schroon Lake; full program; conference center open year-round; Elderhostel sessions.

Word of Life: Director, Mike Calhoun and John Page; 518-532-7111; PO Box 600, Schroon Lake NY 12870. Sessions for girls; boys; coed; adults on an island and at a ranch. Non-denominational Christian camps and full-service conference center. Wide range of indoor, outdoor and team sports; horseback riding. Ages 6–13 at the ranch; 13–18 on the island; 1 week.

CHAMPLAIN VALLEY

Camp Dudley: Director, Wheaton Griffin; 518-962-4720; Camp Dudley Rd., Westport NY 12993. Established in 1885; the oldest boys' camp in the country. Affiliated with the YMCA but operated independently. On Lake Champlain; activities include water sports, hiking, backpacking, golf, soccer, arts, drama, photography, tennis. Ages 10–15; 4 weeks and 8 weeks.

Normandie: Director, Waldemar Kasriels; 518-962-4750; Furnace Point Rd., Westport NY 12993. Established in 1966; coed. Emphasis on water sports: water skiing, windsurfing, kayaking, canoeing, plus land sports and field trips. Ages 9–17; 2, 4, 6, and 8 weeks.

North Country Camps: Lincoln (Boys) and **Whippoorwill** (Girls). Directors, Peter Gucker and Nancy Gucker Birdsall; 518-834-5527; www.nccamps.com; 395 Frontage Rd., Keeseville NY 12944. Winter: 802-235-2908; RR 1, Box 3860, West Rutland VT 05777. Established by the Gucker family in 1920. Strong wilderness program with backpacking, canoeing, sailing, horseback riding; in-camp programs in swimming, windsurfing, kayaking, soccer, science, crafts, dance, music, crafts. Ages 8–15; 5 and 7 1/2weeks.

Pok-O-MacCready Camps: Pok-O-Moonshine (Boys); **MacCready** (Girls); and **Pok-O-MacCready Outdoor Education Center** (Sept.–June). Director, Jack Swan; 518-963-8366 (summer camps); 518-963-7967 (outdoor center); www.members.aol.com/pokomac; Mountain Rd., Willsboro NY 12996. Winter office: 203-775-9865; Box 5016, Brookfield CT 06804. Established in 1905; on Long Pond. Summer sessions highlight horseback riding, sailing, backpacking, gymnastics, lacrosse, tennis, canoeing, rock climbing, archery, crafts, dance, drama. 6 weeks. During fall, winter, and spring, the campus is an outdoor education center for school groups, featuring traditional skills and crafts and earth studies. Nearby is the **1812 Homestead**, a hands-on historical site.

HIGH PEAKS AND NORTHERN ADIRONDACKS

Camp Colby: Director, Dan Capuano; 518-891-3373; www.dec.state.ny.us/website/education/colby; Rte. 86, Saranac Lake NY 12983; winter: Department of Environmental Conservation, Room 505, 50 Wolf Rd., Albany NY

12233. Coed environmental-education camp for New York State teens. Hiking, canoeing, wildlife ecology, arts and crafts. 1 week. This site also hosts **Camp Good Grief**, an excellent program for teens who have gone through the death of a close family member.

Camp Merrill: Directors, Hal Lyons and Laurie Roland; 800-431-1184; www.chateaugay.com; Chateaugay Lake, Merrill NY 12955. Winter office: 203-396-0688; 165 Short Hill Lane, Fairfield, CT 06432. Coed; full or half-summer programs in canoeing, kayaking, windsurfing, horseback riding, sailing, tennis, wilderness trips for teens. Ages 7–15.

Camp Treetops: Director, Brad Konkler; 518-523-9329; www. nct.org/camp; North Country School, PO Box 187, Lake Placid NY 12946. Established 1920; coed. Besides horseback riding, llama trekking, canoe-camping trips, rock climbing, sailing, and a full range of nature and arts programs, the camp is also a working farm, where kids take care of the animals and gardens. Ages 7–13; 7 weeks.

NORTHWEST LAKES

Camp Regis-Applejack: Directors, Michael and Pauline Humes; 518-327-3117; www.campregis-applejack.com; PO Box 245, Paul Smiths NY 12970. Winter office: 914-997-7039; 107 Robinhood Rd., White Plains NY 10605. Coed; established 1946; Quaker philosophy. Based at a former estate on the shore of Upper St. Regis Lake; canoeing, kayaking, sailing, waterskiing; hiking; team sports; arts and crafts; photography; wilderness overnight trips for senior campers; excursions to Montreal, Cape Cod, and Maine. Ages 7–17; 4 weeks and 8 weeks.

Eagle Island: Director, Amy Erickson; 518-891-0928; Eagle Island, Boat Rte. 863, Saranac Lake NY 12983. Winter office: Girl Scout Council of Greater Essex County NJ, 201-746-8200; 120 Valley Rd., Montclair NJ 07042. Established in 1937. Sessions for girls, families, and women. Located on an island in a rustic Great Camp; strong program in water sports; open to non-Girl Scouts, too. Ages 8–17; 2, 4, and 6 weeks.

Star Lake Computer Camp: Director, Dick Leroux; Star Lake SUNY Campus, Star Lake NY 13690. Winter office: 315-267-2167; Raymond Hall, SUNY, Potsdam NY 13676. Coed. Campers explore the natural world around Star Lake, then create databases to develop a guidebook and map; outdoor activities include canoeing, hiking, camping. Ages 9–14; 1 week.

Young Life Saranac Village: Director C. L. Robertson, 518-891-3010; HCR 1, Box 88, Saranac Lake NY 12983. Established in 1970; coed, non-denominational Christian camp for teens. Located in the rustic Great Camp Prospect Point. Programs include all water sports, team sports, Bible studies. 1 week.

CENTRAL ADIRONDACKS

Adirondack Woodcraft Camps: Director, John Leach. 315-369-6031 or 800-374-4840; www.awc1.com; Rondaxe Rd., Old Forge NY 13420. Established 1925. Coed; programs in rock-climbing, riflery, archery, nature, crafts, hiking, map and compass, canoeing, extended wilderness trips. Ages 6–15; 3, 4, and 7 weeks.

Camp Baco Boys; 518-251-2919 and **Camp Che-Na-Wah** Girls; 518-251-3129. Director, Robert Wortman; www.campbaco.com ; Lake Balfour, Minerva NY 12851. Winter office: 516-374-7757; 80 Neptune Ave., Woodmere NY 11598. Camp Baco established in 1923; on private lake. Activities include swimming, canoeing, sailing, waterskiing, tennis, lacrosse, mountain biking, photography, drama, music, crafts. Ages 6–16; 8 weeks.

Camp Mark Seven: Director, Fr. Thomas Coughlin; 315-357-6089; www.campmark7.com; Fourth Lake, Old Forge. Winter: 301-933-1126; 306 Fallsworth Pl., Walkersville MD 21793. Coed; for deaf children, teens, and adults. Canoeing, camping, swimming, water skiing, team sports, arts and crafts. Emphasis on deaf culture and self images; session for children of deaf adults. Ages 10–20, adults and senior citizens; 1 and 2 weeks.

Camp Northwood: 315-831-5700; Rte. 365, Remsen NY 13438. Coed; seven-week sessions for ages 8–18, especially youngsters with low self esteem, attention-deficit disorders, and learning challenges.

Camp Russell: 315-392-3290; Woodgate NY 13494. Winter office: 315-866-1540; Box 128, Herkimer NY 13350. Boys. Established in 1918; affiliated with General Herkimer Council Boy Scouts. Programs include water sports, forestry, riflery, overnight canoeing and camping trips. 1 week.

Cedarlands Scout Reservation: Director, Richard W. Bashant; 518-624-4371; Walker Rd., Long Lake NY 12847. Winter office: 315-735-4437; Oneida Council BSA, 1400 Genesee St., Utica NY 13501. Boy Scouts only. Water sports, crafts, overnight wilderness trips, outdoor skills, rock climbing, conservation. Ages 10–17; 1 week.

Deerfoot Lodge: Director, Charles Gieser; 518-548-5277; Whitaker Lake, Speculator NY 12164. Winter office: 518-966-4115; RD 2 Box 159B, Greenville NY 12083. Boys; non-denominational Christian camp. Activities include water sports, hiking, wildlife study, survival skills, overnight canoeing and camping trips. Ages 8–16; 2 weeks. Also **Tapawingo**, for girls, at Camp of the Woods; 518-548-5091; Rte. 30, Speculator.

4-H Camp Sacandaga: Director, James Tavares; 518-548-7993; Cornell Cooperative Extension; Page St., Speculator NY 12164. Winter office: 518-853-3471; Cooperative Extension, PO Box 1500, Fonda NY 12068. Coed; established in 1945; originally a Civilian Conservation Corps camp. Programs include environmental education, creative arts, horseback riding, sailing, water sports. Campers need not be current 4-H members. Ages 8–19; 1 week.

Fowler Camp and Conference Center: Director, Kent Busman; 518-548-6524;

Sacandaga Lake, Speculator NY 12164. Winter office: 518-374-4573; 1790 Grand Blvd., Schenectady NY 12309. Coed; established 1954. Affiliated with the Reformed Church in America. Water sports, hiking, crafts, nature study, overnight canoeing and camping trips. Late summer and fall sessions for adults in Adirondack history and environment. Ages 9–18; 1 week.

CAMPING

Sleeping under the stars on a remote island, in the bugless confines of a recreational vehicle, or nestled within the cozy comfort of a backpacking tent deep in the forest — camping possibilities in the Adirondacks cater to all tastes. The Department of Environmental Conservation (DEC) operates 40-some public campgrounds, most of which are on beautiful lakes or peaceful ponds, and all of which are open from Memorial Day through Labor Day. Many campgrounds open earlier, and some stay in operation late into the fall. Most state campgrounds now have informative brochures showing individual sites and local services, which can be found in nearby towns.

The smaller places (those with 100 sites or fewer) tend to be quieter; some campgrounds accommodate upwards of 400 groups and can resemble little cities in the woods. However, camping in the North Country is still very much a family experience. The only hassles you may encounter might be from persistent chipmunks and red squirrels who regard your picnic table as their personal lunch counter.

Facilities at state campgrounds include a picnic table and grill at each site, water spigots for every 10 sites or so, and lavatories. Not every campground has showers. Many facilities have sites for mobility-impaired campers, with hard-surface areas, water spigots at wheelchair height, and ramps to rest rooms.

State campgrounds like Golden Beach have been serving travelers for 70 years.

Courtesy of Edward Comstock Jr.

Camping is also permitted year-round on state land, but you need a permit to stay more than three days in one backcountry spot or if you are camping in a group with more than 10 people. These permits are available from local forest rangers. Some locations such as Stillwater Reservoir, Lows Lake, or Lake Lila have designated primitive camping spots with fire rings and/or privies, but you may camp elsewhere provided you pitch your tent at least 150 feet from any trail, stream, lake, or other water body. (Check the information on low-impact camping, below.) Also, along the Northville–Lake Placid Trail and on popular canoe routes you'll find lean-tos for camping. These three-sided log structures are a trademark of the Adirondack wilds. A handy guide with useful tips for family trips as well as destinations is Barbara McMartin's book *Adventures in Backpacking* (North Country Books, 1996).

Reservations can be made for a site in the state campgrounds by calling **Reserve America** (800-456-CAMP), a computerized reservation service, but by all means check out their Worldwide Web page (www.ReserveAmerica.com). It shows amazing detail for every state campground, so you can see for yourself if site #4 at Lake Durant is on the water. (It is.) You can likewise check www.Adirondack.com/reference/sitemaps for similar information. You may reserve a place for a single night or as long as three weeks and charge it to your credit card. DEC campgrounds will cheerfully take you on a first-come, first-served basis if space is available; before July 4 and after September 1, it's usually easy to find a nice site without a reservation. Campsites cost about $10–$15 per night in 1999; the reservation fee is $7.50. Day-use fees are about $5 per carload, and at most places bicyclists or hikers can enter at no charge.

DEC public campgrounds do not supply water, electric, or sewer hook-ups for recreational vehicles; if you require these amenities, there are privately owned campgrounds in many communities. Check Chapter Five, *Lodging*, for these facilities. Also, some towns offer public camping; check with local tourist-information offices, listed in Chapter Eight, *Information*.

PUBLIC CAMPGROUNDS

LAKE GEORGE AND SOUTHEASTERN ADIRONDACKS

Eagle Point (518-494-2220; U.S. Rte. 9, 2 mi. N. of Pottersville) 3-day minimum stay for reserved sites; boat launch; showers; swimming.

Hearthstone Point (518-668-5193; Rte. 9N, 2 mi. N. of Lake George Village) On Lake George. 3-day minimum for reserved sites; showers; swimming.

Lake George Battleground (518-668-3348; Rte. 9, 1/4 mi. S. of Lake George Village) Historic site. 3-day minimum for reserved sites; showers. Easy walk to downtown and tour boat docks.

Lake George Islands (518-644-9696; numerous sites on Narrows Islands, Glen Islands, Long Islands) Access by boat; tents only; swimming. No dogs allowed.

The Bear Truth

As humans have become enamored of sleeping out in the wilds, some wild animals have learned to recognize coolers, packs, tents, even open car trunks as potential food sources. Hungry black bears or pesky raccoons may not be in evidence when you set up camp, but it's best to take all precautions. If your site has a metal locker for food storage, use it. Otherwise, stash your supplies and cooking gear well away from your tent: put it in a pack or strong plastic bags and suspend it between two trees with a sturdy rope at least 20 feet off the ground. Tie it off by wrapping several times around one tree and tie a complicated knot; bears have been known to swat down food stashes within their reach, climb saplings, and even bite through ropes. Don't try to outsmart bruin by putting your food in an anchored boat away from shore; bears swim well. The campsite caretaker can give you an update on the bear situation.

If a bear does visit your camp, loud noises (yelling, banging on pots, loud whistles) usually discourage it. Attacks are extremely rare in the Adirondacks; do keep your dog under control in the event of a close encounter of the ursine kind.

Luzerne (518-696-2031; off Rte. 9N, Lake Luzerne) On Fourth Lake. 3-day minimum for reserved sites; showers; swimming; canoe and rowboat launch; no powerboats allowed.

Rogers Rock (518-585-6746; Rte. 9N, 3 mi. N. of Hague) On Lake George. Historic site. 3-day minimum for reserved sites; boat launch.

CHAMPLAIN VALLEY

Ausable Point (518-561-7080; Rte. 9, N. of Port Kent) On Lake Champlain. 3-day minimum for reserved sites; showers; swimming; boat launch. Near wildlife refuge; good place to explore by canoe.

Crown Point Reservation (518-597-3603; off Rte. 9N, near the bridge to Vermont) On Lake Champlain. Showers; boat launch. Across from fort.

Lincoln Pond (518-942-5292; County Rte. 7, 6 mi. S. of Elizabethtown) 3-day minimum for reserved sites; swimming; showers; canoe or rowboat rentals; no powerboats allowed.

Paradox Lake (518-532-7451; Rte. 74, 2 mi. E. of Severance) Swimming; showers; canoe or rowboat rentals; boat launch.

Poke-O-Moonshine (518-834-9045; Rte. 9, 6 mi. S. of Keeseville) Showers; access to hiking and rock climbing on Poke-O-Moonshine Mountain.

Putnam Pond (518-585-7280; off Rte. 74, 6 mi. W. of Ticonderoga) Swimming; showers; canoe or rowboat rentals; boat launch. Access to Pharaoh Wilderness Area.

Sharp Bridge (518-532-7538; Rte. 9, 15 mi. N. of Schroon Lake) Showers; access to Hammond Pond Wild Forest.

HIGH PEAKS AND NORTHERN ADIRONDACKS

Buck Pond (518-891-3449; off Rte. 30 near Onchiota) Swimming; showers; canoe or rowboat rental; boat launch.

Lake Harris (518-582-2503; Rte. 28N Newcomb) Swimming; showers; boat launch.

Meacham Lake (518-483-5116; Rte 30, 9 mi. N. of Paul Smiths) Swimming; showers; horse trails and barn; some primitive sites accessible by foot only; boat launch. Good place to see bald eagles in summer.

Meadowbrook (518-891-4351; Rte. 86 near Ray Brook) Showers, no swimming. Closest campground to downtown Lake Placid.

Saranac Lake Islands (518-891-3170; off Rte. 3 S.W. of Saranac Lake Village) Access by boat; tents only.

Taylor Pond (518-647-5250; Silver Lake Rd., 9 mi. N.W. of Au Sable Forks) Boat launch.

Wilmington Notch (518-946-7172; Rte. 86, Wilmington) On the West Branch of the Ausable River. Great area for fly fishing.

NORTHWEST LAKES

Cranberry Lake (315-848-2315; off Rte. 3, 1 mi. S. of Cranberry Lake Village) 2-day minimum stay for reserved sites. Swimming; showers; rowboat or canoe rentals. The easy hike up Bear Mountain begins from this campground.

Fish Creek Pond (518-891-4560; Rte. 30, 12 mi. E. of Tupper Lake) 3-day minimum for reserved sites. Swimming; showers; canoe or rowboat rentals; boat launch; nature and Beginner Camper programs.

Rollins Pond (518-891-3239; Rte. 30, near Fish Creek Pond campsite) 3-day minimum for reserved sites. Showers; canoe/rowboat rentals; boat launch.

CENTRAL ADIRONDACKS

Alger Island (315-369-3224; off South Shore Rd., W. of Inlet) 2-day minimum stay for reserved sites; on Fourth Lake; access by boat; tents only.

Browns Tract Ponds (315-354-4412; Uncas Rd. W. of Raquette Lake) 2-day minimum for reserved sites. Swimming; canoe or rowboat rentals; no powerboats allowed.

Caroga Lake (518-835-4241; Rte. 29A S. of Caroga Lake) 2-day minimum for reserved sites. Swimming; showers; boat launch.

Eighth Lake (315-354-4120; Rte. 28, between Raquette Lake and Inlet) 3-day minimum for reserved sites. Swimming; showers; canoe or rowboat rentals; boat launch.

Forked Lake (518-624-6646; North Point Rd., off Rte. 30 near Long Lake) 2-day minimum. Primitive walk-in or canoe-in sites; launch for cartop boats.

Golden Beach (315-354-4230; Rte. 28, 3 mi. E. of Raquette Lake) On Raquette Lake; swimming; showers; boat or canoe rentals; boat launch.

Indian Lake Islands (518-648-5300; off Rte. 30, 11 mi. S. of Indian Lake hamlet) 3-day minimum for reserved sites; access by boat; tents only; boat launch.

Lake Durant (518-352-7797; Rte. 28/30, 3 mi. E. of Blue Mtn. Lake) 3-day minimum for reserved sites. Swimming; showers; canoe rentals; boat launch; handicap-access campsite. Access to Blue Ridge Wilderness and Northville-Placid Trail.

Lake Eaton (518-624-2641; Rte. 30, 2 mi. N. of Long Lake bridge) 2-day minimum for reserved sites. Swimming; showers; canoe or rowboat rentals; boat launch.

Lewey Lake (518-648-5266; Rte. 30, across from Indian Lake Islands access) 2-day minimum for reserved sites. Swimming; showers; canoe or rowboat rentals; boat launch.

Limekiln Lake (315-357-4401; Limekiln Lake Rd., off Rte. 28 E. of Inlet) 2-day minimum stay for reserved sites. Swimming; showers; canoe or rowboat rentals; boat launch.

Little Sand Point (518-548-7585; Piseco Lake Rd., off Rte. 30, Piseco) 2-day minimum for reserved sites. On Piseco Lake; swimming; canoe or rowboat rentals; boat launch.

Moffit Beach (518-548-7102; off Rte. 8, 4 mi. W. of Speculator) 3-day minimum for reserved sites. On Sacandaga Lake; swimming; showers; canoe or rowboat rentals; boat launch.

Northampton Beach (518-863-6000; Rte. 30, 2 mi. S. of Northville) 3-day minimum for reserved sites. On Great Sacandaga Lake; swimming; showers; canoe or rowboat rentals; boat launch.

Point Comfort (518-548-7586; Piseco Lake Rd., Piseco) 2-day minimum for reserved sites. On Piseco Lake; swimming; showers; canoe or rowboat rentals; boat launch.

Poplar Point (518-548-8031; Piseco Lake Rd.) 2-day minimum for reserved sites. On Piseco Lake; swimming; canoe or rowboat rental; boat launch.

Sacandaga (518-924-4121; Rte. 30, 4 mi. S. of Wells) 2-day minimum for reserved sites. On Sacandaga River; swimming; showers; no powerboats.

Tioga Point (315-354-4230; Raquette Lake) 2-day minimum for reserved sites. On Raquette Lake; access by boat; some lean-tos, although it's best to bring a tent. Beautiful spot.

CANOEING AND KAYAKING

Paddlers agree: the Adirondack Park offers some of the best canoeing and kayaking in the Northeast. Some might argue that the region rivals the Boundary Waters Canoe Area in Minnesota for excellent backcountry tripping. For thrill seekers, there's serious whitewater (up to Class V) on the Upper

Mark Kurtz

Canoeing on lakes, rivers, ponds, and streams is a three–season Adirondack pleasure.

Hudson, the Moose, portions of the Schroon, and other rivers; for flatwater fans, there are long trips linking lakes, such as the 44-mile route from Long Lake to Tupper Lake, the 35-mile trip from Old Forge to Blue Mtn. Lake, or the 25-mile trip from Osgood Pond to Lake Kushaqua. In the St. Regis Canoe Area it's possible to paddle for weeks on end and visit a different pond or lake each day. There's even a 3-day race, the Adirondack Canoe Classic, that covers 90 miles of water in a long diagonal from the Fulton Chain of Lakes to Saranac Lake village (see the listing under "Annual Events" in this chapter).

Options have improved considerably in recent years, with New York State's acquisition of beautiful, motorless, Little Tupper Lake and Rock Pond (1998), and the myriad whitewater rivers that formerly belonged to Champion International Company (1999). Four-mile-long Little Tupper Lake offers gorgeous paddling, swimming, and loon-watching, with several primitive campsites you can reserve from the registration box at the parking lot. The Champion purchase is primarily in the northern Adirondacks, and includes some very challenging Class IV–V runs on the Deer, St. Regis, and other rivers. The Department of Environmental Conservation's Northville office (518-863-4545) has an excellent guide to the William C. Whitney Area, which encompasses Little Tupper Lake; field staff at DEC's Ray Brook headquarters (518-897-1200) may have a similar publication on the Champion lands in summer 2000.

Given that the possibilities seem unlimited, you may wonder how a newcomer chooses where to go. Three guidebooks cover Adirondack destinations for human-powered watercraft: *Adirondack Canoe Waters: North Flow* by Paul Jamieson and Donald Morris, updated to include the purchases mentioned above (Adirondack Mountain Club); *Adirondack Canoe Waters: South and West Flow* by Alec Proskine (Adirondack Mountain Club); and *Fun on Flatwater: Family Adventures in Canoeing* by Barbara McMartin (North Country Books). Both *Adirondac* and *Adirondack Life* magazines frequently publish articles describing canoe trips; check a local library for back issues or contact the publications (listed in Chapter Eight, *Information*). There's also a fine topo sheet, *Adirondack Canoe Waters,* published by Adirondack Maps, in Keene Valley, that shows several routes; it's available in regional bookstores and sporting goods stores.

The Department of Environmental Conservation (518-891-1200; Rte. 86, Ray Brook NY 12970) has recently revised its series of pamphlets that describe various canoe routes including the Bog River area near Tupper Lake, Stillwater Reservoir, and many others; ask for *Adirondack Canoe Routes* or the "official map and guide" of the area you wish to paddle. The excellent 24-page booklet *Guide to Paddling Adirondack Waterways* is available by calling 800-487-6867. Canoeing on Niagara Mohawk Power Company's impoundments on the Beaver, Raquette, Sacandaga, and Oswegatchie rivers is outlined in a free brochure available at information booths or by calling NiMo (315-474-1511). Some tourist information offices, such as the Saranac Lake Chamber of Commerce (518-891-1990), offer useful brochures and maps, too; ask for *Canoe Franklin County*. Searching online for the "William C. Whitney Area" and other new public lands leads to basic access information, but note that these simplified charts are not suitable for navigating. Always consult U.S. Geological Service topographic maps for the area you're traveling through.

When you're planning for any trip, allow an extra day in case the weather doesn't cooperate. Remember that you're required to carry a life jacket for each paddler; lash an extra paddle in your canoe, too. Bring plenty of food and fuel, a backpacker stove, and rain gear. A poncho makes a good coverall for hiking, but you're far better off with rain jacket and pants in a canoe, since a poncho can become tangled if you should dump the canoe. Do sign in at the trailhead registers when you begin your trip.

If you're still overwhelmed by making a decision about where to go, consult one of the outfitters or guides listed below. (These are folks specializing in canoeing or kayaking and offer lightweight, good-quality equipment; many boat liveries and marinas also rent aluminum or Coleman canoes.) On the World Wide Web, consult www.Adirondack.com/canoekayak for links to several canoe operations.

And if you're anxious to try canoeing, but just aren't sure of your abilities, there are plenty of places where you can get lessons in flatwater or whitewater techniques. Inlet's *Paddlefest* (315-357-6672) in mid-May, has demonstrations and more than a hundred different boats to try. For lessons, hire a guide for one-on-one sessions or check with your local Red Cross office for water safety courses and basic canoe instruction. You can also contact the Tri-Lakes office of the American Red Cross (518-891-3280; 52 Broadway, Saranac Lake NY 12983) for workshop dates.

Don't Drink the Water

The cool, clear water may seem like the ideal thirst quencher, but please resist the temptation to drink freely from Adirondack lakes, rivers, ponds, and streams. Sadly, due to careless campers and occasional animal pollution, these wild waters may harbor a microscopic parasite known as *Giardia lamblia*, which can cause bloating, diarrhea, cramping, and vomiting. Giardiasis — also known as Beaver Fever — is easily diagnosed (with a stool sample) and treated (with quinicrine or Flagyl), but it's better to avoid the ailment in the first place. Practice good campsite sanitation. Treat all drinking water by boiling 10 minutes, by using a specially designed giardia-proof filter, or with chlorine or iodine tablets.

CANOE OUTFITTERS AND TRIP GUIDES

LAKE GEORGE AND SOUTHEASTERN ADIRONDACKS

Adirondack Mountain Club (518-668-4447; www.adk.org; Luzerne Rd., Lake George) Spring, summer, and fall canoe workshops in different locations; guided canoe tours for women, youth, and Elderhostel groups.

W.I.L.D./W.A.T.E.R.S. (518-494-7478; Rte. 28, The Glen) Canoe and kayak instruction for youth and adults; whitewater clinics for men and women; kayak camp for youth; lodging available.

HIGH PEAKS AND NORTHERN ADIRONDACKS

Adirondack Lakes and Trails (518-891-7450 or 800-491-0414; 168 Lake Flower Ave., Saranac Lake) Canoes, kayaks, tents, and gear to buy or rent; paddling instruction.

Adirondack Rock and River Guide Service (518-576-2041; Alstead Hill Rd., Keene) Whitewater kayaking instruction; guided trips; lodging.

All Seasons Outfitters (518-891-3548; 168 Lake Flower Ave., Saranac Lake) Guided day and overnight canoe trips; flatwater canoe lessons; complete trip outfitter.

Jones Outfitters Ltd. (518-523-3468; 37 Main St., Lake Placid) Canoe rentals and sales.

Middle Earth Expeditions (518-523-9572; www.Adirondackrafting.com; Rte. 73, Lake Placid) Guided wilderness trips.

Tahawus Guide Service; 518-891-4334; Box 424, Lake Placid) Guided canoe and traditional guideboat trips.

Young's Foothills (518-891-1221; Box 345, Saranac Lake) Guided canoe trips.

NORTHWEST LAKES

Adirondack Canoes and Kayaks (518-359-2174 or 800-499-2174; www.capital.net/com/adkcanoe; 96 Old Piercefield Rd., Tupper Lake) Their website asks: "Why are you on the Internet when you should be paddling?" Rentals, tours, car shuttles, paddling instruction.

McDonnell's Adirondack Challenges (518-891-1176; www.Adirondackoutdoorguide.com; Rte. 30, Lake Clear) Complete year-round outfitter and guide service; wilderness education; scheduled trips.

Northern Pathfinders (800-882-PATH; Box 214, Lake Clear) Guided canoe trips; shuttle service.

Raquette River Outfitters (518-359-3228; Rte. 30 near the Moody Bridge, Tupper Lake) Complete trip outfitter; canoe repairs; guided trips; car shuttles.

St. Regis Canoe Outfitters (518-891-1838 or 888-SR KAYAK; www.canoeoutfitters.com; Floodwood Rd., Lake Clear) Trip outfitter; guided trips; canoe instruction; car shuttles. Call or write for the catalog of trips and supplies.

CENTRAL ADIRONDACKS

Blue Mountain Outfitters (518-352-7306/352-7675; Box 144, Blue Mtn. Lake) Complete trip outfitter; guided trips; car shuttles; sporting goods shop; canoe rental and sales.

Free Spirit Adventures (518-924-9275; Rte. 30, Wells) Kayaks, canoes, and outdoor gear. Guided paddling trips — even in winter!

Moose River Company (315-369-3682; Main St., Old Forge) Guided trips.

Mountainman Outdoor Supply Company (315-357-6672; www.mountainmanoutdoors.com; Rte. 28, Inlet) Kayaks, canoes, camping gear, books, maps. Primary sponsor of the annual Paddlefest at Inlet's Arrowhead Park.

Stillwater Shop (315-376-2110; Stillwater Rd., Stillwater Reservoir) Canoe rentals; camping supplies for sale.

Tickner's Moose River Canoe Outfitters (315-369-6286; off Rte. 28, Old Forge) Complete trip outfitter; canoe instruction; canoe rentals and sales; special River and Rail excursion with Moose River paddle and return via the Adirondack Scenic Railroad.

Whitewater Challengers (315-369-6699; Rte. 28 4 miles south of Old Forge) canoes and kayaks for sale and rent; 3-hour guided kayak ecotour to view wildlife for children and adults; day-long ecoexpeditions for adults. Also summer rafting trips with picnics.

DIVING

No amount of wishful thinking could turn the chilly Adirondack depths into crystal-clear Caribbean seas, but there is plenty to discover beneath the waves in Lake George. In fact, it's the site of New York's first underwater heritage preserve and home to numerous 18th- and 19th-century shipwrecks; request the guide for *The Sunken Fleet of 1758* from local tourism offices or the conservation department (518-897-1200) to learn more. New in 1999 is the *Lake George Underwater Classroom*, with interpretive signs for vegetation, fish, and a wreck or two. **Batteaux Below**, a maritime historic preservation group (518-587-7638) sponsors an annual underwater weekend in the fall; past speakers have included Clive Cussler, author of *Raise the Titanic*.

Rentals, instruction, and air service are available at **Divers' World** (518-644-2094; Rte. 9N, Bolton Landing), **Lake George SCUBA Center** (518-798-4486, Bay Rd., Lake George), **Northern Lake George Resort** (518-543-6528; Rte. 9N, Silver Bay), and **Ward's Dockside Marina** (518-543-8888, Rte. 9N, Hague).

FAMILY FUN

Courtesy of the Adirondack Museum

Spectacular Ausable Chasm has been open to tourists since the 1870s.

Besides countless pristine natural attractions, the Adirondack Park offers plenty of manmade amusements and privately owned curiosities. Ausable Chasm, a spectacular gorge of carved sandstone cliffs near the park's northeastern corner, is one of the country's oldest tourist meccas, dating back to 1870. Since the 1930s, visitors have filled their pockets with glittering garnets at the Barton Mines tour. Santa's Workshop, near Whiteface Mountain, is touted as the oldest theme park in the world, dating back to 1946, and it is *the* place to mail your Christmas cards from since the postmark reads "North Pole NY." Frontier Town, near North Hudson, combines Adirondack historic sites, like a working iron forge and a gristmill, with Wild West zest. On the other end of the spectrum, there are new-wave fun parks with towering water slides and pools that generate their own whitecaps. The Olympic Regional Development Authority (518-523-1655; www.orda.org) offers *Go for the Gold*, a reasonably priced all-in-one pass for watching freestyle ski practice, ski-jumping, skating, the Olympic Museum, Whiteface chairlift, and Whiteface highway. If sliding down a frozen chute is something the kids want to try and the bobsled pricetag is a bit much, Lake Placid's **toboggan run**, near the Mirror Lake beach, is a cheap thrill. It's open winter weekends, weather permitting; check with the North Elba Parks Department (518-523-2591).

You'll find miniature-golf courses listed under a separate heading, Olympic spectator events outlined under "Olympic Sports," and annual races and competitions later in this chapter. Described below is a potpourri of places to go and things to do.

Price Code			
Adult Admission:	**Inexpensive**	**Moderate**	**Expensive**
(Children's tickets are less.)	**under $8**	**$9–$15**	**over $15**

LAKE GEORGE AND SOUTHWESTERN ADIRONDACKS

House of Frankenstein Wax Museum (518-668-3377; Canada St., Lake George) From the Phantom of the Opera to modern horrors. Open daily Memorial Day–Columbus Day. Inexpensive.

Magic Forest (518-668-2448; Rte. 9, Lake George) Rides and games; Santa's Hideaway; home to the Adirondack Park's only diving horse, Rex, and a flock of trained parrots. Open Memorial Day–Labor Day. Moderate.

Movieworld Wax Museum (518-668-3077; Canada St., Lake George) Elvis and Batman in the lobby; lots of other wax figures and movie memorabilia. Open Memorial Day–Labor Day. Inexpensive.

Natural Stone Bridge & Caves (518-494-2283; www.stonebridgeandcaves.com; Stone Bridge Rd., Pottersville) 5 caves; stone archway; mineral shop. Open daily Memorial Day–Columbus Day. Inexpensive.

Water Slide World (518-668-4407; Rtes. 9 and 9L, Lake George) Wave pool; water slides; bumper boats. Daily mid-June–Labor Day. Expensive.

CHAMPLAIN VALLEY

Ausable Chasm (518-834-7454; Rte. 9, Ausable Chasm) Deep sandstone gorge, known as a tourist attraction since the 1870s. Hike through the formations, then ride a raft or inner tube down two miles of rapids. Daily mid-May–mid-Oct. Moderate.

Frontier Town (518-532-7181; off Northway Exit 29; North Hudson) Politically correct? Not a chance. Wild West theme park with Indians and cowboys, dancehall show, pony rides. Daily Memorial Day–Labor Day. Expensive.

HIGH PEAKS AND NORTHERN ADIRONDACKS

Adirondack Park Visitor Interpretive Centers (518-327-3000; Rte. 30, Paul Smiths and 518-582-2000; Rte. 28N, Newcomb) Great places for hiking well-marked trails, with lots of workshops and programs for preschoolers to senior citizens. Open daily except Thanksgiving, Christmas, and New Year's Day; no admission charge for trails or exhibits. Recommended.

High Falls Gorge (518-946-2278; www.highfallsgorge.com; Rte. 86; Wilmington) Waterfalls and trails on the Ausable River. July–Aug. Moderate.

Santa's Workshop (518-946-2212; Rte. 431, Wilmington) Reindeer; craft demonstrations; corny singing and dancing; Santa; rides. Daily Memorial Day–Columbus Day; some winter weekends. This is the only place in the Adirondacks where you can buy a personalized magic wand. Moderate.

Whiteface Mountain Chairlift Ride (518-946-2223; Rte. 86, Wilmington) Recommended for fall foliage. Late June–Columbus Day. Inexpensive.

CENTRAL ADIRONDACKS

Adirondack Scenic Railroad (315-369-6290; Rte. 28, Thendara) Excursions from Thendara to Minnehaha or Carter Station, about 4 and 6 miles, respectively, extending to Big Moose Station by 2001. Bike and rail or canoe and rail combinations. Train robberies, Halloween ride, other special events. May–Nov. Inexpensive.

Barton Garnet Mine Tours (518-251-2706; Barton Mines Rd., North River) Tours of open-pit mines; rock collecting; mineral shop. July–Aug. Inexpensive.

Calypso's Cove (315-369-2777; Rte. 28, Old Forge) Bumper boats, batting cages, driving range, go-karts. Memorial Day–Columbus Day. Moderate.

Easy Rolling Skate Park (315-369-6924; North St., Old Forge) Rink for roller and in-line skaters. Year-round. Inexpensive.

Enchanted Forest/Water Safari (315-369-6145; Rte. 28, Old Forge) New York's largest water theme park; a real blast for teenagers *and* younger kids. Try the Black River if you like your rides dark, wet, and fast. Quite the place for people-watching, since everyone wanders around in bathing suits and beach towels. Daily Memorial Day–Labor Day. Expensive.

Gore Mountain Gondola Rides (518-251-2411; Peaceful Valley Rd., North Creek) Fall weekends. Inexpensive.

McCauley Mountain Chairlift Ride (315-369-3225; McCauley Mtn. Rd., Old Forge) Chairlift ride; lots of tame deer. Daily June 25–Labor Day; weekends Memorial Day–June 24; Labor Day–Columbus Day. Inexpensive.

Upper Hudson Scenic Railroad (518-251-5334; Depot St., North Creek) New in 1999, eight-mile trip from North Creek to Riparius. Ride the round-trip or bike to Riparius and ride back. Plans are in the works for kayak and canoe shuttles back upstream. May–Oct. two runs daily. Inexpensive.

BEYOND THE BLUE LINE

New York's largest theme park — **Great Escape Fun Park** (518-792-6568; Rte. 9, Lake George) — is visible from the Northway, just south of Lake George village. It's an awesome complex with 100 rides, shows, and attractions; the newly restored Comet roller coaster is regarded as one of the world's classic thrills. The park is undergoing major changes in 2000 and beyond, with plans to develop its own hotel, conference center, and restaurants. Open daily June–Labor Day, plus some spring and fall weekends. Expensive.

FISHING

Brook trout, lake trout, landlocked salmon, muskellunge, great northern pike, pickerel, walleye, smallmouth bass, largemouth bass, bullhead, whitefish, and assorted panfish are all native to Adirondack waters; toss in the exotics like brown trout, rainbow trout, splake, tiger musky, and kokanee, and an angler's alternatives approach Neptune's harvest. Of course, we offer no guarantees that you'll actually catch anything. But with preparation — like reading a guidebook or calling one of the hotlines or spending a day with a guide on remote waters — you may be able to tell the story about the big one that *didn't* get away.

Quite the catch!

Courtesy of the Adirondack Collection, Saranac Lake Free Library

Begin your fishing education with the *New York State Fishing Regulations Guide* published by the Department of Environmental Conservation and available at DEC offices, sporting-goods stores, tourist information centers, online (www.dec.state.ny.us/huntfish) or by mail (DEC, 50 Wolf Rd., Albany NY 12233). The free booklet details all the seasons and limits for various species. Everyone over age 16 who fishes in the Adirondacks must have a New York fishing license, which can be purchased at sporting-goods stores and town offices. Nonresidents can get special 5-day licenses; state residents over 70 are eligible for free licenses.

In general, trout season runs from Apr. 1–Sept. 30; bass season from the third Saturday in June–Nov. 30; northern, walleye, and pickerel from the first Saturday in May–Mar. 15. There are helpful hotlines for fishing tips describing what's hitting where on which kind of bait. For the southern part of DEC Region 5, including Lake George, lower Lake Champlain, Schroon Lake, and the Central Adirondacks, call 518-623-3682; for the High Peaks and Northwest Lakes area, call 518-891-5413.

If you'd like to read about fishing, county and town tourism offices listed in Chapter Eight, *Information* have the lowdown on local angling. There are a couple of books that you can find in book stores: *Good Fishing in the Adirondacks* (Backcountry Books) by Dennis Aprill and *Fishing in the Adirondacks* (Adirondack Sports Publications) by Francis Betters.

To get in the proper frame of mind for fishing, nothing beats a trip to a local fish hatchery. In ***Lake George and Southeastern Adirondacks***, the **Warren County Fish Hatchery** (518-623-4141; Hudson St., Warrensburg) is open daily. In the ***Champlain Valley***, the **Essex County Fish Hatchery** (518-597-3844; Creek Rd., Crown Point) is also open every day. The only fish ladder in the park is on the Boquet River (518-963-7266; School St., Willsboro); if you time it just right in the fall, you can watch big salmon ascend the watery staircase. In the ***Northwest Lakes*** the **Adirondack Fish Hatchery** (518-891-3358; Rte. 30, Saranac Inn) specializes in raising landlocked salmon for stocking lakes.

Acid rain has had an effect on fishing in the southwestern quadrant of the Adirondack Park, where there's more precipitation and thinner soils. About 200 lakes and ponds that once supported fish are now dead; research has shown it's not the direct effects of low pH levels, but acidic waters leaching toxic minerals from the soil that are to blame. Efforts to combat acidification by applying lime have shown some effect on small ponds. Biologists are also breeding trout that can survive in more acidic waters, but as yet these creatures have not been widely stocked. The good news is that more than two thousand lakes and ponds and countless miles of rivers and streams have stabilized at pH levels that support fish and all kinds of wildlife. For more information about acid rain, its effects, and what you can do to offset its spread, contact your local chapter of Trout Unlimited, or the DEC.

FISHING GUIDES, SCHOOLS, AND OUTFITTERS

LAKE GEORGE AND SOUTHEASTERN ADIRONDACKS

Adirondack Fishing Adventures (Rob Gilchrist; 518-494-5770; www.Adirondackcharters.com; Schroon River, Chestertown) Charter boat on Lake George and Schroon Lake, fly-fishing guides for interior ponds.

Ann's Bait & Tackle Shop (518-644-9989; Norowal Rd., Bolton Landing)

Gibaldi Guide Service (518-494-7059; Schroon River Rd., Warrensburg) Guided trips on Lake George, Lake Champlain, or to wilderness waters.

Lake George Camping Equipment (518-644-9941; Rte. 9N, Bolton Landing) Charter boat for salmon, trout, or bass on Lake George.

Lockhart Charter Fishing & Guide Services (518-623-2236; 70 Library Ave., Warrensburg) Ice-fishing and regular season trips on Lake George for salmon, lake trout, and northern pike; backcountry trips.

The Outdoorsman Sport Shop (518-668-3910; Rte. 9N, Diamond Point) Bait and tackle.

Sand n' Surf Charter Service (518-668-4622; Rte. 9N, Diamond Point) Charter boat for salmon, lake trout, bass on southern Lake George; 1 night free lodging with half-day off-season charter.

Ted's Charter Fishing Service (518-668-5334; Rte. 9N, Diamond Point) Charter boat for salmon, lake trout, bass on southern Lake George; 1 night free lodging with half-day off-season charter.

CHAMPLAIN VALLEY

Adirondack-Champlain Guide Service (518-963-7351; RR 297, Willsboro) Guided trips on Lake Champlain and backcountry lakes.

HIGH PEAKS AND NORTHERN ADIRONDACKS

Adirondack Mountain Club (518-523-3441; Adirondak Loj, Lake Placid) Fly-fishing workshops.

No-Kill Fishing

Angling for fun rather than for the frypan is catching on across the country, especially in trout waters. If you'd like to match wits with a wild piscine, and then send it back to live for another day, here are some tips for catch-and-release fishing.

Use a barbless hook or take a barbed hook and bend down the barb with a pair of pliers. Be gentle landing your fish; some anglers line their nets with a soft cotton bag. When removing the hook, it's best not to handle the fish at all, since you can disturb the protective coating on the skin. If you have to touch the fish, wet your hands first, don't squeeze the body and don't touch the gills. If you can, extract the hook without touching the fish by holding the hook's shank upside down and removing it. Usually, the creature will swim happily away. If your fish is tired, you can cradle it gently facing upstream so that water flows through the gills, or if you're in a lake, move it back and forth slowly as a kind of artificial respiration.

A five-mile-long section of the West Branch of the Ausable River between Lake Placid and Wilmington is designated for catch and release fishing only. With the no-kill rules in effect for more than five years, the action on the river has been transformed; the fly-fishing here can be the stuff dreams are made of. Also, Little Tupper Lake — home to a rare strain of brook trout — is designated for artificial lures and catch and release only. Don't even whisper the word "baitfish" if you plan to wet a line in Little Tupper or nearby Rock Pond.

Blue Line Sport Shop (518-891-4680; 82 Main St., Saranac Lake) Tackle and camping gear.

Francis Betters Guide Service (518-946-2605; 518-647-8418; www.Adirondack-flyfishing.com; Rte. 86, Wilmington) Fly fishing on the Ausable River; fly-fishing and fly-tying instruction; tackle shop.

Hungry Trout (518-946-2217; Rte. 86, Wilmington) Fly shop; fly-fishing instruction; access to private section of the Ausable River.

Jones Outfitters (518-523-3468; 37 Main St., Lake Placid) Fly-fishing instruction; guide service; rod and reel repairs; Orvis shop.

The Mountaineer (518-576-2281; Rte. 73, Keene Valley) Fly-fishing school.

Pat Gallagher Guide Service (518-523-9727; Box 306, Lake Placid) Wilderness fishing trips.

Placid Bay Ventures Guide & Charter Service (518-523-1744; 70 1/2 Saranac Ave., Lake Placid) Charter boat on Lake Placid; wilderness fishing trips.

River Road Bait & Tackle (518-891-2128; off Rte 3, Bloomingdale) Trout flies; rods and reels.

Tahawus Guide Service (518-891-4334; Rte. 86, Ray Brook) Fishing trips to remote streams; corporate retreats.

Young's Foothills (518-891-1221; Box 345, Saranac Lake) Guided trips for trout, bass, and pike; ice fishing.

Whiteface Guide Service (518-946-7258; Wilmington) Guided half- or full-day trips for landlocked salmon, lake trout, rainbow trout.

NORTHWEST LAKES

Tip Top Sport Shop (518-359-9222; 40 Park St., Tupper Lake)

CENTRAL ADIRONDACKS

Adirondack Mountain & Stream Guide Service (518-251-3762; Hardscrabble Rd., Olmstedville) Wilderness fishing trips.

Beaver Brook Outfitters (518-251-3394; Rtes. 8 and 28, Wevertown) Guided trips, Orvis equipment, fly-tying and fly-fishing lessons.

Ed's Fly Shop (518-863-4223; Rte. 30, Northville)

Moose River Company (315-369-3682; Main St., Old Forge) Fishing tackle and fly-fishing gear; outdoor equipment.

North Country Sports (518-251-4299; Thirteenth Lake Rd., North River) Wilderness fishing trips; tackle; books and videos; hand-tied flies.

Thomas Akstens (518-251-2217; Bartman Rd., Bakers Mills) Fly-fishing instruction; Adirondack patterns for bass and trout flies.

Wharton's Adirondack Adventures (518-548-3195; Box 544, Lake Pleasant) Guided wilderness fishing trips.

GOLF

Courtesy of the Adirondack Museum

Folks have been playing golf at the Ausable Club for more than a 100 years.

Savor the green rolling hills, craggy peaks, deep blue lakes, and bracing air — the Adirondacks do recall Scotland's landscape just a wee bit. Perhaps then it's no surprise that there are dozens of courses tucked in mountain valleys throughout the park. Once upon a time, there were even more golf clubs than are open today, links that were attached to grand hotels and exclusive private clubs. The book *Adirondack Golf Courses . . . Past and Present* (Adirondack Golf, 1987), compiled by Peter Martin, outlines the history of regional golf with dozens of old photographs and anecdotes. The annual publication *New York Golf* (Divot Communications) describes course upgrades, tournaments, and personnel and is available at selected pro shops in the region. To preview a number of tracks via the Internet, check out www.roundthebend.com/ Adirondacks/dackgolf. For a smorgasbord approach to play, the Golf-A-Round card (800-755-9706) entitles two to play for the price of one at nearly two dozen Adirondack courses. The only ongoing golf school near the Adirondacks is the Adirondack Foothills Golf Academy (315-831-5222; www.golfAdirondacks.com; Alder Creek Golf Course, Rte. 12, Alder Creek), with two- and three-day packages that include lodging in Alder Creek's elegant old clubhouse, meals, and instruction.

Adirondack golf courses today range from informal, inexpensive, converted cow pastures to challenging, busy, championship links. At most places, you don't have to reserve a tee time, and at only a few are golfers required to rent carts. If you want to try the ultimate caddy experience, hire a llama to carry your bags at Loon Lake; one beast can bear two bags. Contact Doreen Hayes (518-891-5887) to reserve a llama.

Price Code

Greens Fees:	**Inexpensive**	**Moderate**	**Expensive**	**Very Expensive**
(9 holes)	**under $15**	**$15–$25**	**Over $25**	**Over $40**

LAKE GEORGE AND SOUTHWESTERN ADIRONDACKS

Bend of the River Golf Course (518-696-3415; Rte. 9N, Hadley) 9 holes; par 35; 2,700 yards. Inexpensive. One of the first courses to open in the spring.

Cronin's Golf Resort (518-623-9336; Golf Course Rd., Warrensburg) 18 holes; par 70; 6121 yards. Opens early season; stays open past Halloween. Inexpensive.

Green Mansions (518-494-7222; Darrowsville Rd., Chestertown) 9 holes; par 36; 2700 yards. Moderate.

Sagamore Resort & Golf Club (518-644-9400; www.thesagamore.com; Federal Hill Rd., Bolton Landing) 18 holes; par 70; 6900 yards. Very Expensive. Designed by Donald Ross; challenging.

Schroon Lake Municipal Golf Course (518-532-9359; Hoffman Rd., Schroon Lake) 9 holes; par 36; 2958 yards. Inexpensive.

1000 Acres Golf Club (518-696-5246; Rte. 418, Stony Creek) 9 holes; par 35; 3900 yards. Inexpensive.

Top of the World (518-668-2062; Lockhart Mtn. Rd., Lake George) 9 holes; par 36; 2900 yards. Inexpensive to moderate.

CHAMPLAIN VALLEY

Cobble Hill Golf Course (518-873-9974; Rte. 9, Elizabethtown) 9 holes; par 34; 3000 yards. Inexpensive. Completed in 1897; great views of the High Peaks.

Moriah Country Club (518-546-9979; Broad St., Port Henry) 9 holes; par 32; 3000 yards. Inexpensive.

Port Kent Golf Course (518-834-9785; Rte. 373, Port Kent) 9 holes; par 30; 2047 yards. Inexpensive.

Ticonderoga Country Club (518-585-2801; Hague Rd. Ticonderoga) 18 holes; par 71; 6300 yards. Moderate.

Westport Country Club (518-962-4470; Liberty Rd., Westport) 18 holes; par 72; 6200 yards. Moderate. Challenging; beautiful views.

Willsboro Golf Club (518-963-8989; Point Rd., Willsboro) 9 holes; par 35; 3100 yards. Moderate.

HIGH PEAKS AND NORTHERN ADIRONDACKS

Ausable Club (518-576-4411; Ausable Club Rd., St. Huberts) 9 holes; Scottish links-type course. Inexpensive. Open to non-members in Sept. only, Mon.–Thurs.

Ausable Valley Country Club (518-647-8666; Golf Course Rd., Au Sable Forks) 9 holes; par 34; 2700 yards. Inexpensive.

Craig Wood Country Club (518-523-9811; Cascade Rd., Lake Placid) 18 holes; par 72; 6544 yards. Moderate. Named after Lake Placid native Craig Wood, who won both the U.S. Open and Masters in 1941.

Lake Placid Club Resort (518-523-4460; www.lpresort.com; Mirror Lake Dr., Lake Placid) 2 18-hole courses; 1 9-hole course. Expensive. Lunch at the Golfhouse is excellent.

Loon Lake Golf Club (518-891-3249; Rte. 99, Loon Lake) 18 holes; par 70; 5600 yards. Inexpensive. Completed in 1895, one of the oldest courses in the Adirondacks. Call one day ahead to arrange for llama caddy.

Saranac Inn Golf & Country Club (518-891-1402; Rte. 30, Saranac Inn) 18 holes; par 70; 6500 yards. Moderate. Beautifully maintained course.

Saranac Lake Golf Club (518-891-2675; www.saranacinn.com; Rte. 86, Saranac Lake) 9 holes; par 36; 6100 yards. Moderate.

Whiteface Club Golf Course (518-523-2551; Whiteface Inn Rd., Lake Placid) 18 holes; par 72; 6500 yards. Moderate. Challenging course designed by Walter Hagen and John VanKleek; beautiful views.

NORTHWEST LAKES

Clifton-Fine Golf Course (315-848-3570; Rte. 3, Star Lake) 9 holes; par 36; 2854 yards. Inexpensive.

Tupper Lake Golf & Country Club (518-359-3701; Country Club Rd., Tupper Lake) 18 holes; par 71; 6250 yards. Inexpensive.

CENTRAL ADIRONDACKS

Brantingham Golf Course (315-348-8861; Brantingham Rd., Brantingham Lake) 18 holes; par 71; 5300 yards. Inexpensive.

Cedar River Golf Course (518-648-5906; Rtes. 28/30, Indian Lake) 9 holes; par 36; 2700 yards. Inexpensive.

Inlet Golf Course and Country Club (315-357-3503; Rte. 28, Inlet) 18 holes; par 72; 6000 yards. Moderate.

Lake Pleasant Golf Course (518-548-7071; Rte. 8, Lake Pleasant) 9 holes; par 35; 2900 yards. Inexpensive.

Nick Stoner Golf Course (518-835-4211; Rte. 10, Caroga Lake) 18 holes; par 70; 5800 yards. Moderate.

Sacandaga Golf Club (518-863-4887; Rte. 30, Sacandaga Park, Northville) 9 holes; par 36; 3000 yards. Inexpensive.

Thendara Golf Club, Inc. (315-369-3136; off Rte. 28, Thendara) 18 holes; par 72; 6000 yards. Moderate. Designed by Donald Ross.

Wakely Lodge & Golf Course (518-648-5011; Cedar River Rd., Indian Lake) 9 holes; par 34; 2600 yards. Inexpensive.

HIKING AND BACKPACKING

Walk on the wild side. The Adirondack Park has more than 2,000 miles of marked hiking trails leading to pristine ponds, roaring waterfalls, spectacular peaks, ice caves, and hidden gorges; perhaps the toughest choice for an Adirondack visitor is selecting where to go. There are dozens of guidebooks to help you make that decision. The *Discover the Adirondacks* series (Lakeview Press and Backcountry Publications) by hiker-historian Barbara McMartin divides the park into 11 geographical regions and describes the natural and human histories of dozens of different destinations; besides marked trails, she suggests some basic bushwhacks to reach great views. The guidebooks published by the Adirondack Mountain Club (ADK) slice the Adirondacks into six regions; there's also a volume dedicated to 132-mile Northville–Lake Placid Trail. Dennis Aprill's *Paths Less Traveled* (Pinto Press) suggests dozens of small peaks to scale and notes interesting wildlife or natural features. For details on these books, check the bibliography in Chapter Eight, *Information*, and for local sources, consult the bookstore section in Chapter Seven, *Shopping*.

For even more reading on tramps and treks, there's *Adirondac* magazine, published by ADK; *Adirondack Life*, especially the Annual Guide, outlines plenty of good long walks; and the Department of Environmental Conservation has free guides to trails in the various wilderness and wild forest areas.

Buzz Off

Springtime in the Adirondacks can be lovely, but this earthly paradise has a squadron of tiny, persistent insects to keep humans from overwhelming the countryside. We speak here of blackflies. Bug season is usually late May through June, although its duration depends on the weather. If you are planning an extended hike, golf outing, streamside fishing trip, horseback ride, or similar activity, you'll want to apply insect repellent, wear light-colored clothing (blue, especially dark blue, seems to attract blackflies), and tuck in your pantlegs and shirt: the Adirondack red badge of courage is a bracelet of bites around the ankles or waist. Avoid using perfume, shampoo, or scented hairspray — these products broadcast "free lunch!" to hungry little buggers.

There's a pharmacy of lotions and sprays that use varying amounts of DEET (diethyl-meta-toluamide) as the active ingredient, but note that products containing more than 25% DEET should not be applied to children's skin. DEET should not be used on infants. Avon's Skin-So-Soft bath oil has remarkable powers of insect repellency without mysterious chemical additives. Fabric softener sheets, like Bounce, can be tucked into your hatband to keep flies away from your face. Some Adirondackers prefer pine-tar based bug dopes, like Ole Woodsman, that also have the lasting aroma of authenticity; after a good dose of Ole Woodsman, your pillows and sheets will be scented, too.

Postcard of Blue Mtn. Courtesy of Edward Comstock Jr.

Generations of hikers have enjoyed the views from Adirondack fire towers.

Some towns offer hiking maps; for example, if you're in the Blue Mountain Lake vicinity, ask for the trail map at the post office, or at the Tupper Lake Chamber of Commerce, ask for their sheet on nearby mountains to hike.

If you're searching in cyberspace, the Great Outdoor Recreation Pages (www.gorp.com) have a good selection of Adirondack hikes listed by area, like Keene Valley or Old Forge. Descriptions include length, difficulty, and directions to trailheads, but this information should be supplemented by a real topographical map. The Saranac Lake homepage (www.saranaclake.com/hiking) contains a bunch of "short and relaxing" walks plus more strenuous local hikes, like Mount Baker, an easy summit with a great view.

The Adirondack woods are free of many of the natural hazards that you need to worry about in other locales. There's some poison ivy in the Champlain Valley, but very little in the High Peaks, Northwest Lakes, and Central Adirondacks. Rattlesnakes are found only in isolated parts of the Tongue Mountain range near Lake George, and rarely in the Champlain Valley; keep your eyes open when crossing rock outcrops on warm, sunny days. These Eastern timber rattlers are quite shy and nonaggressive, but do take care not to surprise one.

In some parts of the park, you can leave the trailhead and not see another person until you return to your car and look in the rearview mirror. The Five Ponds Wilderness Area, between Stillwater Reservoir and Cranberry Lake, is especially remote. Parts of the Northville–Placid trail are many miles from the nearest road; passing through the West Canada Lakes or Cold River areas, you might go several days with just the cry of the loon or howl of the coyote for company. Going end-to-end on this long trail requires a minimum of 10 days, and a solid amount of backcountry knowledge, but you can pick shorter sections of the trail for three-day junkets. Parts of the High Peaks — especially from southern access points — offer similar overnights. It's possible to find solitude even in the middle of the busy summer season if you select the right destination. Lest we make it sound too daunting, there are plenty of easy hikes in the 2- to 5-mile length that traverse beautiful terrain in all sections of the park. Note that the High Peaks Unit Management Plan — which limits group size, prohibits campfires, and requests that dogs be leashed in this 226,000-acre wilderness — was approved in 1999; contact the DEC's Ray Brook office for the rules.

Don't assume that just because the Adirondacks don't reach the height of the Rockies that it's all easy strolling; paths can be steep and rocky; weather can be changeable. Wherever you choose to go, be prepared. Your pack should contain a flashlight, matches, extra food and water, map, compass, and extra clothes (wool or fleece for warmth; leave the cotton at home). At many trailheads, there's a register for signing in. Forest rangers use this data to estimate how much use a particular area receives; and, in the unlikely event that you get lost, the information about when you started, where you were planning to go, and who you were with would be helpful to the search team.

Tick, Tick, Tick

A few cases of Lyme Disease have been recorded in the Adirondacks in recent years, and hikers should take precautions against exposing themselves to deer ticks (*Ixodes dammini*). The ticks can be found in deep woods although they prefer to stay on their host animals, whitetail deer and deer mice. Dogs — especially exuberant ones that go crashing through the brush — are more at risk than humans; have your pet inoculated against Lyme Disease.

New York State has approved the sale of Permanone, a tick repellent that can be applied to clothing. Be careful! It's a very strong material that should not be placed on your skin or pets. You can minimize your exposure to ticks by wearing long pants (with cuffs tucked into your boots) and long-sleeve shirts, using a good insect repellent, and staying on the trail. If you wear light-colored clothing, the ticks are easier to spot, and you can check yourself and your kids for the vermin while you're in the woods.

Deer ticks are very tiny, no bigger than a sesame seed. They don't fly. If you find an eight-legged crawling creature on your body, it could be a spider, a wood tick (not a carrier of Lyme), or an arachnid locally called a "ked," which, despite its scary-looking crablike pincers, is harmless.

Humans face the highest risk of tick contact in June and July. If you find a tick attached to your skin, pull it out steadily with a pair of tweezers or your fingers, grasping as close to the tick's mouth as you can. Save the creature in a jar — your doctor will probably want to see it. Apply a topical antiseptic to the bite. A tick must feed for several hours before the disease is transmitted.

If you see on your skin a clear area encircled by a red rash and are feeling flu-like symptoms, you may have been exposed to Lyme Disease. Visit your doctor or a medical center for a Lyme test, but be aware that it takes several weeks after exposure for your body to show antibodies. Lyme symptoms mimic many other ailments so it's difficult to get an accurate diagnosis; most medical practitioners will begin a course of antibiotics if they believe you've been exposed.

For neophyte hikers, the trails at the Visitor Interpretive Centers at Newcomb and Paul Smiths are ingeniously designed to offer a wide range of nature in a relatively short distance, and you won't be too far from the building no matter how long you travel. You can join a guided trip to learn about wildflowers, mushrooms, trees, or birds. There are also wheelchair-accessible trails at both centers. See *Family Fun*, above.

Several organizations and guide services lead trips and offer map-and-compass, woodcraft, and low-impact-camping workshops.

HIKING GUIDES AND ORGANIZATIONS

Adirondack Discovery (315-357-3598; Box 545, Inlet) Guided day hikes to places of historical and geological interest in July and Aug.

Adirondack Mountain Club (518-668-4447; www.adk.org; Luzerne Rd., Lake George) Hikes with naturalists; fall foliage hikes; wilderness overnights;

Low-Impact Camping

Wilderness camping in the not-too-distant past relied on techniques like digging deep trenches around tents, cutting balsam boughs for backwoods beds, sawing armloads of firewood, and burying garbage and cans. For camp clean-up, we used to think nothing of washing dishes in the lake, and scrubbing ourselves vigorously with soap as we cavorted in the shallows. All of these activities left a lasting mark on the woods and waters; today it's important to leave no trace of your visit.

Low-impact camping is perhaps easier than old-fashioned methods once you know a few of the basics. Most of the skills are simply common sense: think of the cumulative effects of your actions when you set up camp and you're on your way to becoming a responsible wilderness trekker.

Choose a site at least 150 feet away from the nearest hiking trail or water source, and try to select a place that will recover quickly after you leave. Separate your tent from your cooking area to avoid attracting animals to your bedside and to distribute the impact of your stay. When you leave, tidy up. Be sure the spot is absolutely clean of any trash — even stuff we commonly regard as biodegradable — and spread dirt or dead leaves around any trampled areas.

Use a portable stove for backcountry cooking rather than a campfire. (You can use only dead and down wood in the forest preserve; cutting trees on state land is prohibited.) Plan your meals ahead so that you don't have extra cooked food; if no one in the party can assume the role of "master of the clean plate club," then pack out all your leftovers. Wash your dishes and your body well away from streams and lakes using a mild vegetable-based soap.

How to s—t in the woods is something to consider; nothing kills that "gee, isn't it terrific out here in the wilderness" feeling more than finding unmistakable evidence of other humans. Bring a shovel or trowel and bury that hazardous waste at least six inches down and 150 feet from the nearest water. Lean-tos and some designated backcountry campsites have privies; use them.

weekends for women, youth, and senior citizens. Many programs in the High Peaks at Adirondak Loj (518-523-3441).

Adirondack Park Visitor Interpretive Centers (518-327-3000; Rte. 30, Paul Smiths; 518-582-2000; Rte. 28, Newcomb) Guided hikes; nature trails; ecology programs for adults and children.

Ara-Ho Outfitters (315-357-3306; www.araoutfitters.com; Rte. 28, Inlet) Guided backpack trips in Ha-de-ron-dah and other wilderness areas, good camping gear for rent.

Birchbark Tours (518-891-5704; 32 Glenwood, Saranac Lake) Wildflower and bird hikes; special-needs backpack trips; historical trips.

Headwaters Guide Service (518-882-6855; www.headwatersguides.com; base camp near Stony Creek) nature education, family backpacking, camping in canvas yurts.

McDonnell's Adirondack Challenges (518-891-1176; Rte. 30, Lake Clear) Backpack trips.

Middle Earth Expeditions (518-523-9572; HCR 01 Box 37, Lake Placid) Backpack and day trips.

Wilderness Education Association (518-891-2915; North Country Community College, Saranac Lake) Excellent workshops and seminars in wilderness issues and techniques for trip leaders.

HORSEBACK RIDING AND WAGON TRIPS

New York's North Country may not have the wide, open spaces of the Wild West, but there are hundreds of miles of wilderness horse trails to explore, and plenty of outfitters to put you on a suitable mount. The possibilities range from hour-long rides to three-day guided backcountry forays; if you have your own horse, the Department of Environmental Conservation (DEC) has trail networks across the park, and even operates campgrounds that accommodate man and beast. For a handy booklet describing these trails, contact the DEC, 518-897-1200; Ray Brook NY 12977. One rule applies for bringing in out-of-state horses: proof of a negative Coggins test is necessary. If you plan to camp more than three nights in the forest preserve, or in a group of 10 or more, you'll need a permit from the local forest ranger.

Hay rides, sleigh rides, and wagon trips are available in many communities. You can ride a carriage through Lake George Village, or around Mirror Lake in Lake Placid; there's no need to make a reservation. Listed below are outfitters and teamsters who offer wagon trips and places to ride. In general, local stables are open only during warm weather.

If you enjoy just watching horses, there are two excellent annual horse shows in Lake Placid, located a canter away from the Olympic ski jumps: the **Lake Placid Horse Show** in late June, and the **I Love NY Horse Show** (518-

523-9625; North Elba Town Hall, Lake Placid) in early July. At both, the emphasis is on Olympic-level competition for hunters, jumpers, and riders. There are weekend polo games at the Bark Eater Inn (518-576-2221; Alstead Hill Rd., Keene) starting in late June. Admission is free; the Adirondackers play against teams from Saratoga Springs and Vermont. If you're an accomplished rider, you may even be able to join in a pick-up game.

A legacy of the dude-ranch days in the southeastern Adirondacks, **Painted Pony** (518-696-2421; Howe Rd., Lake Luzerne) presents professional rodeo competitions Wednesday, Friday, and Saturday nights in July and August, rain or shine. This is the home of the country's oldest weekly rodeo, complete with trick riding and roping, clowns and novelty acts, and there's more rodeo action at **1000 Acres** (518-696-2444; Rte. 418, Stony Creek).

OUTFITTERS AND STABLES

LAKE GEORGE AND SOUTHEASTERN ADIRONDACKS

Bailey's Horses (518-696-4541; Rte. 9N, Lake Luzerne) Western trail rides; lessons; hay wagon or carriage rides around Lake Vanare; winter trail rides; trips to Lake George horse trails by reservation.

Bennett Stables (518-696-4444; Rte. 9N, Lake Luzerne) Trail rides.

Circle B Ranch (518-494-4074; Atateka Rd., Chestertown) Wagon, sleigh, and hay rides.

Circle L Ranch (518-623-9967; High St., Athol) Horse-pack outfitter; 1/2 and full-day trips.

Saddle Up (518-668-4801; Rte. 9N, Lake George) Trail rides.

1000 Acres (518-696-2444; Rte. 418, Stony Creek) Guided trail rides.

CHAMPLAIN VALLEY

Essex Farms (Bill Raus; 518-963-7593; Rte. 22, Essex) Percheron farm. Wagon trips and sleigh rides by appointment.

HIGH PEAKS AND NORTHERN ADIRONDACKS

Circle 7 (518-582-4011; Rte. 28N, Newcomb) Wagon trips to Santanoni Preserve by reservation only; hunting and fishing pack trips.

Sentinel View Stables (518-891-3008; Harrietstown Rd., Saranac Lake) English and Western lessons; jumping instruction; bridle trails.

Tom Dillon (518-582-2414; Rte. 28N, Newcomb) Wagon trips to Santanoni.

XTC Ranch (518-891-5674; www.dude-ranches.com; Forest Home Rd., Lake Clear) Horseback riding, sleigh rides, equestrian camp.

Wilson's Livery Stable (518-576-2221; Alstead Hill Rd., Keene) Western or English trail rides by the hour or day; wagon and sleigh rides; polo games; open year-round.

NORTHWEST LAKES

Cold River Ranch (518-359-7559; Rte. 3, Tupper Lake) All-day rides by reservation only; pack-horse trips for fishing, hunting, and camping; no children under 14. Recommended. Lodging.

CENTRAL ADIRONDACKS

Adirondack Saddle Tours (315-357-4499; Uncas Rd., Inlet) Trail rides into Pigeon Lake Wilderness Area; pack-horse trips into Moose River Recreation Area; cookout rides to Cascade Lake. Most half-day rides include a swim; bring your own picnic lunch. Recommended.

T & M Equestrian Center (315-357-3594; Rte. 28, Inlet) Guided trail rides, Western only; hay and sleigh rides by reservation; overnights to Moose River Recreation Area.

PUBLIC HORSE TRAILS

LAKE GEORGE AND SOUTHEASTERN ADIRONDACKS

Lake George Trail System: E. side of Lake George, off Pilot Knob Rd.; 41 mi. of carriage roads on an old estate; lean-tos.

Lake Luzerne: Off Rte. 9N near Lake Luzerne hamlet; on Fourth Lake; campsite (518-696-2031), with corral; 5 mi. of trails on state land that connect with many miles of privately owned trails.

Pharoah Lake Horse Trails: Pharoah Lake Wilderness Area, E. of Schroon Lake. 12 mi. of sandy woods roads; lean-tos.

HIGH PEAKS AND NORTHERN ADIRONDACKS

Cold River Horse Trails: 6 mi. E. of Tupper Lake off Rte. 3; 13- and 32-mile-loop dirt trails; lean-tos and corral. Connects with Moose Pond Trail and Santanoni trails.

Meacham Lake: 3.5 mi. N. of Paul Smiths, off Rte. 30; 10 miles of trails; lean-tos and barn.

Moose Pond Trail: Starts at Santanoni trailhead just N. of Newcomb off Rte. 28N; 10 miles.

Raquette Falls Horse Trail: Branches off Cold River Trail; 2 miles.

Santanoni Trail: N. of Newcomb off Rte. 28N; 10-mile round-trip. Popular in hunting season.

NORTHWESTERN LAKES

Saranac Inn Horse Trail System: Off Rte. 30 near Saranac Inn; several short trails to ponds in the St. Regis Canoe Area; 11-mile round-trip on the Fish Pond Truck Trail.

CENTRAL ADIRONDACKS

Independence River Wild Forest: Off Number Four Rd. near Stillwater Reservoir; assembly area at Chases Lake Rd., off Rte. 12, Greig. 28 miles of sand roads; connects with Otter Creek; barn.

Moose River Recreation Area: Between Indian Lake and Inlet off Rte. 28, 28-mile dirt road plus many miles of old logging roads; campsites.

Otter Creek Trails: Near Greig, off Rte. 12; nearly 50 miles of sandy roads; connects with Independence River. Recomended.

William C. Whitney Area: Between Tupper Lake and Long Lake, off Rte. 30. Horse campsites and more trails in development; sandy roads.

HUNTING

Native Americans, colonial scouts, and 19th-century travelers regarded the Adirondacks as happy hunting grounds. Early accounts describe shooting deer year-round for cooking at camp and for swank Manhattan restaurants. Old pictures show small groups of men displaying dozens of bucks; the moose — never truly abundant in the Adirondacks — probably disappeared in part due to overhunting. (Other factors were loss of habitat and diseases transmitted by deer.) Market hunting has been outlawed for a century. The Adirondack Guides Association was a major force in pushing the state to enact hunting laws that would ensure that deer would not face the same fate as the moose.

A successful Adirondack hunt in the 1890s.

Courtesy of the Adirondack Museum

Many Adirondack counties now hold more resident whitetail deer than year-round humans, and hunting is a popular, regulated pursuit each fall. Beside deer, there are seasons for black bear (the 1999 bear take for the Adirondack Park was more than 400), snowshoe hare, coyote, bobcat, and other small mammals, plus ruffed grouse, woodcock, wild turkey, and waterfowl. The booklets outlining game seasons are available from Department of Environmental Conservation offices, through the agency's website (www.dec.state.ny.us/huntfish), or by writing to DEC, 50 Wolf Rd., Albany NY 12233; licenses can be purchased from sporting goods stores, town offices, or DEC. Non-residents may purchase special 5-day licenses. If you have never had a New York State hunting license, you must show proof that you have attended a hunter education course. Turkey hunting requires a special stamp from DEC; waterfowl hunters must possess a Federal Migratory Bird Hunting Stamp.

In general, big-game seasons begin with early bear (mid-Sept.–mid-Oct.); archery for deer or bear (late Sept.–mid-Oct.); muzzleloading for deer or bear (one week in mid-Oct.); and regular big-game season (third Saturday in Oct. through the first Sunday after Thanksgiving.) Bow and black-powder hunters may take antlerless deer; during regular season, it's bucks only in the Adirondack Park.

Wilderness, primitive, and wild-forest areas of the forest preserve are all open to hunting. Hunters — even if they have a brand-new, state-of-the-art GPS unit — should be proficient with map and compass. Global-positioning units don't always work well in thick forest, and batteries do wear out.

Paper companies, which own about a million acres, also offer memberships and leases for hunting and fishing privileges; contact Finch Pruyn & Co. (518-793-2541; 1 Glen St., Glens Falls) or the Empire State Forest Products Association (518-463-1297; 123 State St., Albany) for information. While hunting, please respect the boundaries of private posted lands.

Listed below are some licensed guides who specialize in hunting.

HUNTING GUIDES

LAKE GEORGE AND SOUTHEASTERN ADIRONDACKS

Lake Luzerne Guide Service (518-696-4646; 2101 Lake Ave., Lake Luzerne) Big game.

Trout Brook Guide Service (518-532-7089; Main St., Schroon Lake) Big and small game.

CHAMPLAIN VALLEY

Adirondack–Champlain Guide Service (518-963-7351; Long Pond, Willsboro) Big game, grouse, and snowshoe hare.

HIGH PEAKS AND NORTHERN ADIRONDACKS

Middle Earth Expeditions (518-523-9572; Cascade Rd., Lake Placid) Big game; lodging.

Placid Bay Ventures (518-523-2001; 70 Saranac Ave., Lake Placid) Big game; lodging.

Stillwaters Guide Service (518-523-2280; Cascade Rd., Lake Placid) Big game; bow hunting; snowshoe hare with beagles.

Young's Foothills (518-891-1221; Box 345, Saranac Lake) Black-powder and bow hunting.

NORTHWEST LAKES

Cold River Ranch (518-359-7559; Rte. 3, Tupper Lake) Pack-horse hunting trips.

CENTRAL ADIRONDACKS

Adirondack Mountain & Stream Guide Service (518-251-3762; Hardscrabble Rd., Olmstedville) Big game; snowshoe hare with hounds.

Adirondack Saddle Tours (315-357-4499; Uncas Rd., Inlet) Pack-horse hunting trips.

Foxfire North (518-494-4545; www.foxfirenorth.com; Box 30, Riparius) Deer, turkey, and rabbit hunting; tracking; fishing; corporate retreats.

Wharton's Adirondack Outfitters (518-548-3195; Box 544; Lake Pleasant) Big game.

ICE SKATING

Considering that the surface of Adirondack waters exist more months of the year in solid rather than liquid state, it's no wonder that ice skating is a popular pastime here. The modern sport of speed skating was launched in Saranac Lake and Lake Placid: in the early 1900s, more world records were set — and broken — by local bladesmen than at any other wintry place. Nowadays, there's backcountry skating on remote lakes and ponds or skating on plowed rinks in the towns and even indoor figure skating or hockey on Zamboni-maintained ice sheets.

If you'd like to try wilderness skating, wait until January. Cold, clear, still weather produces the most consistent ice. Ice that's two inches thick will support one person on skates, but it's better to wait for at least three inches to form, since currents and springs can create weak spots. Ice is thinner near shore, and steer clear of inlets, outlets, and other tributaries. In the ***Champlain Valley***, Webb-Royce Swamp near Westport is a terrific place to skate. Ponds in the ***High Peaks*** are often good for skating by New Year's Day, especially if there's been little snow. You can scout Chapel Pond, off Rte. 73 south of Keene Valley, or the Cascade lakes, on the same road, north of Keene, or Heart Lake, at the end of the Adirondak Loj Road. Ask locally for more favorite places.

Many towns offer lighted rinks with warming huts; check with tourist offices for hours. ***Long Lake***'s public rink is one of the better ones, and it's conveniently located on Rte. 30 between a diner and a hotel. At ***Indian Lake***, the town has built a great new hockey rink at the foot of the ski hill, off Rte. 30, which will be a skateboard park in the summer. There's free skating under the lights in Fern Park, in ***Inlet*** (315-357-5501), and in ***Old Forge***, on North Street (315-369-6983). Lake Champlain towns such as ***Ticonderoga*** and ***Westport*** often have good (or not so good, depending on the weather) skating. In ***Lake Placid***, you can enjoy terrific ice outdoors most evenings at the **Olympic Speed Skating Oval**, on Main St., or you can skate in the Olympic Arena (518-523-1655) at scheduled times for a small charge. If you want to try speed skating, you can get rental skates, a lesson, and ice time in Lake Placid for about five bucks. ***Tupper Lake*** (518-359-2531; McLaughlin St.) maintains rinks for hockey and skating; **Saranac Lake's Civic Center** (518-891-3800) has good ice indoors.

A few local shops specialize in hockey and figure skates, outfits, and equipment: **Ice Time** (518-523-9626; next to the Hilton Hotel, Lake Placid); **Skater's Patch Pro Shop** (518-523-4369; inside the Olympic Arena, Lake Placid); the **Cobbler's Shop** (518-523-3679; Main St., Lake Placid); and **The Edge in Sports** (518-523-9430; in front of the Olympic Arena, on Main St.). You can rent skates from the latter two for gliding around the speed oval, and from **High Peaks Cyclery** (518-523-3764; Saranac Ave., Lake Placid). Many of the sporting-goods stores throughout the region stock skates for children and adults.

MINIATURE GOLF

If the thought of all that howling wilderness makes your kids scream for more familiar entertainment, perhaps one of the many mini-golf links can fill the bill. Throughout the park, there are countless opportunities to sink little bitty putts after avoiding windmills, Vikings, and loop-de-loops; several are listed below, but you may want to call ahead for hours. Historians take note: miniature golf was launched in downtown Lake George at the intersection of Beach Rd. and Rte. 9 in the early years of this century (but the course was recently dismantled). ***Lake George*** remains the Pebble Beach of Adirondack minis, and half a dozen courses are nearby. You can try **Around the World in 18 Holes** (518-668-2531; Rte. 9); **Fort Mini Golf** (518-668-5471; Fort William Henry Commons); **Gooney Golf/Haunted Castle** (518-668-2589; Rtes. 9/9N); **Magic Castle Indoor Golf** (518-668-3777; Canada St.). Further up the road, it's the **Narrows Pizza Miniature Golf Course** (518-532-7591; Rte. 9, Schroon Lake), and you won't have to worry about what's for dinner after the round.

For the *High Peaks and Northern Adirondacks* area, mini golf is an international affair at Around the World in 18 Holes (518-523-9065; Saranac Ave., Lake Placid). In the *Central Adirondacks* go to ***Old Forge*** to choose from **Magic Mountain** (315-369-6602; Main St.), **Nutty Putty Miniature Golf** (315-369-6636; Main St.), or **Over the Rainbow** (Rte. 28).

OLYMPIC SPORTS

James Swedberg

Free–style aerial skiing, Lake Placid.

Lake Placid is the only place in North America that has hosted two Winter Olympic Games, in 1932 and 1980. During the '32 games, the American team won the bobsledding events, took silver and bronze medals in speed skating, hockey, figure skating, and bobsledding, and thus was regarded as the unofficial Olympic champion. In 1980, Eric Heiden garnered five gold medals in speed skating, and the U.S. hockey team won the tournament following a stunning upset over the Russians in the semifinal round. The legacy of Olympic glory lives on here, at the training center on the Old Military Road, where hundreds of athletes eat, sleep, and work out in a high-tech setting, and in several specialized sports facilities in and around Lake Placid. In every season competitors come to town for coaching and practice. In February 2000, the inaugural **Goodwill Winter Games** comes to Lake Placid, followed quickly by the **Senior Olympics**, which both take advantage of brand-new facilities at Whiteface Mountain and Mount Van Hoevenberg.

There's just one place in the Northeast where you, too, can ride a real bobsled on an Olympic run: Mount Van Hoevenberg, just a few miles from downtown Lake Placid. This thrill does not come cheap; it's $25 for the longest minute you'll ever spend. (Note that the sleds are piloted by professional drivers.) Rides are available Tues.–Sun. afternoons from Christmas through early March depending on the track conditions, and it's a good idea to call ahead. The "Summer Rocket," a bobsled with wheels, shoots down the track when there's no ice on it. For $15 you can navigate a luge through some wicked curves, even in summer. The Olympic Regional Development Authority (ORDA) is the place to call for details on all of the Olympic venues and winter sports schedules (518-523-1655; www.orda.org; Olympic Center, Lake Placid).

Watching international luge, skeleton, and bobsled competitions is almost as exciting as trying it yourself, and perhaps easier on the cardiovascular system. Races are held nearly every winter weekend. Dress warmly for spectating; you'll want to walk up and down the mile-long courses in order to see and hear the sleds zoom through. At some vantage points, the sleds fly by nearly upside-down, and the racket of the runners is a lesson in the Doppler effect. You'll definitely want to see several starts, too, where track stars have a decided advantage.

In the Olympic Arena, at the center of Lake Placid, you can watch Can/Am ice hockey tournaments, professional exhibition games, figure-skating competitions, and skating exhibitions, year-round. Since 1993, stars such as Kristy Yamaguchi and Scott Hamilton have come to Lake Placid in November and December to practice for national touring shows; ask at the arena about watching rehearsals. Indoor short-track speed-skating is incredibly exciting, or you can watch longer-distance speed-skating races at the outdoor oval.

Ski jumping on the 70- and 90-meter jumps is thrilling to see; watching people fly through the air is far more impressive in person than the sport appears on television. The annual **New Year's and Master's Ski Jump** is the last weekend in December, and world-team trials and meets are later in the winter; contact ORDA for a schedule. Dress warmly for spectating here too, since the bleachers are exposed to the elements. Surprisingly, this is one winter event that you can also enjoy in the summer: you can ride a chairlift to the base of the 90-meter jump, then go up the elevator to the top, for a small fee. The jump tower is open mid-May to early October, and the view is great. An annual favorite is the **Independence Day Ski Jump** sponsored by ORDA (518-523-1655); this is one Lake Placid spectator event you *don't* have to dress warmly for. Also, at the jumping complex (known as MacKenzie-Intervale), you can watch the U.S. freestyle skiers training in summer and fall. The skiers go off jumps, tumble through the air, and land in a huge tank of water with their skis still attached.

At Whiteface Mountain, you can see the ballet and mogul portions of the **Freestyle World Cup** in late January, and occasional international downhill and slalom races. Or you can try the Olympic Mountain for yourself — look further in this chapter for skiing inspiration.

RACES AND SEASONAL SPORTING EVENTS

Events are listed in chronological order within each region.

LAKE GEORGE AND SOUTHEASTERN ADIRONDACKS

New Year's Day Polar Bear Swim (518-668-5755; Shepard Park, Lake George) No experience necessary!

Prospect Mountain Road Race (518-668-2195; Prospect Mtn. Memorial Highway, Lake George) 5.5 miles uphill all the way, in early May.

Adirondack Distance Run (518-793-9848) 10-mile road race from Lake George to Bolton Landing in early July.

Summerun (518-532-7675; Box 741, Schroon Lake) 5- and 10-km run through downtown Schroon Lake and kids' fun run, on the first Saturday in Aug.

Adirondack Marathon (518-532-7676) Sanctioned qualifier for the big marathons on a beautiful course that circles Schroon Lake in late Sept.

CHAMPLAIN VALLEY

Rotary International Fishing Classic (518-561-5030) Sponsored by Plattsburgh Rotary Club, covering all of Lake Champlain; weigh stations at Port Henry, Westport, and Willsboro; in late May.

Montcalm Mile Run (518-585-6619; Ticonderoga) Footrace down Ticonderoga's main street on July 4th.

24-hour Marathon (518-962-4446; Westport) 10-person relay teams, with each member running a mile every hour; ultramarathon for solo runners. Noon Saturday to noon Sunday at the Essex County Fairgrounds, in Westport in late July.

HIGH PEAKS AND NORTHERN ADIRONDACKS

Crack of Noon Race (518-891-1990) 10-km cross-country fun races at Dewey Mtn., Saranac Lake, on Jan. 1.

Bobcat Snowshoe Race (518-327-6389; Paul Smith's College Sports Annex, Paul Smiths) Sprint and distance snowshoe races in mid-Jan.

Adirondack International Mountaineering Festival (518-576-2281; the Mountaineer, Keene Valley) Clinics and lectures by renowned ice and rock climbers in mid-Jan.

Lake Placid Loppet (518-523-1655; Olympic Regional Development Authority, Lake Placid) 25- and 50-km citizens' races at Mount Van Hoevenberg in late Jan.

Woodchuck Shuffle (518-327-6389; Paul Smith's College) 20-km snowshoe race in early Feb.

Empire State Winter Games (518-523-1655; ORDA, Lake Placid) Figure skating, luge, bobsled, speed skating, ski jumping, cross-country skiing, and other events, in Lake Placid in early Mar.

Dewey Mountain Slip 'n' Slide (518-891-2697; Dewey Mtn., Saranac Lake) Races on snow, slush, or mud, using skis, snowshoes, whatever. Early Mar.

Whiteface Mountain Cocoa Butter Open (518-523-1655; Whiteface Mtn. Ski Area, Wilmington) Citizens' downhill, slalom, and fun races in late Mar.

Ice Breaker Canoe Race (518-891-1990; Saranac Lake Chamber of Commerce, Saranac Lake) 5-mile race on the Saranac River in late Mar.

Ausable River Whitewater Derby (518-946-7200) Sponsored by the Ausable Valley Jaycees. 6-mile downriver canoe race on the East Branch of the Ausable River from Keene to Upper Jay on the last Sunday in Apr.

'Round the Mountain Canoe Race (518-891-1990; Saranac Lake Chamber of Commerce, Saranac Lake) 10-mile canoe race on Lower Saranac Lake and the Saranac River in early May.

Whiteface Mountain Uphill Footrace (518-946-2255; Wilmington) 8.3-mile race up the Whiteface Mountain Veterans' Memorial Highway on the second Sunday in June.

Willard Hanmer Guideboat and Canoe Races (518-891-1990; Saranac Lake Chamber of Commerce, Saranac Lake) Races on Lake Flower for guideboats, canoes, rowing shells, war canoes, and kayaks in early July.

Ironman USA (518-523-2665; www.ironmanusa.com; Lake Placid) The real deal: 2+ mile swim in Mirror Lake; 112-mile bike race from Lake Placid to Keene and back, twice; followed by a marathon. The best international competitors converge for this grueling event. July.

Mike Flanagan Cycling Classic (518-523-3764; High Peaks Cyclery, Saranac Ave., Lake Placid) Loop race and tour near Lake Placid in late July.

Casio Mountain-Bike Series (518-523-1655; ORDA, Lake Placid) Cross-country races at Mount Van Hoevenberg in July and Aug.

Can-Am Rugby Tournament (518-891-1990; Saranac Lake Chamber of Commerce, Saranac Lake) North America's largest rugby meet, with more than 100 teams competing in fields throughout Lake Placid and Saranac Lake in early Aug.

Summit Lacrosse Tournament (518-439-3071) Teams of kids, old-timers, men, women compete at the North Elba Horse Show Grounds in mid-Aug.

Adirondack Century Ride (518-523-3764; High Peaks Cyclery, Saranac Ave., Lake Placid) 100-mile 1-day bike tour from Lake Placid to different destinations. Fall.

Flatwater Canoe and Guideboat Races (518-582-3211) Races for adults and children on Lake Harris, near Newcomb, mid-Sept.

NORTHWEST LAKES

Flatwater Weekend (518-359-3328) Sponsored by Tupper Lake Chamber of Commerce. 11-mile canoe race on the Raquette River near Tupper Lake on

Saturday; 44-mile canoe race from Long Lake to Tupper Lake village on Sunday, on the second weekend in June.

St. Regis Invitational (518-891-1990) Sponsored by the Saranac Lake Chamber of Commerce. 7-mile race for canoes, kayaks, and guideboats starting and ending at Paul Smith's College. June.

Tin Man Triathlon (518-359-3328) Sponsored by Tupper Lake Chamber of Commerce. 1.2-mile swim, 56-mile bike, 13.1-mile run beginning at the Tupper Lake Municipal Park; third weekend in July.

24-Hour Marathon (518-359-3328) Tupper Lake Chamber of Commerce. 10-person relay teams each run 1-mile laps at the Tupper Lake High School track on the second weekend in Aug.

Fall Foliage Canoe and Kayak Race (518-359-3328) 11-mile race on the Raquette River and Piercefield Flow, Tupper Lake. Late Sept.

Boo Bash & Dash (518-891-1900) Mountain-bike races at Big Tupper Ski Area , Tupper Lake and Dewey Mtn., Saranac Lake. Late Oct.

CENTRAL ADIRONDACKS

Jeff Meneilly Memorial Cross-Country Ski Race (315-357-5501) Sponsored by Inlet Chamber of Commerce. 5-km citizens' cross-country ski race; Empire State Games qualifier; late Jan.

Piseco Airport Race (518-548-4521) Sponsored by Speculator Chamber of Commerce. 10-km citizens' cross-country ski race in Piseco on the first Saturday in Feb.

Le Shoe de Blue (518-648-5112) Snowshoe race up and down Blue Mountain during the Indian Lake Winter Festival in Feb.

Kunjamuk Kick (518-548-4521) 10-km citizens' cross-country ski race near Speculator, sponsored by the International Paper Company and the Speculator Chamber of Commerce in late Feb.

Sisu Cross Country Ski Race (518-863-4974; Lapland Lake Cross Country Ski Center, Storer Rd., Benson) 25-km citizens' ski race in late Feb.

Snowflake Derby (315-369-3225; McCauley Mtn. Ski Area, Old Forge) Community downhill races in early Mar.

Whitewater Derby (518-251-2612) Sponsored by North Creek Chamber of Commerce. Slalom race for canoes and kayaks on the Hudson River near North River on Saturday; downriver canoe race from North Creek to Riparius on the Hudson on Sunday; first weekend in May.

Paddlefest (315-357-6672; www.mountainmanoutdoors.com) Canoe and kayak weekend with instruction, boats to try, film festival, mid-May, in Inlet.

Adirondack Deer Run (315-369-6983) 5 and 10km trail running race, early June, Old Forge.

Black Fly Challenge (315-357-5501; www.inletny.com) Mountain-bike races through the Moose River Plains, in June.

Piseco Triathlon (518-548-4521) Sponsored by Speculator Chamber of Commerce. Swim, road bike, and run circumnavigating Piseco Lake on the third Sat. in July.

Lane Lake Run (518-548-4521) Sponsored by the Speculator Chamber of Commerce. 10-km footrace around Lake Pleasant on the second Sun. in Aug.

The annual 90-mile Adirondack Canoe Classic starts in Old Forge.

Mark Kurtz

Adirondack Canoe Classic (518-891-1990) Sponsored by the Saranac Lake Chamber of Commerce. 90-mile 3-day canoe race from Old Forge to Saranac Lake village in early Sept.

Mountain Bike Festival (315-357-6672; Inlet) Bike polo, distance races in the Moose River Recreation Area, other NORBA-sanctioned events in late Sept.

Moose River Festival (315-369-6983) Extreme race for kayaks and closed canoes through Class IV and V rapids. Sponsored by American Whitewater and the Central Adirondack Association in mid-Oct.

Reindeer Roundup (518-863-4974; Lapland Lake Cross Country Ski Center, Benson) 10-km citizens' cross-country ski race; Empire State Games qualifier, before Christmas.

ROCK CLIMBING

Plenty of steep, challenging rock walls can be found in the ***High Peaks***, and scattered cliff faces are hidden in the ***Central Adirondacks***. Possibilities for rock and ice climbers abound, from non-technical scrambles up broad, smooth slides to gnarly 700-foot pitches in the 5.11+ difficulty range. Adirondack climbers — from wannabes to folks with permanently chalky palms — all depend on a thick green guidebook, *Climbing in the Adirondacks: A Guide to Rock and Ice Routes in the Adirondacks* (Adirondack Mountain Club) by Don

The High Peaks

Dozens of mountaintops rise 4,000 feet or more above sea level in the Adirondack Park. You don't need to be a technical climber to enjoy the views, but you should be an experienced, well-prepared hiker capable of putting in at least a twelve-mile round trip. For trail descriptions and access points, consult the *Guide to Adirondack Trails: High Peaks Region* (Adirondack Mountain Club) or *Discover the Adirondack High Peaks* (Backcountry Publications). The following "Forty-Six" are in the area bounded by Newcomb on the south, Elizabethtown on the east, Wilmington on the north, and the Franklin County line on the west.

Peak	Elevation	Peak	Elevation
1. Mount Marcy	5344 feet	24. Mount Marshall	4380
2. Algonquin Peak	5115	25. Seward Mountain	4347
3. Mount Haystack	4961	26. Allen Mountain	4347
4. Mount Skylight	4924	27. Big Slide Mountain	4249
5. Whiteface Mountain	4866	28. Esther Mountain	4239
6. Dix Mountain	4839	29. Upper Wolf Jaw	4185
7. Gray Peak	4830	30. Lower Wolf Jaw	4173
8. Iroquois Peak	4830	31. Phelps Mountain	4161
9. Basin Mountain	4826	32. Street Mountain	4150
10. Gothics Mountain	4734	33. Sawteeth Mountain	4150
11. Mount Colden	4734	34. Mount Donaldson	4140
12. Giant Mountain	4626	35. Cascade Mountain	4098
13. Nippletop Mountain	4610	36. Seymour Mountain	4091
14. Santanoni Peak	4606	37. Porter Mountain	4085
15. Mount Redfield	4606	38. Mount Colvin	4085
16. Wright Peak	4580	39. South Dix Mountain	4060
17. Saddleback Mountain	4528	40. Mount Emmons	4040
18. Panther Peak	4442	41. Dial Mountain	4020
19. Table Top Mountain	4413	42. East Dix Mountain	4006
20. Rocky Peak Ridge	4410	43. Blake Peak	3986
21. Hough Peak	4409	44. Cliff Mountain	3944
22. Macomb Mountain	4390	45. Nye Mountain	3944
23. Armstrong Mountain	4390	46. Cousachraga Peak	3820

(Elevations from *Of the Summits, Of the Forests*, Adirondack Forty-Sixers, 1991)

The **Adirondack Forty-Sixers** is an organization dedicated to these High Peaks. To earn the members' patch, you must have climbed all of the mountains listed above. The group performs trail work and education projects; for information, write to Adirondack Forty-Sixers, RFD 1 Box 390, Morrisonville NY 12962.

Mellor. This book is indispensable since the approaches to many of the best climbs involve a hike or bushwhack to the base. It also outlines hundreds of

And More Peaks

In other parts of the park there are mountains nearly as high, with sweeping vistas of forests and lakes. A short list of pinnacles with marked trails and open summits or fire towers follows. Note that there are plenty more mountains in the park; ask locally for favorite vantage points.

Peak	**Elevation**	**Closest Town**
Snowy Mountain	3899 feet	Indian Lake
McKenzie Mountain	3832	Lake Placid
Lyon Mountain	3830	Chazy Lake
Wakely Mountain	3770	Indian Lake
Blue Mountain	3759	Blue Mtn. Lake
Hurricane Mountain	3678	Elizabethtown
Pillsbury Mountain	3597	Speculator
Ampersand Mountain	3552	Saranac Lake
Vanderwhacker Mountain	3386	Minerva
Crane Mountain	3254	Johnsburg
Pharoah Mountain	2557	Schroon Lake

climbs and explains the local ethic on clean wilderness climbing: leave as little trace as possible and place a minimum of bolts.

Climbers can get tips in a few places. The **Mountaineer** (518-576-2281; Rte. 73, Keene Valley) sells climbing gear, topo maps, and guidebooks; advice is free, but don't monopolize the sales staff with time-consuming questions. Anyway, many of your answers can be found at the **International Mountaineering Festival** each January, sponsored by the Mountaineer. Hardware and software for climbing can also be found in Lake Placid at **Eastern Mountain Sports** (518-523-2505; 51 Main St.) and **High Peaks Cyclery** (518-523-3764; Saranac Ave.), which has an indoor climbing wall. In North Creek, **The Mountain and Boardertown** (518-251-3111; Main St.) opened with a bang in December 1997, with a huge selection of equipment and a state-of-the-art indoor wall with all kinds of handholds.

To learn the basics of climbing or to polish your skills if you've had some experience, a handful of guide services specialize in helping you climb higher:

Adirondack Alpine Adventures (518-576-9881; Rte. 73, Keene) Rock- and ice-climbing guide service; instruction for women, small groups, or individuals.

Adirondack Mountain Club (518-523-3441; Adirondak Loj, Lake Placid) Weekend workshops for beginners and intermediates; lodging.

Adirondack Rock and River (518-576-2041; Alstead Hill Rd., Keene) Rock- and ice-climbing guide service; instruction for beginners to experts; natural indoor climbing wall; lodging.

ROWING

The Adirondack guideboat is the preeminent rowing machine for the region, and you'll find a selection of boatbuilders in Chapter Six, *Shopping*. **Adirondack Rowing** (518-585-7870; Trout Lake) sells all kinds of modern shells and offers lessons.

Most of the small-to-medium-size Adirondack lakes are especially suitable for rowing. Quiet lakes — Indian, Paradox, Forked, Star, Long, Lake Pleasant, and others — offer several miles of open water, yet have less powerboat traffic than say, Lake George or Schroon Lake. You'll also find that early morning or early evening, when the winds are relatively calm, are the best times to row. Do carry a flashlight if you go out at dusk. Mirror Lake, on the backside of downtown Lake Placid, is not open to motorboats, so there's another fine possibility for rowers. You might even be able to match a few strokes with Olympic athletes as they train; the U.S. Canoe and Kayak Team moved to town in 1997.

SAILING

The big lakes — George, Champlain, and Great Sacandaga — offer good sailing in the midst of beautiful scenery and have marinas for an evening's dockage or equipment repairs. In fact, any lake with a public launch is open to sailboats; the most suitable craft for bouldery-bottomed Adirondack lakes are those with centerboards you can pull up readily. Even then, remember to keep an eye out for unmarked rocks! Sailing on these island-studded waters can be tricky, since in the lee of an island you stand a good chance of being becalmed. Wind can whip shallow lakes into whitecapped mini-oceans, too. A portable weather radio should be included in your basic kit; Adirondack forecasts (out of Burlington Vermont) can be found at 162.40 megahertz.

You can purchase Coast Guard charts for Lakes George and Champlain, but not for most of the small interior lakes. Some USGS topographical maps have troughs and shoals marked, but these maps are of limited use to sailors. Your best bet is to ask at boat liveries for lake maps, or at least find out how to avoid the worst rocks.

For hardware, lines, and other equipment you may need, check in the beginning portion of this chapter for a list of marinas. In the ***Lake George*** area, **Yankee Yacht Sales** (518-668-2862; Rte. 9N, Diamond Point), is well stocked with everything from the essentials to brand-new boats. They also offer sailing instruction and rent day-sailers and cruisers. On ***Lake Champlain***, **Westport Marina** (518-962-4356; Washington St., Westport) has a good selection of sailing supplies.

SCENIC FLIGHTS

If climbing a mountain isn't for you, yet you still seek a bird's-eye view of the territory, why not charter a small plane to soar above the wilds? Several pilots offer sightseeing flights at a reasonable cost: a 15- to 20-minute flight covering about 50 miles of territory costs less than the average evening out. You can make special arrangements for longer flights, but a typical short trip costs about $50 for a family of four. Seaplane services are also equipped to take canoeists, fishermen, and hunters into ponds and lakes.

Listed below are a few fixed-wheel and seaplane services for private charters; you *must* call ahead for a reservation. Just beyond the border of the park, you can arrange for floating on air with Adirondack Balloon Flights (518-793-6342; Glens Falls).

Adirondack Flying Service (518-523-2473; Cascade Rd., Lake Placid) Scenic flights over the High Peaks; glider rides; air taxi.

Bird's Seaplane Service (315-357-3631; Sixth Lake, Inlet) Scenic flights; hunting and fishing charters.

Helms Aero Service (518-624-3931; Town Beach, Long Lake) Scenic seaplane flights; hunting and fishing charters.

Payne's Air Service (315-357-3971; Seventh Lake, Inlet) Scenic flights; hunting and fishing charters.

SCENIC HIGHWAYS

We may be biased, but we think that most Adirondack byways are pretty darn scenic: even Interstate 87 — the Northway — won an award as

The most amazing eight miles in the Adirondack Park, Whiteface Memorial Highway.

James Swedberg

"America's Most Beautiful Highway" the year it was completed. Specifically, we're talking here about roads up mountains so that everyone can enjoy the view. In the ***Lake George*** area, **Prospect Mountain Memorial Highway** (518-668-5198; off Rte. 9 near Lake George village) snakes up a small peak to offer a terrific 100-mile view stretching from the High Peaks to Vermont and the Catskills. Not too far from ***Lake Placid***, **Whiteface Mountain Veterans Memorial Highway** (518-946-7175; off Rte. 431, Wilmington) has a great view, too, looking down on other summits and silvery lakes. Both are state-operated toll roads open daily from late May through the fall.

SKIING: CROSS-COUNTRY AND SNOWSHOEING

The Adirondack Park is paradise for cross-country skiers. Most winters there's plenty of snow, upwards of 100 inches, especially in the higher elevations or west of the Champlain Valley. A wide range of destinations entices skiers, from rugged expeditions in the High Peaks to gentle groomed paths suitable for novices, plus hundreds of miles of intermediate trails in between. Many of the marked hiking trails on state land are not only suitable for cross-country skiing or snowshoeing, they're actually better for winter recreation since swampy areas are frozen, and ice-bound ponds and lakes can be easily crossed.

For suggestions on backcountry ski trails, consult *Classic Adirondack Ski Tours* by Tony Goodwin (Adirondack Mountain Club), or any of the books in the *Discover the Adirondacks* series (Backcountry Publications and Lakeview Press) by Barbara McMartin. Both *Adirondack Life* and *Adirondac* magazines outline ski treks in their winter issues; if your local library has back issues, a treasure trove of potential ski trips is at your fingertips.

Many of the designated wilderness and wild-forest areas (described below) offer great ski touring on marked but ungroomed trails. State campgrounds — closed to vehicles from November through May — offer quiet, woodsy, snow-covered roads with gentle grades; places like Lake Durant, near Blue Mountain Lake, and Lake Eaton, near Long Lake, are popular with local skiers and usually have set tracks. The Adirondack Challenge, a hiking-canoeing-skiing program sponsored by the Visitor Interpretive Centers (518-327-3000) describes several trips in a handy brochure. Another option for exploring the wild wintry woods is to hire a licensed guide; check under "Hiking and Backpacking" earlier in this chapter for backcountry trip leaders.

Before setting out on any of these wilderness excursions, prepare your pack with quick-energy food; a thermos filled with hot tea or cocoa; extra hat, socks, and gloves; topo map and compass; matches; flashlight; and space blanket. Dress in layers of wool, polypropylene, or synthetic pile. Don't travel alone. Sign in at the trailhead register. Let friends know your destination and when you plan to return.

Many towns maintain cross-country ski trails, and the **Visitor Interpretive Center** at Paul Smiths (518-327-3000) has many miles of easy trails. At the **Newcomb VIC** (518-528-2000), the trails are not quite so great for skiing, but you can try snowshoeing at no charge; the Tubbs company has donated 50 pairs of new snowshoes for the public to enjoy. Throughout the park, snowshoeing is enjoying a burst of popularity, as witnessed by a series of citizen races in Paul Smiths, Indian Lake, and Blue Mtn. Lake.

Gore Mt. is the perfect hill for intermediate skiers.

James Swedberg

The **Jackrabbit Trail** (518-523-1365; Lake Placid) is a superb local resource, some 35 miles of groomed trails connecting Keene with Lake Placid, Saranac Lake, and Paul Smiths; eventually the route will extend to Tupper Lake. The trail combines old logging roads and trails and is named for Herman "Jack Rabbit" Johannsen, who laid out many of the routes in the 1920s. From some of the hotels in downtown Placid, you can strap on your skis and just head out for the woods. There's even guided inn-to-inn skiing sponsored by some lodgings; check with your host if you're staying in the High Peaks. The Jackrabbit Trail joins with many of the commercial ski-touring areas, and traverses the McKenzie Mountain Wilderness Area between Whiteface Inn and Saranac Lake. Note that dogs are not welcome on groomed portions of the Jackrabbit Trail, nor at the privately owned ski centers.

Besides wilderness trails and informal town ski trails, there are some excellent cross-country ski areas with meticulously groomed tracks and rental equipment. You'll find a variety of ski areas listed below, and we suggest calling ahead for current information about snow cover. Many of the touring centers offer lessons, and the **Adirondack Mountain Club** (518-523-3441; Adirondak Loj, Lake Placid) schedules backcountry- and telemark-skiing workshops.

CROSS-COUNTRY SKI CENTERS AND TRAIL NETWORKS

LAKE GEORGE AND SOUTHEASTERN ADIRONDACKS

Caroline Fish Memorial Trail (518-494-2722; Rte. 8, Chestertown) 11-km town trail.

Rogers Rock State Campsite (518-543-6161; Rte. 9N, Hague) 10-km ungroomed trails.

Schroon Lake Ski Trails (518-532-7675) Backcountry skiing in Pharaoh Lake and Hoffman Notch wilderness areas.

Warren County Trails (518-623-5576; Hudson Ave., Warrensburg) 16-km trails along the Hudson River.

HIGH PEAKS AND NORTHERN ADIRONDACKS

Adirondak Loj (518-523-3441; Adirondak Loj Rd., Lake Placid) 12-km backcountry trails; connect with numerous challenging wilderness trails; guided tours; lessons; food; lodging.

Bark Eater X-C Ski Center (518-576-2221; Alstead Hill Rd., Keene) 20-km groomed trails; connects with Jackrabbit Trail; rentals; lessons; lodging.

Cascade Ski Touring Center (518-523-9605; www.cascadeski.com; Rte. 73, Lake Placid) 20-km groomed trails; connects with Jackrabbit Trail; night skiing; rentals; lessons; ski shop.

Cunningham's Ski Barn (518-523-4460; Main St., Lake Placid) Groomed trails on Lake Placid Club property; connects with Jackrabbit Trail; rentals; lessons; full ski shop.

Dewey Mountain (518-891-2697; Rte. 30, Saranac Lake) 20-km groomed trails; night skiing; lessons; guided tours.

Lake Placid Lodge (518-523-2700; Whiteface Inn Rd., Lake Placid) 20-km groomed trails; full shop; lessons.

Mount Van Hoevenberg (518-523-2811; Rte. 73, Lake Placid) 50-km groomed Olympic trails; connects with Jackrabbit Trail; rentals; lessons; ski shop.

NORTHWEST LAKES

Cranberry Lake Trail (315-386-4000; Rte. 3, Cranberry Lake) Backcountry trails.

Deer Pond Loop (518-359-3328; Rte. 30, Tupper Lake) 15-km backcountry loop.

CENTRAL ADIRONDACKS

Adirondack Woodcraft Ski Touring Center (315-369-6031; Rondaxe Rd., Old Forge) 15-km groomed trails; night skiing; rentals; ski shop.

Fern Park Recreation Area (315-357-5501; South Shore Rd., Inlet) 20-km groomed trails; 2 km night skiing.

Garnet Hill Cross-Country Ski Center (518-251-2821; www.garnethill.com;

Cold, Cold, Cold

In the old days, folks caught unprepared in the wilds occasionally died of "exposure." Today, we call that same condition hypothermia (literally "low temperature"), and it remains a serious concern in cool, moist climates year-round. Even on a summer day, a lightly clad hiker can suffer from hypothermia after being caught in the rain. In winter, unaccustomed strenuous exercise coupled with the wrong kind of clothing can lead to hypothermia.

Hypothermia is caused when the body loses warmth faster than it can produce heat. The normal body-core temperature of 98.6°F decreases to a dangerous level, which happens when the body is inadequately insulated by clothing. Precipitating events can be a dunking in cold water or soaking in steady drizzle. To compensate for heat loss, the body tries to produce more warmth, which burns up energy. As energy reserves dwindle and muscles become exhausted, hypothermia sets in.

Signs of hypothermia arrive in stages: first, the person feels and acts cold. He or she may shiver, have trouble with manual dexterity, or show bluish skin color. Next, shaking becomes uncontrollable, and the person starts to behave erratically, acting sluggish, apathetic, or cranky. The victim may stagger or seem off balance. Some folks refer to the "Umble Rule" — watch out when a companion begins to stumble, mumble, grumble, and fumble.

The final stage of hypothermia is a true medical emergency. The person feels cold to the touch; shivering has stopped; limbs may be frostbitten. The victim may seem uncaring about survival. The treatment of all stages of hypothermia is basically the same — add warmth. Warm the person with your hands, body-to-body contact, a fire. Provide hot liquids: tea, soup, cocoa, or any nonalcoholic beverage. For a person in severe hypothermia, prevent further heat loss and get the victim to a medical facility quickly.

A few ounces of prevention go a long way in avoiding hypothermia. Dress in layers, especially clothing made of wool, polypropylene, or synthetic pile, all of which insulate when wet. ("Cotton kills," forest rangers say.) Bring spare hats, mittens, socks, overpants, windbreaker. Pack plenty of high-energy food and warm liquids. Put an "instant heat" packet in a pocket. Watch out for your friends and be honest about your abilities. Know when to turn back.

Frostbite and its cousin, frostnip, are not hypothermia. The terms refer to flesh actually freezing, and it's usually fingers, toes, ears, nose, or chin that are affected. Frostbite can occur quickly, especially on areas exposed to the wind; look for skin appearing waxy. One test for frostbite is to pinch the affected part gently and watch for the color to change. Unaffected flesh will revert to its normal color, but frozen parts remain whitish and feel hard and cold.

At the first sign of frostbite, warm the affected part at body temperature. You can warm your hands by sticking fingers in your mouth, by placing them in an armpit or between your legs; ears and cheeks can be warmed with a dry hand; feet can be warmed up with the help of a buddy's body. Do not rub a frostbitten part; you can cause severe tissue damage since there are actual ice crystals in the cells. Don't use temperatures above 110°F for warming, as excessive heat can cause greater damage. (Be very careful using a pocket handwarmer.) Avoid refreezing frostbitten parts.

Deep frostbite should not be thawed. It sounds grim, but it's better to walk out on frozen feet than it is to thaw them and then try to shuffle along. Severe frostbite is a medical emergency that will need evacuation and lengthy hospitalization to repair circulatory damage.

13th Lake Rd., North River) 50-km groomed trails; connects with trails in Siamese Ponds Wilderness Area; rentals; lessons; ski shop; food; lodging. Hire a guide for a great backcountry trip that goes off the back side of Gore Mountain Ski Center, past Highwinds Inn, and down to Garnet Hill.

Gore Mountain (518-251-2411; Peaceful Valley Rd., North Creek) 10-km groomed trails; rentals; ski shop; food.

Lapland Lake (518-863-4974; www.laplandlake.com; Storer Rd., Benson) 40-km groomed trails; rentals; lessons; ski shop; food; lodging.

Long Lake (518-624-3077; www.longlake-ny.com) Backcountry trails; excellent map available for Long Lake and Raquette Lake area trails.

McCauley Mountain (315-369-3225; www.oldforgeny.com/mccauley; McCauley Mtn. Rd., Old Forge) 20-km groomed trails at downhill area plus skiing at Thendara Golf Club; rentals; lessons; food.

Speculator Cross-Country Ski Trails (518-548-4521; Elm Lake Rd., Speculator) Backcountry trails.

CROSS-COUNTRY SKI OUTFITTERS AND SHOPS

HIGH PEAKS AND NORTHERN ADIRONDACKS

Blue Line Sport Shop (518-891-4680; 82 Main St., Saranac Lake) Ski rentals and sales; sporting goods; maps.

Eastern Mountain Sports (518-523-2505; 51 Main St., Lake Placid) Cross-country, telemark, and backcountry equipment; gear; guidebooks; maps.

High Peaks Cyclery (518-523-3764; Saranac Ave., Lake Placid) Cross-country, telemark, and backcountry equipment for sale and rent; snowshoe and skate rentals; outdoor gear and books.

The Mountaineer (518-576-2281; Rte. 73, Keene Valley) Cross-country, telemark, and backcountry equipment; gear; guidebooks; maps.

NORTHWEST LAKES

Tip Top Sport Shop (518-359-9222; 40 Park St., Tupper Lake) Downhill and cross-country ski equipment; skates.

CENTRAL ADIRONDACKS

Beaver Brook Outfitters (518-251-3394; Rte. 28, Wevertown) Cross-country ski and snowshoe sales and rentals; outdoor clothing; guidebooks.

Boardertown (518-251-3111; Main St., North Creek) New in winter 1998, with backcountry skis, cold-weather clothing, and snowboards.

Cunningham's Ski Barn (518-251-3215; Rte. 28, North Creek) Downhill and cross-country ski sales and rentals; clothing.

Free Spirits Adventures (518-924-9275; Rte. 30, Wells) Telemark lessons; guided backcountry trips; cross-country and camping gear; wooden skis.

Inlet Ski Touring Center (315-357-6961; South Shore Rd., Inlet) Racing and touring equipment; trails connect with Fern Park.

Mountainman Outdoor Supply (315-357-6672; Rte. 28, Inlet) Hiking, camping, and cross-country ski gear.

Sporting Propositions (315-369-6188; Main St., Old Forge) Downhill and cross-country ski sales and rentals; clothing.

BEYOND THE BLUE LINE

Fall Line Ski Shop (518-793-3203; Quaker Rd., Glens Falls) Downhill and cross-country ski sales and rentals.

Inside Edge (518-793-5676; 624 Upper Glen St., Glens Falls) Downhill and cross-country ski sales and rentals; best local source for racing supplies.

Wooden Ski and Wheel (518-561-2790; Rte. 9, Plattsburgh) Cross-country ski equipment; outdoor gear.

SKIING: DOWNHILL AND SNOWBOARDING

Skiing has been a part of Adirondack life since the 1930s. Weekend ski trains from New York's Grand Central once brought thousands of folks to North Creek, where they could "ride up and slide down." The "ride up" was in school buses equipped with wooden ski racks mounted on the outside, and the "slide down" was on twisty trails carved out of the forest near Barton Mines, across from the present-day slopes on Gore Mountain.

Today there are a couple of high-profile mountains with challenging slopes and extensive snowmaking: Whiteface and Gore, both operated by the Olympic Regional Development Authority. There are also a number of nice little mountains where the emphasis is on family fun rather than on the trendiest gear. A few towns, like Indian Lake and Newcomb, operate free downhill areas for residents and guests. Of course, you won't find manmade snow there, and you'll have to remember dormant skills for managing a poma lift or a rope tow, but you can have a blast with the kids and beat the crowds.

Naturally downhill season in the Adirondacks depends on the weather. Often snowmaking begins in November, and some trails may open by mid-December, but it can be Christmas week before the snow is reliable throughout an entire ski area. Many people prefer spring conditions when there's corn snow and bright sunshine. Whatever the weather, it's not a bad idea to call ahead for the ski conditions before you go.

Compared to ski areas in Vermont or the Rockies, the Adirondack ones seem undeveloped. The emphasis at the hills is on skiing, not on hot-tub lounging, nightlife, or après-ski ambiance. At the base of a mountain, you won't find condos or designer restaurants; for fancy meals and lodging, you have to go to town. Listed below are some downhill ski areas within the Adirondack Park.

Price Code

Downhill Ski Areas	**Inexpensive**	**Moderate**	**Expensive**
(Weekend lift tickets for an adult)	**under $20**	**$20–$35**	**over $35**

LAKE GEORGE AND SOUTHEASTERN ADIRONDACKS

HICKORY HILL
518-623-2825.
Hickory Hill Rd., off Rte. 418, Warrensburg NY 12883.
Summer address: Box 9004, Schenectady NY 12309.
Trails: 14 (1 beginner, 7 intermediate, 6 expert).
Lifts: 1 rope tow; 1 T-bar; 2 poma lifts.
Vertical drop: 1200 ft.
Snowmaking: No.
Tickets: Inexpensive.
Open: Sat.–Sun. 9am–4pm.

In the late 1940s, Hans Winbaur and friends began carving out slopes on a conical mountain overlooking the Schroon and Hudson rivers near Warrensburg. Today, Hickory retains a folksy, hand-hewn approach, and in fact, it was the first ski area in the country to be owned and operated by its stockholders — a cooperative downhill area. Volunteers work on the trails, service the lifts, and raise money to keep the hill afloat.

Runs named Windfall, Hare, Grand Teton, and Topnotch are steep, expert slopes, but there are gentler ridge trails and traverses for intermediates. There's a certified ski school, a base lodge, and a professional patrol. Hickory Hill depends on natural snow cover, so call ahead.

HIGH PEAKS AND NORTHERN ADIRONDACKS

MOUNT PISGAH
518-891-0970.
Mt. Pisgah Rd., off Trudeau Rd., Saranac Lake NY 12983.
Trails: 1 main trail; some side trails.
Lifts: 1 T-bar.
Vertical drop: 300 ft.
Snowmaking: Yes.
Tickets: Inexpensive.
Open: Tues.–Sun.; weekdays 3–9pm; Sat. 9am– 6pm; Sun. 12–6pm.

If you've read *The Bell Jar*, you're acquainted with Mount Pisgah. Sylvia Plath skied there in the fifties and chronicled her spectacular tumble in the book. Since then, the hill was operated on-again, off-again until the late 1980s, when volunteers rebuilt the hill, and their efforts encouraged public officials to revitalize the slope. The mountain today is still very much a family ski area, with a friendly atmosphere and slopes geared to intermediate skiers. One section called "Suicide" falls somewhere between a modest drop-off and a mini-headwall; 10-year-olds think it's awesome. Telemark skiers take note: an annual affair called the **Telethon** (February) is citizen racing at its finest, with a rubber chicken presented to the skier who fails to drop down in the true arms extended, knee-to-the-ground "Mammy" position.

There's snowmaking covering most of the hill, thanks to local fundraising efforts, and a ski school, patrol, and base lodge. Pisgah is one of the few places left in the Adirondacks where you can enjoy night skiing; local residents often hit the slopes after work, when a lift ticket (good from 6–9pm) costs about $6.

WHITEFACE MOUNTAIN
518-946-2233.
www.lakeplacid.com/whiteface or www.whiteface.com.
Rte. 86, Wilmington NY 12997.
Trails: 65 (17 expert, 25 intermediate, 17 novice).
Lifts: 8 chairlifts (6 double chairs, 2 triple chairs); new high-speed gondola.
Vertical drop: 3216 ft.
Snowmaking: 95%.
Tickets: Expensive.
Open: Daily 9am–4pm.

New York governor Averill Harriman dedicated Whiteface Mountain, a state-owned facility, in 1958; the event was marred slightly when the chairlift he was riding came to a dead halt, and Harriman had to be rescued by ladder from his lofty perch. Not to worry, modern skiers — Whiteface lifts are totally reliable now.

The Olympic mountain has the longest vertical drop in the East and lots of intense, expert skiing. Cloudspin, one of the black-diamond trails, is long and hard with big bumps; Wilderness, another toughie, is the site of international mogul competitions. Intermediate skiers have dozens of challenging trails, with the three-mile-long Excelsior at the top of the list. Whiteface is big enough — but not a place you can get lost in — to accommodate scads of skiers without building up long lift lines. Improvements made in 1999, like the addition of the Cloudsplitter, a high-speed gondola, to Little Whiteface should move the crowds in comfort and style.

There's an excellent play-and-ski program for tots and a first-rate ski school led by Ed Kreil. Whiteface also sponsors races ranging from low-key events like the Cocoa Butter Open and pond-skimming contests to Olympic qualifiers.

There are three lodges for food, drink, and discussing the slopes, plus a full ski shop with rentals for skiers of all sizes and abilities. Although a weekend adult ticket is more than $40, there are sizable mid-week discounts, special promotions, and ladies' days.

CENTRAL ADIRONDACKS

GORE MOUNTAIN
518-251-2411.
www.goremountain.com.
Peaceful Valley Rd., off Rte. 28, North Creek NY 12853.
Trails: 59.
Lifts: 7 (1 8-person gondola, 1 triple chair, 3 double chairs, 2 surface lifts).
Vertical drop: 2100 ft.
Snowmaking: 97%.
Tickets: Expensive.
Open: Daily 9am–4pm.

Near North Creek, the cradle of North Country alpine skiing, is the other state-owned Adirondack ski hill: Gore Mountain, which opened in the early sixties. Beginning in 1984, Gore has been managed by the Olympic Regional Development Authority, as is Whiteface Mountain. Since that time, snowmaking has been installed over most of the mountain and trails have been widened.

Gore is intermediate heaven, with wide-open cruising runs, such as Showcase, Sunway, and Twister, on the lower part of the mountain, accessible from the high-speed triple chair. Mogul mavens and expert skiers can find good sport on Chatiemac and Hawkeye. A new high-speed gondola replaced the perky little red bucket ride in 1999; it's a godsend on frigid days. Also new for the millennium are four great trails (Sagamore, Kill Kare, Pine Knot, and Fairview) on Bear Mountain. Shredders have plenty to get excited about at Wild Air, the state-of-the-art snowboard park sponsored by Boardertown. By summer 2000 a huge Great Camp-inspired lodge will finally offer a nice place to linger partway up the mountain, with food, beverages, fireplaces, and a heck of a view.

The mountain has an excellent nursery, a ski-and-play program for preschoolers, and a ski school for all ages. The base lodge has a cozy lounge, but the cafeteria is cavernous. There's a full ski shop and rentals on the ground floor. Citizen racers can join in NASTAR competitions every weekend, while snurfer wannabes can take snowboarding lessons. At the tail end of the season is the annual **Pole, Pedal, Paddle** race for cross-country and downhill skiing, road biking, and canoeing, with teams of four or five or solo competitors.

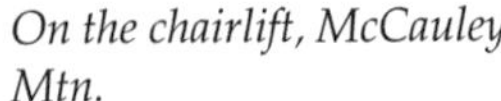

On the chairlift, McCauley Mtn.

John Caruso

MCCAULEY MOUNTAIN
315-369-3225.
www.oldforgeny.com/mccauley.
McCauley Mtn. Rd., off Bisby Rd., Old Forge NY 13420.
Trails: 14 (3 expert, 5 intermediate, 6 novice).
Lifts: 5 (1 double chair, 2 T-bars, 1 rope tow, 1 poma lift).
Vertical drop: 633 ft.
Snowmaking: 65%.
Tickets: Inexpensive.
Open: Daily 9am–4pm.

Hank Kashiwa, the international racing star and ski designer, learned his first snowplow turns here; his brilliant career is something folks in Old Forge still talk about. Actually, the Town of Webb school has produced three U.S. Olympic ski-team members, thanks to good coaches and the welcoming intermediate slopes at the local hill.

This little mountain has heaps of natural snow, due to a micro-climate that can produce 200 inches or more during an average winter. Helmers and Olympic, both of which have snowmaking, are the most difficult slopes. Intermediates can sample Upper God's Land, a ridge trail; Sky Ride, a wide route serviced by the double chair; or the gentle, sweeping Challenger. The lift crew feeds the deer here, so even non-skiers can enjoy a visit. You'll find all the amenities at McCauley: a ski school, rentals, food, and drink.

OAK MOUNTAIN
518-548-7311.
Elm Lake Rd., off Rte. 30, Speculator NY 12164.
Trails: 13.
Lifts: 3 T-bars.
Vertical drop: 650 ft.
Snowmaking: No.
Tickets: Inexpensive.
Open: Fri.–Sun. 9am–4pm.

Just a yodel away from Speculator's busy corner is Oak Mountain, built in 1948. Norm and Nancy Germain run an exemplary family ski hill here that offers diverse slopes for intermediates and novices. There are steep woodland trails, broad gentle runs, and a few options in between. Telemarkers love the place.

Townsfolk work as lift attendants in exchange for skiing privileges; the nearby public schools offer free ski lessons here for students. There's a base lodge that resembles an overgrown log cabin, with dozens of wooden picnic tables, and overall, the philosophy of the place — that downhill skiing is for everybody — remains as clear today as it was forty years ago. Plans unveiled in 1999 will upgrade facilities considerably.

BEYOND THE BLUE LINE

There's good skiing just outside the Adirondack Park, too. Near Glens Falls, you'll find **West Mountain** (518-793-6606; West Mtn. Rd., Queensbury), with 23 trails and 1000-foot vertical. **Titus Mountain** (518-483-3740; www.titus mountain.com; Rte. 30, Malone) has 26 trails, 1200 vertical feet, and snowmaking on 90 percent of the runs. To the west, **Snow Ridge** (315-348-8456; www.snowridge.com; off Rte. 26, Turin) has 22 trails and gets about 250 inches of natural snow a year. Snowmaking has been installed on some trails.

SNOWMOBILING

Deep blankets of snow, miles of old roads, active clubs, and support from town trail-maintenance programs add up to excellent snowmobiling in many parts of the park. A hub of snowmobile activity is Old Forge, which issues more than 12,000 snowmobile permits each winter. (Permits are available from the Tourist Information Center on Rte. 28 in the center of town or by going to www.oldforgeny.com/snowmobile.) Trails in Old Forge spread out like a river with numerous tributaries. You can connect with the Inlet trails to the east, or the Independence River Wild Forest and Big Moose trails to the north, and Forestport and Boonville routes to the south. These trails meet still other trails, so that you can continue further east from Inlet to Indian Lake or Speculator, and then from Speculator to Wells, or you can go from Inlet to Raquette Lake,

Snowmobiling is a mainstay of winter in Old Forge

John Caruso

and then on to Long Lake and Newcomb. Confused? There's information listed below to help you track down maps and brochures, or even find a guide.

Besides the Old Forge–Inlet area, which receives more than 15 feet of snow during an average winter, there are more than 400 miles of snowmobile trails in the Tupper Lake–Saranac Lake–Lake Placid area, and near Cranberry Lake, there are scores of miles of trails. Many trail networks throughout the park cross private timberlands as well as the state forest preserve. Public lands designated as wild forest areas are open to snowmobiling; wilderness areas are not. (You'll find descriptions of these areas near the end of this chapter.)

As with any winter pursuit, planning and preparation help make a successful outing. Know your machine; carry an emergency repair kit and understand how to use it. Be sure you have plenty of gas. Travel with friends in case of a breakdown or other surprise situation. Never ride at night unless you're familiar with the trail or are following an experienced leader. Avoid crossing frozen lakes and streams unless you are *absolutely certain* the ice is safe. Some town or county roads are designated trails; while on such a highway, keep right, observe the posted snowmobile speed limit, and travel in single file.

Your basic pack should contain a topographic map and compass as well as a local trail map; survival kit with matches, flashlight, rope, space blanket, quick-energy food, and something warm to drink; extra hat, socks, and mittens. Although a sip of brandy may give the illusion of warming you up, alcohol impairs circulation and can hasten hypothermia. And an arrest for snowmobiling under the influence carries with it severe penalties.

SNOWMOBILE RENTALS AND GUIDES

Guided snowmobile tours are a relatively new service here, and for getting around unfamiliar territory during a full day's riding, a knowledgeable leader is a real asset. In some communities, you can rent a sled, but this service is not widespread. For example, in Lake Placid you can rent snowmobiles from **Adirondack Snowmobile Rentals** (518-523-1388) and **Lake Placid Sports Unlimited** (518-523-3596); **Adirondack Adventure Tours** (518-523-1475) offers guided expeditions. Near Lake Clear, **XTC Ranch** (518-891-5684; www. Adirondack snowmobiling.com) offers guided trips.

To explore the wild forest around Cranberry Lake, contact **Woods Adventure Rentals** (315-848-5005). The company rents snowmobiles and offers a guide service for day trips.

Near Old Forge, several dealers rent snowmobiles: **Old Forge Sports Tours** (315-369-3796) and **Big Moose Yamaha** (315-357-2998, Eagle Bay). **Don's Polaris** (315-369-3255; Rte. 28, Old Forge) and **Smith Marine** (315-369-3366, Old Forge) sell and repair sleds.

For information about snowmobiling in specific areas, contact county and town tourist-information offices listed in Chapter Eight, *Information*.

WHITEWATER RAFTING

The wild, remote Upper Hudson River provides some of the East's most exhilarating whitewater: nearly 17 miles of continuous Class III–V rapids. From about 1860 to 1950, river drivers sent logs downstream every spring to sawmills and pulp mills, and they followed along behind the churning, tumbling timber in rowboats to pry logjams loose. Since the mid-1970s, the Hudson's power has been rediscovered for recreational purposes, with several rafting companies making the trip from Indian River, just south of Indian Lake, to North River.

Reliable water levels are provided by a dam release below Lake Abanakee, courtesy of the Town of Indian Lake. Releases begin about April 1 and last through Memorial Day, and most years, there are summer and fall seasons, with scheduled dam releases on weekends.

Although you don't need whitewater paddling experience to enjoy a trip down the Hudson, you do need to be over age 14, in good physical condition, and a competent swimmer. The outfitters supply you with wetsuit, paddle, life jacket, and helmet; they also shuttle you to the put-in, give on-shore instructions in safety and paddling techniques, and supply a hot meal at the end of the trip. Rafters should bring polypropylene underwear to wear under the suits; wool hats, gloves, and socks; sneakers; and dry, warm clothing for after the trip. (Springtime Adirondack air can be chilly, and the water temperature is truly frigid).

The Sacandaga River offers mild — not wild — rafting, great for kids.

Melody Thomas

A licensed guide steers each raft and directs the crew. This trip is not for passive passengers; you're expected to paddle — sometimes hard and fast — as the guide instructs. The Hudson Gorge is an all-day adventure, containing four to five hours of strenuous exercise, with the 2000 price $75–$85 per person.

Several rafting companies also offer short, fun trips on the Sacandaga River near Lake Luzerne. These junkets float 3.5 miles and last about an hour. Dam releases make the stream navigable all summer, and the cost is about $15 per person. On the other end of the spectrum is the Moose River from McKeever to Port Leyden; this is a 14-mile beast absolutely for experienced whitewater paddlers only. The Moose is runnable after spring ice-out, and the charge is about $80–$95 per person.

WHITEWATER OUTFITTERS

ARO (800-525-RAFT; Box 649, Old Forge) Trips on the Hudson and Moose rivers in spring; Black and Sacandaga rivers in summer.

Adirondack Wildwaters Inc. (518-696-2953 or 800-933-2468; Box 801, Corinth) Hudson River trips in spring; Moose River trips in Apr.

Adventure Sports Rafting Company (800-441-RAFT; Main St., Indian Lake) Hudson River trips in spring and fall.

Hudson River Rafting Company (518-251-3215 or 800-888-RAFT; www.hudsonriverrafting.com; Rte. 28, North Creek) Hudson River trips in spring and fall; Sacandaga River trips in summer; Moose River trips in Apr.

Middle Earth Expeditions (518-523-9572; www.Adirondackrafting.com; Cascade Rd., Lake Placid) Hudson River trips in spring; overnight float-in fishing trips in fall.

W.I.L.D./W.A.T.E.R.S. Outdoor Center (518-494-7478; Rte. 28, The Glen) Hudson River trips in spring; Moose River trips in spring and fall as water levels allow; Sacandaga River trips in summer.

WILDERNESS AREAS

"Where man is only a visitor who does not remain," is a phrase contained within legislation that defined the 15 wilderness areas of the Adirondack Park in the early 1970s. These portions of the forest preserve are 10,000 acres or larger and contain little evidence of modern times. Wilderness areas are open to hiking, cross-country skiing, hunting, fishing, and other similar pursuits, but seaplanes may not land on wilderness ponds, nor are motorized vehicles welcome. Listed below are Adirondack wilderness areas.

Note that new state-land purchases like the 15,000-acre William C. Whitney Area, near Long Lake, and more than 100,000 acres of Champion International lands, in the northern Adirondacks, have not been classified as this book went to press. It is anticipated that Whitney will remain a motorless parcel (wilderness or primitive), but that Champion will be primarily Wild Forest.

LAKE GEORGE AND SOUTHEASTERN ADIRONDACKS

Pharaoh Lake: 46,000 acres; E. of Schroon Lake hamlet. Extensive trail system; 36 lakes and ponds; lean-tos; views from Pharaoh and other nearby mountains.

HIGH PEAKS AND NORTHERN ADIRONDACKS

Dix Mountain: 45,000 acres; S.W. of Keene Valley. Adjacent to High Peaks wilderness; rock climbing at Chapel Pond; views from Noonmark, Dix, and many other mountains.

Giant Mountain: 23,000 acres; between Elizabethtown and Keene. Roaring Brook Falls; extensive hiking trails; views from Rocky Peak Ridge, Giant, and other mountains.

High Peaks: 226,000 acres; between Lake Placid and Newcomb. Excellent trail network; rock climbing at Wallface and other peaks; small lakes and ponds; views from Mount Marcy, Algonquin, and numerous other summits. Some interior destinations (Lake Colden and Marcy Dam) and peaks are very popular, to the point of being overused; more than 12,000 people climb Mount Marcy every year.

Jay Mountain: 7,100 acres; E. of Jay. Difficult access due to surrounding private lands; no official trails at this writing.

McKenzie Mountain: 38,000 acres; N. of Ray Brook. Trails for hiking and cross-country skiing; Saranac River; views from McKenzie and Moose mountains.

Sentinel Range: 23,000 acres; between Lake Placid and Wilmington. Small ponds for fishing; few hiking trails; views from Pitchoff Mountain. This area is remote and receives little use.

Waterfalls

Throughout the Adirondacks, the combination of streams and rivers and mountainous terrain provides numerous waterfalls. Some are spectacularly high, like T-Lake, which is taller than Niagara; others, like Buttermilk Falls, near Long Lake, are just a two-minute walk from the car. Listed below are just a few of the cascades you can visit.

Falls name	Description	Nearest town
Auger Falls	Gorge on the Sacandaga River; easy hike from Rte. 30	Wells
Blue Ridge Falls	On The Branch; visible from Blue Ridge Rd.	North Hudson
Bog River Falls	2-tier falls at Big Tupper Lake; visible from County Rd. 421	Tupper Lake
Buttermilk Falls	Raquette River; easy hike	Long Lake
Cascade Lake Inlet	Rock falls above Cascade Lake; 4-mile hike from Big Moose Rd.	Big Moose
Falls Brook	1-mile hike	Minerva
The Flume	On West Branch Ausable River; visible from Rte. 86	Wilmington
Hanging Spear Falls	Opalescent River; remote wilderness	High Peaks
High Falls	Oswegatchie River; remote	Cranberry Lake
Raquette Falls	Raquette River; remote	Tupper Lake
Rockwell Falls	Sacandaga River	Lake Luzerne
Shelving Rock	On Knapp estate; 4-mile hike	Pilot Knob
Split Rock Falls	Boquet River; access from Rte. 73	Elizabethtown
T-Lake Falls	Steep; remote	Piseco
Wanika Falls	Chubb River; remote	Lake Placid

NORTHWEST LAKES

St. Regis Canoe Area: 20,000 acres; W. of Paul Smiths. 58 lakes and ponds for canoeing; views from St. Regis and other mountains; trail network for hiking and cross-country skiing.

CENTRAL ADIRONDACKS

Blue Ridge: 46,000 acres; S. of Blue Mountain Lake. Contains several miles of the Northville–Lake Placid Trail for hiking and cross-country skiing; Cascade, Stephens, Wilson, Mitchell, and other trout ponds.

Five Ponds: 101,000 acres; between Cranberry Lake and Stillwater Reservoir. Numerous ponds; canoeing on the Oswegatchie River; many acres of old-growth forest; some hiking trails. This area receives little use. Extensive damage from 1995 storm blowdown of thousands of trees; inquire locally before planning a trip.

Ha De Ron Dah: 27,000 acres; W. of Old Forge. Small ponds and lakes; hiking and cross-country ski trails around Big Otter Lake. This area receives little use.

Hoffman Notch: 36,000 acres; between Minerva and the Blue Ridge Rd. Ponds and trout streams; a few hiking trails. This area is used mostly by fishermen and hunters.

Pepperbox: 15,000 acres; N. of Stillwater Reservoir. Few trails; difficult access; mostly wetlands; excellent wildlife habitat.

Pigeon Lake: 50,000 acres; N.E. of Big Moose Lake. Numerous lakes, ponds, and streams; trails for hiking and cross-country skiing.

Siamese Ponds: 112,000 acres; between North River and Speculator. Canoeing on Thirteenth Lake; Sacandaga River and numerous trout ponds; trails for hiking and cross-country skiing.

Silver Lake: 105,000 acres; between Piseco and Wells. Silver, Mud, and Rock lakes; southern end of the Northville–Placid trail. This area receives little use.

West Canada Lakes: 157,000 acres; W. of Speculator. Cedar, Spruce, West Canada lakes, and 160 other bodies of water; portions of the Northville– Placid trail and other hiking trails. One of the largest roadless areas in the Northeast.

WILD FOREST AREAS

More than a million acres of public land in the park are designated as wild forest, which are open to snowmobile travel, mountain biking, and other recreation. Some of the wild forest areas are listed below.

LAKE GEORGE AND SOUTHWESTERN ADIRONDACKS

Lake George: On both the E. and W. shores of the lake, N. of Bolton Landing. Contains the Tongue Mountain Range on the west, and the old Knapp estate, with 40+ miles of hiking and horse trails, on the east.

Wilcox Lake: W. of Stony Creek. Miles of snowmobile trails and old roads; ponds and streams for fishing.

CHAMPLAIN VALLEY

Hammond Pond: Between Paradox and Moriah, with old roads for hiking and ponds for fishing.

HIGH PEAKS AND NORTHERN ADIRONDACKS

Debar Mountain: Between Loon Lake and Meacham Lake. Horse trails; hiking; fishing in the Osgood River.

Saranac Lakes: W. of Saranac Lake village. Excellent canoeing; island camping.

NORTHWEST LAKES

Cranberry Lake: Between Cranberry Lake and Piercefield. Snowmobile and hiking trails; trout ponds.

CENTRAL ADIRONDACKS

Black River: Between Otter Lake and Wilmurt. Ponds and streams.
Blue Mountain: N.E. of Blue Mountain Lake. Contains part of the Northville–Placid trail; Tirrell Pond; views from Blue Mountain.
Ferris Lake: Between Piseco and Stratford. Dirt roads for mountain biking and driving through by car; numerous ponds and streams.
Independence River: S. of Stillwater Reservoir. Dirt roads; Independence River; snowmobile trails; beaver ponds.
Jessup River: Between the south end of Indian Lake and Speculator. Miami and Jessup Rivers, and Lewey Lake; views from Pillsbury Mountain; trails for snowmobiling, hiking, and mountain biking.
Moose River Plains: Between Indian Lake and Inlet. Dirt roads; numerous ponds and streams; Cedar River and Cedar River Flow; primitive car-camping sites; snowmobile trails. If you want to see moose, this is the place.
Sargent Ponds: Between Raquette Lake and Long Lake. Trout ponds; hiking trails; canoe route between Raquette Lake and Blue Mountain Lake.
Shaker Mountain: E. of Canada Lake. Dirt roads; hiking, cross-country skiing and mountain-biking routes.
Vanderwhacker Mountain: N.W. of Minerva. Fishing on the Boreas River; views from Vanderwhacker Mountain.

WILDLIFE

Viewing the bears at the town dump was a time-honored Adirondack pastime for generations of tourists, but local landfills closed during the early 1990s and ended this quaint practice. To be honest, watching a sow and her cubs rip through garbage bags wasn't all that pleasant an experience. Nowadays, the Adirondack Park offers a great variety of wildlife in their natural habitats to observe.

With marsh and mountain, field and forest to explore, experienced birders might be able to see a hundred different species in day. (Back in the 1870s, young Theodore Roosevelt and a friend compiled and published a bird guide to the northern Adirondacks listing some 90+ native birds they had seen.) In late spring, warblers in all colors of the rainbow arrive, and the best places to watch for them is along edges where habitats meet, such as woods on the border of a wetland, or along the edge of a brushy field. A variety of songbirds, including kingbirds, flycatchers, grosbeaks, waxwings, thrushes, wrens, and sparrows all nest here.

Many interior lakes and ponds are home to kingfishers, ducks, herons, and loons; listen and watch for that great northern diver in the early morning and at dusk. Peregrine falcons and bald eagles, absent from the park for much of the 20th century, have been reintroduced. Cliffs in the High Peaks are now falcon eyries, and you should be able to spot a bald eagle or two in the Northwest Lakes part of the park. In the evening, listen for owls: the barred owl, known by its call, "Who cooks for you, who cooks for you," is quite common. In the fall, look up to see thousands of migrating Canada and snow geese. Wild turkeys — absent from the Adirondacks until the 1990s — are positively ubiquitous, especially along roadsides in the central Adirondacks.

Small mammals are numerous: varying hares, weasels, mink, raccoons, fisher, pine martens, otters, bobcats, porcupines, red and gray fox. Coyotes, with rich coats in shades of black, rust, and gray, can be seen in fall, winter, and spring, and their yips and yowls on a summer night can be thrilling to the backcountry campers' ears. (Recent studies from Canada's Algonquin Park indicate that the Adirondack coyote may actually be an eastern red wolf.) About 50 lynx from the Northwest Territories have been released in the High Peaks in the 1980s, in an attempt to restore the big cats to their former range, but it appears now that few survived.

Whitetail deer are seemingly everywhere, especially in the early spring before the fawns are born. In Old Forge, even in front yards facing busy Main Street, does are as common as common as squirrels.

Several couple dozen moose (bulls first) have wandered into the park since the 1980s; more and more cows and calves are sighted each year, with the resident population now somewhere north of 60. The best place to see moose is — no surprise — Moose River Recreation Area, where bulls can be seen in fall from woods roads. If you encounter one of these draft-horse size guys, do not approach! They tend to be very cranky during rutting season.

Many of the state campgrounds are good places to observe wildlife, especially aquatic birds and mammals. Ask the caretaker about where to see resident otters, ducks, loons, ospreys, and you may be rewarded with a wonderful vacation experience.

Don't Touch That Critter!

In recent years rabies cases have been reported in the northern and southeastern corners of the Adirondacks. The disease seems to be spread by raccoons, foxes, and skunks in upstate New York.

If you come across a wild animal acting unafraid or lying passively, by all means stay away from it. Don't touch dead creatures you may find. However, humans are not at great risk for rabies exposure since contact with sick wildlings can be avoided.

Dogs must be inoculated against rabies. Keep your pet under control when traveling through the woods.

CHAPTER SEVEN

Woodsy Whimsy to Practical Gear

SHOPPING

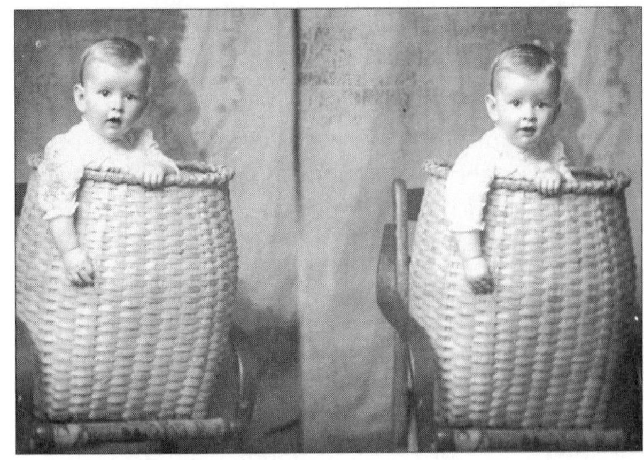

Courtesy Edward Comstock Jr.

An Adirondack pack basket can carry your gear, your game, your grandkids.

Designer-label devotees, mall rats, and outlet gypsies may find themselves at sea on an Adirondack vacation. You'll find the shopping here ranges from quirky to funky to woodsy, with nary a Prada in sight. True Adirondack style — favored by ordinary folks who chose substance over style and function over form — predates the Ralph Lauren look by a century. Today, in shops across the park, you can get hearty woolens and practical gear without worrying whether you are setting or following the trend.

Emblematic of the region's classic designs is the always-in-season Adirondack chair, available from woodworkers in shops large and small. You can get the country seat in basic pine or beautiful native hardwoods, with rockers or anatomically curved backs, as a settee or porch swing, or even with hinges so the whole thing folds for storage.

Rustic furniture, from simple tables to sculptural headboards, remains an authentic product crafted by artisans who search the woods for the right piece of crooked yellow birch, the perfect shaggy cedar sapling. For a song (almost), you can purchase a rustic picture frame — or you can spend a small fortune on a museum-quality piece. Adirondackana (a term used describe housewares with a woodsy motif, historic collectibles, prints, books, and native crafts) is the specialty of some fine shops that have been in business since the 1950s.

During the past twenty-five years, handcrafts have enjoyed a renaissance. Typical items range from ash-splint pack baskets to drapey chenille scarves to contemporary jewelry depicting miniature fishing lures. Some artisans rely on Adirondack wood to fire their kilns, or Adirondack wool for their yarns, or even quills from native porcupine for their jewelry. Other craftspeople are here for quiet lifestyles and natural inspiration. Items can be purchased in shops and galleries, at artisans' studios and fairs, all of which are described further in this chapter.

For book lovers, there are shops offering contemporary novels, trashy paperbacks for a rainy day, wholesome stories for kids, and a plethora of how-to, where-to, and why-to publications. If you can't find it on the shelves, just ask — these independent bookstores can order most anything in print. In some emporiums, you'll find new and old books combined with other things like health foods, tobacco, or hardware, making for an excellent afternoon's browsing.

Dozens of antique shops are located in the park, with concentrations around Warrensburg, the Champlain Valley, and Lake Placid. From Stickley rockers to postcards, moose antlers to Georgian silver, squeeze boxes to cheese boxes, there's bound to be the dealer who has just what you're looking for at a fair price. Don't miss the first-rate antique shows, which you'll find listed under "Fairs and Flea Markets."

General stores are still the real item in North Country towns, supplying the goods for daily life from fresh milk to rain ponchos to crescent wrenches, and maybe even a wedding present. We like to think that the definition of an authentic general store would be a place where you could buy truly everything — from socks to dessert — you'd need for a week in the wilds.

The waters of the Adirondack Park attract many small-craft aficionados to special gatherings and to the fine traditional-boat exhibit at the Adirondack Museum (described in Chapter Four, *Culture*). Boatbuilders who make guideboats — a sleek rowboat — along with craftsmen who build everything from ultralight canoes to runabouts are listed in this chapter.

The one thing you won't find inside the Adirondack Park is the modern suburban shopping mall. For that consumer experience you need to go south, to Aviation Mall (off I-87, Glens Falls), or north, to Champlain Centres (off I-87, Plattsburgh), or west, to Watertown, Utica, Syracuse, and beyond. Schroon Lake and Lake Placid have old-fashioned main streets that you can stroll for serious window shopping; in recent years the historic village Essex has blossomed into a delightful shopper's destination with galleries and boutiques featuring quality crafts, antiques, and gifts. Canada Street, Lake George's main drag, is a day-glo kaleidoscope of T-shirt shops, ice cream stands, and souvenir joints; if you can't decide what to get the folks back home there's a psychic advisor who might be able to help. A few towns like Ticonderoga, Tupper Lake, Saranac Lake, and Lake Placid have plazas with grocery, discount, liquor, and hardware stores, but in general, Adirondack shopping is a relaxed, folksy pastime. If you're looking for a general mail-order source of all things Adirondack, request *The Pack Basket* (877-ADKPACK; www.adirondackpack basket.com), which has a good selection of regional crafts.

ADIRONDACKANA

The word defines all kinds of material things that complement the countryside and evokes textures: bark, wood grain; smells: balsam, cedar; tastes: maple, apple; forest colors: deep green, gold, sienna. For a real sampling of Adirondackana, you need to travel to the heart of the park.

HIGH PEAKS

Keene Valley

The Birch Store (518-576-4561; Rtes. 9N/73, Keene Valley, near the Noon Mark Diner) Antiques, hip clothing, and interesting jewelry combined with traditional Adirondack camp furnishings: blankets, birch-bark baskets and frames, chairs, balsam pillows, and wicker ware in a classy vintage storefront. Open daily June 15–Labor Day, and some fall, winter, and spring weekends.

Lake Placid

Adirondack Decorative Arts & Crafts (518-523-4545; 104-6 Main St.) Delightful two-story shop with a huge inventory — everything from birch-bark-patterned table linens to one-of-a-kind twig furniture, oiled canvas jackets, bark picture frames, jewelry, and even a full-size rustic doghouse. The best source for woodsy cabinet hardware. Open all year; worth a visit.

Adirondack Store and Gallery (518-523-2646; 109 Saranac Ave., W. of Cold Brook Plaza) This place launched the Adirondackana trend decades ago. If you're looking for anything — pottery, wrapping paper, doormats, sweaters, stationery, cutting boards — emblazoned with loon, trout, pinecone or birch motifs, search no further. There's an excellent selection of Adirondack prints by Winslow Homer and Frederic Remington; antique baskets and rustic furniture; camp rugs and blankets; woodsy ornaments for the Christmas tree, including minute Adirondack chairs. Be sure to visit the basement. Open daily year-round.

Adirondack Trading Company (518-523-3651; Main St., across from the Northwoods Inn) Doodads from the woods: cedar-scented sachets, rustic doll-house furniture, pine-cone-covered picture frames, silk-screened totebags shaped like fish; flannel night shirts printed with leaping deer silhouettes; goofy bear-foot slippers. Tables, bookshelves, and dressers with painted tops and white-birch legs and trim are reasonably priced. Open daily year-round.

CENTRAL ADIRONDACKS

Northville

Adirondack Country Store (518-863-6056; 252 N. Main St., Northville; www.adirondackcountrystore.com) Stick furniture and accessories, regional books, local crafts, food products, clothing. Open year-round; catalog available.

Old Forge

Moose River Trading Company (315-369-6091; Rte. 28, Thendara) Pack baskets, canvas hats, Duluth packs, maps, compasses, bug dope, camp cookware and blankets, Adirondack chairs, and Guide's Coffee — what more could you need for an Adirondack expedition or creating your own Great Camp room? Open year-round; mail-order catalog, too.

Peace of the Forest (315-369-2684; Main St.) Rustic furniture, antler lamps and sconces, birchbark mirrors and picture frames, pottery, carved wildlife jewelry. Open daily in summer. Similar stock at sister store, **Arrowhead Trading Post** (315-357-2140; Main St. Inlet).

ANTIQUES

While traveling along rural routes in the Northeast, we just expect to find barns full of milk-painted country furniture, salt-glazed crocks, and marvelous hand tools. But these artifacts don't always relate to the territory we're passing through for reasons of history, culture, and climate. When you're antiquing in the Adirondacks, keep a thumbnail sketch of the region's past in your mind, and that will guide you to old things true to the countryside.

Expect to find artifacts relating to logging and farming days and good-quality mass-produced 19th-century furniture. Local pottery, except in the far southern part of the park is quite rare; Redford glass, made in the Saranac River valley during the early 1800s, is highly prized and extremely hard to find. Vintage rustic furniture, which was discarded willy-nilly in the fifties as camp owners modernized, is scarce, but Old Hickory pieces have the right look and feel and are widely available. If you're on track for a pair of snowshoes or antlers to hang at home, you shouldn't have any trouble finding them here.

Many shops stock wood engravings and hand-tinted etchings of Adirondack scenes; these prints — many of them by Winslow Homer or Frederic Remington — which appeared in *Harper's Weekly*, *Every Saturday*, and other magazines, are usually inexpensive. Stereo views of the grand hotels, postcards from 1910–1930, and photographs by George Baldwin, H.M. Beach, "Adirondack" Fred Hodges, and others are charming and not too dear. For photographs of the lakes, mountains, and resorts by Seneca Ray Stoddard, a contemporary of William Henry Jackson and Matthew Brady, you can expect to pay more, but the images are exceptional. Another name on the list for ephemera fans is Verplanck Colvin: mountain panoramas, diagrams, and maps from his 1870–90 surveys are meticulous curiosities.

Another aspect of the Adirondack past to keep in mind is that the area has been a tourist destination since the Civil War. There's a brisk trade in historic souvenirs and small things relating to bygone transportation networks: embossed-brass luggage tags from steamboat and stagecoach lines are one example. Besides items designed to catch a visitor's eye or track his or her property, you can find objects that summer folk brought with them from back home or around the world to decorate camps great and small. These 19th-century part-time residents amassed an eclectic variety of knickknacks, musical instruments, rugs, silver, and china that have become part of the antique scene as modern families spurned the elephant-foot humidors, Japanese lanterns, and other peculiar things the Victorians adored.

A few publications can help you find antique dealers: *Antiques, Collectibles, Handcrafts* (Box 19, Olmstedville NY 12857) describes shops in the North Creek–Riparius–Olmstedville area. Or consider a trip south to Fulton County (information 800-676-3858), where there are numerous shops in the Sacandaga and Mohawk basins. In Glens Falls, not too far from I-87, Glenwood Manor (518-798-4747; Quaker Rd.) is a group undertaking with 40 dealers, who have filled four dozen rooms with quality antiques; the mansion is open year-round. In Whitehall, try the Antique Center (518-499-2501; Rte. 4), where numerous dealers share 8,000 square feet in a shop that's open all year.

The best fair is unquestionably the *Adirondack Antiques Show* at the Adirondack Museum (518-352-7311; Rte. 28/30, Blue Mtn. Lake) in September; dealers from across the country flock there with their absolute best woodsy wares. Also recommended is the July show and sale benefiting the *Adirondack Medical Center* (518-891-1990; Harrietstown Hall, Saranac Lake NY 12983). Both affairs feature dozens of booths showcasing primitive furniture, decoys, jewelry, books, glass, clocks, dolls, and of course, Adirondackana.

A sampling of the antique shops you'll find in the Adirondack Park is described below. Most are open several days a week in July and August and on weekends in spring and fall; some are open year-round. Many dealers frequently travel to shows, so it's always a good idea to call ahead.

LAKE GEORGE AND SOUTHEASTERN ADIRONDACKS

Adirondack

Country Cottage Antiques and Gifts (Carl Pratt; 518-494-2051; 9 Church St.) Oriental rugs, country furniture, and collectibles. Open daily July–Aug.; weekends in spring and fall; call ahead.

Bolton Landing

Black Bass Antiques (Henry Caldwell and Kate Van Dyck; 518-644-2389; Main St. near Ben & Jerry's) Books, antique fishing tackle, Lake George souvenirs and photographs, general Adirondack items.

Brant Lake

Fox Hill Antiques, Brant Lake, sells everything from old farm implements to vintage clothing.

James Swedberg

Fox Hill (518-494-4974; on Brant Lake Mill Pond, Rte. 8) Interesting shop with general antiques, vintage clothing, and smalls. Closed Wed. in summer; open weekends in fall.

Chestertown

Atateka Books & Collectibles (Mark Walp; 518-494-0042; 1329 Friends Lake Rd., near Rte. 8) Paper ephemera, books, and smalls; call ahead.

Lake George

Ralph Kylloe Antiques and Rustics Gallery (518-696-4100, Lake Luzerne Rd.) Established in 1995, enormous shop with exceptional rustic furniture, quality smalls, and sporting antiques. Open year-round; worth a special trip.

Waterborne (Skip and Lynn Gauger; 518-656-9248; Brayton La.) Antique boats, motors, marine art. By appointment.

Schroon Lake

High Tor (Gloria and Irwin Diamond; 518-532-9835; Rte. 74 3 mi. E. of Northway Exit 28) Delightful century-old house filled with furniture, glass, books, linens, mirrors, games, and prints from the Victorian era through Art Deco. Open May–Nov.

Warrensburg

Cleverdale Antiques (518-623-4181; 3273 Main St., near the Ford dealer) Lots of 19th century furniture, some smalls. Call ahead in off-season.

Discoveries (518-623-4567; Rtes. 9 & 28 1 mile north of town center) Real miscellany from kitchen to bath, but occasional gems in furniture. Open year-round.

Donegal Manor Antique & Gift Center (518-623-3549; 117 Main St.) Behind Donegal Manor Bed and Breakfast; Irish linen, furniture, coins, postcards, books, pocket watches; Victorian jewelry, glass, prints. Open year-round; daily in summer.

Ed and Pearl Kreinheder (518-623-2149; 197 Main St.) Rare books; country furniture and accessories. Open year-round, Mon.–Sat. Call ahead.

Field House Antiques (Virginia Field; 518-623-9404; 179 Main St.) In the carriage house you'll find furniture, country ware, toys, china, and glass. Open year-round; daily in summer; call ahead.

Riverside Gallery (Lenore Smith; 518-623-2026; 2 Elm St., 1 block W. of Rtes. 9 & 28) Old prints; paintings; reproduction furniture; picture framing. Open year-round Mon.–Sat.

Sherman & Locke (518-762-3156 or 518-494-5100; 3729 Main St.) Vintage Adirondack souvenirs; fine porcelain; silver, paintings, prints. Open year-round; call ahead.

Tamarack Shoppe (518-623-3384; 148 Main St., at the bandstand) Fiesta ware, jewelry, glass, books, and some furniture, mixed in with new brass, table linens, rugs, and imported china. Open daily, year-round.

CHAMPLAIN VALLEY

Elizabethtown

Pleasant Valley Collectibles (Janice and Conrad Hutchins; 518-873-2100; Upper Water St.) "Interesting old stuff from a pack-rat's attic — everything priced to sell." Open by chance or appointment.

Essex

Margaret Sayward's Antiques & Untiques (518-963-7828; South Main St.) Excellent shop taking up entire house in the heart of Essex. Furniture, glassware, clocks, collectibles, clothing from the 1930s. Open daily June–Oct., winter and spring by chance or appointment.

Summer Shop (Colin Ducolon; 518-963-7921; Rte. 22) Painted furniture, early pressed glass, 19th-century textiles, coin silver. Open June–Oct.

Ticonderoga

Lonergan's Red Barn Antiques (Craig Lonergan; 518-585-4477; Rte. 9N) Old barn packed to the roof beams with things you've been looking for — books, china, furniture, photos, prints, Lake Champlain souvenir plates, Fiesta ware, crocks, tinware, trunks, farm implements, horse-drawn equipment, guns — or, as the flyer says, "Useful Stuff for Man and Beast." Open daily Memorial Day–Columbus Day; weekends in spring and fall.

Past Lives Antiques (518-585-9066; 111 Montcalm St.) Vintage clothing and linens, used books, kitchenware, some furniture. Open year-round.

Robin Hill Antiques (518-585-6675; Roger St.) Oil lamps, vintage jewelry, pottery, furniture. Open Thurs.–Sun. in summer or by appointment. Closed winter.

Wild Angels (Sue Borho; 518-585-9796; Montcalm St.) Vintage fabrics, antiques, and crafts. Open year-round.

Willsboro

Ben Wever's Farm (Dare Van Vree Wever; 518-963-8372; 221 Mountain View Dr.) Ten rooms of antiques in a beautifully restored farmhouse: pine, cherry, walnut, and mahogany furniture; fine china, porcelain, and silver; rugs; paintings; lamps; glass; Adirondackana, Americana, and Victoriana. Open daily late June–Labor Day; also Memorial Day weekend.

Brown House Antiques (Suzanne Medler; 518-963-7396; Main St.) Six rooms of linens, prints, pine and mahogany furniture, china, books, Fiesta ware, toys and dolls, wicker, Adirondack collectibles. Open late June–Aug. Tues.–Sat; weekends in Sept. by chance.

HIGH PEAKS AND NORTHERN ADIRONDACKS

Au Sable Forks

Don's Antiques (Marge and Don Denette; 518-647-8422; North Main St.) Furniture, Depression and patterned glass, clocks, stoneware, postcards, "ancestral paraphernalia." Open year-round by chance or appointment.

Bloomingdale

Buyer's Paradise (518-891-4242; Rte. 3) Antiques, used furniture, horse-drawn equipment, and more inside and outside an old roadhouse. If you're fed up with precious prices and uptight dealers, go here for serious rummaging. Open year-round.

Germaine Miller (518-891-1306; Rte. 3) Country and small Adirondack furniture, painted cupboards, Majolica and Quimper, china, glass, silver. By chance or appointment; practically next door to Buyer's Paradise.

From sleighs and wagons to picture frames and tables — you can find almost anything at Buyer's Paradise.

James Swedberg

Sign of the Fish Studio & Gallery (Henry and Virginia Jakobe; 518-891-2510; Rte. 3 just north of town hall) Furniture, books, paintings and prints, glass, china from the 19th century to the 1950s. Open July–Aug., or by appointment.

Keene Valley

George Jaques Antiques (518-576-2214; Main St., Keene NY 12942) Rustic furniture, advertising art and signs, antique taxidermy, porch furniture, pack baskets. Open Memorial Day–Columbus Day.

Keeseville

Granny Appleseed's (518-834-5418; Rte. 9N between Au Sable Forks and Keeseville) Nice roadside shop with books, advertising art, and some furniture, plus homemade pies. Open daily in summer.

Lake Placid

Log Cabin Antiques (Greg Peacock; 518-523-3047; 86 Main St.) Furniture, prints, kitchenware, Adirondackana, some reproduction stuff mixed in. Open year-round.

Alan Pereske (home phone 518-891-3733; shop address 81 Saranac Ave.) Quality oak, pine, and rustic furniture; paintings and prints of local interest; glass, toys; ephemera. Open weekends spring and fall. Mon.–Sat. summer.

Loon Lake

Arden Creek Designs (518-891-4518; Box 77) Excellent selection of antique baskets and rustic furnishings in vintage Adirondack camp. Call ahead.

The Old Art Gallery (518-891-3249; Loon Lake Golf Course) Bins of 19th-century engravings and lithographs plus some framed pieces. Open daily mid-May–Oct.

Red Barn Antiques (Roberta and Jay Friedman; 518-891-5219; Onchiota Rd.) Furniture, oil lamps, glassware, tools, sheet music, postcards, prints, jewelry, clocks in a grand old barn. Open July–early Sept., plus some spring and fall weekends.

Vermontville

Forest Murmurs (518-891-6933; Rte. 3) General line plus new rustic furniture. Open daily in summer.

NORTHWEST LAKES

Tupper Lake

Nice Twice (Jenny Matlock; 518-359-3256; 95 Park St.) Glass galore at reasonable prices plus good used household items. Note that the decorations change gaily with the seasons: orange and black paper napkins beneath items for Halloween, flag bunting for the Fourth of July. Open year-round.

Sorting Gap (Kathleen Bigrow; 518-359-3463; 359-2567; 123 Park St.) Named for a narrows on the Raquette River where logs were sorted according to the brands burned on their butt end. Rustic furniture, old books, glass, pottery, toys, games. Open daily in summer.

CENTRAL ADIRONDACKS

Inlet

Lake View Antiques (Barb and Walt Wermuth; 315-357-4722; Rte. 28) Clocks and clock repair; house full of furniture, paper, postcards, china, Oriental rugs. Open late June–Sept.

Johnsburg

Carriage Shed (518-251-2140; Crane Mt. Rd. about 5 miles off Rte. 8) Antiques, linens, country furniture, collectibles; call ahead for directions.

Minerva

Mountain Niche Antiques (John and Kathy Feiden; 518-251-2566; Rte. 28N, 2 mi. N. of Minerva post office) Excellent assortment of country furniture, textiles, books, prints, tools, pottery, glassware. Open most days year-round; call ahead.

North Creek

You can decorate your dream cabin at Hudson River Trading.

James Swedberg

Hudson River Trading Co. (518-251-4461; Main St.) Furniture, pottery, antique sporting goods, prints, and advertising art in a nicely restored livery stable. Open year-round.

Northville

Red Barn (518-863-4828; 202 N. Main St.) Furniture, prints, collectibles, baskets, taxidermy animals. Open spring–fall: daily in summer, otherwise by chance or appointment.

Wheels of Time (Joan Crean; 518-863-2267; 112 Van Arnham Ave.) General line of antiques and collectibles. Open weekends May–June; Weds.–Sun. July–Aug.

Old Forge

Antiques & Articles (Mary Diamond; 315-369-3316; 19 Main St.) Oak, wicker, rustic, and pine furniture; baskets; books; Fiesta ware, Depression glass; toys. Open daily July–Aug.; fall weekends.

Indian Summer Antiques (315-369-3899; Rte. 28 across from Bald Mt. trailhead) Camp furnishings, sporting antiques, prints, smalls in an old roadside tourist stop. Open May–Sept.; call ahead.

Old Stuff and Such (Rte. 28 across from Adirondack Bank) Kitchen items, glass, and smalls; Memorial Day–Labor Day.

Olmstedville

Board 'n' Batten (Floss and Bob Savarie; 518-251-2507; Main St.) Furniture, country items, Adirondack postcards, buttons, steins; focus on quality glass and pottery. Open daily July–Aug.; or by chance or appointment.

Riparius

Clen's Collectibles (Donalda and Clennon Ellifritz; 518-251-2388; River Rd.) Large, bright shop across from the Riparius train station with a general line of antiques and smalls; vintage clothing; Adirondack postcards and prints. Open year-round by chance or appointment; daily in summer. Recommended.

ART GALLERIES AND PAINTERS' STUDIOS

The best 19th-century American painters came to the Adirondacks to interpret wild scenery on paper and canvas, and many artists still rely on the great outdoors for inspiration. Listed here you'll find local artists in residence as well as fine-arts galleries representing painters from different eras and regions.

LAKE GEORGE AND SOUTHEASTERN ADIRONDACKS

Lake Luzerne

Art Center at Rockwell-Harmon Cottage (518-696-3011; 37 Main St. next to Papa's Ice Cream) Paintings, folk art, woodcarvings, ironwork, weavings, with occasional demonstrations by the artists. Open Thurs.–Sun. in summer.

Lynn Benevento Gallery (518-696-5702; 4 Bridge St., next to Rockwell Falls) Local landscapes, wildflowers, and town scenes available as original paintings or limited-edition prints. Open daily in summer.

CHAMPLAIN VALLEY

Westport

Atea Ring Gallery (Atea Ring; 518-962-8620; Sam Spears Rd.) A modern professional fine-arts gallery like you'd expect to find in a major city, located instead in an out-of-the-way farmhouse. One-person and group exhibitions of paintings, quilts, prints. Past shows have included works by Harold Weston; realist Paul Matthews; primitive paintings by Edna West Teall (who was the Grandma Moses of Essex County); and Lake Champlain fish decoys. Open June–Sept.

Willsboro

East Side Studio (Patricia Reynolds; 518-963-8356; 390 Point Rd.) Watercolor and oil landscapes of Lake Champlain and the Adirondacks; lovely flower paintings from the artist's extensive perennial gardens; usually a hundred or so works on hand. Open by chance or appointment year-round. Her paintings are often for sale at the Westport Yacht Club (518-962-8777).

HIGH PEAKS AND NORTHERN ADIRONDACKS

Keene

Adirondack Studio (518-576-9213; Old Gristmill Rd. near Rte. 73) New in 1999, group gallery featuring painter John Hudson, jeweler Jodi Downs, sculptor Pax Lemmon, and others. Call ahead.

Heritage Gallery (Bruce and Annette Mitchell; 518-576-2289; corner Spruce Hill and Hurricane Rds.) Oil and watercolor paintings of Adirondack and Vermont scenes; limited-edition wildlife, floral, and landscape prints. Open Mon.–Sat. June–Nov. 14.

Saranac Lake

Small Fortune Studio (Timothy Fortune; 518-891-1139; 71 Main St.) Realistic Adirondack landscapes by an internationally regarded artist; works range from tiny, charming scenes to massive triptychs. Open year-round Tues.–Sat.

North Country Artists Guild (518-891-2615; 74 Main St. near Adirondack Bank) New gallery started by photographer Mark Kurtz, sculptor Ralph Prata, and other local artists of note, with changing exhibitions. Open year-round.

NORTHWEST LAKES

Cranberry Lake

End of the Pier Studio (Jean Reynolds; 315-848-2900; Rte. 3, at The Emporium) Watercolor paintings of Cranberry Lake and Adirondack vistas; limited-edition prints. Open by chance or appointment.

Gabriels

Point of View Studio (Diane Leifheit; 518-327-3473; Hunt Building, Rte. 86) Meticulous pen-and-ink drawings of noteworthy Adirondack buildings; special commissions. Call ahead.

Tupper Lake

Casagrain Studio and Gallery (Gary Casagrain; 518-359-2595; Rte. 3, across from Massawepie Cooperative Area, 10 mi. W. of Tupper Lake village) Oil paintings and limited-edition prints of Adirondack scenes and wildlife. Open year-round; call ahead.

CENTRAL ADIRONDACKS

Edinburg

Dodge House Studio (Constance Dodge; 518-863-2201; S. Shore Rd.) Oil paintings and mixed-media drawings; portraits from photographs. Open Tues.–Sun. in summer or by appointment.

Old Forge

Gallery North (315-369-2218; Main St., across from the school) Limited-edition wildlife and Adirondack prints, posters, and woodcarvings; picture framing. Open year-round.

BOATBUILDERS

The interconnected waterways of the region led to the development of a specialized craft, the Adirondack guideboat. Traditional guideboats, which first appeared after the Civil War, are smooth-skinned rowboats with quarter-sawn cedar or pine planks, and have naturally curved spruce roots for ribs. These delicate-looking craft are fast on the water and easy to carry between ponds, lakes, and rivers. In the 19th century, a handmade boat cost $30 or $40.

Beside guideboats, a number of local boatbuilders have developed their own special designs, from ultralight pack canoes to cold-molded multipurpose sport boats. Listed below you'll find a variety of water-craftsmen; it's always a good idea to call ahead. Also, you may find that there's a waiting list of other prospective buyers. Beautiful things take time to create.

CHAMPLAIN VALLEY

Ticonderoga

Hacker Craft Boats (Bill Morgan; 518-543-6731; former Newberry Dept. Store, Montcalm St.) Showroom for mahogany speedboats made a few miles away in Silver Bay from original Hacker Craft plans. Prices $30,000–$85,000.

HIGH PEAKS AND NORTHERN ADIRONDACKS

Saranac Lake

Hathaway Boat Shop (Christopher Woodward; 518-891-3961; 9 Algonquin Ave.) A long line of boatbuilders has occupied this shop on the edge of town, including Willard Hanmer, whose boats are displayed at the Adirondack Museum. Chris learned the trade from Carl Hathaway, who was taught by Willard himself. Traditional wooden Adirondack guideboats; boat repairs. Traditional guideboats with oars and yoke: $7,500–$10,000.

Spencer Boatworks (Spencer Jenkins; 518-891-5828; www.antiqueandclassicboats.com; Bloomingdale Rd.) Inboard wooden boats built along classic runabout lines with modern epoxy lay-up; models include cruisers and utility boats 18 to 26 feet long; prices $38,000–$92,000. Also wooden boat and inboard-motor repairs.

NORTHWEST LAKES

Lake Clear

Jim Cameron builds just a few traditional guideboats each year.

Mark Kurtz

Boathouse Woodworks (James Cameron; 518-327-3470; Upper St. Regis Lake) Traditional wooden Adirondack guideboats built to order; 16-foot guideboat with oars and yoke: $6,000–$7,000. Seat caning; boat restoration.

Tupper Lake

Spruce Knee Boatbuilding (Rob Frenette; 518-359-3228; Rte. 30 near Moody Bridge) Rushton-design wooden canoes and rowboats, guideboats, and sailboats all built to order; wooden boat repairs; seat caning. New boats start at $3,000; traditional guideboats with complete outfit: $7,000 and up.

CENTRAL ADIRONDACKS

Indian Lake

Adirondack Guide Boat Shop (John B. Spring; 518-648-5455; Rte. 28 near Cedar River Golf Course) New wood-and-canvas canoes in 15-foot Rushton designs and 17-foot traditional models; $3,000 and up. Restored guideboats and antique canoes in stock. Wooden boat repairs; seat caning.

Long Lake

Adirondack Goodboat (Mason Smith; 518-624-6398; North Point Rd.) This craft, which won the "Great Versatility Race" at Mystic Seaport's annual small-boat gathering, is a car-toppable multipurpose (row, sail, or motor) wooden boat, built with modern materials for easy maintenance and strength without weight. Other models are the Lakesailer and the Chipmunk canoe; kits available. Price range: $1,700–$5,500.

Olmstedville

Hornbeck Boats (Peter Hornbeck; 518-251-2764; Trout Brook Rd.) Nessmuk (George Washington Sears) pioneered the go-light outdoor movement in the 1880s, and Pete has brought his designs into the 21st century. Kevlar pack canoes in 9-, 10 1/2-, and 12-foot lengths, perfect for tripping into remote ponds, weigh only 12–19 pounds; Kevlar guideboats and ultralight sea kayaks are available by special order. Price range: $550–$2,000.

BOOKS

Within the Adirondack Park, there are about a dozen independently owned bookstores. Each place has its own personality: some highlight nature books; others offer art supplies and crafts too.

CHAMPLAIN VALLEY

Ticonderoga

Fort Ticonderoga (518-585-2821; off Rte. 74) In a huge log cabin at the entrance to the museum, if you go beyond the bins of souvenirs, you'll find books, prints, monographs, maps, and audiotapes pertinent to 18th-century military history. Open daily mid-May–mid-Oct.

HIGH PEAKS AND NORTHERN ADIRONDACKS

Keene Valley

Keene Valley Book Store (518-576-4736; Rte. 73) Restored farmhouse with an impressive selection of regional and children's books; contemporary novels, how-to, nature guides, and cheerful service. Upstairs, Celtic harps. Coffee bar, Adirondack folk music tapes and CDs, too. Open daily in summer; closed mid-week fall–spring.

The Mountaineer (518-576-2281; Rte. 73) Good selection of outdoor, international adventure travel, nature, and Adirondack titles; topo maps. Open year-round Mon.–Sat.

Lake Placid

The Bookstore Plus (518-523-2950; 89 Main St.) Racks of paperbacks; good how-to guides; contemporary fiction; regional histories and guidebooks; cookbooks; children's books; coffee-table books; art supplies; stationery and cards. Open year-round Mon.–Sat.

Eastern Mountain Sports (518-523-2505; 51 Main St.) Adirondack and outdoor guidebooks, camping cookbooks, and adventure travel tales; maps; gear and garb. Open year-round Mon.–Sat.; daily in summer.

Nature Unlimited (518-523-TREE; 59 Main St.) Books, nature tapes, science toys, rocks, and minerals. Open Mon.–Sat. all year.

A New Leaf (518-523-1847; Hilton Plaza, Main St.) New Age and self-help books; cards and stationery; tea, coffee, and cappuccino. Open daily year-round.

With Pipe and Book (Julie and Breck Turner; 518-523-9096; 91 Main St.) Landmark shop with new and rare Adirondack books; a huge selection of used books; antique postcards, prints, and maps; pipe tobaccos and imported cigars. Worth a visit just to browse books from their lovely porch overlooking Mirror Lake. Open year-round; closed midweek in winter.

Saranac Lake

Fact & Fiction Book Shop (518-891-8067; 17 Broadway across from Mailboxes Etc.) Compact but well stocked independent bookshop. Open year-round Mon.–Sat.

North Country Community College (518-891-2915; Winona Ave.) College bookstore; general interest; magazines. Open fall–spring Mon.–Sat.

James Swedberg

Fact & Fiction Bookshop, in downtown Saranac Lake, is compact and complete.

NORTHWEST LAKES

Paul Smiths

Paul Smith's College Bookstore (518-327-6314; Rte. 30, Paul Smith's College, below the snack bar) Regional guides and histories; forestry books; topo maps; magazines. Open year-round Mon.–Sat.

Tupper Lake

Hoss's Country Corner (518-359-2092; 111 Park St.) Adirondack titles; outdoor recreation and natural history guides; cookbooks; Christian books; maps; clothing; gifts. Open year-round Mon.–Sat.

CENTRAL ADIRONDACKS

Blue Mountain Lake

Adirondack Museum Gatehouse Shop (518-352-7311; Rtes. 28/30) Complete assortment of Adirondack histories and guidebooks; books on antique boats and furniture; children's books; Adirondack folk music and storytelling on tape and CD; prints, postcards, stationery, and gifts. Open daily late May–Columbus Day. Mail-order catalog available.

Long Lake

Hoss's Country Corner (518-624-2481; Rte. 30) Adirondack histories and guidebooks, Christian books and tapes, children's nature books, general store. Hoss's sponsors Adirondack book-signing parties in July and August showcasing dozens of regional authors — worth a visit. Open year-round Mon.–Sat.

Old Forge

Old Forge Hardware (315-369-6100; Main St.) Way in the back of this enormous emporium is a huge bookstore with Adirondack histories and guidebooks, cookbooks, nonfiction, children's books, paperbacks, and art supplies. Open year-round Mon.–Sat.; daily in summer.

Speculator

Charles Johns Store (518-548-7451; Rte. 30) Between fresh produce and the deli counter are aisles of regional books, maps, and posters. Open daily, year-round.

BEYOND THE BLUE LINE

In ***Gloversville***, **Mysteries on Main** (518-725-7373; 43 N. Main St.) has an excellent selection of regional books, plus novels, children's books, magazines, and contemporary nonfiction. Surprisingly, at this writing, ***Glens Falls*** does not have a general-purpose bookstore at all. In ***Saratoga Springs***, **Craven Books** (518-583-0025; 440 Broadway) stocks thousands of titles, along with maps, magazines and cards; the regional section features folklore, history, guides, and natural history. Open daily year-round. Also in ***Saratoga***, **Lyrical Ballad** (518-584-8779; Phila St.) has a great assortment of old books and prints, and **Borders** plans to open a store on Broadway in 2000. Heading north to ***Plattsburgh***, the **Corner-Stone Bookshop** (518-561-0520; Corner Margaret and Court Sts.) has some 50,000 used books plus a good selection of regional titles; open all year.

Several regional publishers specialize in books of local interest and have mail-order catalogs: Countryman Press (802-457-1049; Box 175, Woodstock VT 05091), North Country Books (315-735-4877; 18 Irving Place, Utica NY 13501), Syracuse University Press (315-443-5534; 1600 Jamesville Ave., Syracuse NY 13244-5160), and Purple Mountain Press (800-325-2665; Box E-3, Fleischmanns NY 12430).

CLOTHING

Hunting for designer bargains in "shop till you drop" mode is best pursued outside the Adirondack Park. Here you'll find classic woolens, practical sportswear, and high-tech outer gear. Lake Placid's Main Street, which has a pleasant parade of shops and outlets, is described here; also listed below you'll find haberdasheries plus interesting new places and clothing designers.

LAKE GEORGE AND SOUTHEASTERN ADIRONDACKS

Bolton Landing

Bolton Bay Traders (518-644-2237; Main St.) Quality sportswear for men and women, including Merrill and Nike hiking boots; Columbia, Big Dog, and Sierra Designs jackets, shirts, pants, and shorts; outdoor guidebooks. Open year-round.

Lake George

Leather Outlet (518-668-3601; www.leathercompany.com; Rte. 9, 2 miles south of village) Jackets, motorcycle gear, gloves, belts, bags. Open daily in summer.

CHAMPLAIN VALLEY

Crown Point

Fritelli & Lockwood (518-597-3910; Rte. 22) Handwoven chenille and woolen fabrics made into tailored jackets, vests, and ties. By appointment only.

Essex

Natural Goods & Finery (Sharon Boisen; 518-963-8109; Main St.) Handmade cotton dresses; interesting jewelry; lovely fragrances and personal-care products. Like a shop you'd find on Martha's Vineyard. Open daily mid-June–mid-Sept.

HIGH PEAKS AND NORTHERN ADIRONDACKS

Lake Placid

The Bear Haus (518-523-3848; 23 Main St.) Men's and women's clothing, swimwear, and skiwear; Royal Robbins, Obermyer, and other quality labels. Open Mon.–Sat. year-round.

Eastern Mountain Sports (518-523-2505; 51 Main St.) Outdoor clothing and footgear by Woolrich, Patagonia, Merrill, Nike, and EMS. Open Mon.–Sat. year-round; daily in summer.

Far Mor's Kids (518-523-3990; 1 Main St.) "Far Mor" means grandmother in Swedish; picture an indulgent, tasteful granny and you've got a glimpse of this shop. Designer infant and children's clothes; educational toys and puzzles; quilts. Open year-round.

The Gap (518-523-4651; 55 Main St.) Hip outfits for all ages in flannel, denim, fleece, and khaki. Open daily year-round.

Great Range Outfitters (518-523-1650; 71 Main St.) Well-chosen men's and women's clothing; great selection of woolen outerwear and sweaters. Open daily year-round.

The In Step (518-523-9398; 35 Main St.) Designer shoes, stockings, and bags, featuring wool clogs to Mootsie's Tootsies. Open Mon.–Sat. year-round.

Ruthie's Run (518-523-3271; 11 Main St.) Men's and women's clothing, from Cambridge Dry Goods, Ruff Hewn, Tango, and such. Open Mon.–Sat. year-round.

Where'd You Get That Hat? (518-523-3101; 155 Main St.) The question friends back home are bound to ask. . . . Headgear of all descriptions; great selection of Converse high tops. Open year-round.

Saranac Lake

Cinderella's (518-891-4431; 44 Broadway) Handmade fashions for infants to teenagers; special-occasion dresses. Open Mon.–Sat. year-round.

T.F. Finnigan (518-891-1820; Main St., near the Adirondack Bank) Men's clothing, including Cross Creek, Nautica, B.D. Baggies; formal-wear rental and sales. Open Mon.–Sat. year-round.

Major Plowshares (518-891-7214; 28 Broadway) A surplus store, yes, but also the outlet for Wild Oats locally made children's clothing in woodland prints, corduroys, and denim. Open Mon.–Sat. year-round.

Mountain Gypsy (518-891-2770; 47 Broadway) Vintage clothing, fabrics, handbags. open Tues.–Sat.

Northern Light (Mercado del Sol, Rte. 86 across from Casa del Sol) Imported sweaters and clothing. Open Mon.–Sat. year-round.

NORTHWEST LAKES

Tupper Lake

Hoss's Country Corner (518-359-2092; 111 Park St.) From outerwear to expedition underwear for men, women, and children, plus outdoor supplies. Open Mon.–Sat. year-round.

CENTRAL ADIRONDACKS

Old Forge

Homecoming (315-369-2828; Main St. near the school) Nice new ladies' wear shop in a lovely old home. Great selection of summer linens and cotton dresses, beautiful sweaters. Closed winter.

Stuff from Other Countries (no phone; Main St.) Cotton and silk clothing from Guatemala, India, etc. Open Memorial Day–Columbus Day.

Speculator

From fleece to fine woolens, you can outfit the family at Speculator Department Store.

James Swedberg

Speculator Department Store (518-548-6123; Rte. 8) Just past the intersection with Rte. 30 is this 50-year-old landmark selling Woolrich sweaters, Jantzen swimwear, Lee jeans, and more Pendleton woolens than you can shake a spindle at. Open daily.

BEYOND THE BLUE LINE

They call it the "Million Dollar Half Mile," and it's just a quick toss of the gold card from ***Lake George Village***. Four separate plazas on both sides of U.S. Rte. 9 (near its intersection with Rte. 149) add up to outlet heaven for the dedicated shopper. On the west side of the road is **French Mountain Commons Outlet Center** (518-792-1483); on the east is **Log Jam Factory Stores** (518-792-5316), **Adirondack Factory Outlet Mall**, and **Lake George Plaza Factory Stores**. You'll find everything from Fieldcrest towels and Oneida flatware to lingerie, Nine West shoes, and Big Dog shirts.

In ***Plattsburgh***, the north and south **Champlain Centres** (518-561-8660) are close to the Northway and contain chains like Sears and Penneys plus dozens of other clothing stores. Off I-87 close to the Canadian border is **Miromar Factory Outlet Center** (518-298-3333) with 40-some shops.

CRAFT SHOPS

Functional handmade items have always been part of Adirondack life; in the last few decades, the region has attracted contemporary craftspeople from outside, and encouraged local folks to rediscover old-time products. Part of this renaissance has been nurtured by the Adirondack North Country Association (ANCA), a non-profit group that published the first "Craft Trails" map highlighting studios and stores more than fifteen years ago and operated a huge store in Lake Placid for several years. For a free copy of the map, write to ANCA (183 Broadway, Saranac Lake).

Listed below you'll find craft shops showcasing a variety of media. Many of the studios are in private homes, so it's a good idea to call ahead. Further on in this chapter you'll find fiber and fabric artists and basket makers; carvers of wood, plaster and other materials; and furniture makers.

LAKE GEORGE AND SOUTHEASTERN ADIRONDACKS

Bolton Landing

Trees (518-644-5756; Rte. 9N) Adirondack chairs; wooden toys, baskets, balsam items; regional books, prints, and photos. Open mid-June–Columbus Day.

Chestertown

Chestertown's Harness Shop Artisans has prints, posters, paintings, and pottery.

James Swedberg

Harness Shop Artisans (518-494-3295; Main St.; www.harnessshop.com) Quilts, carvings, toys, jewelry from more than a hundred craftspeople. Huge selection of framed paintings, drawings, and photographs. Meet selected artists, photographers, authors, and craftspeople on Saturdays in July and August; big tent sale on Labor Day weekend. Open daily July–Oct.; Fri.–Sun. Nov.–June. Small mail-order catalog available.

Miss Hester's Emporium (518-494-7940; Main St., next to the Main St. Ice Cream Parlor) Songbirds made by local carvers, quilts and wallhangings, baskets, antiques, cards, and gifts. Open year-round.

Diamond Point

Hearthside Artisans II (518-668-2172; Rte. 9N) Quilts, pottery, woodenware, toys, Christmas items, and handcrafted goods by some 65 area artisans. Open Thurs.–Sun. spring and fall; daily June–Oct.

CHAMPLAIN VALLEY

Elizabethtown

River Run Gifts (518-873-6574; Water St.) Paintings by regional artists; local crafts and toys. Open daily mid-June–Oct.

Studio Showcase (518-873-6836/2311; Water St.) Baskets, handmade clothing, jewelry, and toys. Open Mon.–Sat. mid-May–Oct.

Essex

Adirondack Chandler (518-963-4923; Main St.) Hand-dipped candles made in the shop, plus cool jewelry made locally from European glass, gifts. Open daily in summer, fall and winter weekends.

The Store in Essex (518-963-7551; 1 Main St.) This 1810-vintage stone building next to the Lake Champlain ferry landing houses an eclectic assortment of contemporary jewelry and clothing, African masks and baskets, designer glass and pottery, plus gourmet food from Vermont and the Adirondacks. Definitely fun, especially if you're traveling with 13-year-old girls. Open daily mid-May–late Oct.

Peru

Yarborough Square (518-643-7057; Bear Swamp Rd. 1/4 mi. west of Northway Exit 35) Works by 150+ North Country and Canadian artisans; open all year.

Ticonderoga

Hancock House Gallery (518-585-7868; Moses Circle) Works by local artists; historical souvenir items. Open Weds.–Sat. year-round.

<u>*Westport*</u>

Artifacts and Westport Trading Co. (Kip Trienens; 518-962-4801; Main St.) Bark and twig baskets, pottery, jewelry, contemporary furniture, stained glass, and eclectic crafts. Open year-round, most of the time.

HIGH PEAKS AND NORTHERN ADIRONDACKS

<u>*Keene*</u>

Evergreen Trading Company (518-576-9141; Rte. 73 in same building as A Piece of Cake) Quilts, pottery, toys, candles, cards. Open year-round.

Keene Trading Post and North Country Taxidermy (518-576-3549; Rte. 73) You can't miss this place — there's usually a full-size stuffed creature out front. Bring a camera so the kids can pose next to the moose or mountain lion. If you'd like to buy a souvenir antler or two, there are boxes full of them, plus rustic furniture, birchbark items, etc. Bearskin rugs are a specialty. Open year-round.

<u>*Lake Placid*</u>

Adirondack Crafts Center (518-523-2062; 93 Saranac Ave.) More than 250 upstate New York craftspeople are represented here. Jewelry made of silver, porcupine quills, semiprecious stones, butterfly wings, and feathers; designer clothing for dolls, children, and adults; leather bags and backpacks; quilts; handmade paper; woodcarvings of fish, birds, folk figures; baskets; pottery; rustic and contemporary painted furniture; prints; photographs; stationery. Open Mon.–Sat. year-round; daily in July–Aug.

Caribou Trading Co. (518-523-1152; Hilton Plaza, Main St.) Pottery, jewelry, kites and mobiles, woodenware, handwovens. Open year-round.

Guadalupe's Mexican Imports (518-523-9845; 132 Main St.) Tinware, glass, textiles, pottery, sweaters, and jewelry from Mexico and Central America. Open Mon.–Sat. year-round.

Nature Unlimited (518-523-8733; Main St., near the Gap) Polished rock plates, paperweights, bookends, etc.; jewelry; nature toys. Open year-round.

Po Polsku (518-523-1311; 12 Saranac Ave., at the Ramada Inn) Folk crafts imported directly from Poland: embroidered clothing; wooden boxes and plates; dolls and toys; textiles; paper cutouts. Open year-round; daily in summer. Catalog available.

<u>*Saranac Lake*</u>

Smith's Taxidermy (518-891-6289; Saranac Ave. near Luna Java coffeehouse) Rustic furniture by Thomas Phillips and the Smith brothers; antler chandeliers, pottery, baskets. Open year-round.

NORTHWEST LAKES

Childwold

Leather Artisan (Tom Amoroso; 518-359-3102; www.leatherartisan.com; Rte. 3) Classic leather handbags, wallets, belts, and backpacks made on the premises; quality crafts; Naot shoes and Minnetonka moccasins. If you want a gorgeous made-to-order leather golf bag, look no farther. Open year-round; closed midweek in winter.

Harrisville

Tripp's Adirondack Gift Shop (315-543-7112; Rte. 812, off Rte. 3) Black-ash baskets made here, also balsam products, rustic furniture, and more. Open daily in summer.

CENTRAL ADIRONDACKS

Blue Mountain Lake

Blue Mtn. Designs (Lory Wedow; 518-352-7361; Rte. 30) Blue Mtn. Lake's old-time schoolhouse is packed with contemporary jewelry, fine rustic and camp-style furniture, wrought iron, woodenware, pottery, handwovens, silk-screen prints, photographs, etchings, stationery, candles, toys, leather, and clothing. Also Lory creates custom-cast hardware for Adirondack guideboats. The problem of how to entertain the kids while parents do some serious shopping has been solved amusingly at Blue Mtn. Designs: there's a big wooden sluiceway outside for gem mining. A sack of sand and assorted precious pebbles costs about five bucks and can avert a meltdown, especially when followed by an ice cream bar or fresh-squeezed lemonade from the adjacent stand. Open daily mid-May–mid-Oct.; weekends before Christmas.

Long Lake

Mountain Medley (Ed Wight; 518-624-4999; Rte. 30 next to Hoss's Country Corner) Adirondack chairs, stoneware pottery, rocking horses, loon and Canada goose planters, lamps, and more all made by Ed, plus baskets, jewelry, quilts, dolls, toys, candles, and so on from regional artisans. Open daily mid-June–mid-Oct.

Mayfield

Havlick Snowshoe Co. (Richard Havlick; 518-661-6447; Rte. 30) Handmade snowshoes and snowshoe furniture, Adirondack pack baskets, and outdoor gear. Open daily, year-round.

Northville

Adirondack Country Store (518-863-6056; 252 N. Main St.) Rambling old home filled with quality local crafts: hickory and oak rockers made by Amish woodworkers, quilts, handwovens, jewelry, hand-spun yarns, baskets, pottery, toys, decoys, Adirondack books. New in 1997 is a small but excellent mail-order catalog. Open daily Memorial Day–Columbus Day; Tues.–Sun. Columbus Day–Dec. and Apr.–Memorial Day; winter weekends.

Old Forge

The Artworks (315-369-2007; Main St.) Cooperative gallery featuring North Country artisans. Ash-splint baskets, stained glass, hooked rugs, woodcarvings, patchwork quilts and pillows, toys, and jewelry. Open year-round.

The Broom Man (315-369-6503; 1146 Main St.) Handmade brooms, rakes, and pitchforks; hand-loomed rugs; sweaters; baskets; wagons. Open daily Memorial Day–Labor Day; weekends in spring and fall.

Hand of Man Gallery (315-369-3381; Main St., near the Town of Webb school) Trendy glass, pottery, and jewelry; handmade lampshades, turned woodenware. Open daily Memorial Day–fall.

Mountain Peddler (315-369-3428; Main St.) Quilts, tinware, baskets, woodenware, gifts. Open year-round; daily Memorial Day–Columbus Day.

Raquette Lake

Sagamore Bookstore (315-354-9905; at Sagamore Lodge) Rustic furniture and miniatures; ash-splint baskets, stained glass, wrought iron, carved and painted shelf fungus, handmade paper. Available by special order are place settings of the Vanderbilts' woodsy china, reissued by Syracuse China in 1997. Open daily Memorial Day–Labor Day; spring and fall weekends.

Speculator

Red Leaf Designs (888-584-8010; Rte. 30 across from Mountain Lakes Real Estate) Packbaskets, pottery, furniture and shelves, photographs, custom-embroidered clothing. Open daily in summer.

FAIRS AND FLEA MARKETS

For a true shopping adventure, consider the outdoor extravaganzas: from May through Columbus Day, many Adirondack communities sponsor craft fairs and flea markets. At one end of the spectrum are juried craft shows with high-quality items, while flea markets and town-wide garage sales escape succinct categorization as to just what you can expect to find. But that's the fun of those affairs — nosing past the velvet paintings and tube socks to discover a box of stereo views of Ausable Chasm. Listed below are some annual events arranged by region and date; check local newspapers for information about other festivals. The "Inside & Out" calendar of events in *Adirondack Life* (www.adirondacklife.com) is another good source of information.

LAKE GEORGE AND SOUTHEASTERN ADIRONDACKS

Hobby Fair (518-532-7675; Town Park, Schroon Lake) 50+ craft booths, music, rustic-furniture building and other demonstrations, third Sat. in July. Also that day in Schroon Lake, the Community Church Bazaar, on Rte. 9.

Riverview Arts & Crafts Festival (518-696-3423; Lakeside Park, Lake Luzerne) Craft fair, third Sat. in July.

Quality Antique Show–Under the Big Top (518-644-3831; Bolton Central School Ballfield, Bolton Landing) Antique show with 30+ dealers, first weekend in Aug.

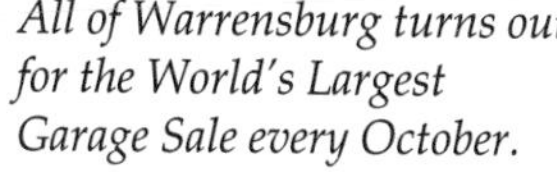

All of Warrensburg turns out for the World's Largest Garage Sale every October.

James Swedberg

World's Largest Garage Sale (518-623-2161; throughout Warrensburg) The traffic backs up to Northway Exit 23 for this town-wide blow-out; more than 500 dealers, plus many local families offer a bewildering array of items for sale. Plan to walk once you get to town; there are shuttle buses from the parking lots. First weekend in Oct.

CHAMPLAIN VALLEY

Marigold Festival (518-962-8383; Main St., Westport) Craft fair on the library lawn, games and events for children. Memorial Day weekend.

Old-Time Folkcraft Fair (518-963-4478; Paine Memorial Library, Willsboro) Last Sat. in July.

Champ Day (518-546-7261; Main St., Port Henry) Craft-and-food fair with activities for children celebrating "Champ," Lake Champlain's legendary monster, first Sat. in Aug.

Downtown Essex Day (518-963-4287; Main St., Essex) Craft fair, games, and races, first Sat. in Aug.

HIGH PEAKS AND NORTHERN ADIRONDACKS

Craftfest (518-891-1489; The Lodge, Lake Clear) Juried craft show featuring furniture, pottery, baskets, jewelry, stained glass, and more, third weekend in July.

Peak of Summer Country Fair (518-946-2255; Wilmington Town Park, Wilmington) Craft fair and games for children, third Sat. in July.

Adirondack Antiques Show and Sale (518-891-4141; Harrietstown Town Hall, Main St., Saranac Lake) A high-summer tradition and one of the best around. Late July.

Kiwanis Crafts Fair (518-946-2551; Village Green, Jay) Outdoor craft fair, second weekend in Aug.

Artisans' Studio Tours (518-946-2445) Craftspeople in the Jay–Wilmington–Upper Jay area open their studios to the public, in mid-Aug.

High Peaks Arts and Antiques Show (518-576-4719; Marcy Airfield, Keene Valley) Large assortment of crafts and regional antiques in late Aug.

Adirondack Antiques Auction (518-523-2445; Horse Show Grounds, Lake Placid) Boats, rustic furniture, camp kitsch, prints, and photos in late Sept. usually the day after the Adirondack Museum Antiques Show.

NORTHWEST LAKES

Backwoods Craft Fair and Flea Market (315-848-2391; Rte. 3, Cranberry Lake) Dozens of local artisans selling their wares and demonstrating their skills plus flea market, third weekend in July.

Eastern Star Flea Market (518-359-2542; Municipal Park, across from the A&P, Tupper Lake) More than 300 dealers — everything from Adirondack ephemera to used furniture and new footwear, plus fried dough, sausage-and-pepper sandwiches, and other delicious, artery-clogging carnival chow, third weekend in Aug.

CENTRAL ADIRONDACKS

Neighbor Day (315-369-6411; Arts Center, Old Forge) Craft fair with music, special exhibitions, chicken barbecue, and events for children, second Sun. in June.

Central Adirondack Craft Fair (315-369-6411; sponsored by the Arts Center, Old Forge) Craft fair with 75+ exhibitors, first weekend in July.

Caroga Historical Museum Craft Fair (518-835-4400; Caroga Historical Museum, London Bridge Rd., Caroga Lake) Annual outdoor craft fair, second Sat. in July.

Antique Show and Sale (518-624-3077; Town Hall, Long Lake) Mid-July.

Arts in the Park Craft Fair (315-357-5501; Arrowhead Park, Inlet) Outdoor craft fair, third weekend in July.

Speculator Flea Market (518-548-4521; Ballfield, Speculator) 50+ vendors, third Sat. in July.

Piseco Craft Fair (518-548-8732; Piseco Community Hall, Piseco) 50+ craft booths, last Sat. in July.

Adirondack Gem and Mineral Show (518-251-2612; Gore Mt. Ski Area, Peaceful Valley Rd., North Creek) 20+ rock dealers, plus gem-cutting demonstrations and lectures, first weekend in Aug.

Heart of the Park Craft Fair (518-624-3077; Mount Sabattis Park Pavilion, Long Lake) Craft fair "under the big top," first Sun. in Aug.

TWIGS Arts and Crafts Show (518-548-4521; Rte. 30, Speculator) 75+ craftspeople, second Thurs. in Aug.

Town-wide Garage Sale (518-624-3077; throughout Long Lake) Long Lake introduces drive-by shopping, second Sat. in Aug.

Rustic Furniture Makers' Fair (518-352-7311; Adirondack Museum, Blue Mtn. Lake) Showcase of more than 40 rustic furniture builders, early Sept. Museum admission required for fair visitors.

Adirondack Antiques Show (518-352-7311; Adirondack Museum, Blue Mtn. Lake) Ephemera, quilts, furniture, photographs from some 90 dealers, on the grounds of the Adirondack Museum, late Sept.

Antique Show & Sale (315-369-6411; Arts Center/Old Forge) First weekend in Oct.

FIBER AND FABRIC; BASKETS AND BALSAM

Fiber arts encompass more than things made of thread and yarn; handmade paper relies on wood and other plant fibers, while traditional and modern baskets use wood splints, grasses, leaves, and ropes. The needle arts in the true Adirondack sense of the word include sweet-smelling pillows and sachets; balsam fir *(Abies balsamea)* needles are gathered, dried and stuffed into calico fabric bags and pillows. Listed below you'll find an assortment of quilters, basket makers, paper makers, spinners, weavers, and balsam crafters from across the park. (Check under "Clothing" in this chapter for handmade ready-to-wear items.) If you'd like to visit sheep, goat, and rabbit farms, there's an annual **Washington County Wool and Fiber Tour** held on the last weekend in April; Glens Falls newspapers usually publish a map of participating farms. If you'd like to experience an old-fashioned balsam bee — from chopping the needles to hand-stitching pillows — the **Big Moose Community Chapel** (315-357-5841;

Big Moose Rd.) holds one in late July; the extra-fresh pillows are sold at the annual bazaar, held on the first Saturday in August.

North of the Adirondack Park border, on the St. Lawrence River, is Akwesasne, home of many Mohawk families, an excellent place to look for baskets woven of ash splints and sweetgrass. The **Akwesasne Cultural Center Museum** (315-346-2240; Rte. 37, Hogansburg) has a shop selling all kinds of baskets, from tiny thimble cases to full-size pack baskets, plus moccasins decorated with beadwork and porcupine quills. Call for hours and directions; a group of Mohawk artisans is putting together a catalog of fine crafts.

LAKE GEORGE AND SOUTHEASTERN ADIRONDACKS

Putnam Station

Hawk Mountain Crafts (518-547-9511; Box 28) Angora and mohair yarns from their own goats.

Warrensburg

Blue Heron Designs (Charlene Leary; 518-623-3189; Truesdale Hill Rd.) Fine handwovens and women's clothing from her fabrics. Call ahead.

CHAMPLAIN VALLEY

Crown Point

Fritelli & Lockwood Textiles (518-597-3910; Rte. 22) Colorful and elegant handwoven fabrics made into tailored jackets, vests, and scarves, available from retail craft shops in the region. By appointment.

Elizabethtown

Studio Showcase (518-873-6836/2311; Water St.) Baskets made by six different weavers; handmade clothing, jewelry and toys. Open Mon.–Sat. mid-May–Oct.

Essex

Pioneer Weave (Mary Beth Brennan; 518-963-8067) Traditional finely woven rag rugs in assorted sizes and made to order; available at Natural Goods & Finery and Third Time Around, both in Essex. Call ahead.

Willsboro

Alice Wand and Dennis Kalma (518-963-4582; 44 Spear Rd.) Handmade paper sculptures and wall pieces. Call ahead.

HIGH PEAKS AND NORTHERN ADIRONDACKS

Lake Placid

Mark Kurtz

Main Street, Lake Placid.

Quaker Mtn. Studio (Annoel Krider; Box 163) Exceptional tapestries and naturally inspired rugs, featured on the cover of *Adirondack Life* magazine. Works displayed at the Lake Placid Lodge. Commissions by appointment.

Newcomb

Upper Hudson Woolery (Judy Blanchette; 518-582-2144; Rte. 28N) Hand-spun yarns from Judy's own sheep; hand-knit sweaters; spinning wheels; spinning lessons. Open daily year-round.

Saranac Lake

Asplin Tree Farms (518-891-5783; Rte. 86) The best-smelling store in the Adirondacks, filled with balsam pillows and products. Open daily June 1–Dec. 24.

A Basket Case (518-891-2423; 800-263-0480; Beechwood Dr.) Pack baskets, gift baskets, baskets filled to order. By appointment.

NORTHWEST LAKES

Paul Smiths

Adirondack Mountain Basketry (Tracy Santagate; 518-327-3665; HCR Box 37) Willow and reed baskets; traditional Adirondack ash-splint pack baskets; lessons. By appointment only; mail-order brochure available.

Tupper Lake

Edith Mitchell (518-359-7830; 4 Wawbeek Ave.) Traditional and contemporary quilts in all sizes by one of the leading artists in the Adirondacks. By appointment only.

Genevive Sutter (518-359-2675; Raquette River Dr.) Choice pictorial quilts of North Country scenes and historic sites. By appointment only.

Thomas and Judy Phillips (518-359-9648; Star Rte. 2) Ash-splint melon, apple, and potato baskets in various sizes; big-bellied pack baskets; rustic furniture. By appointment only.

CENTRAL ADIRONDACKS

Blue Mountain Lake

Woven with Wood (Tracy Meehan; 518-352-7721; Durant Rd.) Ash-splint baskets including fine Shaker-style baskets; workshops; demonstrations; by appointment.

Indian Lake

Homemade Quilts and Crafts (Kathleen Herrick; 518-648-5360; Rte. 28) Tied quilts, patchwork pillows, dolls, baskets, balsam pillows. Open daily Memorial Day–Columbus Day; other times by chance or appointment.

Long Lake

Adirondack Basket Case (Patty Farrell; 518-624-2501; Rte. 28N at Northwoods Garden Center) Ash-splint baskets of all sizes and styles. Open daily in summer; weekends in fall and winter.

FURNITURE

Regional woodworkers create furniture in a variety of styles, from Shaker-inspired designs, to rugged sculptural pieces, to the straightforward Adirondack chairs that now come in an infinite range of permutations. Several of the rustic workers listed below have brochures or catalogs that you may request by mail; if you're planning to visit an individual's shop, call ahead. Note that many studios are in private homes, so don't expect a large ready-made inventory on hand. For a cyberspace overview, check out www.adirondackwood.com. It's updated weekly and includes sources for quality hardwood lumber if you wish to build your own furniture. For classes in furniture-making, include rustic methods, the arts centers listed in Chapter Four, *Culture*, offer hands-on workshops.

LAKE GEORGE AND SOUTHEASTERN ADIRONDACK

Adirondack

Lean-2 Studio (518-494-5185; 800-554-5185; Pease Hill Rd.) Table lamps, hanging lamps, and beautiful hand-painted shades, some with leaves and pine needles embedded in vellum. By appointment.

Bolton Landing

Thomas W. Brady, Furnituremaker (518-644-9801; 87A North Bolton Rd.) Elegant contemporary furniture in cherry, walnut, and figured maple: screens, bedsteads, desks, blanket chests, tables, and chairs, some with painted motifs or in Shaker designs. Color flier available; open year-round by appointment only.

Chestertown

Chester Creek Woodworks (518-494-0003; Friends Lake Rd.) Furniture and useful wooden ware. Open weekends or by appointment.

Diamond Point

Pine Plank (Don Farleigh; 518-644-9420) Adirondack chairs, benches, and tables in pine. Open year-round Tues.–Sun.

S. T. Siadak (518-644-9703; Timlo Dr.) Mission-style Adirondack light fixtures for interior and exterior use. By appointment.

Lake George

American Guild of Rustic Masters (518-668-0443; Rtes. 9 & 9N south of Lake George village) Three-story house featuring furniture by Barry Gregson, Barney Bellinger, Jean Armstrong, and leading rustic makers from across the country like Daniel Mack. Closed Mon. in summer. Call for off-season visits.

Ralph Kylloe Gallery (518-696-4100; www.mediausa.com/ny/lg/rkylloe; Rte. 9N 2.7 miles south of the Northway) Huge old log cabin packed with antlers, twigs, bark, and leather in and on every kind of antique; worth a detour. Open year-round; call ahead.

Moose Creek Ltd. North (518-745-7340; www.moosecreekltd.com; Intersection Rtes. 9 & 149) Interior design service, rugs, accessories, new and antique Mission and rustic furniture. Open daily year-round.

Schroon Lake

Furniture-maker Barry Gregson in his Schroon Lake studio.

James Swedberg

Adirondack Rustics Gallery (Barry Gregson; 518-532-9384; Charley Hill Rd.; www.adkrustic.com) Rustic tables, chairs, settees, beds, corner cupboards, and sideboards, made of burls, cedar, white-birch bark, and assorted woods. Clocks, frames, and selected items by Jerry and Jessica Farrell, Jean Armstrong, and others. Worth a special trip; open summers Tues.–Sat.; call ahead.

CHAMPLAIN VALLEY

Keeseville

Willsboro Wood Products (518-834-5200; Ausable St.) Sturdy and comfortable beds, tables, chairs, dressers, mirrors, benches, and settees made of white cedar; you've seen these in the L.L. Bean catalog. Color catalog available; open Mon.–Fri. year-round.

Mineville

Essex Industries (518-942-6671; Pelfisher Rd.) Canoe and guideboat accessories: backrests, caned seats, yokes; folding canvas camp stools and shopping bags. Flier and price list available; open Mon.–Fri. year-round.

HIGH PEAKS AND NORTHERN ADIRONDACKS

Cadyville

Wood Grain Furniture (518-293-6268; www.adirondackfurniture.com; Rte. 3) Unfinished chairs, tables, beds, outdoor furniture in Shaker, country French, and Adirondack styles. Open year-round.

Jay

Earth Works (David Douglas; 518-647-1279; North Jay Rd.) Mirrors, lamps, shelves, and more made from birch bark and twigs. By appointment.

Rusted Rock (Paul Bodean; 518-647-5475; North Jay) Great source for birch-bark frames, mirrors, etc.; buy the frame stock cut to your specifications. By appointment.

Rustic Woodworks (Wayne Ignatuk; 518-946-7439; 55 Trumbulls Corners Rd. off Rte. 9N) Sculptural furniture with fine dovetailing and mortise and tenon construction; color catalog available. Call ahead.

Keene

Hurricane Mountain Industries (518-576-2015; Hurricane Rd.) Amusing rustic clocks with wildlife dioramas, lamps, desks, chairs. Call ahead.

Lake Placid

Adirondack Furniture (David Hall; 518-523-2697; 105 Saranac Ave.) Cherry, maple, and birch tables, chairs, desks, dressers, beds, picture frames, and mirrors. Open year-round.

North Country Wood Works (518-523-4531; Rte. 86 W. of town) Unfinished pine Adirondack chairs, tables, wall cabinets, shelves, planters. Open Mon.–Sat. year-round.

Twigs (518-523-0055; Sentinel Rd. near the Horse Show Grounds) Big shop with rustic furniture by several makers; look for the giant chair. Open year-round; closed Tues.

Newcomb

Truly Adirondack Crafts (Bruce Wight; 518-582-3581; Rte. 28N) Rustic coat hooks, towel bars, etc., plus simple furniture. Call ahead.

Saranac Lake

Adirondack Antler Art (Charles Jessie; 518-891-5383; McKenzie Pond Rd.) Chandeliers, lamps, and sconces made from moose and whitetail deer antlers. Call ahead.

Vermontville

Forest Murmurs (Glenn Bauer; 518-327-9373; Rte. 3) Wall secretaries and shelves with antlers; birch-bark signs for your home or camp; lamps, mirrors, frames, and sconces. Price list and brochure available; open summer weekends; call ahead.

NORTHWEST LAKES

Lake Clear

Jay Major Dawson (518-891-5075; off Rte. 30) Need a rustic gate or archway over the entrance to your own Great Camp? Jay's the guy. He'll also make custom railings, built-in furniture, and lawn pieces. By appointment.

Paul Smiths

Train Brook Forest (David Woodward; 518-327-3498; Easy St.) Travel trunks and document boxes made of wood and leather; wrought-iron fireplace screens with wildlife silhouette designs; fireplace accessories; iron lighting fixtures in Arts-and-Crafts designs. Open year-round; by appointment only.

Tupper Lake

Jean Armstrong (518-359-9983; Big Wolf Lake) Rustic boxes, frames, and furniture, fungus art. Summer only, by appointment.

Michael Trivieri (518-359-7151; Moody Rd.) Burl bowls and tables; woodcarvings; mantels; custom railings and rustic trimwork done on site. By appointment.

Thomas and Judy Phillips (518-359-9648; Star Rte. 2) Ash-splint baskets with sculptural branch handles; twig-style and birch-bark chairs, tables, benches, and beds; cedar outdoor furniture; rustic furniture restoration. Price list available; open by appointment only.

CENTRAL ADIRONDACKS

Indian Lake

Backwoods Furnishings (Ken Heitz; 518-251-3327; Rte. 28) A Paul Bunyan-size log chair arches over Ken's driveway, marking the home of one of the originators of the Adirondack rustic revival. Twig, birch-bark, and cedar beds, tables, sideboards, settees, rockers, and custom orders. Ken's furniture has been featured in *House Beautiful, House and Garden, Gourmet,* and many other publications. Color brochure available; open year-round by appointment only.

Long Lake

Cold River Gallery (Jamie Sutliffe; 518-624-3581; www.coldriverwoodworks.com; Deerland Rd.) Painted arch-top trunks; carved furniture, mirrors and frames with wildlife designs; custom doors and signs. Open year-round by appointment only.

Mountain Medley (Ed Wight; 518-624-4999; Rte. 30) Curved back, classic, and child-size Adirondack chairs in stock or by special order. Open daily late June–Columbus Day.

North Country Designs (James Howard; 518-624-3813; Newcomb Rd.) Bark-and-twig hutches, desks, corner cupboards; burl tables, rocking chairs. Open year-round.

Mayfield

Sampson Bog Studio (Barney and Susan Bellinger; 518-661-6563) Twig mosaic and birch-bark tables, desks, wall shelves, benches with fine hand-painted details and graceful lines. Call ahead.

Northville

Peter Winter's Rustic Studio (518-863-6555; 132 Division St. near the Grand Union) Rustic furniture and accessories, open daily in summer.

Old Forge

Old Forge Woodmaker (315-369-3535; Main St.) Adirondack chairs and benches; tables, bookshelves, and wooden toys. Open Weds.–Mon. Memorial Day–Labor Day; weekends in spring and fall.

Speculator

Jerry's Wood Shop (518-548-5041; www.adirondack.net/products/woodshop; Rte. 30) Adirondack chairs and settees that fold for storage; picnic tables; lawn furniture. Open daily year-round.

GENERAL STORES

In a town that shall remain nameless, there's an abandoned cobblestone building with a sign proclaiming that it's the "Shop of Three Wonders: Wonder Where It Came From, Wonder What It Costs, and Wonder How Long It's Been Here." Those kinds of intellectual exercises make an expedition to a real general store fun. Chances are you'll find odd things like nail pullers and chick-feeding troughs right alongside the glass percolator tops and sugar shakers and an aisle over from the suspenders and boot socks, around the corner from the chips and salsa. Don't worry about the dust; don't be afraid to ask the price. If you can't find it here, you can probably live without it.

Some general stores really take the word "general" to heart, so that you can pick out a nice graduation gift as well as the fixings for an afternoon picnic, including sunglasses, bug dope, and sustenance. Each shop has its own personality, and they all occupy a hallowed place within the community.

LAKE GEORGE AND SOUTHEASTERN ADIRONDACKS

Adirondack

Adirondack General Store (Joan and Dick Lomnitzer; 518-494-4408; East Shore Dr.) There's a fine line between country-looking places that try too hard and end up cutesy, and those authentic country stores that mix the antique and the modern — and turn out charming. This place, which was the company store for a tannery dating back to the 1850s, hits the nail on the head. You can hang out by the wood stove when it's cold, read the paper on the porch when it's warm, buy a nice gift, or get milk, eggs, bread, and such for camping in Pharaoh Lake Wilderness Area. The deli is very good, Joan's homemade soups are scrumptious, and if there are any pies left, grab one. They're the best around. Open year-round.

Brant Lake

Daby's General Store (518-494-4039; Rte. 8) Along with the Freihofer's donuts, videos, cold beer, and wristwatches are display cases and shelves with 1940s-vintage dolls, old bottles and toys, fancy knives (for looking at, not for sale). You can find just about everything here, and even if you only buy some Popsicles, the view down Mill Pond toward the cobblestone library perched out over the water is worth the trip. Open year-round.

HIGH PEAKS AND NORTHERN ADIRONDACKS

Bloomingdale

Norman's Wholesale Grocery (518-891-1890; Rte. 3) Norman's has been in the same family since it began in 1902, and display drawers still have ornate hardware and lettering declaring "Socks and Mittens" or "Silks and Laces." For retail customers, the stock is mainly convenience-store items, but the place still feels very much like the old times when the stagecoach stopped here. Open year-round.

NORTHWEST LAKES

Cranberry Lake

The Emporium (315-848-2140; Rte. 3) Tiny place crammed with souvenirs, maps, fishing tackle, announcements of coming attractions, canned goods, frozen treats, and T-shirts, but there's even more — the Emporium is a marina with gas pumps, water taxi, and a big long weathered wooden dock. This kind of place used to be common in the Adirondacks, and the Emporium is one of the few lakeside general stores that remains. Open daily year-round.

CENTRAL ADIRONDACKS

Indian Lake

Pine's Country Store (518-648-5212; Rte. 28) Clothing, garden equipment, extensive hardware and houseware selection. Also renting yard equipment, bikes, etc. Open year-round.

Long Lake

Hoss's Country Corner (John and Lorrie Hosley; 518-624-2481; corner Rtes. 30 & 28N) Exemplary modern general store with aisles of groceries, fresh meats and deli items; Woolrich clothing for men and women, camp furnishings; stuffed animals; quilts, rugs, and baskets galore; cold beer; topo maps; Adirondack, outdoor, children's, and Christian books; jewelry; soaps and candles; out-of-town newspapers; film . . . the list is nearly endless, as is the rambling frame building that goes up, down, and around. Open Mon.–Sat. year-round.

Minerva

Murdie's General Store (518-251-2076; Rte. 28N) If you're on the Teddy Roosevelt Memorial Highway retracing his 1901 midnight ride to the presidency, and find that you need gas, nightcrawlers, crusher hat, six-pack, transmission fluid, ice cream, spaghetti, or maps, well, look no farther. Open year-round.

Old Forge

Old Forge Hardware (315-369-6100; Main St.) A visit to Old Forge Hardware is to Adirondack shopping as a trip to the Adirondack Museum is to regional history. This coliseum-size landmark bills itself as the "Adirondacks' Most General Store," a title with which we can't argue. Need a pack basket?

Old Forge Hardware — nearly a city block long — is a destination even during mud season.

James Swedberg

Bamboo steamer for your wok? Spar varnish? Snowshoes? Reflective dog collar to fit a Newfoundland? Authentic shade for your antique Aladdin lamp? Spiles for maple sugaring? Replacement handle for your peavey? You can spend an entire day here. Open year-round.

Raquette Lake

Raquette Lake Supply (315-354-4301; downtown) The Dillon family has owned Raquette Lake Supply in one manifestation or another for more than a century. The building is huge, with the post office, a bakery, and the Tap Room on one side; a Laundromat on another; the store takes up most of the floor space facing the water. There's a soda fountain, meat counter, dairy case, and groceries, plus toy tomahawks, vintage postcards, and fish poles. This is the only place in the park where you can get honest-to-gosh, cut-from-the-lake ice for your cooler; the huge bluish blocks come with a frosting of sawdust that a quick plunge in the lake rinses off. Open year-round. If you're around in February for the annual ice-cutting weekend, drop by for a glimpse of a time-honored process.

Sabael

The Lake Store (Eris Thompson; 518-648-5222; Rte. 30) Toys, gifts, sports gear, souvenirs, moccasins, and clothing, plus a summertime soda fountain, year-round deli, and all the major food groups. Open year-round.

Stillwater

Stillwater Shop (315-376-2110; Stillwater Rd. at the boat launch) A true wilderness outpost, with food, gear, boat rentals, gas, snowmobile rentals, and a seaplane base. Open year-round.

GLASS

A handful of glass workers ply their trade in the Adirondacks, making custom beveled or stained-glass windows. In ***Westport***, visit ***Westport Trading*** (Kip Trienens; 518-962-4801; Main St.) for architectural stained-glass windows, panels, and mirrors in stock or made to order; repairs for antique stained glass. Kip's shop is open most of the time, year-round; drop-ins welcome. In ***Old Forge***, for Tiffany-style shades and lamps, the venerable ***Meyda Stained Glass Studio*** (315-369-6636; Main St.) has a great selection, plus planters, jewelry boxes, and mirrors. Open daily Memorial Day–Labor Day.

JEWELRY & GEM SHOPS

Many of the craft shops listed above carry silver, gold, or porcelain jewelry by local artisans; the jewelers and mineral shops described below specialize in contemporary designs or native gemstones.

LAKE GEORGE AND SOUTHEASTERN ADIRONDACKS

Pottersville

Natural Stone Bridge and Caves (518-494-2283; off Rte. 9N) Extensive mineral shop plus sluiceway where the kids can pan for gems. Open daily in summer.

HIGH PEAKS AND NORTHERN ADIRONDACKS

Lake Placid

Arthur Volmrich (518-523-2970; 99 Main St.) Amusing earrings and necklaces mixing antique charms, buttons, and stones with modern components; turquoise bracelets and watchbands; custom rings; repairs and resettings. Open Mon.–Sat. year-round.

Darrah Cooper Jewelers (518-523-2774; www.mountain-air.com/jewelry; 10 Main St., next to the Hilton) Delightful sterling silver and gold charms and earrings representing miniature North Country objects: pack baskets, canoe paddles, guideboats, oars, pine cones, and Adirondack chairs. Also rings, bracelets, and necklaces in precious stones, silver, and gold. Open Mon.–Sat. year-round.

Spruce Mountain Designs (518-523-9212; Box 205) Adirondack wildflowers in sterling silver and gold. By appointment only.

CENTRAL ADIRONDACKS

Blue Mountain Lake

At Blue Mt. Designs, youngsters can pan for gems while parents seek out quality crafts.

James Swedberg

Blue Mtn. Designs (Lory Wedow; 518-352-7361; Rtes. 28/30) Classic contemporary cast and hand-fabricated silver and 14k gold: rings, earrings, handmade chains, pins, bracelets, Adirondack charms, and necklaces. Also cast hardware for antique boats. Open daily Memorial Day–Columbus Day, plus fall and winter weekends.

Long Lake

Minerals Unlimited (518-624-5825; Deerland Rd. next to Blueberry Hill Motel) Geodes, crystals, silver jewelry with semiprecious stones made by Leslie Knoll. Open daily in summer plus fall weekends.

North River

Gore Mountain Mineral Shop (518-251-2706; Barton Mines Rd., 5 mi. off Rte. 28) Garnet jewelry; faceted gemstones; rocks and minerals from around the world; garnet mine tours; gem-cutting demonstrations on Sun. and Mon. Open daily late June–Labor Day.

Jasco Minerals (Jim Shaw; 518-251-3196; Rte. 28) Specializing in native garnet, plus fossils and semiprecious stones from around the world; custom jewelry orders. Open daily May–Dec.

OUTDOOR GEAR

Many shops in the Adirondack Park offer sports equipment, outdoor clothing, and camping supplies; you'll find them listed in Recreation under specific headings like Camping, Fishing, Rock and Ice Climbing, or Skiing.

POTTERY

LAKE GEORGE AND SOUTHEASTERN ADIRONDACKS

Chestertown

Red Truck Clayworks (Bill Knoble; 518-494-2074; Darrowsville Rd.) Truly fine stoneware, from everyday dishes to paella pans, casseroles, salad bowls, and more. Call ahead to see the whole wood-fired operation. Open daily in summer.

CHAMPLAIN VALLEY

Essex

James Swedberg

Sugar Hill Pottery operates all summer in a historic storefront in Essex.

Sugar Hill Pottery (Judith Koenig; 518-963-7068; Main St.) Hand-thrown stoneware pottery. Open daily late May–Columbus Day.

Wadhams

New Moon Pottery (Joe Dinapoli; 518-962-4045; Youngs Rd.) Contemporary stoneware, raku, and porcelain in a historic carriage barn. Open most days in summer; fall ahead.

HIGH PEAKS AND NORTHERN ADIRONDACKS

Saranac Lake

Kate Mountain Pottery (518-891-2726; 41A Main St.) Stoneware with graceful Adirondack motifs; handspun yarns and alpaca-wool hats from Windchill Hill Llamas; antiques. Open Mon.–Sat. summer and fall.

Jay

Jay Crafts Center (Lee Kazanas and Cheri Cross; 518-946-7824; Rte. 9N) Pottery lamps, bowls, vases, and dinnerware made by Lee and Cheri; wooden toys; ash-splint baskets; silver jewelry; prints; custom matting and framing. Open Apr.–Dec.

Youngs' Studio and Gallery (Sue and Terrance Young; 518-946-7301; Rte. 86) Wonderful pottery (raku and stoneware) made by Sue; limited-edition etchings of Adirondack landscapes by Terry; other local crafts. Open year-round Tues.–Sat.

CENTRAL ADIRONDACKS

Blue Mountain Lake

Blue Mountain Pottery (Bill Knoble; 518-352-7611; Rtes. 28/30, S. of the Blue Mtn. Lake Service Center) Platters, bowls, vases, and place settings in a gorgeous variety of glazes and geometric designs by a dozen first-rate potters, plus large-format photographs, handmade musical instruments, and works by local artists. Open daily mid-June–Labor Day.

SCULPTURE

Architectural-design elements, folk-art figures, realistic wildlife, and modern concrete sculpture are just a few of the things shaped by Adirondack hands. Listed below you'll find a sampling of decorative items for indoors and out.

LAKE GEORGE AND SOUTHEASTERN ADIRONDACKS

Lake Luzerne

Chicken Coop Forge (Mike Parwana; 518-798-9194; 992 E. River Rd.) Wrought-iron stairways made to order, light fixtures, fireplace screens, architectural elements. Call ahead.

HIGH PEAKS AND NORTHERN ADIRONDACKS

Bloomingdale

Ralph Prata (518-891-2417; West Main St.) Abstract concrete carvings: free-standing sculptures, wall reliefs, and framed limited-edition works. Brochure available; open by appointment only.

Rainbow Lake

Wolf Den Woodworks (John Lefebvre; 518-891-4022; www.mountain-air.com/wolfden; Rainbow Lake Rd.) Mohawk designs in stone and wood, plus carved jewelry. By appointment.

NORTHWEST LAKES

Tupper Lake

Michael Trivieri (518-359-7151; Moody Rd.) Burl bowls and tables; bas-relief sculptures of Adirondack wildlife; commissions. Many of Mike's woodland scenes are prominently featured in the dining room at the Lake Placid Lodge. Call ahead.

CHAPTER EIGHT
Nuts, Bolts, and Free Advice
INFORMATION

Itsuzo Sumy photograph courtesy of the Town of Chester Museum of Local History

Checking the latest news in Chestertown.

Consult this chapter to find the answers to questions about important community services and organizations, and for an array of miscellaneous facts and figures.

AMBULANCE, FIRE, STATE, AND LOCAL POLICE

There is no unified emergency-assistance system that operates throughout the Adirondack Park, though efforts are ongoing to get some form of 911 to as many locations as possible. In Warren County, which includes Lake George, Warrensburg, North Creek, Lake Luzerne, Pottersville, Johnsburg, and several other communities, you can dial 911 for help. Inlet and Old Forge also use 911 for emergencies. If you're traveling on I-87, the Northway, there are solar-powered emergency phones spaced about every two miles along the shoulders that automatically contact dispatchers.

Clinton County, which covers the northeastern portion of the Adirondack Park, has enhanced 911 service; this means that when you call, your name and address pop up on a display screen at the safety center. Ticonderoga (585) and Lake Placid (523) telephone exchanges have basic 911 service.

Elsewhere in the Adirondacks, you should dial 0 to reach the operator; stay on the line and you'll be connected to the appropriate agency. If you're lucky enough to have a telephone book nearby when you run into trouble, check the inside front cover for emergency listings for individual towns.

The New York State Police has offices throughout the Adirondacks. If no local officer is available calls are forwarded to a 24-hour central dispatcher. Numbers are:

Chestertown	518-494-3201
Elizabethtown	518-873-2111
Indian Lake	518-648-5757
Keeseville	518-834-9040
Moriah	518-546-7611
Old Forge	315-369-3322
Ray Brook	518-897-2000
Schroon Lake	518-532-7691
Ticonderoga	518-585-6200
Tupper Lake	518-359-7677
Westport	518-962-8235
Willsboro	518-963-7400

The number for Central New York Poison Control, covering the 315 area code, is 800-252-5655. Hudson Valley Poison Control, covering 518 area code, is 800-336-6997.

AREA CODES

The area code for the eastern two-thirds of the Adirondacks, including Lake George, Warrensburg, Schroon Lake, Elizabethtown, Westport, Keene, Lake Placid, Saranac Lake, Tupper Lake, Long Lake, Blue Mountain Lake, Indian Lake, North Creek, Speculator, Wells, and Northville is 518. For communities in the northwestern and west-central Adirondacks, such as Cranberry Lake, Star Lake, Raquette Lake, Inlet, Eagle Bay, Big Moose, and Old Forge, the area code is 315.

Be aware that in late 1999, it was announced that a new area code would either be carved out of 315 or integrated into the same geographical area. No time frame was given.

BANKS AND AUTOMATIC TELLER MACHINES

Most days of the week many Adirondack banks still keep the proverbial "banker's hours," so don't count on transactions after 3pm. Only a few banks are locally owned; several are associates of Fleet, Charter One, or Marine Midland chains, and will honor checks drawn on accounts from member banks.

For a vacation-time cash crunch, some banks may advance money on charge cards. Automatic teller machines are not associated with every bank, as they often are in urban areas; in parts of the Adirondack Park ATMs are actually quite rare. However, you can find NYCE Cashere terminals at Stewart's Shops throughout the park. These booths honor NYCE, or can give you an advance on VISA, Mastercard, American Express, or Discover cards, but don't expect the machine to dispense greenbacks. The NYCE terminal furnishes a paper receipt that you present to the cashier, who then gives you the money.

BIBLIOGRAPHY

Diverse authors have been inspired by the Adirondacks, from Robert Louis Stevenson, who completed the *Master of Ballantrae* when he was a tuberculosis patient in Saranac Lake, to Nathanael West, who penned part of *Miss Lonelyhearts* during a sojourn in Warrensburg. Sylvia Plath chronicled her ski accident at Mt. Pisgah in *The Bell Jar*. Alix Kates Shulman spent a season as a waitress in Lake Placid; her *Memoirs of an Ex-Prom Queen* has plenty of juicy details about a wild summer in the mountains. Ian Fleming's *The Spy Who Loved Me* is set in a dreary motor court near Lake George; L. Sprague DeCamp's horror-fantasy *The Purple Pterodactyls* has a definite Adirondack flavor. Mystery writer John D. MacDonald, of Travis McGee fame, even wrote a book about his cats spending their summers in Piseco.

The two lists that follow are collections of recent books and out-of-print volumes that may be read at several local libraries. The latter books don't circulate; an appointment may be necessary in order to peruse a special collection. For a list of libraries with special sections of Adirondack literature, consult Chapter Four, *Culture*. For where to buy Adirondack books, check Chapter Seven, *Shopping*.

BOOKS YOU CAN BUY

Literary Works

Banks, Russell. *Cloudsplitter*. NY: HarperFlamingo, 1998. 540 pp., $27.50. Novel about abolitionist John Brown and his sons.

Cooper, James Fenimore. *The Last of the Mohicans*. Numerous paperback editions. NY: Bantam Classics, 1982. 384 pp., $3.50.

Doctorow, E. L. *Loon Lake*. NY: Random House, 1980. 258 pp., $11.95.

Dreiser, Theodore. *An American Tragedy*. Paperback editions available. NY: Signet Classics, 1964. 832 pp., $4.95.

LaBastille, Anne. *Woodswoman*. NY: E.P. Dutton, 1976. 277 pp., $7.95.

Architecture and Decorative Arts

Kaiser, Harvey. *Great Camps of the Adirondacks*. Boston: David Godine, 1986. 240 pp., color photos, maps, index, $35.

Kylloe, Ralph. *Rustic Style*. NY: Harry N. Abrams, 1998. 160 pp., 175 color plates, $39.95.

O'Leary, Ann Stillman. *Adirondack Style*. NY: Clarkson Potter, 1998. 180 pp., 210 color plates, $37.50.

History

Bellico, Russell. *Chronicles of Lake Champlain*. Fleischmanns, NY: Purple Mountain Press, 1999. 415 pp., historic vignettes, photos, maps, drawings, index. $29. Likewise, *Chronicles of Lake George*. (1997).

Bond, Hallie. *Boats of the Adirondacks*. Blue Mountain Lake, NY: Adirondack Museum, 1995. 334 pp., $49.95.

Brumley, Charles. *Guides of the Adirondacks*. Utica, NY: North Country Books, 1994. 320 pp., photos, list of guides, index, $35 cloth, $20 paper.

Donaldson, Alfred L. *A History of the Adirondacks*. 2-volume set originally published in 1921; reprinted Fleischmanns, NY: Purple Mountain Press, 1993. 766 pp., $58.95.

Jerome, Christine. *An Adirondack Passage: The Cruise of the Canoe Sairy Gamp*. Lake George, NY: Adirondack Mountain Club, 1999. 246 pp., photos, maps, index, $12. Wonderful essay about a long canoe trip.

McMartin, Barbara. *The Great Forest of the Adirondacks*. Utica, NY: North Country Books. 1994, 266 pp., photos, charts, index, $27.50.

Schneider, Paul. *The Adirondacks*. NY: Henry Holt, 1997. 340 pp., $25 cloth. Well-written retelling of regional history.

Starbuck, David. *The Great Warpath: British Military Sites from Albany to Crown Point*. Hanover, NH: University Press of New England, 1999. 206 pp., photos, sketches, diagrams, $19.95.

Terrie, Philip G. *Contested Terrain*. Blue Mountain Lake and Syracuse, NY: Adirondack Museum and Syracuse University Press, 1997. Political history contrasting the real vs. imagined Adirondacks.

Todd, John. *Long Lake*. Pittsfield, MA: 1845; reprinted in 1997 by Purple Mountain Press. Glimpses of pioneer life; perfect companion to *Contested Terrain*.

Natural History

North Country Books, in Utica, publishes a series of field guides on native birds, mammals, trees and shrubs, wildflowers, and mushrooms. All of the books are paperbacks with numerous color photos; prices are $12.95 each for the mushroom and wildflower guides, and $13.95 each for the bird, mammal, and tree guides.

DiNunzio, Michael. *Adirondack Wildguide*. Elizabethtown, NY: Adirondack Conservancy/Adirondack Council, 1984. 160 pp., illus., $14.95.

Kalinowski, Tom. *Adirondack Almanac: A Guide to the Natural Year*. Utica, NY: North Country Books, 1999. Illus. Month-by-month descriptions of typical wildlife. $16.95.

McMartin, Barbara. *The Adirondack Park: A Wildlands Quilt*. Syracuse, NY: Syracuse University Press, 1999. 94 pp., color photos, maps, $24.95. Highlights wilderness, wild forest, and canoe areas.

Stager, Curt. *Field Notes from the Northern Forest*. Syracuse, NY: Syracuse University Press, 1998. 272 pp., illus. $26.95.

Terrie, Philip G. *Wildlife and Wilderness: A History of Adirondack Mammals*. Fleischmanns, NY: Purple Mountain Press, 1993. 176 pp., photos, index. $14.50.

Photographic Studies

Bogdan, Robert. *Exposing the Wilderness: Early 20th Century Adirondack Postcard Photographers*. Syracuse, NY: Syracuse University Press, 1999. Photos, index, $39.95.

Heilman, Carl E. II. *Adirondacks: Views of an American Wilderness*. NY: Rizzoli Press, 1999. 160 pp., color photos, $45.

Oppersdorff, Mathias. *Adirondack Faces*. Syracuse, NY: Syracuse University Press/Adirondack Museum Book, 1991. 108 pp., $34.95.

Winkler, John. *A Bushwhacker's View of the Adirondacks.* Utica, NY: North Country Books, 1996. 118 pp., $27.50, paper. Color photographs of the High Peaks.

Winkler, John. *A Cherished Wilderness: The Adirondacks.* Utica, NY: North Country Books, 1998. 118 pp., $37.50. Color photographs of the region.

Recreation

There are two main sources for Adirondack guidebooks for hiking, snowshoeing, and cross-country skiing: the Adirondack Mountain Club (ADK), based in Lake George, NY, and North Country Books, out of Utica, NY. The *Forest Preserve Series* by various ADK authors covers seven different regions of the park, from the High Peaks to the Northville–Lake Placid Trail; these $14.95 pocket-size paperbacks have plenty of detail and each comes with a separate topo map showing trails. North Country Books distributes the *Discover the Adirondacks Series,* written by historian/hiker Barbara McMartin. These are more lively to read, with notes on the human and natural history of a particular destination, and cost between $9.95 and $14.95.

Two recent guidebooks intended for young readers by Barbara McMartin are *Adventures in Hiking* and *Fun on Flatwater,* available from North Country Books; another is *Kids on the Trail,* equal parts how-to and where-to, published by the Adirondack Mountain Club in 1998. If you can't decide on which region to trek, read Barbara McMartin's *Fifty Hikes in the Adirondacks: Short Walks, Day Trips, and Extended Hikes Throughout the Park,* published by Backcountry Publications in Woodstock, VT ($12.95).

Aprill, Dennis. *Good Fishing in the Adirondacks.* Stackpole Books, 1999. 224 pp., photos, maps, $15. Also, *Paths Less Traveled.* Elizabethtown, NY: Pinto Press, 1998. 181 pp., maps, photos. Descriptions of good hikes on smaller mountains.

Goodwin, Tony. *Classic Adirondack Ski Tours.* Lake George, NY: Adirondack Mountain Club, 1996. 127 pp., maps, index. $10.95.

Jamieson, Paul and Morris, Donald. *Adirondack Canoe Waters: North Flow.* Lake George, NY: Adirondack Mountain Club, 1999. Includes new state acquisitions. 368 pp., maps, index, $15.95.

Kick, Peter. *25 Mountain Bike Tours in the Adirondacks.* Woodstock, VT: Backcountry Publications, 1999. 190 pp., photos, maps, $14.95.

McKibben, Halpern, etc. *25 Bike Rides in the Adirondacks: Bicycle Adventures in the East's Largest Wilderness.* Woodstock, VT: Backcountry Publications, 1995. 174 pp., $13.

Mellor, Don. *Climbing in the Adirondacks: A Guide to Rock & Ice Routes.* Lake George, NY: Adirondack Mountain Club, 1996. 318 pp., photos, maps, index, $24.95.

Out-of-print Adirondack books can be found in places like the Raquette Lake Library.

James Swedberg

Travel

Brown, Phil. *Longstreet Highroad Guide to the New York Adirondacks*. Atlanta, GA: Longstreet Press, 1999. 338 pp., photos, illustrations, maps. $18.95.

Folwell, Elizabeth and Godine, Amy. *Adirondack Odysseys*. Lee, MA and Blue Mountain Lake, NY: Berkshire House Publishers and the Adirondack Museum. 220 pp., $16.95. Guide to museums and historic sites from the Mohawk Valley to the St. Lawrence River.

Stoddard, Seneca Ray. *The Adirondacks Illustrated*. Glens Falls, NY: Chapman Historical Museum, 1983. Reprint of 1874 guidebook. 204 pp., illus., index, $15.

BOOKS YOU CAN BORROW

Barnett, Lincoln. *The Ancient Adirondacks*. NY: Time-Life Books, 1974. 184 pp., photos, index. An excellent introduction to the Adirondack Park by a Westport resident and former *Life* magazine editor.

Colvin, Verplanck. *Report on a Topographical Survey of the Adirondack Wilderness of New York*. Albany, NY: 1873. Sounds dull, but it reads like an adventure story. Many engravings and maps.

Deming, Philander. *Adirondack Stories*. Boston, MA: 1880. Gritty short stories.

CLIMATE AND WEATHER INFORMATION

"Nine months of winter and three months of poor sledding" sums up an Adirondack year if you happen to ask a native in, say, mud season. A typical twelve months has about 190 days of subfreezing temperatures. The western Adirondacks, including Old Forge, Eagle Bay, Big Moose, Inlet, and north to Cranberry Lake and Star Lake, get considerably more snow than the eastern Adirondacks, with about ten feet falling in an average winter, much of it from lake-effect storms off Lake Ontario.

Spring in the Adirondacks can be elusive. March is winter, despite the date of the vernal equinox. April weather bounces between brief flashes of hot and dry, or sustained snow and cold, or mixtures of mild and moist. May tends to be reliably above freezing during the daytime, although in 1976, nearly two feet of snow fell on May 19. June temperatures can be sweltering, with plenty of bug activity.

July and August days are usually in the 70s and 80s, with occasional hotter spells, but evenings cool off pleasantly. Early September often brings the finest dry weather for outdoor activities, with highs in the 70s and lows in the 50s.

Fall can be brilliantly sunny, providing great leaf-peeping opportunities from about September 20 through October 15, depending on the elevation. Or autumn can be dismally rainy, with the only chance to see fall colors by looking in mud puddles. There's a toll-free hotline for fall foliage reports, 800-CALL-NYS.

Generalities about the weather are one thing; getting an accurate forecast is another. There is no nearby National Weather Service station. Predictions for Albany, Syracuse, or Burlington, VT, need temperatures to be adjusted downwards by five or ten degrees, with a corresponding change for precipitation — 40 degrees and rain in the Albany area usually means subfreezing temperatures and sleet or snow in the Adirondacks.

The Lake Placid radio station, WIRD (105.5 FM), has a weatherman on staff who provides good information for the area from Tupper Lake to Keene; there's a 24-hour telephone weather report available at 518-523-1363. If you're hiking anywhere near the High Peaks, call 518-523-3518 for the Adirondack Mountain Club's recorded weather forecast, plus a word or two about what to expect on mountaintops and the trails that lead there.

North Country Public Radio WSLU-FM (see below for frequencies), broadcasting out of St. Lawrence University, in Canton, airs extensive forecasts that cover much of the Adirondacks. The "Eye on the Sky" weather update from Vermont Public Radio, WVPR (107.9 FM), tends to be fairly reliable for the eastern Adirondacks. The Albany television station, WRGB, also has a weather forecast at 518-476-WRGB, which covers the southern Adirondacks.

On the World Wide Web, Rainorshine (www.rainorshine.com) shows five-day forecasts for Lake George and Lake Placid. The Weather Channel (www.weather.com) allows you to plug in a Zip code and receive current conditions and a five-day forecast, though it may not work for Zips of smaller Adirondack towns — for example, Old Forge's Zip yields nothing. Weather Underground (www.wunderground.com) has the same feature but the five-day report comes from the nearest weather station, which doesn't account for topographical differences (plug in Old Forge and get a forecast for Watertown, well outside the Adirondack Park).

North Country Public Radio's website (www.ncpr.org) has links to weather

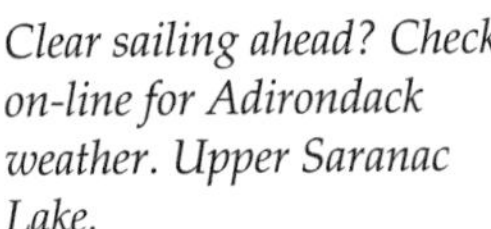

Clear sailing ahead? Check on-line for Adirondack weather. Upper Saranac Lake.

James Swedberg

information by county, and Paul Smith's College has a weather page (www.paulsmiths.edu/aai/eet/weather.html) which shows current conditions, though the forecast button links back to Weather Underground.

GUIDED TOURS

There are hundreds of licensed Adirondack Guides for fishing, hunting, hiking, and climbing trips; you'll find information about them in Chapter Six, *Recreation.* Several communities in the Champlain Valley have self-guided walking and driving tours for historic-preservation buffs; check "Architecture," in Chapter Four, *Culture,* for the details. Guided bus tours of the Olympic facilities are available from Lake Placid Sightseeing Tours, on Mirror Lake Dr., 518-523-4431.

HANDICAPPED SERVICES

For disabled New Yorkers, free passes to state-operated camping, swimming, golf facilities, and historic sites are available by applying to the Office of Parks, Recreation and Historic Preservation. Write to OPRHP at Agency Building 1, Empire State Plaza, Albany, NY 12238, or call 518-474-0456.

Some of the nature trails at the Visitor Interpretive Centers, at Paul Smiths and Newcomb, are designed for the mobility-impaired. The Adirondack Mountain Club (see "Bibliography," above) has appendices on appropriate trails for wheelchairs in some of its hiking guidebooks.

Cultural institutions, such as the Adirondack Museum or Lake Placid Center for the Arts, libraries, and theaters are generally accessible; some historic buildings are not. Chapter Four, *Culture,* provides more information. Restaurants that are accessible are described in Chapter Five, *Restaurants & Food Purveyors;* lodgings with handicapped facilities are listed in Chapter Three, *Lodging*.

HEALTH CENTERS AND HOSPITALS

Most local health centers are open weekdays; Hudson Headwaters centers are open Saturdays as well. Many town health centers have answering services that can help with emergencies any time, day or night.

LAKE GEORGE AND SOUTHEASTERN ADIRONDACKS

Bolton Health Center, 518-644-9471; Cross St., Bolton Landing
Chester Health Center, 518-494-2761; Main St., Chestertown
Glens Falls Hospital, 518-792-3151; 100 Park St., Glens Falls
Schroon Lake Health Center, 518-532-7120; North Ave., Schroon Lake
Warrensburg Health Center, 518-623-2844; Main St., Warrensburg

CHAMPLAIN VALLEY

Champlain Valley Physicians Hospital Medical Center, 518-561-2000; 75 Beekman St., Plattsburgh
Elizabethown Community Hospital, 518-873-6377; Park St., Elizabethtown
Mineville Health Center, 518-942-6661; Hospital Rd., Mineville
Moses-Ludington Hospital, 518-585-2831; 2 Wicker St., Ticonderoga
Ticonderoga Health Center, 518-585-6708; Old Chilson Rd., Ticonderoga

HIGH PEAKS AND NORTHERN ADIRONDACKS

Adirondack Medical Center, 518-523-3311; Church St., Lake Placid
Adirondack Medical Center, 518-891-4141; Lake Colby Dr., Saranac Lake
Mountain Health Center, 518-576-9771; Rte. 73, Keene

NORTHWEST LAKES

Adirondack Health Center (formerly Mercy Health Care), 518-359-3355; 115 Wawbeek Ave., Tupper Lake
Clifton-Fine Hospital, 315-848-3351; 1014 Oswegatchie Trail, Star Lake

CENTRAL ADIRONDACKS

Central Adirondack Family Practice, 315-369-6619; South Shore Rd., Old Forge
Indian Lake Health Center, 518-648-5707; Rte. 28, Indian Lake
Long Lake Medical Center, 518-624-2301; Rte. 28N, Long Lake
Nathan Littauer Hospital, 518-725-8621; 99 E. State St., Gloversville
North Creek Health Center, 518-251-2541; at Adirondack Tri-County Nursing Home, Ski Bowl Rd., North Creek

LATE NIGHT FOOD AND FUEL

Most towns with more than a few hundred people now have convenience stores open until 11pm, offering gas, food, and personal-care essentials. From Lake George to Lake Placid to Old Forge, look for Cumberland Farms, Nice n' Easy, Stewart's Shops, or Sugar Creek plazas. All Stewart's stores, and most others, also have cash machines.

MAPS

A standard road-atlas page showing New York State shrinks the Adirondack Park down to a postage stamp and indicates maybe three highways. The Adirondack North Country Association publishes an excellent full-size road map that shows just the park and adjacent counties; send $2.00 (check or money order) and a stamped, self-addressed legal-size envelope to ANCA, 183 Broadway, Saranac Lake NY 12983, to receive one. JiMapco, in Round Lake, NY, publishes individual county maps that are widely available in grocery stores and book shops. The *New York State Atlas and Gazetteer* ($19.95) published by De Lorme Mapping Co., Freeport, ME, uses a topographical map format to show areas in still greater detail; these can be found in most area bookstores, and larger stores elsewhere.

MEDIA: MAGAZINES AND NEWSPAPERS; RADIO STATIONS

Magazines & Newspapers

Adirondac 518-668-4447; RD 3, Box 3055, Lake George NY 12845; bimonthly magazine. Published by the Adirondack Mountain Club, with articles on local history, outdoor recreation, and environmental issues.

Adirondack Explorer 518-891-9352; 36 Church St., Saranac Lake NY 12983; tabloid paper issued ten times a year. Short pieces on travel destinations, current issues, wildlife, and personalities.

Adirondack Life 518-946-2191; www.adirondacklife.com; Box 410, Jay NY 12941; award-winning bimonthly magazine, plus two special issues: Annual Guide to the Outdoors and Collectors Issue. Known for excellent color photography; publishes essays, short stories, columns, and features on history, outdoor recreation, architecture, culture, local life, regional products, politics, and environmental issues by nationally known writers.

LAKE GEORGE AND SOUTHEASTERN ADIRONDACKS

Glens Falls Post Star 518-792-3131; P.O. Box 2157, Lawrence and Cooper Sts., Glens Falls NY 12801; daily newspaper covering the Adirondacks from Lake George to Long Lake.

CHAMPLAIN VALLEY

Plattsburgh Press-Republican 518-561-2300; 170 Margaret St., Plattsburgh NY 12901; daily paper covering Clinton, Franklin, and Essex counties, with news bureaus in Lake Placid (518-523-1559) and Ticonderoga (518-585-4070).

Valley News 518-873-6368; Denton Publishing Co., Elizabethtown NY 12932; weekly paper for Elizabethtown, Westport, Willsboro, Essex, Keene, Keene Valley, and Jay.

HIGH PEAKS AND NORTHERN ADIRONDACKS

Adirondack Daily Enterprise 518-891-2600; 61 Broadway, Saranac Lake NY 12983; daily paper for Lake Placid, Saranac Lake, Paul Smiths, and Tupper Lake area; the Friday Weekender insert has a good regional calendar of events plus local history features.

Lake Placid News 518-523-4401; Mill Hill, Lake Placid NY 12946; weekly paper for Lake Placid, Keene, Keene Valley, Wilmington, and Au Sable Forks.

NORTHWEST LAKES

Tupper Lake Free Press 518-359-2166; 136 Park St., Tupper Lake NY 12986; weekly paper covering Tupper Lake, Piercefield, Cranberry Lake, and Long Lake.

Watertown Daily Times 315-782-1000; 260 Washington St., Watertown NY 13601; daily paper covering Thousand Islands/Lake Ontario area, including the northwestern Adirondacks.

On the Internet

Adirondack organizations, artisans, and tourist destinations have established themselves on the Internet in earnest in recent years; look for information on their services, products, and special events. World Wide Web sites describe everything from ski-jump competitions at Lake Placid to facts about Mount Marcy, New York's highest peak. A sampling of where to look for Adirondack materials in cyberspace follows, but note that this is just the beginning — new domains are being established almost every day. Internet addresses for lodgings and restaurants described in Chapters Three and Five are listed with the phone numbers.

The **Adirondack Mountain Club** (www.adk.org) uses its website to promote outdoor workshops and describe the club's activities and facilities, and includes listings of ADK events and lodgings.

AdirondackNet (www.adirondack.net.) has many listings of interest to travelers about golf courses, Lake George boat cruises, whitewater rafting, lodgings, museums, attractions, and so forth in the Lake George region and southeastern Adirondacks, Champlain Valley, and High Peaks.

Adirondacks.com (www.adirondacks.com) is the most comprehensive site for regional resorts, real estate, maps, events, and attractions, with a photo gallery and links to specific communities and businesses. This is not to be confused with Adirondack.com (www.adirondack.com), which has extensive recreation listings, plus lodging, business, and other links.

Adirondacks.org (www.adirondacks.org) is the website of the Adirondack Regional Tourism Council, with information by town, county, and region, events, a map, park history, and lodging links. Also at www.adk.com.

Mount Marcy has at least one Web page dedicated to it (www.americasroof.com/ny.html.); it contains background on this mile-high mountain, with photos and links to everything from weather to other Adirondack sites.

The **Olympic Regional Development Authority** (www.orda.org.) describes downhill and cross-country-skiing facilities, bobsled and luge races, speed-skating events, and useful Lake Placid tourist information.

(see *Tourist Information* section for individual chambers of commerce websites)

CENTRAL ADIRONDACKS

Adirondack Express 315-369-2237; Box 659, Old Forge NY 13420; weekly newspaper with coverage from Blue Mountain Lake to Otter Lake.

Hamilton County News 518-548-6898; Rte. 30, Speculator NY 12164; weekly newspaper for Long Lake, Blue Mountain Lake, Indian Lake, Speculator, Wells, Piseco, and Benson.

North Creek News 518-251-3012; 288 Main St., North Creek NY 12853; weekly paper for Johnsburg, Bakers Mills, Minerva, Olmstedville, North Creek, and North River.

Radio Stations

National Public Radio: Three NPR affiliates reach different parts of the Adirondacks:

WAMC-FM, 90.3, 518-465-5233; Albany NY; also translator WANC, 103.9 (Ticonderoga) and WCEL, 91.9 (Plattsburgh)

WSLU-FM, 89.5 (Canton), 90.9 (Malone), 91.3 (Blue Mountain Lake and Thousand Islands), 91.7 (Long Lake, Lake Placid, Tupper Lake), 90.5 (Saranac Lake), 88.3 (Peru), 89.7 (Keene), 89.9 (North Creek), 88.1 (Lowville), 315-229-5356; www.ncpr.org; Canton NY. The best news and feature coverage for the entire Adirondack Park by any media outlet; recently launched an Adirondack News Bureau at Paul Smith's College.

WVPR, 107.9, 802-655-9451; Colchester, VT. News coverage for the eastern Adirondacks and relatively reliable weather forecasts.

Commercial Radio Stations

WIRD-FM, 105.5, 518-523-3341. Lake Placid. General. (Signal broadcasts through WRGR-FM, 102.3, Tupper Lake as well.)

WNBZ-AM, 1240, 518-891-1544. Saranac Lake. General.

WSLK-FM, 106.3, 518-891-1544. Saranac Lake. Country.

Television Stations

There are no television stations broadcasting from within the Adirondack Park, and TV reception in areas not covered by cable or satellite service can be awful. The Plattsburgh NBC-affiliate, WPTZ, reports on news from Lake Placid, Saranac Lake, and elsewhere in the eastern Adirondacks during the "Today Show" and in evening slots. WCAX, the Burlington, VT, CBS-affiliate, has a reporter filing stories from the Adirondacks on a relatively regular basis.

REAL ESTATE

Because the population of the region has been fairly stable over the last century, there are often older farmsteads and village homes for sale, as families build new houses to meet their needs. If you're not afraid of the "handyman's special," the Adirondacks could provide some challenges and rewards for you, with perhaps some acreage to boot. Townhouses and condominiums are a relatively new local phenomenon, and after intense initial speculation, prices have stabilized at a level that shouldn't be too shocking to a typical New England urbanite. Waterfront — on just about any lake, river, or pond inside the Blue Line — tends to be scarce and very pricey: the going rate can be as high as $1000 per running foot of shoreline just for the land. Add a summer cottage, or a real winterized house plus a decent driveway, a boathouse, or a garage, and the figures start to escalate.

Even crossroads that don't have grocery stores have real-estate offices. Weekly newspapers usually have some real-estate listings, and many Realtors publish bimonthly buyers' guides. *Adirondack Life* magazine has a large real-estate section in each issue. An added bonus for the visitor: most realtors offer private rentals of well-equipped lakefront homes and ski chalets.

RELIGIOUS SERVICES AND ORGANIZATIONS

St. John's in the Wilderness Church, Lake Clear.

Michael Kahn

Churches throughout the Adirondacks anchor the communities and provide a network of help and social life along with spiritual guidance. Several local churches are interesting for their architecture and are listed on the National Register of Historic Places; a few seasonal chapels are located on lovely islands accessible only by boat. Some churches even put on great, inexpensive dinners (see Chapter Five, *Restaurants & Food Purveyors*, for advice on chicken barbecues and church suppers). Check the papers for listings of church services. Inside the park, Lake Placid has the only active synagogue; Temple Beth Joseph, in Tupper Lake, is open as a historic building and occasionally offers services.

ROAD SERVICE

For AAA members, there are local offices in Glens Falls, 518-792-0088; Johnstown, 518-762-4619; and Plattsburgh, 518-563-3830. For non-AAA members, some towing and automotive services are listed below:

LAKE GEORGE AND SOUTHEASTERN ADIRONDACKS

Lakeview Automotive, Lake George	518-668-9267
Pottersville Garage, Pottersville	518-494-3631
Thomson's Garage, Lake George	518-668-5337
Warrensburg Car Care, Warrensburg	518-623-2135

CHAMPLAIN VALLEY AND NORTHEASTERN ADIRONDACKS

Chesterfield Truck Stop, Keeseville	518-834-7407
Pierce's Service Station, Lewis	518-873-2065/962-8971 evening
R.B. Motors, Ticonderoga	518-585-7774

HIGH PEAKS AND NORTHERN ADIRONDACKS

Central Garage, Lake Placid	518-523-3378
Madden's Towing, Saranac Lake	518-891-1100/891-2544 evening
Smith's Towing & Recovery, Malone	518-483-0776/483-0505 evening
Woodruff Towing, Saranac Lake	518-891-3423

NORTHWEST LAKES

Counter's Garage, Tupper Lake	518-359-7514/359-2370 evening or if no answer
Eric's Auto & Truck Repair	518-359-7809/359-8628

CENTRAL ADIRONDACKS

Eldridge Automotive, Indian Lake	518-648-0086
King's Collision and Auto Maintenance, Indian Lake	518-648-6327
Morin's Collision, Old Forge	315-369-3396
Speculator Auto, Speculator	518-548-8102

TOURIST INFORMATION

Old Forge's tourism offices are near the covered bridge.

James Swedberg

Taking care of visitors is the number-one industry in the Adirondacks, and communities have become quite skilled at educating the public about their unique offerings. Warren County (which encompasses Lake George and the southeastern Adirondacks) publishes a colorful guide with a calendar of events, lists of hiking trails, boat-launch sites, museums, libraries, attractions, campgrounds, and much more; call 518-761-6366 for a copy. Likewise, the Lake Placid/Essex County Visitors Bureau (518-523-2445) has an extensive promotional packet.

Franklin County publishes a four-color booklet with general background information plus publications detailing services and outdoor recreation; these are available from the tourism office, at 518-483-6788. Clinton County offers a magazine-size guide, available by calling 518-563-1000. Hamilton County has a series of pamphlets about hunting and fishing, snowmobiling, craft shops, dining, and lodging, plus a magazine-format booklet, available by calling 518-648-5239.

A selection of chambers of commerce and visitor information centers are listed below; check out www.adirondacks.com or www.adirondacks.org for links to these towns and areas.

LAKE GEORGE AND SOUTHEASTERN ADIRONDACKS

Bolton Landing: Box 368, Rte. 9N, Bolton Landing NY 12814; 518-644-3831; www.boltonchamber.com.

Chestertown-Brant Lake-Pottersville: P.O. Box 490, Rte. 8, Chestertown NY 12817; 518-494-2722 or 888-404-2722

Hague-Silver Bay: Rte. 9N, Hague NY 12836; 518-543-6353; www.hagueticon deroga.com.

Lake George: P.O. Box 272, Rte. 9, Lake George NY 12845; 518-668-5755 or 800-705-0059; www.lgchamber.com.

Lake Luzerne: Box 222, Lake Luzerne NY 12846; 518-696-3500; www.lakeluzernechamber.org.

Schroon Lake: P.O. Box 726, Main St., Schroon Lake NY 12870; 518-532-7675; www.schroonlake.org.

Stony Creek: Box 35, Stony Creek NY 12878; 518-696-4563

Warrensburg: 136 Main St., Warrensburg NY 12885; 518-623-2161

CHAMPLAIN VALLEY

Essex County Visitors Information Center, Bridge Rd., Crown Point NY 12928; 518-597-4646; www.lakeplacid.com.

Ticonderoga–Crown Point: Box 70, Ticonderoga NY 12883; 518-585-6619.

Westport: General Delivery, Westport NY 12992; 518-962-8383; www.west portny.org.

HIGH PEAKS AND NORTHERN ADIRONDACKS

Lake Placid Visitors Bureau: Main St., Lake Placid NY 12946; 518-523-2445 or 800-44PLACID; www.lakeplacid.com.

Saranac Lake: 30 Main St., Saranac Lake NY 12983; 518-891-1990 or 800-347-1992; www.saranaclake.com.

Whiteface Mountain Regional Visitors Bureau: Rte. 86, Wilmington NY 12993; 518-946-2255 or 888-WHITEFACE.

NORTHWEST LAKES

Tupper Lake: 60 Park St., Tupper Lake NY 12986; 518-359-3328; www.tupper lakeinfo.com.

CENTRAL ADIRONDACKS

Blue Mountain Lake Association: Rte. 28, Blue Mtn. Lake NY 12812; 518-352-7659.

Central Adirondack Association: Main St., Old Forge NY 13420; 315-369-6983; www.oldforgeny.com.

Gore Mountain Region: P.O. Box 84, Main St., North Creek NY 12853; 518-251-2612 or 800-880-GORE; www.goremtregion.org.

Indian Lake: Main St., Indian Lake NY 12842; 518-648-5112; www.indian-lake.com.

A cut-out moose lurks on the outskirts of Indian Lake.

James Swedberg

Inlet: P.O. Box 266, Inlet NY 13360; 315-357-5501; www.inletny.com.
Long Lake/Raquette Lake: P.O. Box 496, Rte. 28N, Long Lake NY 12847; 518-624-3077; www.longlake-ny.com or www.centraladirondacks.com.
Speculator–Lake Pleasant–Piseco: Rte. 30, Speculator NY 12164; 518-548-4521; www2.telenet.net/community/adrkmts.

IF TIME IS SHORT

B. Folwell

Rock Pond Outlet, William C. Whitney Area.

A whirlwind tour to see the Adirondacks can mean an awful lot of time spent in the car rather than getting to know a few nice places. Maybe it's best to carefully consider your tastes and concentrate your energy within a forty-mile area.

If you're a history buff and want to stroll through attractive, well-preserved towns and old forts, then head for the Champlain Valley, especially Ticonderoga, Crown Point, Westport, and Essex. Great restaurants and lovely bed and breakfast accommodations in Essex and Westport offer an excellent counterpoint to more rustic experiences. If you crave sweeping mountain vistas, aim your sights at the High Peaks, highlighting Keene Valley, Keene, and Lake Placid. The view from downtown Lake Placid, with chains of craggy peaks marching around the village, is unlike any other town in the park. If you like clean, island-dotted lakes, use Upper Saranac, Cranberry, Long, Blue Mountain, Indian, Raquette, Piseco, or Lake Pleasant as a base. For a terrific overview — literally — charter a floatplane from Long Lake or Inlet or take flight above the High Peaks from Lake Placid.

Recommended drives include Rte. 22 along Lake Champlain, Rte. 73 between Keene and Lake Placid, Rte. 30 between Long Lake and Lake Pleasant, and the Blue Ridge Rd. between the Interstate 87 (the Northway) and Newcomb. Take a trip up the toll roads on Prospect or Whiteface mountains; the views before you get to the summit are amazing, and accessible. Incidentally, the Northway offers quite possibly the most scenic high-speed road experience in the Northeast.

A few suggestions for places to see or stay:

LODGING

The Sagamore Hotel (518-644-9400; Sagamore Rd., Bolton Landing) is at a particularly beautiful spot on Lake George and is a thoroughly luxurious modern resort with an exceptional 18-hole golf course, three gourmet restaurants, spa, huge indoor pool, and tennis. Do take a cruise on the Morgan, a handsome wooden tour boat that leaves from the Sagamore dock.

Lake Placid Lodge (518-523-2700; Whiteface Inn Rd., Lake Placid) is a marvelously elegant rustic hotel with massive stone fireplaces in each room, lovely furnishings, gorgeous views of Lake Placid and the High Peaks, and one of the finest restaurants in upstate New York. Recently renovated cabins on the property are wonderful, and you can bring your dog.

CULTURAL ATTRACTIONS

The Adirondack Museum (518-352-7311; Rtes. 28/30, Blue Mtn. Lake) is generally open from late May through Columbus Day, and no visit to the Adirondack Park is complete without spending a whole day here. The scope of the exhibits ranges from classic watercraft to fine arts to indigenous crafts. Construction begun in fall 1999 may delay the 2000 season; please call ahead to be sure the museum is open.

Adirondack Park Visitor Interpretive Centers (518-327-3000, Rte. 30, Paul Smiths and 518-582-2000, Rte. 28N, Newcomb) offer exhibits on the park's natural history; interpretive trails for hiking, skiing, and snowshoeing; and numerous programs for adults and children from preschoolers to teens. Open year-round.

Fort Ticonderoga (518-585-2821; Fort Rd., Ticonderoga) is a handsomely restored fortress that played important roles in the French and Indian Wars and the American Revolution; it's in a beautiful promontory on Lake Champlain. Plan your visit on a nice day so you can enjoy the view. Open early May through late October.

Sagamore Great Camp (315-354-5311; Sagamore Rd. 4 miles off Rte. 28, Raquette Lake) is the real deal, a grand rustic estate in the heart of the wilderness. Guided tours are offered twice daily in summer; inquire about May–October schedule. Concerts, workshops, and theatrical performances are offered on many weekends.

RESTAURANTS

Le Bistro Laliberté (518-523-3680; 51 Main St., Lake Placid) has an innovative menu of new American cuisine and awesome desserts. In the summer you can sit on the private deck overlooking Mirror Lake and watch the sunset. Open year-round.

Tail O' the Pup (518-891-5092; Sara-Placid Hwy., Ray Brook) is a no-frills roadside eatery with good barbecue at great prices; you can't pick a better place to bring the family. Open May through October.

The William West Durant (315-354-5532; Pier One, Raquette Lake) is a wonderful tour boat that presents a movable feast as it cruises Raquette Lake, the fourth-largest lake in the Adirondacks. Open May through October.

Index

LODGING BY PRICE CODE

Price Codes (per night, double occupancy):

Very Inexpensive:	*under $40*
Inexpensive:	*$40–$70*
Moderate:	*$70–$100*
Expensive:	*$100–$200*
Very Expensive:	*Over $200*

CENTRAL ADIRONDACKS

Inexpensive

Inexpensive–Moderate

RESTAURANTS BY PRICE CODE

Price Codes:

Inexpensive:	*up to $15*
Moderate:	*$15–$20*
Expensive:	*$20–$35*
Very Expensive:	*Over $35*

RESTAURANTS BY CUISINE

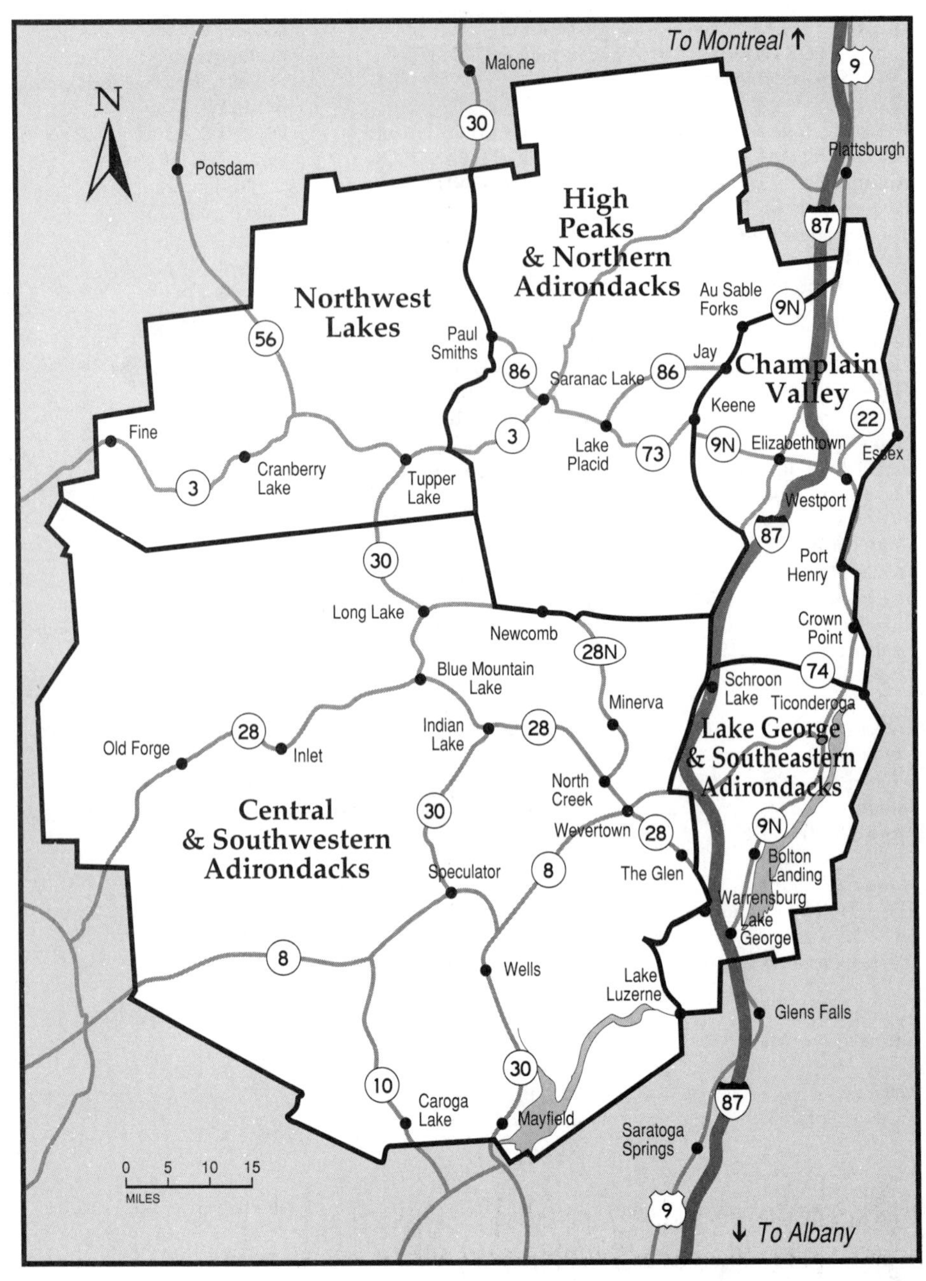

THE ADIRONDACKS IN FIVE REGIONS

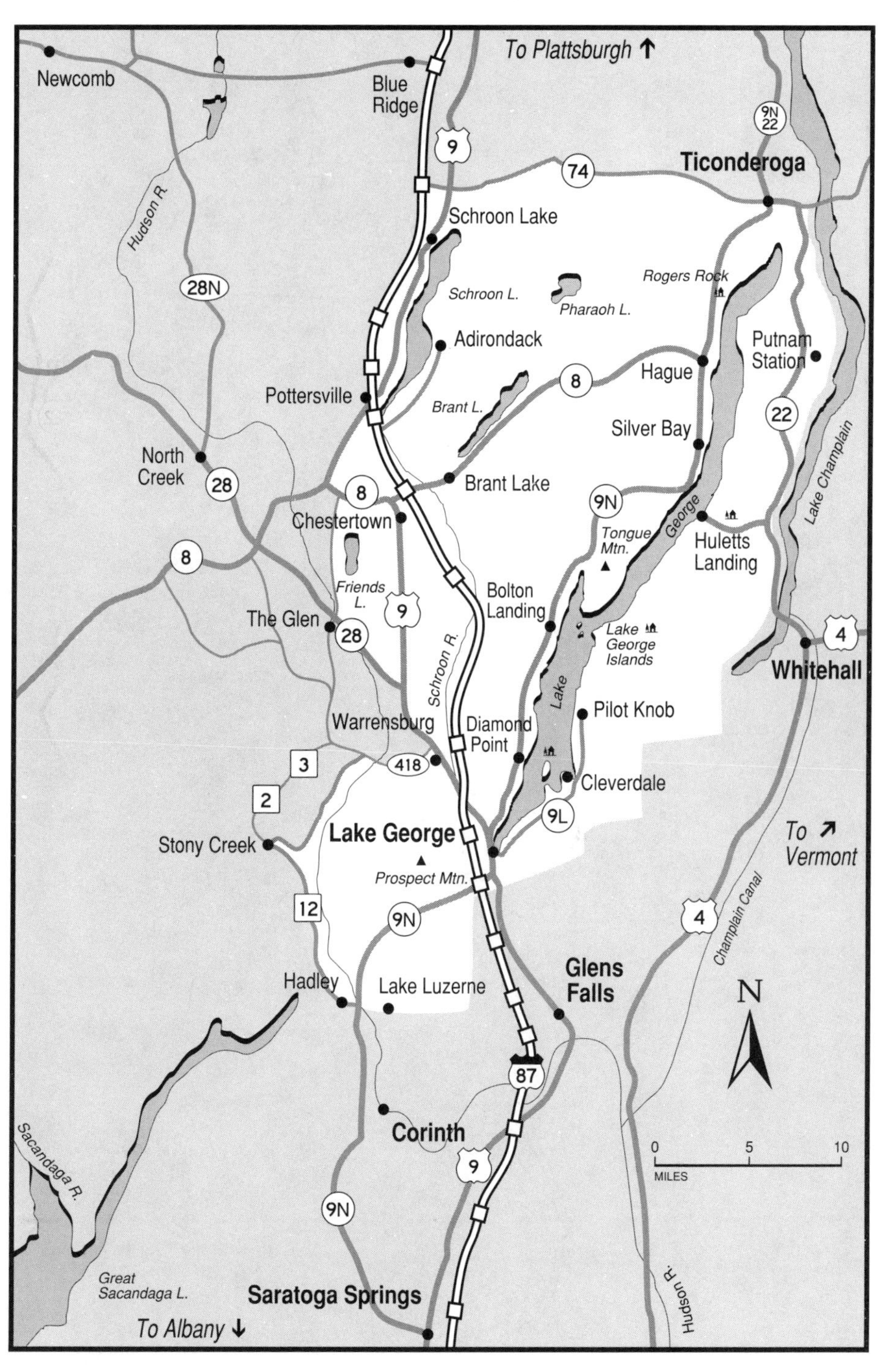

LAKE GEORGE AND SOUTHEASTERN ADIRONDACKS

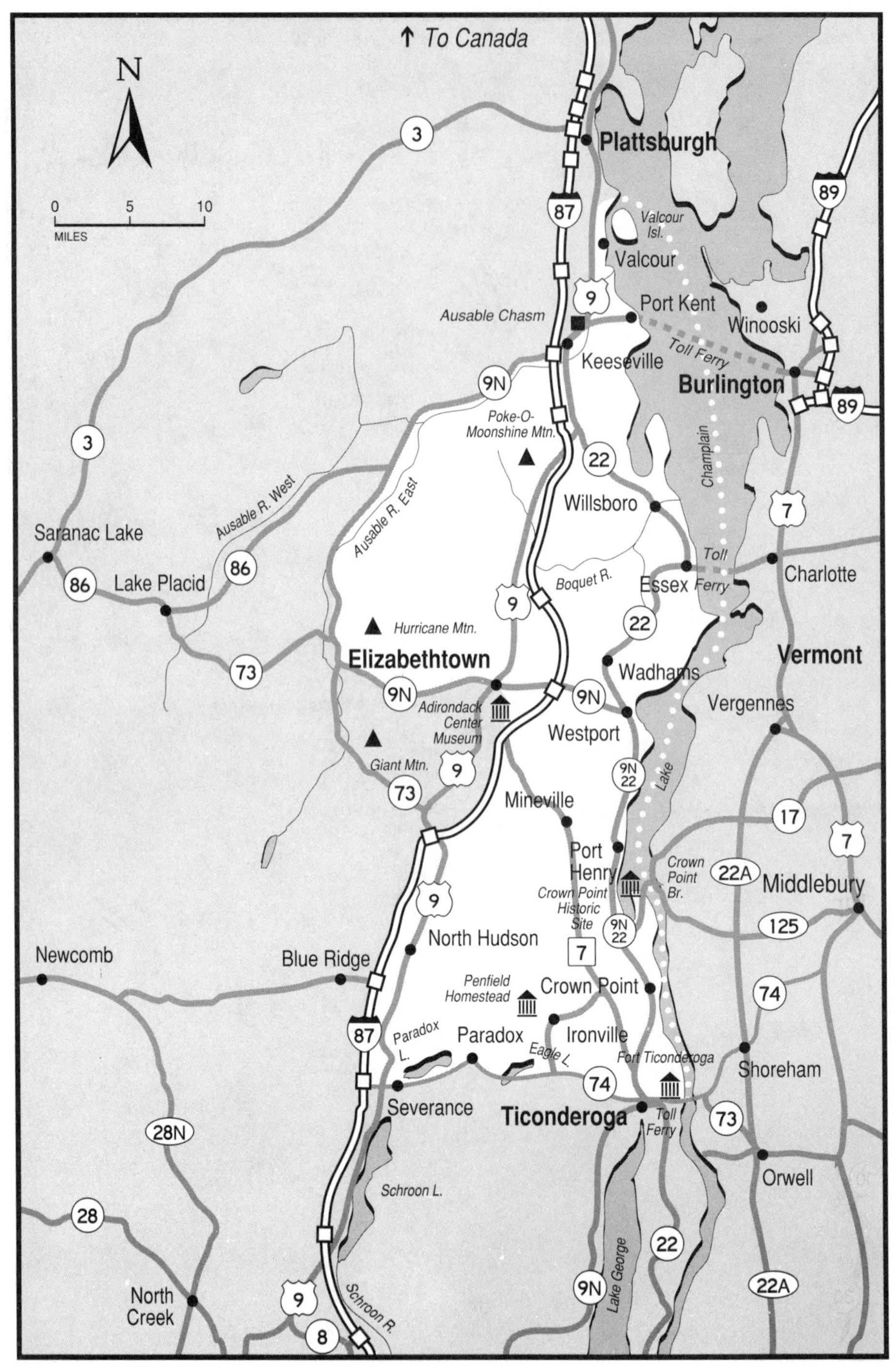

CHAMPLAIN VALLEY

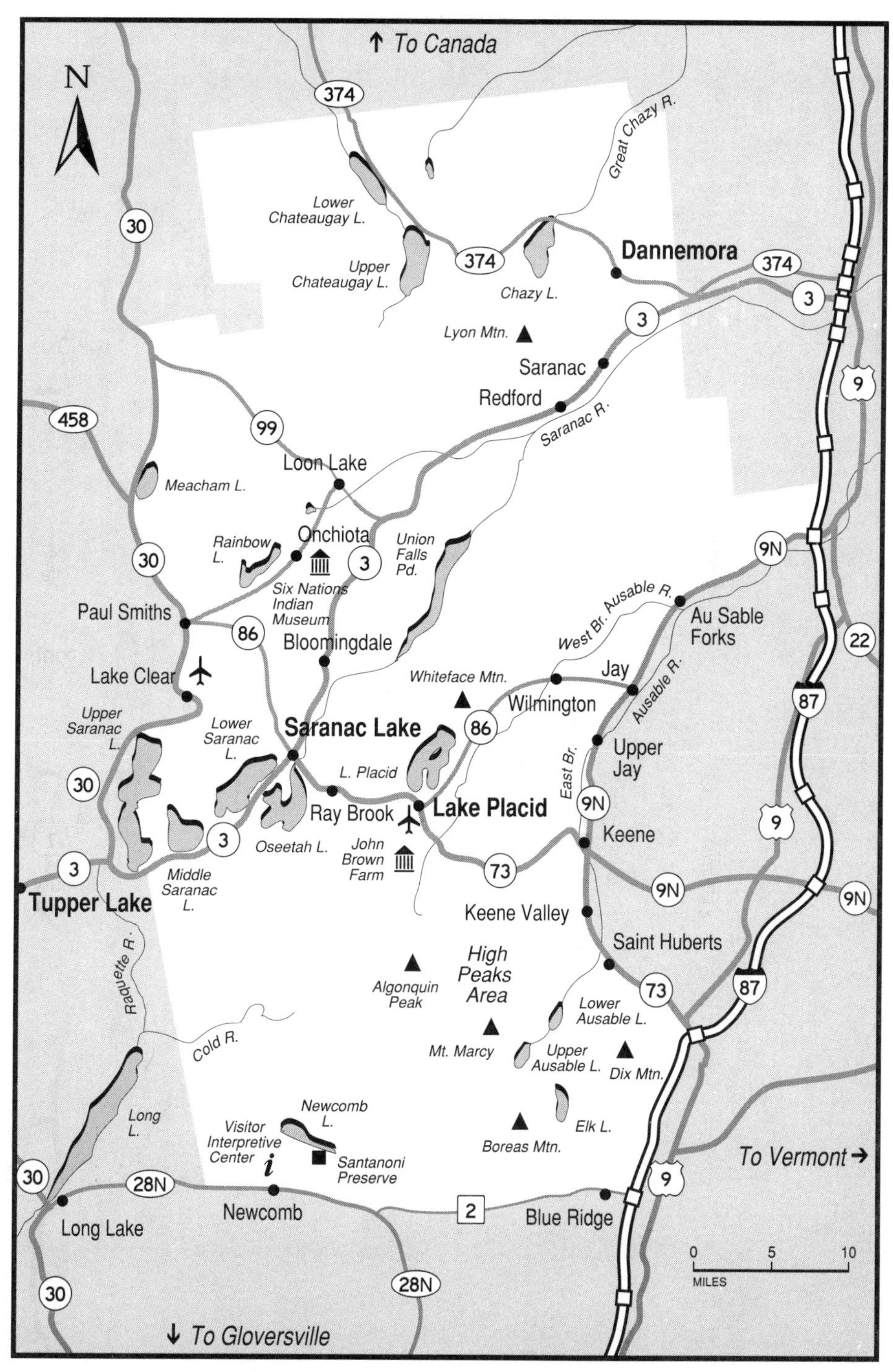

HIGH PEAKS AND NORTHERN ADIRONDACKS

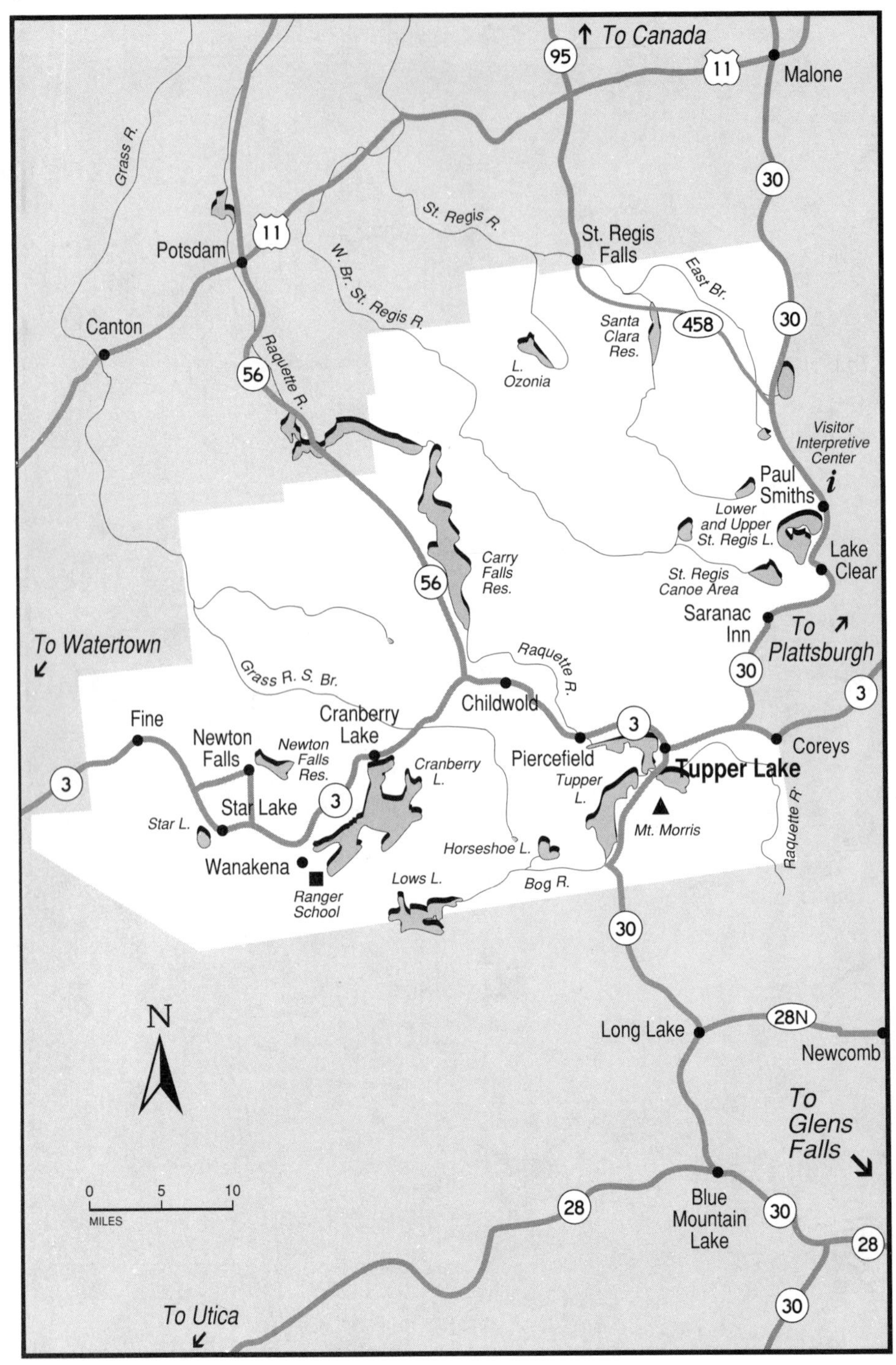

NORTHWEST LAKES

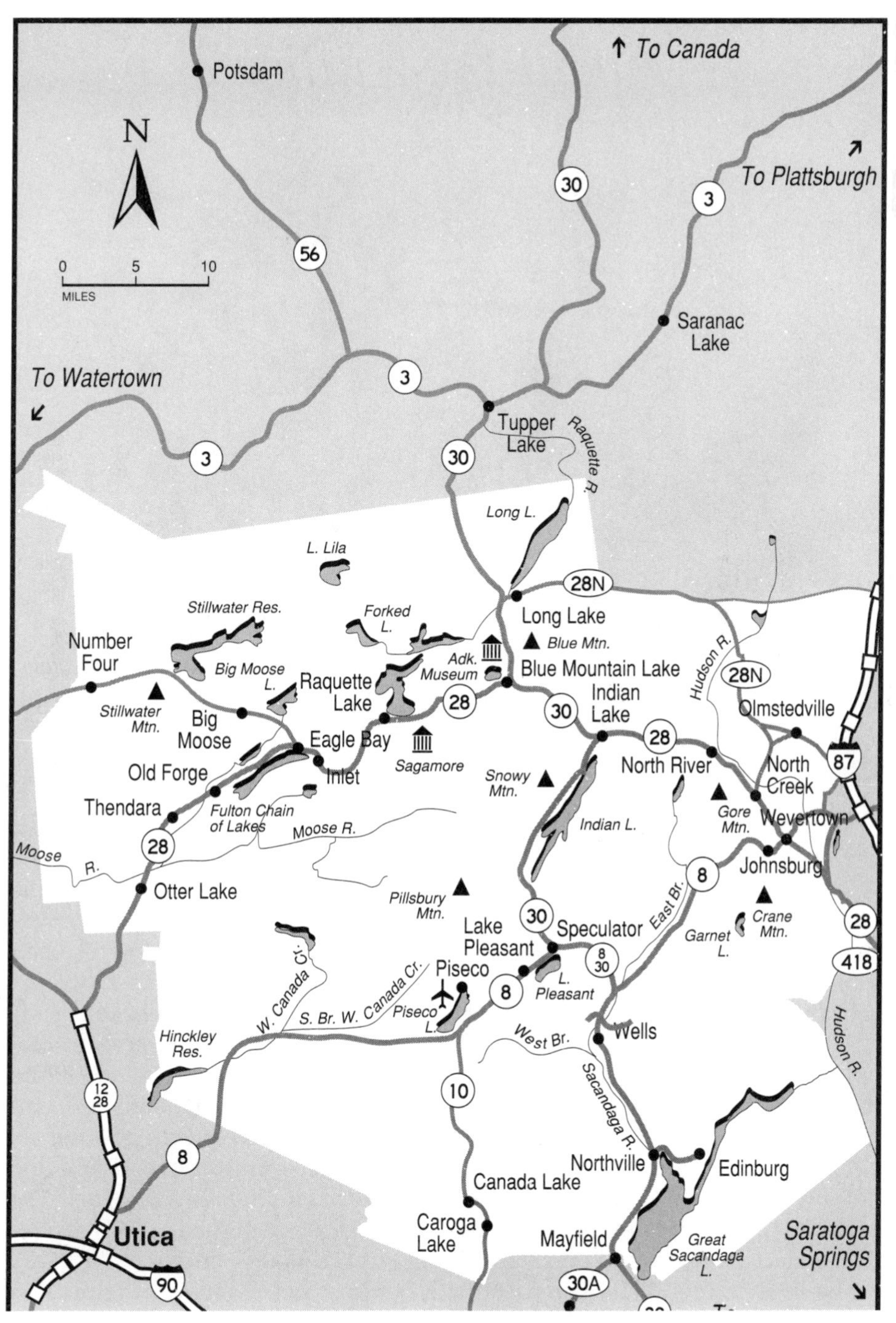

CENTRAL ADIRONDACKS

About the Author

Judy Natal

Since moving to the mountains in 1976, Elizabeth Folwell has worked in a variety of Adirondack places, serving as education coordinator of the Adirondack Museum in Blue Mountain Lake, and as executive director of the Adirondack Lakes Center for the Arts, also in Blue Mountain Lake. Currently she is editor of *Adirondack Life* magazine, based in Jay, New York. She also had a brief career as manager of a general store, and worked as a project coordinator for Travelers Aid during the 1980 Winter Olympics in Lake Placid.

While at *Adirondack Life*, she has written numerous pieces on local history, outdoor recreation, and the environment; her freelance articles on adventure travel, regional history, and indigenous crafts in the Northeast, Southwest, and Caribbean have appeared in the *New York Times* travel section, *National Geographic Traveler*, *Sailing*, *Backpacker*, and other publications. She is the author, with Amy Godine, of *Adirondack Odysseys: Exploring Museums and Historic Places from the Mohawk to the St. Lawrence* (copublished in 1997 by the Adirondack Museum and Berkshire House Publishers).

She lives in Blue Mountain Lake with her husband, Tom Warrington, and two dogs.